WORLD
EVANGELISM

WORLD EVANGELISM

HEARTBEAT OF THE LOCAL CHURCH

TEACHER'S EDITION

EDWARD THAL

Pleasant Word
A Division of WINEPRESS PUBLISHING

Pleasant Word (a division of WinePress Publishing, PO Box 428, Enumclaw, WA 98022) functions only as book publisher. As such, the ultimate design, content, editorial accuracy, and views expressed or implied in this work are those of the author.

Fairfax Baptist Temple
6401 Missionary Lane
Fairfax Station, Virginia 22039-1859
(Telephone) 703-323-8100 (Fax) 703-250-8660
Attention: Copyright Requests

Author: Mr. Edward Thal, Personal Evangelism Director
Edited by: Dr. Troy R. Calvert, Pastor; Dr. Bud Calvert, Pastor Emeritus; Dr. Ted Wieler, Missions Director

Unless otherwise noted, all Scriptures are taken from the King James Version of the Bible.

ISBN 13: 978-1-4141-1089-9
ISBN 10: 1-4141-1089-8
Library of Congress Catalog Card Number: 2007906503

CONTENTS

*Part I and Part II based on a study prepared
by Dr. Bud Calvert for the International
Conference on World Evangelism.

ACKNOWLEDGMENTS

This book was conceived a long time ago in the mind of Dr. Bud Calvert, founder and Pastor Emeritus of Fairfax Baptist Temple (FBT). His passion for world evangelism has supported the growth of a vibrant church that has given birth to dozens of churches in the United States and abroad and has seen the investment of more than $10 million over 37 years to spread the Gospel through missions and church planting.

It has long been Bud Calvert's desire to have world evangelism taught as part of the Bible curriculum in church schools. My prayer is that the impact of this textbook meets his high expectations.

Some of the material contained in these pages has been distilled from the teachings of Fairfax Baptist Temple, in particular from courses made available to prospective pastors and missionary evangelists who attended the FBT Missions Academy.

The daunting task of presenting the material in a coherent and biblically sound textbook format was made infinitely easier by the ever-cheerful encouragement and invaluable assistance of Dr. Ted Wieler, whose writing and editing skills are legendary.

My thanks go also to Dr. Troy Calvert, who continues his father's commitment to spreading the Gospel through the establishment of independent, fundamental, local New Testament churches, and whose support ultimately made possible the publication of this book.

Finally, I thank my students. Their love for Jesus Christ and their hunger to know the truth constantly inspires me.

FOREWORD

The foundational premise upon which this course on World Evangelism rests is that it should be the desire of every Christian to perform faithfully the work that we have been left on this earth to do (see John 17:15–18). The motivating force behind this desire is love—love for God, love for God's people, and love for the lost of the world. Faithfulness in discharging all of the responsibilities we have as believers toward our Savior is nothing more and nothing less than patterning ourselves after Jesus Christ.

Jesus Christ's love for you and your love for Him explain the source of your compassion for people and your passion to act. Most fundamental Baptists readily give mental assent to the fact that the Bible teaches world evangelism; however, faithfulness to God requires more than mere assent. Faithfulness requires each one of us to pray for and desire a heart for missions. It is not enough to know of the need, we must see the need—literally see it. For me, the many trips that I have taken to various mission works in numerous countries have allowed my heart to be affected greatly by what my eyes beheld. The testimony of the members of my congregation who have taken missions trips is the same.

The Spirit of God moved the heart and pen of Jeremiah as he wrote in the book of the Lamentations: "Mine eye affecteth mine heart" (3:51a). There is a similar passage, describing how the eye affects the heart in Matthew 9:35–38. A portion of that passage reads, "But when he [Jesus] saw the multitudes, he was moved with compassion ... Then saith he unto his disciples... Pray ye therefore the Lord of the harvest, that he will send forth labourers."

As the students study the Scriptures together through this course, they will see that God has given the responsibility of worldwide missions to every church, and that every member has a responsibility to ask God to guide his or her participation in that work. Through this course we hope that many of the students will develop a heart for missions. It is this heart that drives and motivates a Christian to engage actively in God's work, to faithfully spread the good news of the gospel message far and wide.

My teenaged daughter has already taken this course. I imagine that most people would expect a "preacher's kid" to have developed a heart that is perfectly attuned to every aspect of the Christian life. I wish that were the case. The truth is that she needed to be specifically and repeatedly challenged to consider how God might be planning to use her in world evangelism. As we talked throughout the year about this course, I was encouraged to see real growth in the expanse and depth of her understanding of the centrality of world evangelism to the Christian life.

We in Christian education often focus on the fact that we teach all of our courses in a Christ-centered manner. That is certainly a good thing, but it is a course such as this that truly separates the church school from secular and even "Christian" schools. This course represents real education and training in ultimate Truth. It is, perhaps, the first course in the high school student's career that helps focus his career thoughts completely toward the work of the ministry.

It is my prayer as you begin this journey around the world that you will come with an open mind and open heart so that you are able to receive all of the blessings that are just waiting for you to gather them. It is a great privilege to be touched by God to participate personally in His work.

Dr. Troy R. Calvert
Pastor, Fairfax Baptist Temple

INTRODUCTION

There is an interesting story about leadership drawn from the experiences of Moses found in Numbers 11. Moses was unable to be the effective personal leader that each of the million or so people needed. The solution was to find other men to help with the task. When questioned by Joshua about a young man acting in a manner that Joshua assumed was a dangerous diffusion of Moses' authority, Moses responded, "Enviest thou for my sake? Would God that all the LORD's people were prophets, and that the LORD would put his spirit upon them!" (Numbers 11:29).

Moses' response teaches us that when the task is huge—such as reaching the world for Christ—it is wise to get some help. Thus, it is the responsibility of the leader, in our case this is the pastor of a local church, to find men that are called of God to help in the work of the ministry, which is in part, church planting. Many young men may have missed God's call to be a church planter simply because no preacher or other person challenged them with the idea. I'm with Moses: I wish that all of our people would be called into the ministry. But how does this happen?

It starts with prayer. Then, the pastor of the local church makes world evangelism a high priority. That includes ensuring that the students in the church's academy are exposed to world evangelism and challenged to find themselves among those blessed few men that respond when they are called by God. What a high honor this is, and the students need to learn that it is so. Pastors and teachers must explain to students that the church's main responsibility is world evangelism and that God's program to accomplish the task is church planting.

Requiring students to immerse themselves in the study of world evangelism in no way interferes with the work of the Holy Spirit. Indeed, it is cooperating with the Holy Spirit in that work. Who called John Mark? Who called Timothy? The Holy Spirit called them through the influence of other godly men.

Let me say a word about our young ladies and the idea of a "call" upon their lives. It is my understanding from study of the Scriptures that God impresses the heart of men and women differently. Men are called to a task. Women are to come alongside men in the work of the ministry. Saying this, I need to quickly add that coming alongside is in no way a lesser role. It is, in fact, impossible for a church, or any ministry for that matter, to function fully unless everyone is behind it and getting involved. Men are called to plant churches. Women are to be yielded to accompany the men in this work. Therefore, this course on world evangelism is as important for our young ladies as it is for our young men.

What a thrill it is to see young men and women who have been moved by the Holy Spirit to enter into His ministry as a full-time passion. This passion must be cultivated. Our children need to be taught to always keep in mind that the people we meet, wherever we go, whether in our neighborhoods or anywhere in the rest of the world, will spend their eternity in hell if they are not saved. God moves in the lives of soulwinners.

It is my prayer, and it is my heart's desire that through the use of this textbook many young men and women will hear the voice of God speaking directly into their hearts. If my prayers are answered then I know the result will be hundreds, even thousands of souls kept safe from the fires of hell.

Dr. Bud Calvert
Pastor Emeritus, Fairfax Baptist Temple.

WORLD EVANGELISM:
AN INTRODUCTORY STUDY COURSE

I. Purpose

- To introduce students in a church/Christian high school to world evangelism and to instill in them an appreciation for this key biblical doctrine and core mission of the local New Testament church.

- To equip students with a framework for understanding the nature and importance of world evangelism and to prepare their hearts to be receptive to a call by God into full-time Christian service.

II. Focus

- The course is suggested for ninth or tenth grade because:
  - ☆ Students at this level are highly impressionable.
  - ☆ These grades leave sufficient time (the remaining high school years) for maturing students in a positive attitude towards world evangelism and to respond to a call by God.

III. Concept

- A challenge to students to assess their lives and find the "good work" God has ordained for them (Ephesians 2:10), which may include the high privilege of full-time work in the ministry, perhaps even with the highest calling in the context of world evangelism, as a missionary evangelist.

- An introduction to the vastness of the world and the lost estate of millions of its peoples to underline the need for personal commitment through full-time service, or some form of part-time service, aimed at supporting World evangelism.

- A familiarity with the heroic lives of missionary evangelists, past and present, to encourage students to adopt and emulate missionary heroes of their own.

  ☆ "Adoption" as a prayer partner of individual missionary families among those supported by the local church to give practical expression to familiarity.

  ☆ Contact with missionary evangelists to be made and maintained primarily through correspondence, but possibly including interviews with visiting missionary evangelists.

  ☆ Study of the biographies of great missionary evangelists.

  ☆ Instruction by missionary evangelists currently on the field or about to follow God's call to the mission field.

IV. Resources

- *Speakers*
  ☆ The church pastor as an occasional lecturer
  ☆ The church missions director or missions secretary as a source of information on the administration of the missions program and contacts with missionary families
  ☆ Visiting missionary evangelists

- ***Required Reading and Book Reports***
  (See Unit 19 for a complete list of suggested books.)

  ☆ *The King James Bible*

  ☆ *Giants of the Missionary Trail*
    A compilation of missionary biographies written by
    Eugene Myers Harrison, published by Fairfax Baptist
    Temple, 6401 Missionary Lane, Fairfax Station, VA
    22039.

  ☆ *Heroes of the Faith* selections
    Missionary biographies, published by Barbour
    Publishing Inc., P.O. Box 719, Uhrichsville, OH
    44683.

- ***Research Resources***
  Please note that reference to these resources should not
  be understood to imply that they carry the endorsement
  of Fairfax Baptist Temple. It should also be noted that
  numbers and statistics contained in this book are often a
  composite of data from several sources, since the purpose
  is less to furnish precise figures than to illustrate general
  dimensions and proportions.

  ☆ *Operation World,* a book and DVD providing de-
    tailed maps and statistics on the state of Christianity
    in the world (Authentic Media, P.O. Box 1047,
    Waynesboro, GA 30830)

  ☆ *From Jerusalem to Irian Jaya,* a biographical history
    of missions written by Ruth A. Tucker (Zondervan,
    1983, 2004)

  ☆ *World Christian Database*
    www.worldchristiandatabase.org

  ☆ *First Bible International*
    www.firstbible.net

☆ *World Christian Missionary Resources*
www.missionaryresources.com

V. Scope And Sequence

- Appendix A

VI. An Outline For Guest Speakers

- Appendix B

INTRODUCTION TO WORLD EVANGELISM

- *Outline of the Course*
- *What Motivates Us?*
- *Introduction to Foundational Concepts*
- *Informal Survey of Students: How many are disposed to full-time Christian service?*

I. Outline of the Course

- Scope and Sequence (See Appendix A)

II. What Motivates Us?

- Vanity—I care only for myself.
- Humanity—I care about others' physical and emotional needs.
- Christianity—I care about spirit, soul, and body.
- Discipleship—I love God with all my heart and my neighbor as myself.

  ← A wise person has said, "He who lives only for himself does not have much to live for."

III. Introduction to Foundational Concepts

A. *Personal Evangelism*
The Purpose and Priority of a Christian
- Luke 14:16–23

1

B. *World Evangelism*
The Purpose and Priority of a Local Church
- Acts 1:8

C. *The Two-Fold Purpose of God for Each Local Church*
Note that one cannot be accomplished without the other!
1. Glorify God—1 Corinthians 10:31
2. Evangelize the World—Mark 16:15

D. *"Missionary" Defined*
1. The word "missionary" is not found in the Bible. The word comes from the Latin word "mitto," which means "I send." It is closely related to the Greek term "apostle," which also means "to send." Thus, a missionary is a messenger (sent one) with a message from God. As used in this course, it is inappropriate to say every Christian is a missionary. Instead, the term is used in a more technical sense of a man leaving his home country to plant churches in a foreign land.
2. In the New Testament, a missionary is an evangelist—a word that literally means "a wisher of well" or "a messenger of good."
3. An evangelist in turn is one who proclaims the gospel, the "good news" (from the Greek *euangelion*—good news, gospel).
4. Christian men may receive a specific calling to full-time work in the Gospel ministry as:
   a. A missionary evangelist—A man commissioned by a local church and usually sent beyond the borders of his country to preach the Gospel and plant new churches. In the initial phase of

Introduction To World Evangelism 3

establishing a church, the missionary will do the work of an evangelist, then of a pastor, but always with the goal in mind of turning the work over to a national pastor.

   b. A pastor—A man sent out from a local church with the intention of establishing a single new church where he will be the pastor. In the initial phase of establishing the church, he will do the work of an evangelist.

5. Note that apart from these unique and specific callings to full-time work in the Gospel ministry, it is the duty of every Christian to be a soulwinner—that is, someone ready at all times to share the Gospel of salvation with family, friends, neighbors, and co-workers. This requires no more confirmation than Jesus' command to the church, represented in the persons of His disciples—the "Great Commission" of Matthew 28:18–20.

E. *The Role of Women*

It is clear from Scripture that men are to lead and direct churches and the Gospel ministry. Men are called to fulfill this task, while women are to come alongside them, to accompany them in the work. This is in no way a lesser role. It is impossible for a church, or any ministry, to function fully unless men and women are equally involved in their different roles. See Ephesians 5:22–32; 1 Timothy 2:11–12, 3:1–12; 1 Peter 3:1–7; 1 Corinthians 14: 34–37.

1. With specific reference to the mission field, women generally go as helpers to their husbands. Mission Boards usually count a husband and wife team as a single unit.

2. Single women may also serve on the mission field as school teachers, administrative assistants, or general missionary helpers.

IV. Informal Class Survey

- By a show of hands, how many students are aware that God is leading them to enter some form of full-time Christian service?
- How many male students are aware that they have been called to be a pastor or a missionary evangelist?
- How many students who have not already raised their hands would like to know that the good work ordained for them by God is to full-time Christian service?

WORLD MISSIONS DEMOGRAPHICS (PART I)

- *The World—nations and populations*
- *World Missions*
- *World Religions*
- *Bible Translations*
- *World Regions/Peoples*
- *The "10/40 Window"*

I. The World

A. *The World's Population*
1. 240 Countries and Territories
2. 6,500 Million People (6.5 billion)
3. 13,000 Population Groups. A population group is a group of people considered unified enough to be reached by a single language. 7,000 of these groups are among the least reached people on earth.

B. *The World's Unsaved*
1. 3,000 million people have not heard the gospel.
2. 1,000 million Muslims
3. 1,000 million Roman Catholics

C. *The World's Saved*
1. Among those who are identified as "Christian," 645 million are classified as "Evangelical" or "Bible believing."

2. These terms usually refer to Christians who believe in salvation by faith in Jesus Christ alone. Baptists are included in this number.

II. World Missions

(Note: The numbers below are misleading in that they do not show how many "missionaries" believe or teach the Scriptures or how many teach salvation by grace through faith alone. Also, Baptists are not Protestants, but they are counted with Protestants in most reference books. The main lesson to be drawn here is that there are relatively few "Christian missionaries" in the world and fewer still who preach the Gospel.)

A. 410,000 missionaries in total
B. 140,000 Protestant missionaries (non-Roman Catholic or Greek Orthodox)
C. 64,000 Protestant missionaries from the USA
1. Includes less than 3,000 missionary families from 12,000 fundamental, independent Baptist churches.
2. There are about twenty-three fundamentalist mission boards in the United States.
D. Distribution of Protestant Missionaries
1. 74% among people already exposed to the Gospel (nominal Christians)
2. 8% among tribal peoples
3. 6% among Muslims
4. 4% among non-religious/atheists
5. 3% among Buddhists
6. 2% among Hindus
7. 2% among Chinese folk religions
8. 1% among Jewish peoples

III. World Religions

A.	Islam	1,400 million
B.	Roman Catholic	1,000 million
C.	Hindu	950 million
D.	"Evangelical" Christian	645 million
E.	Ethnic	360 million
F.	Buddhism	350 million
G.	Chinese Folk Religions	340 million
H.	Tribal Religions	220 million
I.	No known religion	1,000 million

IV. Bible Translations

- Fewer than 400 whole Bibles and fewer than 2,000 New Testaments have been translated for about 13,000 languages or dialects.

V. World Regions/Peoples

A.	Arab	300 million
B.	Asia	3,100 million
	1. East Asia	1,500 million
	2. South Asia	1,400 million
	3. Southeast Asia	200 million
C.	Africa	700 million
	1. North Africa	150 million
	2. Sub-Sahara	600 million
D.	Eurasia (Europe and Russia)	800 million
E.	Latin America	600 million
F.	North America	300 million
G.	Persia	140 million
H.	Pacific Islands	10 million

I.	Tibet/Himalaya	90 million
J.	Turkic	160 million
K.	Jewish	16 million

VI. The "10/40 Window"

The 10/40 Window is a section of the world located between latitudes 10 degrees north and 40 degrees north of the equator. It covers the Middle East, North Africa, and Central and Southeast Asia, and holds two-thirds of the world's population. The window also contains the world's most "unreached people groups" and most of the world's governments which oppose Christianity.

A. Middle East—13 countries, 300 million people

B. North Africa—7 countries, 150 million people

C. Central Asia—5 countries, 100 million people

D. South Asia—12 countries, 2,700 million people

E. Southeast Asia—1,000 inhabited islands, 220 million people

WORLD MISSIONS DEMOGRAPHICS (PART II)

- *To provide context for this unit, show students a map of the world and identify the different continents and major countries.*
- *Christian Outreach in Relation to Population*
- *The Fields Are White Unto Harvest!*

I. Christian Outreach in Relation to Population Growth

A. The world population has grown enormously since the days of the New Testament church, when it is estimated that the total world population was about 200 million.

B. Christianity grew very quickly in the first 300 years A.D., while world population grew slowly, but today the growth in the number of Bible-believing churches and missionary evangelists is declining in relation to world population.

- It took over 1,800 years for world population to grow from 200 million to 1,000 million.
- By 1900 the world population was 1,600 million.
- In 1930 the population reached 2,000 million.
- In 1950 the population reached 2,500 million.
- In 2000 the population reached 6,000 million.

- In 2040 the population is expected to reach just under 9,000 million (nine billion).

C. World Population Distribution, 2005:
- North America, 5%
- South America, 9%
- Europe, 12%
- Africa, 13%
- Asia, 61% (including Middle East and Far East, China, India, Indonesia, Japan, etc.)

D. Note that 99% of people who have never heard the Gospel live outside of the U.S. and Canada.

E. There are only 140,000 Protestant missionaries in the world today (that is, missionaries other than Roman Catholic or Greek Orthodox).
  1. This is one missionary for every 46,000 people on earth.
  2. There are fewer than 3,000 missionary families from fundamental, independent Baptist churches.
     a. Brazil has the highest number of fundamental Baptist missionary evangelists (more than 250 families and missionary helpers).
     b. Mexico, the Philippines, Great Britain, and Canada are also well represented.
     c. More than seventy nations have no U.S. missionary presence. Most of these countries are located in the 10/40 Window.

F. Most missionaries are found in areas that are already heavily evangelized:
  1. The Pacific Islands—550 to every 1 million people
  2. The Caribbean—58 to every million people

3. Latin America—38 per million
4. Africa (south of the Sahara Desert)—34 per million
5. India and China—9 per million
6. The Middle East and Muslim countries in Asia—uncertain, though probably very few

II. The Fields Are White Unto Harvest!

A. An estimated 3,000 million people have never heard the gospel.
   - Each second of the day, approximately two people die.
   - 110 people die each minute.
   - 6,400 people die each hour.
   - 154,000 people die each day.
   - Nearly five million people die each month.
   - 56 million people die each year.
B. In the United States, the adult population grew by 15% from 1991 to 2004. During the same period, the number of adults who do not attend church doubled, from 39 million to 75 million.
   - There are about 300,000 churches in the U.S.
   - 12,000 churches in the U.S. call themselves "independent, fundamental Baptist."
   - The median adult attendance per church service (all churches) is 90.
   - 45% of adults attend church in a typical weekend (down from 49% in 1991).
   - In Europe, the average church-going population is about two percent.

TEST 1

(40 Points)

Note: Where no total point value is given for a question, each correct answer is worth one point.

1. Complete this sentence: "He who lives only for himself
                    does not have much to live for."
2. What is the purpose and priority of a Christian?
   (2 points)
   "Go out into the highways and hedges and compel them to come in" (Luke 14:23).
3. What is the purpose and priority of a local church?
   (2 points)
   "Ye shall be witness unto me both in Jerusalem, and in all Judea, and in Samaria, and unto the uttermost part of the earth" (Acts 1:8).
4. What is the two-fold purpose of God for each local church?
   a) *Glorify God (1 Corinthians 10:31)*
   b) *Evangelize the world (Mark 16:15)*
5. Provide the following statistics:
   • Number of countries in the world: *240*
   • World population: *6,500 million*
   • Number of people who have never heard the gospel:
                    3,000 million

- Number of missionary evangelists from independent, fundamental Baptist churches: *Fewer than 3,000*
- Name the four largest world religions:
    - ☆ *Islam*
    - ☆ *Roman Catholic*
    - ☆ *Hindu*
    - ☆ *Evangelical Christian*

6. What is the number of language groups in the world?
    13,000

7. What is the total number of whole Bibles available?
    400

8. How many people live in the 10/40 Window?
    3,200 million

9. What percentage of people living in the 10/40 Window has never heard the Gospel?
    95%

10. What period in history saw the most rapid growth in population?
    1950–2000

12. Where is more than 60 percent of the world's population found today?
    Asia

13. What is the ratio of missionaries to world population?
    1:46,000

14. Based on our studies what is your response to the fact that 154,000 people die each day (110 each second and 6,400 each hour)?
    (3 points)
    Answers will vary, but the general idea should be that the task of world evangelism is urgent.

15. In your estimation, what percentage of people who die each year are saved and so will not spend eternity in hell?

Note: There is technically no wrong answer to this question since it is a personal estimation. The purpose is to assess the student's awareness of the size of the problem, but since it has already been established that roughly half of the world's population has never heard the Gospel, to be correct the answer must be considerably less than 50%.

16. What percentage of adults attend church each week?
    a. In the United States?   *45%*
    b. In Europe?   *2%*

17. What is evangelism? (2 points)
    Telling other people about the saving power of Jesus Christ and the new life that comes from being united with Him.

18. Name two kinds of evangelism:
    a. *Personal evangelism*
    b. *World evangelism*

19. Describe a motivation for evangelism. (2 points)
    Hell is Real or "Thou shalt love thy neighbor as thyself"

20. What is the message of evangelism? (2 points)
    God provides for man's salvation through the death, burial, and resurrection of His only begotten Son, Jesus Christ. This is the Gospel, the good news about God's salvation plan.

21. True or False: Only pastors are soulwinners. Explain your answer. (4 points)
    False. Every Christian has a responsibility to attempt to reach everyone in a local community with the Gospel of Christ.

GOD'S UNFOLDING PURPOSE FOR HUMANITY

- *God's Purpose*
- *The Progressive Revelation of God to Man*
- *Carrying the Revelation of God to the Ends of the Earth*

I. God's Purpose

A. God's original purpose for humanity—as expressed in Genesis 1:26–28 and 3:8–9—was to rule the earth and have fellowship with Him.

B. This purpose was interrupted by the rebellion of Adam and Eve (Genesis 3:22–24).

C. But God has a plan to fulfill His purpose, despite man's sin. We see this plan unfold in Scripture through:

1. The call of Abraham (Genesis 12:1–3, 22:18)
2. The establishment of Israel (Exodus 3:14–17)
3. The provision of a sacrifice for sin (Exodus 12:2–7, 13; John 1:29)
4. The local church as the vehicle to carry God's message (Matthew 28:19)
5. A new creation (Revelation 21:1–5)

II. The Progressive Revelation of God to Man

A. Immediately after the sin of Adam and Eve, God hinted at the outline of His plan for the salvation of mankind (Genesis 3:15).

17

B. After the Flood, God began to explain His plan for the salvation of mankind by reaching out first to a single man, Abraham (Genesis 12:1–8).

C. Then God revealed a little more of Himself and His purpose to Abraham's family, Isaac and then Jacob (Genesis 26:24, 28:13, 32:9).

D. Then to the tribe of Israel (Exodus 3:6, 13–15, 6:2)

E. Then God established that tribe as a nation in a promised land, with His Word to guide them (Psalm 44:1–4; Psalm 119:105).

F. He made it clear that He wanted this special nation to "declare his glory among the heathen, his wonders among all people" (Psalm 96:3).

G. Then God began to expand the revelation of Himself and His purpose through His Son, Jesus Christ (Matthew 13:16–17, 16:13–18).

H. God provided more of His Word (the New Testament) to teach more about Himself and His purpose and to expand on the Old Testament by showing how the Law is fulfilled in Christ (1 Corinthians 10:6,11; Romans 15:4; Galatians 4:22–26; 1 Peter 1:10–12).

I. Then God revealed more about Himself through the local New Testament church (Ephesians 3:10).

J. Now God wants His people to tell about Him all over the world! (Acts 1:8).

III. Carrying the Revelation of God to the Ends of the Earth

A. In the Old Testament the message was, "Come and see." In the New Testament the message is, "As you go—tell!"

B. Since the commission to preach the Gospel to all the world was first given to Christians, the message has spread far and wide:

1. Early church growth (A.D. 70–300) was primarily through the Middle East, Asia Minor (present-day Turkey), Southern Europe, and North Africa.

2. From 300 to 1600, Christianity spread slowly through Europe and Asia, as far as India, China, and Japan.

3. From 1500 to 1900—the period of the Reformation and beyond—

   a. Baptist and Protestant missionaries preached the gospel in Europe, England, North America, Africa, and Asia.

   b. Roman Catholics focused on Central and South America.

   c. The high-water mark of world missions came during the 1800s.

4. The very rapid growth of world population in the past 100 years requires a redoubled effort by Gospel-preaching Christians to reach the lost.

Unit 6

THE LOCAL CHURCH

- *What Is It?*
- *Who Owns It?*
- *What is the Church's Purpose?*

I.   **What Is It?**

A.   The word "church" in the New Testament comes from the Greek word "ekklesia" which means "called out assembly."

1.   "Ekklesia" can refer to any assembly of people, but in the New Testament, there is only one passage that uses the word without having in mind people meeting as a church (Acts 19:32–41).

2.   In the New Testament the use of "ekklesia" refers primarily to the Lord's assembly. The word appears as "church" or "churches" 113 times.

a.   It is used for a local church (1 Corinthians 1:2).

b.   It is used for a group of churches (Galatians 1:2).

c.   It is used of the church as an institution (Matthew 16:18).

3.   The term is not to be confused with the idea of a "universal" church or an "invisible" church. In

21

Hebrews 12:23 the phrase "general assembly" is from a completely different Greek word that means a "mass meeting." This meeting will take place for the first time at the rapture of the church.

B. The church is not a bricks and mortar building or a denomination. It is a local expression of the life of Jesus Christ in a community of called-out, regenerated people.

1. The local church is called a "body" with Jesus Christ as the Head (Colossians 1:18, Ephesians 1:22–23).

2. The "body" has many members (1 Corinthians 12:12–28).

3. Each individual believer's living body is called a building or a temple (1 Corinthians 3:9, Ephesians 2:19–22).

4. The church is called a bride (2 Corinthians 11:2, Ephesians 5:27).

5. At the rapture, all believers from the Church Age will be gathered into a great assembly as the Bride of Christ.

II. Who Owns It?

A. The local church is created by Jesus Christ, founded by Jesus Christ, paid for by Jesus Christ, built by Jesus Christ, and owned by Jesus Christ.

1. The choosing of the twelve disciples marks the birth of the first church. The disciples were "called out" and "assembled" around Christ their head. They forsook former associations and became followers of Christ. He was their Pastor (Mark 3:14).

   • Note that the already existing church was given power to function at Pentecost.

2. Jesus Christ is the builder of the church (Matthew 16:18).

3. Jesus Christ is the Foundation of the church (1 Corinthians 3:10–11).

4. Jesus Christ purchased the church with His own blood (Acts 20:28).

5. Jesus Christ is the Head of the church (Ephesians 1:22–23).

B. A denomination is a man-made system to control and manage a group of churches that share the same doctrines and aims. There is no biblical charge for this. Note the autonomy of churches in the New Testament and Christ's personal authority over them.

1. The church at Antioch resisted attempts by the church at Jerusalem to exert control over it (Acts 15:1–2).

2. A dramatic picture of Christ's relationship with individual churches is seen in His messages to the seven churches (Revelation 2–3).

   a. He stands among the churches, represented as candlesticks (Revelation 1:12–13, 20).

   b. He is seen holding the pastors of the churches, represented as stars, in His right hand (Revelation 1:16, 20).

3. Denominations arose because of differences in interpretation of the Bible and differences in practice.

III. What Is the Church's Purpose?

The local church has a two-fold purpose: to glorify God and evangelize the world.

1. God is glorified when His people separate themselves from the world (James 4:4) and live in such a way that they are pleasing to Him (1 Corinthians 6:19–20).

2. World evangelism begins with local church members who share the gospel with their neighbors as they go about the daily routines of life, while missionary evangelists go beyond the area of the local church to plant new churches (Acts 1:8).

3. There is no greater spiritual truth than that Christ, the Head of the Church, is dependent upon the members of His body for carrying out His purpose: to seek and to save the lost (Luke 19:10). We are commanded (Matthew 28:19) to win the souls for whom Jesus died and was resurrected to save, for the glory of God the Father (John 17:1–6).

   a. "It was a solemn thing for the Son of God to come to save the world: He had to bear its sins and to die for it. It is equally a solemn thing for us to take part in the work of soulwinning; it requires that we, in faith and love, have a burden for souls…" (Andrew Murray)

   b. "The Son of Man is come to seek and to save that which was lost" (Luke 19:10).

   c. "…teach all nations…" (Matthew 28:19)

   d. "…preach the gospel to every creature…" (Mark 16:15)

   e. "…and ye shall be witnesses unto me both in Jerusalem, and in all Judaea, and in Samaria, and unto the uttermost part of the earth…"(Acts 1:8)

What Is One Soul Worth?

- *A Challenge to Emulate Great Soulwinners*
- *Overcoming the God of This World*
- *The Reality of Hell*
- *Weighing Our Commitment*

I. A Challenge To Emulate Great Soulwinners

- *Jesus Christ* (Isaiah 53:3–5)

What *is* one soul worth? What is your soul worth? From the Bible's description of the trials and sufferings of Jesus Christ, it seems that your soul is worth a lot to God. According to Philippians 2:7–8, Jesus went so far as to lay aside His reputation and become a servant "made in the likeness of men."

Then He humbled Himself further and became obedient to a terrible death on a cross. For me. For you. Our souls are worth a lot to God!

Do you think the soul of the person next to you has equal value in God's eyes? What about your neighbor or the person across the street? What are *their* souls worth?

In the terrible story of a man burning in hell (Luke 16:19–31), Jesus gave a clue to the reason why He was willing to sacrifice His glory, His power, His reputation, and His own body for us. Our Lord and Savior placed so high a value on a human soul because He knew the terrors of hell, and He knew that without His intervention all of us would be doomed to spend eternity there.

Hell is a place of awful, unending torment. Do you think the soul of your neighbor is worth enough for you to walk across the street and tell him about the only sure escape from hell?

- ## *William Carey*

He thought one soul was worth seven years of toil, hardship, and sacrifice in India. That was how long it took for him to lead one soul to Christ. Along the way, he lost a child and his wife. But when he died at the age of seventy-three, he had seen, through his efforts, the Scriptures translated and printed into forty different Indian languages and many, many thousands of souls receive an assurance that they would not go to hell.

- ## *Adoniram Judson*

He was a brilliant young man who could read fluently at the age of three and began to study theology at the age of ten. But when he entered a university at seventeen, he came under the influence of a clever unbeliever and was persuaded that heaven and hell were not real.

Shortly after he graduated, Judson spent the night in a country inn. But he got no rest because of the moans, groans, and fearful cries of someone dying in the next room. The following morning the sleepy young man discovered the identity of his dead neighbor: it was his unbelieving college friend!

Judson decided that he would never again find himself in a position where he was unable to offer help and comfort to someone approaching the gates of hell. He surrendered his life to Christ, and soon after, he and his bride of seven days set sail for India, on their way to the neighboring country of Burma—a country where there was not a single Christian.

His first child died. Then he was arrested as a British spy and spent nearly two years in jail, narrowly escaping execution.

For six hard years he labored with no results, until the first Burmese soul was saved. But when Adoniram Judson died at the age of sixty-two, some thirty-eight years after arriving in Burma, a government survey recorded 210,000 Christians in the country.

- ### Charles Thomas—"CT"—Studd

He was a privileged young man from a wealthy family who represented England in international cricket competition after attending Eton and Cambridge. He was a Christian, having been converted under the preaching of D. L. Moody, and he was satisfied with his comfortable life.

But when his brother George became seriously ill, C.T. was confronted by the question: "What is all the fame and flattery worth, when a man comes to face eternity?"

In answer to the question, he gave away his family inheritance and joined Hudson Taylor as a missionary in China, where for the next ten years he suffered great hardships to reach areas where the gospel had never been preached. Then he pastored a church in India for six years before going to Africa at the age of fifty-three, winning souls in the Sudan and Congo and laboring there for another seventeen years until his death.

C. T. Studd explained his amazing life of sacrifice by saying, "If Jesus Christ be God and died for me, then no sacrifice can be too great for me to make for Him." He said on another occasion, "Let us not glide through this world and then slip quietly into heaven!"

He lamented the lukewarmness of some Christians: "If men hear so loudly the call of gold, and obey it, can it be that the ears of Christians are deaf to the call of God? Are gamblers for gold so many, and gamblers for God so few?"

On the subject of hell he had this to say: "How can a man believe in hell unless he throws away his life to rescue others from its torment?"

But he is perhaps best known for a verse he penned that sums up his whole life:

> *Some wish to live within the sound*
> *Of church or chapel bell.*
> *I want to run a rescue shop*
> *Within a yard of the gates of hell.*

II. Overcoming the God of This World

What is one soul worth? To Jesus Christ, it was worth everything—His glory and power and body. To men like Carey and Judson and Studd, it was worth everything. They rejoiced in the great truth that in gaining souls for God they had great gain as well. No man really sacrifices anything when that man spends his life doing God's work!

What is the worth of one soul to you? Is it worth investing a little of your time or your comfort to make the effort to tell just one other person how to escape the everlasting destruction of hell?

At the very least, reach out and put a tract in someone's hand. Some day, in heaven, you will be glad you did, as some person runs up to you and thanks you for caring about the value of another soul.

Jesus challenges us to make what the world would perhaps call "great sacrifices" but God calls "great gain" (1 Timothy 6:6) to engage in a great spiritual battle raging for the souls of men. According to the Scriptures, those who have not heard and heeded the gospel:

- Have the devil as their father! (John 8:44).
- Are dead to the things of God (Ephesians 2:1)
- Are blinded by the god of this world, the devil (2 Corinthians 4:4)
- Have no hope (Ephesians 2:12)

III. The Reality of Hell

A place of eternal torment awaits those who never receive Jesus Christ as their Savior, for His is the only sacrifice for sin acceptable to God. Those who doubt the reality of hell need only listen to Jesus' graphic description found in Luke 16:19–31.

IV. Weighing Our Commitment

What should be our personal commitment to keeping just one more soul out of such an awful place?

- None?
- Minimal effort?
- Some personal inconvenience?
- The investment of a little time?
- Financial sacrifice?
- Submitting personal ambition to God's will?
- Complete yielding to the call of God?

Where do you fit on this scale? Make a note of your response in the space below:

_____

_____

_____

_____

_____

TEST 2

(34 Points)

Note; Where no total point value is given for a question, each correct answer is worth one point.

1. What was God's purpose for humanity, outlined in Genesis? Provide Scripture references. (4 points)
   To rule the earth and have fellowship with Him.
   Genesis 1:26–28, 3:8–9

2. Mention the eight steps by which God progressively revealed Himself to mankind after the flood.
   a. *To Abraham*
   b. *To Abraham's family*
   c. *To the tribe of Israel*
   d. *To a nation in the Promised Land, with His Word as a guide*
   e. *Through His Son, Jesus Christ*
   f. *Through the New Testament Church*
   g. *Through the complete Scriptures*
   h. *Through world evangelism*

5. Complete these sentences: In the Old Testament the message was, *"Come and See!"*
   In the New Testament the message is, *"As you are going, Tell!"*

6. Which century was the high water mark of missions?
   1800s

7. True or False: The church is a building or a denomination.
   Explain your answer. (5 points)
   *False. The Church is not a bricks and mortar building or
   a denomination. It is a local expression of the life of Jesus
   Christ in a community of people. Each individual Christian
   is the temple of God.*

8. Who owns a local church? (4 points)
   *A local church is paid for by Jesus Christ, built by Jesus
   Christ, and owned by Jesus Christ.*

9. Mention a great spiritual truth with regard to the purpose
   of Jesus Christ, as expressed through the local church.
   (3 points)
   *Jesus Christ is dependent upon the members of His body for
   carrying out His purpose—to save the lost.*

10. How do we know that our souls are very precious to God?
    (2 points)
    *From the Bible's description of the trials and sufferings of
    Jesus Christ.*

11. "C.T." Studd lamented the *lukewarmness* of many
    Christians.

12. Provide the Scripture reference where Jesus Christ gives a
    dramatic description of hell. (2 points)
    Luke 16:19–31

13. What degree of personal commitment are you willing to
    consider as an investment in keeping one soul from hell?
    (2 points)
    Answers will vary

MISSIONS AND WORLD EVANGELISM

- *The Meaning of Evangelism*
- *The Motivation for Evangelism*
- *The Message of Evangelism*
- *Missionary Evangelists*

I.   The Meaning of Evangelism

Evangelism is telling other people about the saving power of Jesus Christ and the new life that follows, wherever you may be as you go through your day. The great "rule" of evangelism is that God desires fellowship with man. There are two kinds of evangelism:

A. Personal evangelism—every member of every local church—every Christian—bearing witness wherever he or she goes to the reality of Jesus Christ and the truth of the Scriptures. When these individuals actively present the Gospel to others and try to win them to salvation in Christ, they are known as soulwinners.

B. World evangelism—God-called evangelists or pastors ordained and commissioned by a local church to preach the gospel.

1. Some minister in their own countries; some go to "the uttermost part of the earth."

2. Those known as *missionary evangelists* aim to plant several new churches.

3. Those known as *pastors* feel called to plant one church and to minister there. Pastors may also be called to minister in an already established church.

C. Note that every missionary evangelist or pastor is a soulwinner, but every soulwinner is not necessarily a missionary evangelist or a pastor. In 2 Timothy 4:5, the apostle Paul instructs Timothy to "do the work of an evangelist." We may assume that in his role as a pastor he was being reminded by Paul about the importance of both personal soulwinning and of sending out church planters to establish works in areas beyond the reach of his local church.

II. The Motivation for Evangelism

A. God's Word: "Thou shalt love the Lord thy God with all thy heart, and with all thy soul, and with all thy mind...and the second is like unto it, Thou shalt love thy neighbor as thyself" (Matthew 22:37, 39).

B. Hell is real. It is a place of **everlasting** torment, an awful lake of fire (Luke 16:19–26; Revelation 21:9), where all unsaved men, women, and children will go. In the time it takes you to read this sentence, two people have died and gone to hell, with no hope of escape, ever. By the time this class is over, 6,400 people will have died and gone to hell. By the time this day is over, 154,000 people will have died and gone to hell. **But we have the words of eternal life!**

III. The Message of Evangelism

God provides for man's salvation from the penalty of sin through the death, burial, and resurrection of His only begotten

Son, Jesus Christ. This is the Gospel, the good news about God's salvation plan.

A. The Gospel offers the only possible escape from the rule of the god of this world, the devil.

B. The Gospel is the only way of escape from the awful punishment in the next world, which is the fate of all those who submit to the devil by failing to accept Jesus Christ as Savior.

    1. Satan's rule stems from Adam's disobedience toward God, who created the world for man to rule. By ignoring God's Word and choosing to believe Satan's lie, Adam and Eve handed the world to the devil (Genesis 1:27–29, 2:15–17, 3:1–24).

    2. Satan exercises control of this world (Luke 4:5–7; 2 Corinthians 4:4).

    3. As a result of Adam's fall and Satan's rule, human history is the story of the outworking of man's self-indulgent sin nature (Romans 3:10–18).

    4. Man deserves death—eternal separation from God—for his sinful disobedience (Romans 1:20–21, 3:23, 6:23a).

    5. God desires restoration of fellowship with man (Romans 5:8–10; 2 Corinthians 5:18–21).

        a. Note that God has given to us the ministry of reconciliation.

        b. Note also that those who speak the word of reconciliation are ambassadors for Christ.

IV. Missionary Evangelists

We have already seen that all Christians are called by God to be witnesses and soulwinners, every day. Some remain in their local church and serve God there while they support themselves, their families, and their church through secular jobs. Others are called by God to devote all their time to the purpose of preaching the gospel, doing church administration, winning souls, and planting new churches.

A missionary—whom the Bible calls an evangelist—is a person sent out from his local church to preach the Gospel for the purpose of starting, or planting, churches. A missionary evangelist **has heard and answered God's call** to devote all his time and energy to be a witness for Him—in his city, in his state, in his country, and, more commonly, *unto the uttermost part of the earth* (Acts 1:8). In this he emulates Jesus Christ, who came from heaven to earth to seek and to save the lost (Luke 19:10).

A. Jesus Christ is the complete representation of God's missionary heart (Matthew 16:18).

B. Paul the apostle (special messenger) proclaimed "our Saviour Jesus Christ, who hath abolished death, and hath brought life and immortality to light through the gospel: whereunto I am appointed a preacher, and an apostle, and a teacher of the Gentiles" (2 Timothy 1:10–11).

   1. Paul felt his calling so strongly that he said, "Woe is unto me, if I preach not the gospel" (1 Corinthians 9:16).

   2. Antioch was the predominant sending church at this time, and it was here that Paul received his training from Barnabas.

   3. He started many churches in Iconium, Lystra, Derbe, Corinth, Philippi, Ephesus, Galatia, Thessalonica, Athens, and Troas.

C. Barnabas and John Mark planted a church in Cyprus (Acts 15: 36–39).

A PERSONAL RESPONSIBILITY FOR A GREAT COMMISSION

- *A Personal Responsibility for Souls*
- *A Great Commission for Soulwinners*
  - ✫ According to Matthew
  - ✫ According to Mark
  - ✫ According to Luke
  - ✫ According to John
  - ✫ According to Acts

I. A Personal Responsibility

A. The "heart" of Christianity is outlined in Paul's first letter to Timothy:

"Christ Jesus came into the world to save sinners... God our Saviour ... will have all men to be saved, and to come unto the knowledge of the truth. For there is one mediator between God and men, the man Christ Jesus" (1 Timothy 1:15, 2:3–5).

B. Jesus Christ identifies Himself as a soulwinner (Luke 4:16–21).

C. He calls His followers to do likewise (Matthew 4:18–19, 28:19–20; John 20:21; Acts 1:8).

D. He has committed to us "the word of reconciliation" (2 Corinthians 5:18–19).

E. We are ambassadors for Christ (2 Corinthians 5:20).

F. If we don't share the gospel, who will? Who else has the complete, yet simple, truth? (Romans 13:11; Acts 20:26).

II. A Great Commission

A. The Commission According to Matthew (28:18–20)
1. **The Power of the King to give it:**
    "All power [authority] is given unto me" (v18)
2. **The Purpose of the King in giving it:**
    "Teach [make disciples of] all nations" (v19)
3. **The Possession of the King for those receiving it:**
    "Baptize [bring them into the local church]" (v19)
4. **The Precept of the King for those believing it:**
    "Teaching [discipling] them to observe all things whatsoever I have commanded you" (v20a)
5. **The Presence of the King with His own:**
    "And lo, I am with you always, even unto the end of the world" (v20b)

B. The Commission According to Mark (16:15–18)
1. **The Method of Missions:**
    "Go ye into all the world and preach the gospel" (v15a)
2. **The Scope of Missions:**
    "To every creature" (v15b)
3. **The Message of Missions:**
    "He that believeth and is baptized shall be saved; but he that believeth not shall be damned" (v16)

C. *The Commission According to Luke (24:44–49)*
1. **The Content of the Gospel:**
   "All things must be fulfilled, which were written in the law of Moses, and in the prophets, and in the psalms, concerning me" (v44).
2. **The Charge of the Gospel:**
   "That repentance and remission of sins should be preached in his name" (v47a).
3. **The Scope of the Gospel:**
   "Among all nations, beginning at Jerusalem" (v47b)
4. **The Instrument of the Gospel:**
   "Ye are witnesses of these things" (v48)
5. **The Dynamic of the Gospel:**
   "Ye be endued with power from on high" (v49)

D. *The Commission According to John (20:21, 21:15)*
1. **The Origination of the Great Commission:**
   "As my Father hath sent me, even so send I you" (20:21).
2. **The Motivation for the Great Commission:**
   "Lovest thou me more than these?" (21:15).
3. **The Object of the Great Commission:**
   "Feed my lambs" (21:15).

E. *The Commission in Acts (Acts 1:8)*
1. **The Ministry of the Holy Ghost:**
   "Ye shall receive power [ability/empowerment] after that the Holy Ghost is come upon you"
2. **The Ministry of the Disciples**
   "Ye shall be witnesses unto me"

3. **The Message Everywhere**

"In Jerusalem [your city], and in all Judea [your state], and in Samaria [the "unwanted" and "unloved" of society], and unto the uttermost part of the earth [the whole world]"

TEST 3

(40 Points)

Note: Where no total point value is given for a question, each correct answer is worth one point.

1. What is the meaning of evangelism? (4 points)
    Evangelism is telling other people about the saving power of Jesus Christ and the new life that follows, wherever you may be as you go through your day.
2. Explain the term "soulwinner". (2 points)
    Someone actively presenting the Gospel to unsaved people and striving to win them to salvation in Jesus Christ.
3. Briefly explain the motive for soulwinning. (4 points)
    Soulwinners love the lost and reach out to them with the gospel of salvation, because hell is real. Soulwinners have the words of eternal life.
4. What is the Gospel of Jesus Christ? (5 points)
    God provides for man's salvation from the penalty for sin through the death, burial, and resurrection of His only begotten Son, Jesus Christ. The Gospel is the good news about God's salvation plan.
5. Explain how Satan came to be the ruler of this world. Provide Scripture references. (6 points)
    God gave the world to man to rule. Man in turn gave the world to Satan by choosing to believe him rather than obey God. Thus, Satan's rule stems from Adam's disobedience toward God by ignoring His Word. Genesis 1:27–29, 2:15–17, 3:1–6.

6. Explain why you have a personal responsibility to be a soul-winner. Provide Scripture references. (6 points)
   Jesus Christ identifies Himself as a soulwinner (Luke 4:16–21) and calls His followers to do likewise (Matthew 4:18–19; Acts 1:8). He has committed to us the "word of reconciliation" (2 Corinthians 5:18–19). Matthew 28:19–20 also applies.

7. Where is the "heart" of Christianity outlined? Provide Scripture references. (3 points)
   In Paul's first letter to Timothy. 1 Timothy 1:15, 2:3–5

8. List the various places in the New Testament where a Great Commission is outlined. Provide the relevant Scripture references. (10 points)
   - *The Commission according to Matthew (28:18–20)*
   - *The Commission according to Mark (16:15–18)*
   - *The Commission according to Luke (24:44–49)*
   - *The Commission according to John (20:21, 21:15)*
   - *The Commission in Acts (1:8)*

THE LINK BETWEEN PERSONAL EVANGELISM AND WORLD EVANGELISM

- *The Meaning of "Personal Evangelism"*
- *The Need for Personal Evangelism*
- *Three Conditions*
- *Prerequisites for Personal Evangelists*

I. The Meaning of "Personal Evangelism"

A. Personal—Person-to-person confrontation with the gospel.

B. Evangelism—Transliterated from the Greek word for "gospel" (the good message or good news). Those who share the gospel are:

1. Declarers of the Good News that Christ died for our sins and rose again (1 Corinthians 15:1–4).

2. Dependent on God (2 Corinthians 3:5–6).

3. Co-laborers together with Christ (1 Corinthians 3:5–9).

4. Familiar with God's Word (2 Corinthians 4:1–2).

C. Personal evangelism and soulwinning is therefore the spreading of the good news of salvation through person-to-person contact and sometimes direct presentation of the Gospel in an attempt to win someone to Christ by the power of God. Personal evangelism and soulwinning are the duty of every Christian.

II. The Need for Personal Evangelism

In the previous lesson we considered biblical commissions that lie at the heart of world evangelism. God's Word provides both the impetus and authority for missionary evangelists to plant churches around the world in the name of Jesus Christ. But a Christian who will not cross the street to tell his neighbor the good news about salvation is unlikely to cross the world to share the same message. Personal evangelism comes before world evangelism.

Another way to view the challenge to be a personal evangelist is to understand that each of the more than six billion people in the world must respond *individually* to Jesus Christ in order to inherit eternal life, starting perhaps with the individual sitting right next to you!

Jesus' strategy for His disciples was very simple and direct: "Follow me, and I will make you fishers of men."

Notice that we must first be followers of Jesus before we can be fishers of men. To be a follower of Jesus means that we conduct our lives in a way that clearly differs from the ways of the world. Ralph Waldo Emerson perhaps framed it best: "What you do speaks so loud that I cannot hear what you say."

Personal evangelism begins with our Christian witness, our testimony, which in turn lays the foundation for our work as soulwinners. Sadly, though many Christians may be careful to maintain a good testimony, very few know (or care to know) how to "fish for men." Church attendance is viewed as sufficient service to Christ rather than preparation for service to Christ. We serve by soulwinning!

III. Three Conditions Must Be Met to Reach the World with the Gospel

A. Individual Christians must accept responsibility.

1. Soulwinning is not the sole responsibility of missionaries or "paid professionals."

2. An individual Christian who may never go to the mission field or enter any field of full-time Christian service is still responsible for sharing the gospel.

B. Individual Christians must be trained as soulwinners.

1. Know the Scriptures.

2. Know how to share the Scriptures.

C. Individual Christians must "tell as they go" in obedience to the Great Commission.

IV. Prerequisites for Personal Evangelists

Soulwinners are not "Super Christians." But they are not weak and defeated Christians either. The following prerequisites are shared by all dedicated soulwinners:

A. *They are prepared!* They have memorized the relevant Scriptures and know how to use them when presenting the gospel. These key soulwinning verses are the minimum that should be memorized:

- John 3:16; Romans 3:23, 5:8, 6:23; Acts 4:12, 20:21; and Romans 10:9, 13.

B. *They are pure!* Charles Spurgeon said there cannot be faith in your heart if there is not holiness in your life—and soulwinners need faith! Souls are not saved by human personality or the power of human argument, but by the power of the Holy Spirit exalting the risen Jesus Christ.

C. *They pray!* Prayer does not prepare us for the greatest work—it is the greatest work!

1. The world is a hostile place where we "wrestle not against flesh and blood, but against principalities,

against the powers, against the rulers of the darkness of this world, against spiritual wickedness in high places" (Ephesians 6:12).

2. Wicked spiritual powers are determined to enslave people and lead them blindly to hell (Matthew 24:4, 5, 11). Thus, prayer is not an option for a Christian, it is a necessity.

THE IMPORTANCE OF A PERSONAL TESTIMONY

- *The Power of a Personal Testimony*
- *Three Reasons for a Personal Testimony*
- *Key Elements of a Personal Testimony*
- *Students Share Personal Testimonies of Salvation*

I. The Power of a Personal Testimony

Every saved Christian has a personal testimony. You may not have theological answers to every question, you may not even know all the Scripture verses you should, but you can speak with enthusiasm and conviction about your personal relationship with Jesus Christ.

If the Jesus you are pointing to in the Scriptures is seen to be alive in you, your hearers will be impressed. The powerful story of the man born blind, told in John 9:1–38, perfectly illustrates this point. The man knew very little about Jesus and could not explain how he was healed—but he did know one thing: once he was blind, and now he could see!

II. Three Reasons For a Personal Testimony

It may not always be appropriate to share your personal testimony, but when you do make use of this tool, there are at least three good reasons why it will enhance your soulwinning efforts.

A. *Your Audience Cannot Disagree With You*
When you share your testimony, it is hard for others to disagree with you since it is *your* personal experience!

B. *You Can Say Things That Might Otherwise Be Offensive*
If you want to communicate a provocative or controversial truth, it is easier to do so as something you have learned, rather than something your audience must learn. So, for example, you might say:

- ☆ "My experience from conversations with many different people is that most have no real purpose in life."
- ☆ "I've discovered that most people don't really know what the Bible says. They may know about some passages but often in the wrong context."
- ☆ "I've learned from personal Bible study that many churches don't teach the truth."
- ☆ "I've discovered that religion doesn't save; obeying God saves."

C. *A Good Testimony Leads Naturally to the Gospel*
Your testimony will not get anyone else saved. Its purpose is to arouse curiosity so that you can present the gospel message that saved you.

III. Key Elements of a Personal Testimony

A. Tell it in two minutes or less. Remember, soulwinning is not about you; it's about Jesus!

B. Tell what you were like before you became a Christian.

C. Tell what happened the day you met Christ.

- ☆ Why did it happen?

☆ How did it happen?

D. Tell how Christ has changed your life.

    ☆ Don't brag—give glory to God.

    ☆ Don't dwell on the bad things you used to do.

      ← You realized you were a sinner.

      ← You discovered that Christ died for your sins.

    ☆ Emphasize your assurance and certainty—merely religious people have no sure hope or certainty in their beliefs

E. Note that if you are fortunate enough to have been raised in a Christian home, you may have been saved at a very early age and not have an awareness of what life was like before becoming a Christian. Likewise, it is unlikely that you will have a sense of a sinful past or a dramatic change that occurred in your life after salvation. However, you should be able to testify with joy and assurance about the reality of a personal relationship with Jesus Christ and the prospect of spending eternity in heaven with Him.

F. Don't get too complicated.

G. Stick to the point—don't get sidetracked.

H. Share your testimony with sincerity.

    ☆ Look at the person you're talking to.

    ☆ Don't talk as if you have memorized a script.

    ☆ Be warm and friendly at all times.

IV. Practicum—Students Share Their Personal Testimonies

Think about your salvation experience and organize your thoughts in writing so that you can share your testimony with your classmates in two minutes or less.

Presenting The Gospel

- *Why We Present the Gospel*
- *How We Present the Gospel*
- *Steps In Presenting the Gospel*

I. Why We Present the Gospel

A God commands all His people to preach the Gospel to everyone (Mark 16:15).

B. Salvation is contained only in the Gospel (2 Corinthians 11:4; Galatians 1:6).

C. Sinners need a Savior (Romans 3:23).

D. Hell is real (Luke 16:19–31).

E. Christians have the words of eternal life—the Gospel (2 Corinthians 5:18–20).

II. How We Present The Gospel

A. It is *history* when we say, "Christ died on Calvary."

B. It is *theology* when we say, "Christ died on Calvary for sins."

C. It is *testimony* when we say, "Christ died on Calvary for *my* sins."

D. It is an offer of *salvation* when we say, "Christ died on Calvary for *your* sins."

E. Salvation is a *personal* experience. We do not meet Jesus Christ when we merely know about Him or speak of Him, but when we sincerely yield to Him as our Lord and Savior.

1. Our responsibility in presenting the gospel is not to debate history or theology but to simply and directly present Jesus Christ as *real* and *present* and the only Savior for lost sinners.

2. We must make the salvation message as clear as possible to those we talk to and depend on the Holy Spirit to use our words to persuade them that they can act immediately by claiming Christ as their Savior.

3. The materialistic and sinful nature of society makes this a difficult task. But it has always been true that regardless of the condition of society or the heart of the individual sinner, the presence and power of the Holy Spirit is the essential component of soulwinning. We are co-laborers with Him (John 16:7–11)—our job is to share the gospel, and His job is first to convict the sinner of his or her need of salvation and then to perform the miracle of new spiritual birth.

4. Note, however, that the Holy Spirit's work is quenched (1 Thessalonians 5:19) if the soulwinner is uncaring and his life is unholy. Concern for the lost, prayer, and holy living must be part of the make-up of the soulwinner (Galatians 5:15–26).

III. Steps in Presenting the Gospel

The heart of the Gospel is very simple:

- People are sinners.

- Sinners need a Savior.
- Jesus Christ is the answer.

This message may be shared in many different ways—one of the most popular is to use the so-called "Romans Road" (because all of the Scriptures come from the New Testament book of Romans). An outline of the gospel message as four steps along this road provides a simple and effective means to lead a sinner to Jesus Christ. These steps should be memorized and practiced so that the soulwinner is able to share the gospel with ease and confidence.

STEP ONE—Everybody Falls Short of God's Standards:

"All have sinned and come short of the glory of God."
(ROMANS 3:23)

The Bible defines sin as falling short of God's perfection. Our first step towards God comes when we understand and agree that we do not live up to His perfect standards. We do things that we know are wrong.

If you know that you're not perfect, then you know that you're a sinner. However, if you believe that you can somehow do enough good deeds to outweigh your bad deeds (an impossibility), or if you're not troubled by the consequences of your sin—in this life and the next—you are not yet ready for God to help you.

STEP TWO—There is a Price to Pay for Sin:

"The wages of sin is death..."
(ROMANS 6:23A)

Sinners are like workers punching a time clock. Each time we "clock in" with a sin, we increase our debt. No sin is free, and no sin is cheap—the Bible says that the payment for our sin is "death." This death is more than a mere physical experience—it is the eternal separation of our soul from God in a terrible place called hell; a place reserved for those who reject God and choose to make their own payment for their sins.

The fact is that those who persist in rejecting God in this life will go in the next life to a place where God is not!

STEP THREE—God has Paid the Price:

> "God commendeth his love toward us, in that, while we were yet sinners, Christ died for us. Much more then, being now justified by his blood, we shall be saved from wrath through him."
>
> (ROMANS 5:8–9)

> "... the gift of God is eternal life through Jesus Christ our Lord."
>
> (ROMANS 6:23B)

God loves you very much. He does not want you to spend eternity in hell. That is why He came to earth as a man called Jesus Christ. He came to live a perfect life in your place and die a horrible death in your place. He took on Himself the full punishment for your sin so that you would never have to pay the price. Instead, you can live forever in heaven with Him.

What's more, Romans 6:23b explains that the eternal life God offers is a gift—you cannot earn it, and you don't have to work for it, you need only to ask for it and accept it.

STEP FOUR—What Will You Do About It?

> "If thou shalt confess with thy mouth the Lord Jesus, and shalt believe in thine heart that God hath raised him from the dead, thou shalt be saved."
>
> (ROMANS 10:9)

Forgiveness that leads to eternal life comes through faith in Jesus Christ, who rose from the dead to prove that He is the only one able to save you. But head knowledge alone is not enough. Knowing that you are a sinner, and knowing that God wants to save you, must motivate your heart to do something about it. You must want to be saved.

This means you want to turn from your old life and choose a new life with Jesus Christ. The Bible calls this repentance (Acts 17:30, 26:20). The new life begins the moment you place your faith in Him alone to save you and sincerely and openly ask Him to do so. The Bible promises that He *will* save you when you call on Him!

> *"For whosoever shall call upon the name of the Lord shall be saved."*
>
> (Romans 10:13)

Introducing The Gospel— and Tying The Knot

- *Getting Started*
- *The Power of a Tract*
- *Door-to-Door Visitation*
- *Answering Questions by Asking Questions*
- *More Questions*
- *Next Steps*

I. Getting Started

Once you are sure you know the outline of the gospel and the key Scripture verses that go with it (Unit 14: Presenting the Gospel), the next step is to find an audience. But as you go, remember that soulwinning is not an intellectual exercise, and people are not saved simply through a change of mind after losing an argument!

Through the presence and work of the Holy Spirit and through the effectual working of the Word of God, lost souls experience the miracle of spiritual rebirth. Thus it is essential for soulwinners to know the Scriptures and to immerse their soulwinning activities in prayer, acknowledging their need of God's help. See John 14:26; John 6:44; Romans 10:17; Hebrews 4:12.

II. The Power of a Tract

The easiest way to witness to others is to hand out tracts. A well-designed gospel tract is a powerful soulwinning tool.

Getting a tract into someone's hand is as easy as walking up to
a stranger, smiling, and saying, "Here's a gift for you!"

Always have tracts with you, and be prepared to use them.
Take advantage of every situation—never let a chance go by.
Tracts may be left anywhere people go—in planes, trains, buses,
restrooms, supermarkets, restaurants, and shopping malls. Leave
them where others can find them, or personally hand them out.
Tracts are so effective because they never get tired, are never
discouraged, remain consistent in every circumstance, and are
always ready to speak to anyone who is ready to listen!

III. Door-to-Door Visitation

When you knock on a door or ring a doorbell, you are calling
the home resident to meet a total stranger—you! Make a good
first impression. Smile. Tell yourself you're glad to be there (it
will show in your eyes). Be as personable as possible so that you
leave a good testimony for your church and for your Savior.
Speak clearly and unhurriedly and say something like this:

- "Hi! My name is *(your name)*, and this is *(your soulwinning partner's name)*. We're from *(name of church)*, and
  we're out visiting in your neighborhood. (Present the
  church tract.) We want to give you a personal invitation
  to visit us sometime."

Try to engage the person in general conversation. Perhaps say
something nice about the house or the neighborhood. Then ask:

- "Do you (does your family) have a church home where
  you attend regularly?"

If the answer is, "Yes, we attend church," your reply should
be:

- "That's wonderful! Having a church home is very
  important—but it's even more important to have a home
  in heaven. **Have you ever come to the place in your
  spiritual life where you know for certain that if you**

**died today you would go to heaven? Or do you have
some doubt?"**

Listen carefully to the answer and look for an opportunity
to share the Gospel. Be friendly. Engage in conversation as long
as the person is willing to give you time. But don't overstay your
welcome, and don't push too hard. Try to make an appointment
for a follow-up visit. Try to get a telephone number.

If the answer is, "We're not interested," smile and look the
person in the eye as you hold out the tract. Then say:

- "We would like you to have this simple explanation of
how you can have a home in heaven. This is something
that means a lot to us, and I trust it will to you too."

Depending on the response, look for an opportunity to ask
the salvation question (in bold) above.

IV. Answering Questions by Asking Questions

Asking questions is an effective way to begin a conversation
about the Gospel under almost any circumstance, whether you're
sitting beside someone on a bus or train or standing in line at
a supermarket or knocking on doors in a neighborhood. In the
latter case, the questions may be posed as a community survey
being conducted by your church or youth group. Wherever you
are, asking a question offers a simple, friendly way to begin a
conversation that will lead to a challenge to hear the Gospel.

Questioning is also a subtle but powerful way to get people
to think about important spiritual issues that most avoid and
will not usually discuss with a stranger.

So the initial purpose in asking questions is to establish a
basis for sharing the Gospel. Here are some typical questions
that may be asked. Notice how they follow a logical order:

- What do you think about religion?
- What do you think about Jesus Christ?

- Do you believe there is a heaven and a hell?
- Where do you think you will go when you die?
- Do you think that a loving God wants you to be absolutely sure about where you will spend eternity? Or will He keep you guessing?
- Was there ever a time when someone showed you from the Bible how you can know beyond any doubt that you have eternal life in heaven?

Listen to the answers to these questions without commenting, since they lead up to a challenge to consider the truth of the Gospel (assuming that the answers indicate that the person to whom you are speaking does not know or understand the way of salvation). The next question is the key:

- The Bible explains simply and clearly how we can be sure beyond any doubt that we have a home in heaven. Would you like to see what the Bible says?

This is the point of decision. Do not say anything more as you wait for a response. Let the Holy Spirit do His work! If it becomes clear that the person does not wish to proceed further, thank him or her for his or her time and hand the person a tract with an invitation to read it when opportunity permits. On the other hand, if the person indicates he or she would like to know more, you now have an opportunity to share the gospel as outlined in the previous lesson.

V. More Questions

As you share the Gospel, asking a question which makes someone think about the answer is a powerful device, because it allows the Holy Spirit to influence the answer. So when you come to the point of sharing a tract, instead of trying to explain the contents, you might point to the first Scripture verse and ask, "What do you think this means?"

From this point on, follow the conversation wherever it leads, being careful to ask open-ended questions (questions that require more than a "yes" or "no" answer). Give the Holy Spirit an opportunity to bring conviction to the sinner's heart through the Word of God. If the tract is well designed, the Scripture verses should lead step-by-step to the point of commitment to Jesus Christ. For example, show Romans 3:23 and ask, "What do you think this means?"

- Wait for a complete answer. Provide gentle guidance as necessary.
- Do not rush this process. Proceed to the next verse only when you are satisfied that your listener grasps the meaning of the present verse.

VI. Tying the Knot

The whole focus of sharing the gospel is to bring your listener to a point of decision regarding Jesus Christ. When you have presented all the verses in the Roman Road and received satisfactory answers, ask this last question:

- Based on what the Bible says, is there any reason you can think of why you would not want to receive Jesus Christ as your personal Savior?

Wait for the answer without further comment. Let the Holy Spirit do His work. If there is any hesitation, do not rush to pray, but seek to clarify what the problem is by asking more questions.

- Do not be sidetracked by irrelevant questions. Politely turn them aside by saying, "I would like to answer you in some detail, but let's settle this issue first and come back to your question later."
- Perhaps the time or location is a problem. If the person is evasive for any reason, hand him or her the tract and ask him or her to read it again when time permits. Make

an appointment to return within the next few days. Be sure to get the person's full name, address, and telephone number, and let the person know that you will be praying for him or her.

- If, on the other hand, you get a positive response to your invitation, explain that it is important not only to place one's faith in Jesus but also to express it (Romans 10:9–11).

- Encourage a prayer out loud, but be careful not to put words in the other person's mouth. Salvation does not come from following a religious formula. The person should be willing to pray on his or her own, using his or her own words.

- Shyness and unfamiliarity with personal expressions of spiritual belief may still prevent the person from praying out loud. In that case, encourage him or her to pray silently while you wait, then ask the person to confirm that he or she has prayed and asked Jesus to save him or her.

VII. Next Steps

A soulwinner's responsibility does not end when someone gets saved! We are exhorted by Scripture both to teach and to make disciples. See the apostle Paul's letters to his converts, especially Romans 1:7–12; Ephesians 1:15–23; Philippians 1:1–11, etc.

You should let your convert know that you are proud of this very important decision and that you will be available to answer questions and provide spiritual assistance in the weeks ahead. Offer to provide a Bible if necessary, and encourage him or her to attend church with you. It is essential that your convert (sooner rather than later) make a public profession of his or her faith, get baptized, and join a good Bible-believing church like the one you attend.

TEST 4

(50 Points)

Note: Where no total point value is given for a question, each correct answer is worth one point.

1. What was Jesus' strategy for teaching His disciples to be soulwinners? (2 points)
    "Follow me, and I will make you fishers of men."
2. True or False: Church attendance is our service to Christ. Explain your answer. (4 points)
    False. Church attendance prepares us for service to Christ. We serve Christ by soulwinning.
3. What three conditions must be met to reach the world with the Gospel? Complete this statement in each case. Individual Christians must…
    a. *accept responsibility*
    b. *be trained as soulwinners*
    c. *"tell" as you are going, in obedience to the Great Commission*
4. Complete this sentence (3 points): Soulwinning is *spreading the good news of salvation through person-to-person confrontation, by the power of God.*

5. List the seven key elements of a personal testimony. (14 points)
   a. *Tell it in two minutes or less.*
   b. *Tell what you were like before you became a Christian.*
   c. *Tell what happened the day you met Christ.*
   d. *Tell how Christ has changed your life.*
   e. *Don't get too complicated.*
   f. *Stick to the point—don't get sidetracked.*
   g. *Share your testimony with sincerity.*

6. Why do we present the Gospel?
   a. *God commands all of His people to preach the Gospel to everyone.*
   b. *Sinners need a Savior.*
   c. *Hell is real.*
   d. *Salvation is contained only in the Gospel.*
   e. *Christians have the words of eternal life.*

7. What is the heart of the Gospel we present?
   a. *People are sinners.*
   b. *Sinners need a Savior.*
   c. *Jesus Christ is the answer.*

8. List four "steps" along the Romans Road and the related Scripture references (8 points):
   a. *Everybody falls short of God's standards. The Bible calls this sin. (Romans 3:23)*
   b. *There is a price to pay for sin—eternal separation from God. (Romans 6:23a)*
   c. *God loves you and has paid the price for your sins. God's payment is offered to you as a gift. (Romans 6:23b)*
   d. *Merely knowing that God loves you and has done so much for you is not enough. You must ask God to save you. (Romans 10:9, 13)*

9. What is a key question that you should ask in order to determine if someone wants to know more about the Gospel? (5 points)

    The Bible explains simply and clearly how we can be sure beyond any doubt that we have a home in heaven. These verses do not agree with your answers. Would you like to see what the Bible says?

10. What question would you ask to bring someone to the point of decision about praying for salvation? (4 points)

    Based on what the Bible says, is there any reason you can think of why you would not want to accept Jesus Christ as your personal Savior?

LESSON BY PASTOR OR VISITING MISSIONARY EVANGELIST

- *Lesson By Pastor or Visiting Missionary Evangelist*
  - ☆ May be inserted at any time during this quarter.

REVIEW AND SCRIPTURE TEST

- *Review Quarter*
- *Test Memorized Scripture Passage*

INTRODUCTION TO STUDY OF GREAT MISSIONARY EVANGELISTS

- *Introduce and Review **Giants of the Missionary Trail***
- *Review List of Books for Book Reports*

I. Briefly Review the Textbook for this Quarter

- *Giants of the Missionary Trail* by Eugene Myers Harrison

II. Book Reports

A. A list of approved biographies is provided below. Many of these are found in the "Heroes of the Faith" series by Barbour Publishing. Where this is not the case, reference to the Internet will provide information on where the books may be obtained.

B. Requirements for Book Reports:

1. Reports must be submitted in the next-to-last week of this quarter (the eighth week).

2. Reports must be between 800 and 1,000 words in length. The word count must be clearly indicated on the report.

3. The first section of the report must be in the form of an outline summary of the story.

4. The greater part of the report must be devoted to a discussion of the student's personal reaction

and views—what was gleaned from the story that inspired, informed, and influenced the student.

III. List of Approved Missionary Evangelists for Study

Biographical information on some Baptist missionaries and pioneering Baptist preachers may be obtained on the Internet at:

- www.geocities.com/baptist_documents/bapt.bios.html

Two recommended biographies from this source are Tarlton Perry Crawford and William Hickman. There is also much other interesting material.

Books listed below, obtainable from Barbour Publishing and other publishers, focus on missionary evangelists, missionary helpers, and individuals who do not fit the biblical definition of a missionary evangelist but whose Christian testimonies as preachers, personal evangelists, or soulwinners made a significant impact for the cause of Christ.

- Brother Andrew
- Gladys Aylward
- Amy Carmichael
- William Carey
- Jim Elliot
- Elisabeth Elliot
- Adoniram Judson
- Eric Liddell
- Florence Nightingale
- Nate Saint
- Francis and Edith Schaeffer
- Mary Slessor

- Charles Spurgeon
- John and Betty Stam
- C.T. Studd
- Hudson Taylor
- John Wesley
- George Whitfield

GIANTS OF THE MISSIONARY TRAIL: HENRY NOTT

- *Henry Nott—Tahiti.*

REVIEW AND TEST: HENRY NOTT

- *Test*
- *Discuss main lessons learned from Henry Nott's story.*
- *Homework: read chapter on William Carey.*

WILLIAM CAREY

- *William Carey—India.*

REVIEW AND TEST: WILLIAM CAREY

- *Test*
- *Discuss main lessons learned from William Carey's story.*
- *Homework: read chapter on George Grenfell.*

George Grenfell

- *George Grenfell—Congo.*

Review and Test: George Grenfell

- *Test*
- *Discuss main highlights from George Grenfell's story.*
- *Homework: read chapter on Adoniram Judson.*

Adoniram Judson

- *Adoniram Judson—Burma.*

Review and Test: Adoniram Judson

- *Test*
- *Discuss main highlights from Adoniram Judson's story.*
- *Homework: read chapter on Samuel Marsden.*

SAMUEL MARSDEN

- *Samuel Marsden—New Zealand.*

REVIEW AND TEST: SAMUEL MARSDEN

- *Test*
- *Discuss main highlights from Samuel Marsden's story.*
- *Homework: read chapter on David Livingstone.*

DAVID LIVINGSTONE

- *David Livingstone—Southern Africa.*

REVIEW AND TEST: DAVID LIVINGSTONE

- *Test*
- *Discuss main highlights from the David Livingstone story.*
- *Homework: read chapter on James Chalmers.*

James Chalmers

- *James Chalmers — New Guinea.*

Review and Test: James Chalmers

- *Test*
- *Discuss main highlights from the James Chalmers story.*
- *Homework: read chapter on Jonathan Goforth.*

Jonathan Goforth

- *Jonathan Goforth—China.*

Review and Test: Jonathan Goforth

- *Test*
- *Discuss main highlights from the Jonathan Goforth story.*

Lesson by the Pastor or Visiting Missionary Evangelist

- *Lesson By Pastor Or Visiting Missionary Evangelist*
  ☆ May be inserted at any time this quarter.

REVIEW AND SCRIPTURE TEST

- *Review*
- *Test Memorized Scripture Passage*

PRESENTATION BY THE PASTOR OR MISSIONS DIRECTOR/ SECRETARY

- *Presentation By Pastor Or Missions Director/Secretary*
  ☆ How our church helps to evangelize the world.

ADOPT A MISSIONARY EVANGELIST

- *Purpose*
- *Correspondence*
- *Project*
- *Form Letters*

I. Purpose

Bring the mission field and the mission experience "close to home" by corresponding with a missionary child of the same age (names and addresses supplied from a list of church-supported missionaries). This correspondence will provide material for monthly reports and a project presentation (see below).

II. Correspondence

Correspondence will be by e-mail and regular mail (see form letters below). At least three different letters must be written before the end of the school year (February, March, and April or May) and each response must be turned in for a grade on the third week of each month. It is the student's responsibility to obtain a response or to provide a valid reason why a response could not be obtained.

III. Project

A display project based on information gleaned from the "adopted" missionary family must be completed by mid-April.

The presentation must be mounted on a science project display board (obtainable at any craft store) and must contain the following (numbers in brackets indicate points earned for each section—the total will add up to the equivalent of two test grades):

- A heading containing the name of the missionary family and the country in which they minister. Next to the information, in smaller type, must be written: Reported By: Your Name [5]
- The favorite Bible verse of the missionary family. [4]
- A photograph of the missionary family and an additional photograph of the missionary child with whom you are corresponding, with captions. [10]
- Personal details about the missionary family—the house they live in, the town they live in, the type of food they eat, favorite activities, things that are similar to life in America, and things that are different. [15]
- A picture of the country's flag. [2]
- A small map showing the region of the world in which the country is located, and a larger map of the country with the capital and major landforms or bodies of water labeled. Also show where the missionary family is located. [10]
- The country's current form of government and the leader's name. [2]
- Size of population and major ethnic/people groups. [2]
- Number of language groups. [2]
- Names of the country's major religions and numbers of adherents. [5]
- Estimated number of missionaries in the country. [3]

- Estimated number of independent fundamental Baptists in the country. [5]
- At least one other interesting fact about the country (strange customs, foods, etc.). [5]
- Layout, neatness, and use of proper display board. [20]
- Spelling and grammar. [10]

IV. Form Letters

- **First Letter:**
  Your address
  Date
  Dear.................

I am a student at [Name] Academy and a member of [Name] Church. I have your name because our church supports your father in his work as a church planting missionary in [Country].

This year in our World Evangelism class, we are learning a lot about missions and missionary evangelists. I'm required to do a project about a missionary family. This letter is to ask if you are willing to participate in this project with me. From the information I have about you, it seems we are almost the same age—so that's a good place to start!

I have a lot of questions to ask about you and your family, where you are located, and what it's like to live there, both for you personally and for your family. However, because this will require some effort on your part, I want to be sure that you have time to help me with my project. Please let me know as soon as possible so that if you are not able to participate in this project with me, I have time to ask someone else.

Thanks a lot. I look forward to hearing from you soon.

Your friend,

(Your name)

• *Second Letter:*
  Dear.............

Thanks for writing back so soon! I appreciate your willingness to participate with me in this project. I'm excited about getting to know you and your family. At the same time I would be happy to answer any questions you might have about me.

Here is a list of the things I would like to know:

1. The names of all the people in your family—and the ages of the children—with pictures, please, including a separate (and recent) picture of you!
2. Your family's favorite Bible verse.
3. Information about where you live—your house, your town, the food you eat, your favorite activities, things that are similar to life in America, and things that are different. Perhaps some funny or strange or exciting adventures you have had.
4. Information about your family's ministry.

I also need to find a lot of information about the country you are in, but I think I can find most of it from reference books or off the Internet. If I need help in this area I will let you know.

I look forward to hearing from you soon.

SO WHAT IN THE WORLD IS THE WORLD LIKE?

- *Introduction*
- *First World and Third World*
- *Civilized and Uncivilized*
- *Hygienic and Unhygienic*
- *Food and Hunger*
- *Personal Space and Other Problems*
- *Language*

I. Introduction

In his letter to the Corinthians, Paul talks about his efforts to reach out to the lost and concludes by saying, "I am made all things to all men, that I might by all means save some. And this I do for the gospel's sake…" (1 Corinthians 9:22–23).

In another place (1 Corinthians 10:25), he says not to ask questions about what you buy in the market to eat "for conscience sake." Paul is here referring to food that might have been offered to idols, but it is generally good practical advice for those who go to foreign fields as missionary evangelists, since exotic customs and cultural differences can often be stumbling blocks to spreading the Gospel.

II. First World and Third World

It may be that God calls you to be a missionary evangelist and church planter in the next city or the next state, where living conditions are no different to yours—but what will you experience if you are called to a Third World country?

Most people live in Third World countries. The term First World applies to countries that are economically developed and industrialized, with established and stable legal systems, like the USA, Canada, Japan, France, England, Australia, etc. Second World countries are developing nations that are relatively stable, like Brazil, South Africa, India, and China. Third World countries are unstable, poverty-ridden, and rely heavily on outside aid. Most of these are found in Africa and Asia and include barely viable nations like Chad, Haiti, Somalia, North Korea, and Uganda.

III. Civilized and Uncivilized

A Third World country may lack First World amenities like dependable water and electricity supplies or a network of paved roads or well-equipped schools, offices, and shops, but that does not make it uncivilized.

"Civilization" is a term that is generally applied to a governed society that has a written language, a recorded history, a defined system of laws, and a culture of religion, arts, and music. Thus, the ancient Greeks and Chinese were civilized, while they still lived in mud huts without TV or hot and cold running water!

IV. Hygienic and Unhygienic

Most Americans hardly pause to consider that the milk and meat they buy at the supermarket does not originate in neat plastic containers. Our highly organized and regulated society ensures that the quite messy process that precedes the appearance of milk, meat, and other foodstuffs on our dinner tables is hidden from view.

What we don't eat immediately, we keep refrigerated. We also take regular baths—in water that has been purified, chlorinated, and fluoridated. Then we walk on pavements or drive on streets that are paved and clean and live in neighborhoods where trash is collected twice a week. Lawns are mowed. Roadkill is quickly removed by the sanitation department.

We wash our hands before each meal. We brush and floss after each meal, and we hide or correct what we find disagreeable about ourselves by the use of deodorants, breath fresheners, orthodontic devices, and plastic surgery.

The rest of the world is not like this. People in Third World countries (and even many First World countries) who bother to give a thought to dental hygiene feel Americans have too much time and money to waste on such nonessentials.

V. Food and Hunger

Americans are very picky about their diets, because they can afford to be picky. For most of the world's population, meals are taken no more than once a day (often less than once a day), and a meal consists of one thing—usually a staple like rice or corn or potatoes. So anything that can be eaten to supplement the diet is welcomed: insects, reptiles, rats, mice, spiders, worms, ants, bats, birds, beetles, and grubs—if it moves and it doesn't kill you first, kill it and eat it!

Meat and fish are highly prized, of course, and when an animal is slaughtered for food, every part of the animal is eaten, from the tip of its nose to the tip of its tail. Nothing is wasted. In a Third World country, heed the Apostle Paul's good advice: don't ask what's in the pot, just eat. It's usually quite tasty.

VI. Personal Space and Other Problems

Many cultures have no concept of "personal space"—that invisible, private, two-foot envelope that surrounds Americans and allows us to comfortably communicate with each other while not touching, smelling, or feeling threatened by each other.

An African or Asian (or even an Italian) may literally "get in your face" to talk to you. In hot countries where there is no air conditioning, there is no use of deodorants, and food is usually cooked with the addition of strong herbs and spices like garlic. This can be a testing experience for the average American.

African men who are good friends often hold hands. But they don't like to shake hands—sticking your hand out towards somebody is a very threatening gesture. Also, they (along with most Arabs) think it an insult when you look them straight in the eye. And they will be doubly insulted if you stand when they come into the room or fail to sit while they are standing or fail to crouch low while they are sitting, since it is very rude to raise yourself above another person who may be your superior.

In addition to these challenges, perhaps the biggest problem American missionaries face on almost any foreign field is that they have so much *stuff!* We need so much with us wherever we go, whether clothes or furniture or books or utilities, so we have to live in big houses.

VII. Language

Language can be a great barrier. Unfamiliar languages should be approached with great caution. Idioms, customs of use, single words that mean one thing in one language and something entirely different in another—all of these present richly-seeded minefields, threatening disaster. Americans should be especially cautious of the use of English! Though it is spoken by many people in all corners of the world, local cultures give meanings to words and expressions that are fraught with danger for the unaware.

GOD'S PURPOSE AND OUR RESPONSE

- *God's Purpose Revealed in Scripture*
- *New Testament Soulwinning in Response to God's Purpose*
- *Our Commission and Response*

I. God's Purpose for Humanity

A. To gather together in one all things in Christ (Ephesians 1:1–12, 2:7). In his letter to the Colossians, Paul expands on the idea of the centrality of Jesus Christ:

1. He is the image of God (Colossians 1:15).
2. He created everything (1:16).
3. Everything was created for Him (1:16).
4. By Him all things consist (1:17).
5. He is the head of the church (1:18).
6. He is preeminent in everything (1:18).
7. All fullness is in Him (1:19).
8. The riches of this mystery must be made known to the unsaved (1:27).
9. Everyone should be presented perfect in Christ (1:28).
10. In Him are hid all the treasures of wisdom and knowledge (2:3).

11. We are complete in Him (2:10).

12. Christ is our Life (3:4).

13. Christ is all, and in all (3:11).

14. We must do everything in the name of Christ (3:17).

B. It is not God's will that any should perish without Christ (2 Peter 3:9). Yet those who do not know Him, and those who resist Him, will suffer a terrible fate (Romans 6:23; Hebrews 10:29–31; Revelation 21:8).

II. New Testament Soulwinning In Response to God's Purpose

A. Jesus, the Founder of missions, was a great personal soulwinner!

1. Peter, Andrew, Philip, Nathanael (John 1:35–49; Matthew 4:18–19)

2. Matthew (9:9)

3. A leper (Mark 1:40–42)

4. A sick woman (Mark 5:24–34)

5. A man at a poolside (John 5:1–9)

6. Zaccheus (Luke 19:1–10)

7. A man born blind (John 9:1–25)

8. Nicodemus (John 3:1–16)

9. The woman at the well (John 4:5–10)

B. The early church, A.D. 33–100, was devoted to soulwinning.

1. Acts 1:82, 2:41, 8:5–6, 25–39, 10:1–6, 11:19–21

2. Acts chapters 13 through 28

3. Note especially Acts 17:6

III. Christians Today Have a Clear Commission to be Soulwinners

- Matthew 28:18–20
- Mark 16:15–18
- Luke 24:46–49
- Have you responded to the call?

GREAT MISSIONARY MOVEMENTS OF THE BIBLE

PART I: JESUS CHRIST, THE FOUNDER OF MISSIONS

Matthew 28:18–20 contains the "Great Commission" to teach all nations about salvation through Jesus Christ. Christians engaged in world evangelism are seeking to declare this good news—the Gospel—to every people group in the world. In many communities (like parts of California or the Washington, D.C. metropolitan area), the people of the world have come to where the Christian is, making the task of participating in world evangelism both easier and more immediately possible.

The fourth chapter of the Gospel of John tells a story that provides a powerful model for this world outreach. The story recounts a meeting at a well between Jesus and a woman who had come to find water.

1. Jesus showed how to reach out to those who are not well liked (4:4). Jews generally despised Samaritans and went out of their way to avoid them.

2. Jesus sought a meeting place where others would have a clear need (4:6).

3. He established common ground by allowing His humanity to show forth (4:6).

4. He showed how to stage an encounter (4:7–15).

   a. His presence at the well aroused the woman's curiosity.

   b. He asked her a question that made her even more curious.

    c. He let her know that He had a very special gift for her.

    d. He indicated the spiritual nature of the gift.

    e. He encouraged her to express her need for this great gift.

5. He confronted the woman with her sinfulness (4:16–18). Note that Jesus did not ignore, cover, or compromise over the woman's sin—yet He did not condemn her to the point that He alienated her.

6. He patiently explained the differences between true and false religion (4:21–24).

7. He did not allow Himself to be sidetracked by religious argument.

8. He plainly stated the truth (4:23–26).

9. He relied on His new convert to help Him to reach others (4:28–30, 39–42). Note a similar occasion where Jesus did the same thing in Luke 8:26–40.

10. Jesus also showed how to train soulwinners (4:27, 31–38).

    a. Note especially His encouragement for us to get our eyes off physical and material things and onto the spiritual (4:31–34).

    b. The spiritual harvest does not require ideal conditions some time in the future. Soulwinners must be active everywhere, anywhere, all the time (4:35–38).

GREAT MISSIONARY MOVEMENTS OF THE BIBLE

PART II: THE APOSTLE PAUL, CHURCH PLANTER—I

The Apostle Paul had a strong motivation and a clear strategy of missions that becomes apparent as we study his activities in preaching the gospel and planting new churches. Carefully consider each of the following Scripture verses for a full appreciation of the practical aspects of Paul's ministry. (Part II of this study of Paul follows in the next lesson.)

I. He had a strong motivation:

1. Paul was very clear about whom he served and why he served (1 Corinthians 1:1; 2 Corinthians 1:1; Galatians 1:1; Ephesians 1:1; Colossians 1:1; 1 Timothy 1:1; 2 Timothy1:1; Titus 1:1).

2. He was completely dedicated to the will of God (Acts 18:21, 21:13–14).

3. He was completely dependent on the Holy Spirit (1 Corinthians 2:1–5).

4. He played to win (1 Corinthians 9:26–27).

5. He knew what the stakes were (2 Corinthians 5:9–10).

6. His motives were pure (Philippians 1:20–21; 1 Corinthians 13:1–3).

7. He was committed to holiness (Philippians 4:8).

8. He had a very clear understanding of sin and its effects (Romans 1:18–2:9, 3:10–18, 6:13, 8:7; Ephesians 2:1–3, 4:17–19).

9. He was committed to the success of his cause:
   a. He believed in success (2 Corinthians 2:14).
   b. He prayed for success (Romans 1:10).
   c. He worked for success (Acts 20:26–27).
   d. He expected success (Romans 15:29).
   e. He achieved success (2 Timothy 4:6–8).

GREAT MISSIONARY MOVEMENTS OF THE BIBLE
PART III: THE APOSTLE PAUL, CHURCH PLANTER—II

In the previous lesson we saw that the apostle Paul had a strong motivation to be a missionary evangelist. As we study his life, it is apparent that he also had a clear strategy of missions as he planted churches over a period of about fifteen years.

II. He had a clear strategy:

1. Concentrating on a specific geographic area—four provinces in what is today Turkey and Greece.
   a. Galatia (Acts 18:23)
   b. Asia (Acts 19:10)
   c. Macedonia (Acts 16:9–10)
   d. Achaia (Acts 18:21)

2. Concentration on major cities. From there the gospel spread to the surrounding country. Cities included:
   a. Ephesus (Acts 19:1–20)
   b. Philippi (Acts 16:12–40)
   c. Thessalonica (Acts 17:13)
   d. Berea (Acts 17:10–12)
   d. Corinth (Acts 18:1–18)
   e. Rome (Acts 28:14–31)

3. He preached boldly! (Romans 1:16).
   a. Wherever Paul went, he attracted attention (Acts 14:3).

      b. He did not plant churches quietly and timidly (Acts 13:46–51, 20:7–21).

      c. He preached openly, expecting a response (Acts 13:50–51).

4. He baptized converts on their confession of faith. No requirements had to be met first (Acts 16:33).

- But note 1 Corinthians 1:14–17, where Paul explains that he personally stopped baptizing converts so that none could claim a special status regarding their baptism.

5. He made use of fellow workers—Barnabas (initially Paul's teacher), John, Mark, Silas, Timothy, etc.

      a. He built leaders (Acts 16:1–6).

      b. He built missionary teams (Acts 18:5).

6. He was flexible enough to become all things to all people, without the compromise of sin (1 Corinthians 9:22).

7. He encouraged the establishment of strong indigenous churches that were:

      a. Self-governing

      b. Self-supporting

      c. Self-propagating

TEST 5

[40 Points]

Note: Where no total point value is given for a question, each correct answer is worth one point.

1. Over what period of years did the apostle Paul plant churches?
   15

2. Looking at a modern map of the world, we would say that Paul planted churches in two geographic areas:
   a. *Asia Minor (Turkey)*
   b. *Europe (Greece)*

3. Paul planted churches in many cities and wrote letters to them all, except to the church in...
   Berea

4. List three characteristics of Paul's preaching:
   a. *He preached boldly.*
   b. *He preached openly.*
   c. *He baptized converts on their confession of faith.*
      He made use of fellow workers.
      He was flexible.

5. Where in Scripture is the "Great Commission" found?
   Matthew 28:18–20

6. Who is the Founder of missions?
   Jesus Christ

7. What is another term for the Gospel?
   The good news

8. How did Jews treat Samaritans?
   They looked down on them and tried to avoid them.

9. In your own words, indicate what you think is the most important or most interesting part of the story of Jesus meeting the woman at the well. Give Scripture references. Write your answer on a separate sheet of paper.(8 points)
   [Answers will vary]

10. Complete this sentence (3 points):
    Soulwinners must be active…*everywhere, anywhere, all the time.*

11. Complete this sentence (3 points):
    In order to be effective soulwinners, we must get our eyes off *physical and material things and onto the spiritual needs of individual people.*

12. What is significant about the way in which the apostle Paul introduced himself in all of his letters? (3 points)
    Paul was very clear about whom he served and why he served.

13. To what was Paul completely dedicated? Give a Scripture reference. (2 points)
    Doing the will of God (Acts 18:21, 21:13–14)

14. On what was Paul completely dependent? Give a Scripture reference. (2 points)
    The Holy Spirit (1 Corinthians 2:1–5)

15. What was Paul's attitude toward the success of his cause? Give Scripture references. (8 points)
    - *He believed in success (2 Corinthians 2:14).*
    - *He prayed for success (Romans 1:10).*
    - *He worked for success (Acts 20:26–27).*
    - *He expected success (Romans 15:29).*
    - *He achieved success (2 Timothy 4:6–8).*

The Person Of The Missionary Evangelist

Part I: Qualifications for the Ministry

- *Spiritual Qualifications*
- *Character Qualifications*

I. Spiritual Qualifications

The Bible admonishes those who are members of the family of God to live in a way that does not bring reproach to Him.

> *Do all things without murmurings and disputings:*
> *that ye may be blameless and harmless,*
> *the sons of God, without rebuke,*
> *in the midst of a crooked and perverse nation,*
> *among whom ye shine as lights in the world.*
> (PHILIPPIANS 2:14–15)

Even higher standards are expected of those who are called to preach the Gospel. 1 Timothy 3:1–7 and Titus 1:5–9 list the qualifications of a "bishop"—a pastor—as follows:

- Blameless—beyond criticism in his life
- The husband of one wife
- Vigilant—careful conduct, sound judgment
- Sober—serious-minded
- Of good behavior
- Given to hospitality

- Apt to teach
- Not given to wine (Note that the word "not" in this passage is a very strong word—No! Never!)
- No striker—either with his hands or his tongue
- Not greedy of filthy lucre—no love of money
- Patient
- Not a brawler—not an aggressive person
- Not covetous—not seeking his own things, but the things of Christ
- One that ruleth well his own house, having his children in subjection with all gravity.
- Not a novice—not a new Christian
- Have a good report of them that are without

II. Character Qualifications

In addition to the qualifications listed in Scripture for a pastor (which apply equally and completely to the missionary evangelist), a missionary evangelist should have certain emotional and character traits that will enable him to be a success on the mission field.

- Emotional stability
- Adaptability:
  - Accept different culture, food, dress, language
  - Not critical of the new culture or too proud of one's own
- A well-developed sense of humor
- Co-operative
- Teachable
- Submissive (to his pastor and home church)
- Humble
- No racial prejudice

THE PERSON OF THE MISSIONARY EVANGELIST

PART II: THE POWER OF PRAYER

- *Prayer is Talking to God*
- *Prayer was Evident in the Life of Jesus Christ*
- *Prayer was Evident in the Life of the Early Church*
- *The Apostle Paul was a Man of Fervent Prayer*
- *Prayer is the Key to Joy, Power, and Fruitfulness*

I. Prayer is Talking to God

Prayer is talking to God and expecting an answer. It is one of the most sacred activities of a Christian, because it acknowledges God, recognizes His power, and demonstrates trust in His personal concern for His people. More than six hundred prayer requests appear in the Bible. All of God's people should talk to Him each day—especially preachers of the Gospel!

Psalm 139 wonderfully reflects the close relationship between a believer and his heavenly Father as the basis for prayer. In the examples below, of prayer in the life of Jesus Christ, the apostle Paul, and the early church, we see that:

A. *Prayer Acknowledges God*
The very act of prayer assumes the existence of God and that He "has ears to hear."

B. *Prayer Recognizes the Power of God*
Help is asked only of those who are assumed to have the power to help!

C. Prayer Demonstrates Trust in God

Many profess to believe in the power of God but do not pray in the expectation that God will respond specifically and benevolently in response to their prayers. In the early church, trust that prayer would be answered flowed from a relationship with God made possible by birth into His family through Jesus Christ.

D. Prayer is always the right response

In every circumstance, whether joyful or sorrowful.

E. Prayer is always possible

Because God is always present.

II. Prayer Was Evident in the Life of Jesus Christ

A. Jesus Christ had much to say on the subject of prayer and set a great example as one who prayed often. Although He was the Son of God and possessed all authority in heaven and earth, He demonstrated His complete dependence on His Father by constantly resorting to prayer.

1. When the multitudes came to be healed by Him, He "withdrew himself into the wilderness, and prayed" (Luke 5:16).

2. Before choosing His disciples, He "continued all night in prayer to God" (Luke 6:12).

3. When He fed the five thousand, He prayed (Luke 9:16).

4. When He faced betrayal and death, He prayed (Luke 22:39–46).

5. As He hung on the cross, three of His seven last utterances were prayers. (Matthew 27:47; Luke 23:34, 46).

B. Since Jesus prayed so much, it is not surprising that He exhorted His followers to pray and found many opportunities to teach them to pray.

1. He taught His disciples that "men ought always to pray" and not to lose heart (Luke 18:1).

2. He urged prayer for more soulwinners (Matthew 9:38).

3. He counseled prayer instead of sleep in order to resist temptation (Luke 22:46).

4. He revealed that prayer and fasting was sometimes necessary to overcome the devil's power (Matthew 17:21).

5. He encouraged prayer for the Holy Spirit's power (Luke 11:13, 24:49).

III. Prayer Was Evident in the Life of the Early Church

A. Immediately after Pentecost, the disciples "continued stedfastly ...in prayers" (Acts 2:42).

B. When threats came, they prayed so fervently that they were filled again with the Holy Spirit! (Acts 4:23–31).

C. Missionaries were commissioned after prayer (Acts 13:2–3).

IV. The Apostle Paul was a Man of Fervent Prayer

A. He prayed especially on behalf of his converts (Romans 1:9–10; Ephesians 1:15–16, 3:14–16; Philippians 1:3–4; Colossians 1:9; 1 Thessalonians 1:2).

B. He spoke of the importance of prayer as a means to wage spiritual warfare (Ephesians 6:10–12, 18).

V. Prayer is the key to joy, power, and fruitfulness

A. When we ask and receive, our joy is made full (John 16:24).

B. Fellowship with Jesus Christ, through prayer, brings joy (1 John 1:3–4).

C. Followers of Jesus Christ—especially pastors and missionary evangelists—are on a mission from God, but they need His power to complete the mission! John 15:16 contains instruction about:

   1. The detail of the mission: "I chose you and appointed you that you should go and bear fruit."

   2. The source of power to complete the mission: "...so that whatever you ask the Father in my name, He may give it to you."

D. The apostle Paul prayed constantly for God's power. See for example: Ephesians 6:19; Colossians 4:3; 2 Thessalonians 3:1.

The Person Of The Missionary Evangelist

Part III: Hindrances

- *The Command to "Teach!"*
- *Hindrances to Going*

I. The Command to "Teach!"

Among the clearest commands in the Bible is Jesus' instruction to His followers to "teach." God builds His kingdom one soul at a time by Christians telling others the wonderful story of salvation. It is not surprising then, that the devil fights this command in every way he can, sowing confusion, discouragement, and disobedience among God's people.

Nevertheless, telling as we're going remains our greatest priority after salvation. Jesus put a lot of emphasis on the purpose of His ministry and His expectation of our purpose.

A. The first recorded words He spoke in public at the start of His ministry, clearly identified His purpose: "The Spirit of the Lord is upon me, because he hath anointed me to preach the gospel" (Luke 4:18).

B. The first recorded words He spoke to His disciples as He called them were just as direct: "Follow me, and I will make you fishers of men" (Matthew 4:19).

C. Later He told them: "You have not chosen me, but I have chosen you, and ordained you, that ye should go and bring forth fruit" (John 15:16).

D. Significantly, His last recorded words before returning to heaven addressed the same theme:
   1. "Go ye therefore, and teach all nations" (Matthew 28:18).
   2. "Go ye into all the world, and preach the gospel to every creature" (Mark 16:15).
E. Given this unmistakable directive, it is surprising that Christians hesitate to teach as they "go"—either around the block or around the world. A country like America, with a strong Christian tradition, will hear the Gospel preached in many Bible-believing churches (if not through door-to-door visitation), so it is the mission field that suffers most as a result of the reluctance of individual Christians to share their faith. Even those who answer a call to full-time Christian service will often resist the thought of doing so in a foreign country.

II. Hindrances to Going

Some reasons people are kept off the mission field:

A. *Misinformation:*
Laboring in a strange foreign country is often seen as difficult—both culturally and economically—because of different customs and foods and poor living conditions.

B. *Marriage:*
Spouses divided in their commitment to serve God do not make good missionaries! All Christians have a duty to God to be very careful in their choice of a marriage partner.

C. *Money:*
Nobody gets rich on the mission field!

D. Debt:

Debt usually indicates a lack of self-discipline. Moreover, a missionary laboring to pay his debts will not be laboring wholeheartedly to serve the Lord.

E. Advanced Education:

A college education is good, but too much education (in the form of Masters or Doctors degrees) may become a stumbling block because of the commitment of additional time, money, and energy that may be put to better use on the mission field. Particular dangers lurk in pursuing higher education through secular colleges. While the education may be technically of a high standard, the godless (and often virulently anti-God and anti-Christian) atmosphere prevailing on almost all secular campuses will be a severe test of faith and detract strongly from the potential benefits of whatever may be offered in the lecture room.

F. Parents:

The greatest opposition sometimes comes from parents who may be unsaved and therefore uncomprehending of the decision to "waste" one's life on a mission field, or from saved parents who simply don't want to cut the apron strings or are fearful of releasing the child into the caring hands of God. The Bible commands us to put God first.

- "He that loveth father or mother more than me is not worthy of me: and he that loveth son or daughter more than me is not worthy of me" (Matthew 10:37).

- "There is no man that hath left house, or brethren, or sisters, or father, or mother, or wife, or children, or lands, for my sake, and the gospel's, but he shall receive an hundredfold now in this time, houses, and brethren, and sisters, and mothers. And children, and lands, with persecutions; and in the world to come eternal life" (Mark 10:29–30).

TEST 6

(35 Points)

Note: Where no total point value is given for a question, each correct answer is worth one point.

1. Give a simple definition of prayer. (2 points)
    Prayer is talking to God and expecting an answer.
2. In what way does prayer recognize the power of God? (2 points)
    Help is asked only of those who are assumed to have the power to help.
3. Why is prayer always possible?
    Because God is always present.
4. In what way did Jesus Christ demonstrate His complete dependence on His Father?
    By constantly resorting to prayer
5. Give one example of Jesus exhorting His followers to pray. Include a Scripture reference. (3 points)
    When the multitudes came to be healed (Luke 5:16); before choosing His disciples (Luke 6:12); when He fed the 5,000 (Luke 9:16); when He faced betrayal and death (Luke 22:29–46); as He hung on the cross.
6. Give two instances where prayer brings joy. Provide Scripture references. (4 points)
    a) *When we ask and receive (John 16:24).*
    b) *Through fellowship with Jesus Christ (1 John 1:3–4).*

7. Provide the Scriptures which lists qualifications for a pastor. (2 points)
   1 Timothy 3:1–7 and Titus 1:5–9

8. In your own words, explain why each of the following qualification is necessary or important for a pastor. (2 points each)

   a) One that rules well his own house

      Answers will vary but should indicate that the student grasps the meaning and importance of each qualification.

   b) Not a novice

   c) Not greedy

9. Why do you think a well-developed sense of humor might be useful for a missionary evangelist? (2 points)
   Answers will vary but should be in line with the unexpected challenges that arise on the mission field.

10. According to your notes, what is the clearest command in the Bible?
    Jesus' instruction to His followers to "teach"

10. How does God build His kingdom? (2 points)
    One soul at a time as the result of Christians telling others the wonderful story of salvation

11. What suffers most when individual Christians have no vision or desire to share their faith?
    The mission field

12. Think again about the qualifications of a pastor and give two reasons why you think pursuing an education in a secular university might be a hindrance to the spiritual growth of a young Christian. (2 points each)

    a) *Answers will vary*

    b)

13. List four hindrances that keep some people off the mission field:
   a. *Misinformation*
   b. *Marriage*
   c. *Money*
   d. *Debt*
   Advanced Education
   Parents

THE MISSION FIELD
PART I—THE WORLD

- *Introduction*
- *Geography and Population*
- *Peoples and Languages*
- *Religions*

I. Introduction

The world is a vast stage on which billions of people play out their lives—people of different ethnic groups, different cultures, different languages, different traditions, and different religious beliefs. But they all have the same spiritual needs. Jesus Christ is the answer, and it is our responsibility to get the answer to them.

When we look at the world as a whole, in all of its vastness and diversity, the task seems impossible. How can we approach this mission field? In the next few lessons we will briefly survey some key geographical and population statistics that present the world in smaller components to make the task less daunting. But first we will take a look at the world as a whole.

II. Geography and Population

A. *Extent*
The world's six continents cover an area of almost 85 million square miles.

1. There are about 240 nations and territories.

    This is a fluid number that changes as new nations are spawned from existing nations or territories, adding to the total. In some cases, the total is reduced as one nation is absorbed by another.

B. Population

At the time of Christ, the total world population is estimated to have been about 200 million. Today it is well over 6 billion (six thousand million). The last hundred years has seen a very rapid population increase.

1. 1950—about 2,500 million

2. 1990—about 5,300 million

3. 2007—about 6,500 million

4. 2020—about 7,500 million (estimated)

C. Cities

Until 100 years ago, most people lived outside of cities. In all parts of the world today, people are flocking to cities. This in turn has led to the rise of so-called urban conurbations or "super cities" where it becomes hard to tell where one city ends and the other begins.

1. There are almost 500 cities in the world with populations of more than 1 million inhabitants.

2. 20 cities have populations of more than 10 million.

3. The largest conurbations are:

    • Tokyo/Yokohama, 28 million

    • Mexico City, 18 million

    • Sao Paulo, over 17 million

    • New York, over 16 million

III. Peoples and Languages

The World Christian Encyclopedia identifies 13,000 people groups, "distinct ethnic and/or cultural peoples that are bonded together by race, tradition, history, and culture."

A. Languages

The 13,000 people groups scattered amongst the world's 240 nations share common language roots, but within each larger group, there may be hundreds of dialects that are often so distinctive as to effectively prevent smaller groups of people from understanding each other. This presents a huge challenge to missionary evangelists who seek to both preach the Gospel and give their hearers the Scriptures in their own tongue.

1. *The World Christian Encyclopedia* estimates the number of dialects at 30,000.

2. Bible translators estimate in turn that they would need to provide the Scriptures in more than 7,000 languages in order to begin to reach most of the people groups.

3. The largest languages are Chinese, English, Spanish, Hindu, Arabic, Bengali, Portuguese, Russian, Turkic, Japanese, and German.

4. Only 35 languages are used for official instruction in all of the world's universities.

5. This indicates that the real need for spreading the Gospel lies amongst the poor and uneducated people of the world.

IV. Religions

The variety of religions and traditions in the world is not as great as the number of people groups, yet the diversity is complex enough to present many challenges to missionary evangelists. The picture is further complicated by the fact that the "Christian religion" is itself so fractured. Many who claim the name "Christian" teach a gospel that is very different from the truth found in Scripture. With this in mind, the following statistics provide a rough guide to the world's major religious affiliations. The numbers are approximate round figures:

1	Christian (inc. Roman Catholic)	2,000 million
2.	Muslim	1,400 million
3.	Hindu	950 million
4.	Buddhist	350 million
5.	Chinese	350 million
6.	Traditional Ethnic	200 million
7.	Sikh	20 million
8.	Jewish	14 million
9.	No known religion	1,000 million

Of the 2 billion so-called Christians, about 1 billion are Roman Catholics. The remainder is made up of Anglican (Episcopalian), Orthodox (primarily Greek and Russian), Independents, and Protestants. The latter group includes Baptists, although Baptists are not Protestants and should be grouped on their own. The number of Baptists in the world is probably considerably less than 50 million.

THE MISSION FIELD
PART II—AFRICA AND EUROPE

- *Parts I and II: Africa and Europe*
- *Geography and Population*
- *Peoples and Languages*
- *Religions*

PART I—AFRICA

I. Geography and Population

A. About 18,883,000 square miles provide a home to 55 countries. Seven countries in North Africa are Arabic speaking, Muslim nations.

B. The population of the entire continent and its surrounding islands is about 800 million. This is projected to increase to over one billion by 2020, although the rate of population increase is uncertain due to the ravages of AIDS, malaria, tuberculosis, famine, and war.

C. More than 80 cities in Africa have populations of over 1 million. Three cities have more than 10 million inhabitants each. About 70 percent of Africans still live in rural areas.

II. Peoples and Languages

Almost 80 percent of Africans are Negroid peoples who live south of the Sahara Desert. The remaining 20 percent are mostly

Arabs who live in the seven countries north of the Sahara Desert. White people of European descent form significant minorities in several countries, but primarily in South Africa. There are 3,500 ethnic groups living in Africa.

A. *Languages*
More than 2,000 languages and thousands more dialects are spoken in Africa. As a leftover of the colonial era, 40 nations have French or English as their official language, but few people are fluent in these European languages.

B. *Bible Translations in African languages*
1. 130 complete Bibles
2. 237 New Testaments
3. 250 portions of Bibles (usually John and Romans)
4. About 370 Bible translations in progress.

III. Religions (Approximate round numbers)

A.	Christian (inc. Roman Catholic)	400 million
B.	Muslim	350 million
C.	Traditional ethnic	70 million
D.	Other or non-religious	12 million
E.	Listed as Christian "Protestant" or "Independent." These would include a small proportion of Baptists.	180 million

PART II—EUROPE

I. Geography and Population

A. This area of 52 countries combines Europe and Russia and covers almost 14,500,000 square miles.

B. The projected population in 2010 is just over 700 million—lower than it was in 2000 and projected to be lower still in 2025, due to low birth rates as Europeans increasingly opt for personal affluence rather than large families.

C. The London metropolitan area, with a population of about 15 million, is the major conurbation. More than 70 percent of Europeans live in urban areas, the highest concentration in the world.

II. Peoples and Languages

Slavs, located primarily in central and eastern Europe, make up the largest ethnic group (about 32%), followed by Latins in southern and southwestern Europe (29%) and Germanic peoples, predominantly in central and northwestern Europe (25%). There are 270 languages indigenous to Europe, of which fewer than 50 have complete Bibles and 13 have New Testaments.

III. Religions (Approximate round numbers)

A. Christian (inc. Roman Catholic)	520 million
B. Non-religious/other	170 million
C. Muslim	37 million
D. Jewish	2 million
E. Listed as Christian "Protestant" or "Independent." These would include a small proportion of Baptists.	70 million

The relatively large numbers of "Christians" must be qualified by noting that the spiritual climate in Europe is very low, with the average church-going population (Catholics included) estimated at about two percent (eight percent in Britain).

The Mission Field
Part III—Asia and Pacific

- *Parts I and II— Asia and Pacific*
- *Geography and Population*
- *Peoples and Languages*
- *Religion*

PART I—ASIA

I. Geography and Population

A. Covering almost 20 million square miles, with 50 countries, this area is the largest in the world and forms the biggest portion of the 10/40 Window.

B. The population is vast. Two countries, India and China, have over 1,000 million people each, and the population for the whole area is projected to exceed 4,000 million by 2010.

C. There are almost 200 megacities, including 14 of the world's largest conurbations, led by Tokyo with almost 35 million people. Despite these impressive statistics, however, only 33% of the population is urbanized (compared to Europe's 70%).

II. Peoples and Languages

There are about 3,550 ethnic groups who make up over 80% of people in the world and who are least-reached by the

Gospel. Over 2,000 distinct languages are spoken, of which only 110 have been translated into complete Bibles. There are an additional 200 languages that have been translated into New Testaments.

III. Religions

Asia is the only continent where Christianity is not the largest religion.

A.	Muslim	900 million
B.	Hindu	800 million
C.	No known religion	700 million
D.	Buddhist	400 million
E.	Chinese	400 million
F.	Christian	300 million
G.	Listed as Christian	100 million

"Protestant" or "Independent."
These include a few Baptists.

PART II—PACIFIC

I. Geography and Population

A. The area includes 25,000 islands scattered over 55 million square miles (larger than Africa, Asia, and Europe combined) but comprising only 5 million square miles of land. It includes the continent of Australia, the relatively large islands of New Zealand and Papua New Guinea, and 26 smaller island states and territories.

B. Total population is expected to reach only 35 million in 2010.

C. There are five megacitities in Australia and one in New Zealand.

II. People and Languages

Despite the small total population, there are more than 1,200 ethnic groups. Europeans form the largest single group, primarily in Australia and New Zealand, with the remainder made up of Melanesians, Polynesians, Micronesians, and Asians. More than 1,300 languages have only 21 complete Bibles, 180 New Testaments, and 200 portions of Scripture.

III. Religions

A. Christian (inc. Roman Catholic)   23 million

B. No known religion   7 million

C. Small numbers of Hindus,
   Buddhists, Muslims, and Spiritists

D. Listed as Christian "Protestants"   8 million

THE MISSION FIELD
PART IV—THE AMERICAS

- *Parts I and II—North America, Latin America and Caribbean*
- *Geography and Population*
- *Peoples and Languages*
- *Religion*

PART I—NORTH AMERICA

I. Geography and Population

A. Only four countries—Canada, Greenland, Mexico, and the United States—cover 14 million square miles. Canada is the world's second largest country; the U.S. is fourth.

B. The population is expected to total just over 330 million in 2010.

C. There are 71 cities of over 1 million inhabitants.

II. People and Languages

Communities from every ethnic group in the world have settled in North America, mostly from Europe. Native Americans form a tiny minority. There are 245 recognized languages, with English being the predominant language of communication. A high proportion of Christians, coupled with a high literacy rate and multilingualism, ensures that virtually all North Americans have access to the Bible.

III. Religions

    A. Christian (inc. Roman Catholic)   260 million

    B. No known religion   32 million

    C. Jewish   6 million

    D. Muslim   5 million

    E. Listed as Christian "Protestant" or   140 million
        "Independent"

    F. Baptists, included in the total above,
        perhaps number as many as 20 million,
        more than anywhere else in the world.

PART II—LATIN AMERICA AND CARIBBEAN

I. Geography and Population

    A. 46 countries and territories—including 25 islands—cover an area of about 13 million square miles. Some of the islands are fairly large—Cuba, Haiti, the Dominican Republic, Puerto Rico, and Jamaica—while most are tiny.

    B. The population is expected to total about 600 million by 2010.

    C. 52 cities have populations of over one million, with Mexico City (18 million) and Sao Paulo (17million) being two of the world's largest.

II. People and Languages

People of European descent make up about 40% of the population, with a further 40% being mixed race European and American Indian. Native Americans and African-Americans (descendents of slaves) comprise the balance.

There are close to 1,000 languages in this area. Spanish is predominant, although the largest country in Latin America, Brazil, is Portuguese-speaking. Complete Bibles are available in 25 indigenous languages, with a further 245 New Testaments and 200 portions of Scripture available in other indigenous languages.

III. Religions

100 years ago, almost the entire Spanish-speaking and Portuguese-speaking populations of South America were considered Roman Catholic. But Protestant missionary activity has made significant inroads in recent years.

A. Roman Catholic	410 million
B. Protestant and "Independent"	60 million
C. Traditional ethnic	15 million
D. Muslim	2 million

TEST 7

[50 Points]

Note: Where no total point value is given for a question, each correct answer is worth one point.

1. What was the estimated world population at the time of Christ?
   200 million
2. What is the estimated world population today?
   Over 6 billion
3. What is an "urban conurbation"? (2 points)
   A "super city" where it is hard to tell where one city ends and the other begins.
4. What is a "people group"? (4 points)
   A distinct ethnic and/or cultural group of people who are bonded together by race, tradition, history, and culture.
5. How many people groups have been identified in the world?
   13,000
6. How many dialects have been identified in the world?
   30,000
7. List three of the world's largest languages:
   a. *Chinese; Hindu; Portuguese; German*
   b. *English; Arabic; Russian; Japanese*
   c. *Spanish; Bengali; Turkic*

8. How many languages are used for official instruction in all of the world's universities? What does this tell us as we consider spreading the Gospel to all the world? (4 points)
   35 languages. This indicates that the real need for spreading the Gospel lies amongst the poor and uneducated people of the world.

9. List the four largest religious groups in the world, with approximate numbers, and the approximate number of Baptists in the world. (8 points)

a.	*Christian*	*2 billion*
b.	*Muslim*	*1.4 billion*
c.	*Hindu*	*950 million*
d.	*Buddhist*	*350 million*
e.	*Baptists*	*50 million*

10. What are the two main people groups of Africa? (2 points)
    Negroid peoples and Arabs

11. How many languages are spoken in Africa, and how many Bibles or portions of Bibles are available? (2 points)
    2,000 languages and a little over 600 Bibles or portions of Bibles.

12. What are the three main people groups of Europe? (2 points)
    Slavs, Latins, and Germanic peoples

13. How many languages are spoken in Europe, and how many Bibles or portions of Bibles are available? (2 points)
    270 languages and about 60 Bibles and portions of Bibles

14. How many people groups are in Asia? What is the most troubling aspect of this number? (3 points)
    3,550 people groups. These groups make up 80% of the people in the world and are the least reached by the Gospel.

15. How many languages are spoken in Asia, and how many Bibles or portions of Bibles are available? (2 points)
    Over 2,000 languages and 310 Bibles or portions of Bibles

16. How many languages have been identified in the Pacific area, and how many Bibles or portions of Bibles are available? (2 points)

    1,300 languages and 400 Bibles or portions of Bibles

17. Explain why virtually all North Americans have access to the Bible. (3 points)

    English is the predominant language. Also a high proportion of Christians, a high literacy rate, and multilingualism

18. What are the two largest population groups in Latin America? (2 points)

    People of European descent and mixed race European and American Indian

19. What is the predominant language spoken in Latin America? What is the total number of languages spoken, and how many Bibles or portions of Bibles are available? (3 points)

    Spanish. 1,000 languages and 470 Bibles or portions of Bibles

20. What is the predominant religion of the entire Spanish-speaking and Portuguese-speaking world? (2 points)

    Roman Catholic (Note: The answer must specify Roman.)

REVIEW AND SCRIPTURE TEST

- *Review Third Quarter*
- *Test Memorized Scripture Passage*

THE HEART OF THE GREAT COMMISSION*: PART I

[*PART I AND PART II BASED ON A STUDY PREPARED BY DR. BUD CALVERT FOR THE INTERNATIONAL CONFERENCE ON WORLD EVANGELISM.]

- *Church Planting is the Heart of the Great Commission*
- *What the Great Commission Is Not*
- *A Better Understanding of Matthew 28*
- *A Better Understanding of Acts 1:8*

I. Church Planting is the Heart of the Great Commission

A. *Problem Areas*

1. Most churches are aware of the Great Commission spelled out in Matthew 28:18–20, but many have never properly defined what it means.
2. Many have never taken it to heart.
3. There is no passion for world evangelism.
4. Churches are satisfied with the status quo.
5. Churches believe that evangelizing the world is the responsibility of mission boards.
6. Most churches have never deliberately started another church.

B. *The Responsibility of Every Church*

1. Church planting is at the heart of the Great Commission and should be in the heart of every church.

2. Every church is known by something—its music program, youth program, preaching, facilities, etc. But every church should seek to be known by God for its church planting program!

II. What the Great Commission Is Not

A. *It is not philanthropic in nature*
Many churches are turning to social programs—but programs that may be very useful to society should not be employed as substitutes for the real thing. The Great Commission is not fulfilled in a hospital or a jail ministry or a homeless shelter or an orphanage.

B. *It is not a ministry to directly benefit a local church*
The Great Commission is not fulfilled in a bus ministry, a TV or radio ministry, a youth camp, or anything that would directly benefit a local church.

C. *It is not street preaching*

D. *It is not tract distribution*

E. *It is not a men's meeting*
The Great Commission is not fulfilled in a ministry like Promise Keepers or city revival meetings.

III. A Better Understanding of Matthew 28:18–20

A. *The Voice*
1. Every church has a clear responsibility to go into all the world and preach the gospel.
2. The word "teach" in verse 19 means "to make disciples."
3. "Make disciples" is the only command in this verse.

4. To "make disciples" of people is to lead them to a saving knowledge of the Teacher, the Lord Jesus Christ.

   a. It is to get others to become what we are!

   b. Moreover, we are to "teach all nations."

5. The word "Go" at the beginning of the verse means "while you are going." In other words, it is assumed that Christians will be interacting with society and winning others to Christ in the normal course of their lives.

   a. From a practical standpoint, this means we should be a witness at work, in our neighborhoods, and in society in general.

   b. Everywhere we go, we should be on a mission to "make disciples" of all people.

   c. Our attitude should be that of someone working on a "Search and Rescue" team—dedicated to our task and going out of our way to help others, while laying aside our personal needs and comforts.

6. As we make disciples, we are to baptize them.

   a. "Baptize" means to dip or immerse.

   b. It is the first step of obedience after a person has been saved.

7. Our final responsibility is to teach our disciples to observe—obey—God's Word.

   a. The Great Commission doesn't stop with someone's salvation.

   b. Teaching takes place in preaching services, Bible study fellowship classes, and one-on-one discipleship.

B. *The Vessel*

  1. To whom was the Great Commission given?

     a. It was not to the apostles. If that were true, the commission died when the apostles died!

     b. It was not given to Christians in general, since there were no other Christians around when Jesus gave the commission.

     c. It was given to the church!

        • Note when the church was founded (Matthew 16:13–18).

        • As further evidence, note that when Jesus selected the twelve apostles (Luke 6:12–13) He set them in the Church, indicating that the Church was already in existence (1 Corinthians 12:28).

  2. To whom was authority given?

     a. "All power (authority)" is given to Jesus Christ, according to Matthew 28:18.

     b. Jesus in turn passes His authority on to the church to carry out the Great Commission.

        • The only way the Great Commission can be achieved is through soulwinning and church planting.

     c. The local church has the power of God.

     d. The local church has the resources.

     e. The local church has the Word of God.

     f. The local church has the people of God.

IV. A Better Understanding of Acts 1:8

A. *The Power*

The Greek word is "dunamis," from which we get our words "dynamite" and "dynamo." The sense is significant: dynamite is an explosive release of energy that is quickly dissipated, while the dynamo is a sustaining power. The changed life at salvation is evidence of the dynamite power. The Spirit-filled life that follows is the dynamo effect. God's work must be done through the power of the Holy Spirit, or it will not be done at all!

B. *The People*
Everyone is to be a witness. The Greek word here is "martus," from which is derived the English word "martyr."

C. *The Philosophy*
Notice the word "both." The great problem of our day is that most preachers and churches interpret this word as meaning "first."

- This is the reason that many churches struggle to get started—their vision is simply too limited! The emphasis of the Bible is not on our "Jerusalem" but on the whole world.

D. *The Program*
1. Jerusalem—reaching your local area.
2. Judea—spreading into surrounding counties and states.
3. Samaria—reaching the unwanted.
   a. Door-to-door visitation programs must not be selective—deciding which ones we invite and which ones we do not invite.
   b. It is our responsibility to reach everyone with the Gospel of Jesus Christ. This includes Hispanics, Asians, blacks, whites, the deaf, the handicapped, children, and the elderly.

4. Uttermost parts of the earth—this is world evange-
    lism. Notice that we are to be ministering in each
    of these areas at the same time.

THE HEART OF THE GREAT COMMISSION: PART II

- *New Testament Church Planting*
- *The Great Commission today*

I. New Testament Church Planting

A. *First Response*
The church in the New Testament did not at first understand its responsibility and obligation towards the Great Commission. In Acts 8:1–4 we see God's unique way of getting the church to spread the Gospel far and wide.

B. *Later Efforts*
Although there is not a lot of detail about the mechanics of early church growth, it is clear that churches were planted as a result of Christians "going everywhere."

1. Philip was preaching (Acts 8:5–8).
2. Samaria was being evangelized (Acts 8:12–14, 25).
3. The church at Antioch became the dominant "sending church" (Acts 11:19–22, 26).
4. More church planters were sent out (Acts 13:1–5).
5. Paul and Barnabas continued their ministry to churches in Lystra, Iconium, and Derbe (Acts 14:19–23, 16:5).
6. Paul and Silas started the church at Philippi (Acts 16).

7. The church at Thessalonica was started (Acts 17).

II. The Great Commission today

A. *The heart of the Great Commission is Church Planting.*

B. *This must be the heart of every church and pastor.*

C. *Every church has the same responsibility.*
1. Evangelize the world.
2. Start other churches.

D. *Never waver in commitment.*
Churches must maintain their commitment to obey God at any cost:
1. Time
2. Money
3. Manpower

E. *Remain true to the vision.*
1. Never replace church planting with any other program.
2. Church planting is not optional with God!
    a. It is a high and holy calling to be a church planter.
    b. Never take this calling for granted.
    c. Never treat this calling lightly.

F. *Satan hates church planters!*

*Therefore, my beloved brethren,
be ye steadfast, unmoveable, always
abounding in the work of the Lord,
forasmuch as ye know that your
labour is not in vain in the Lord.*

(I CORINTHIANS 15:58)

"Grace Giving" In Support Of World Evangelism*

[*Based on a study prepared by Dr. Bud Calvert for the International Conference on World Evangelism]

- *A Plan to Fulfill the Program*
- *Grace Giving Goes Beyond the Tithe*
- *Grace Giving From the Heart*
- *Grace Giving: How Much?*

I. A Plan to Fulfill the Program: 2 Corinthians 8:1–7

God designed the program of world evangelism using church planting and a financial plan to carry it out. We may not all be called to *go* (to a foreign land), but we are all called to *give!* The financial plan funds the program—it is what the Bible calls "grace giving" (also known as "faith promise giving").

A. Grace giving is in addition to tithes and offerings.

B. Grace giving is based on our faith in God's ability.

C. Grace giving is a partnership with God that will change the life of the individual and of the local church.

II. Grace Giving goes Beyond the Tithe

Tithing is a deeply spiritual act of worshipful consecration to God. It has nothing to do with Old Testament law and everything to do with our perception of who God is and our relationship with Him.

A. The first accounts of tithing in Genesis, long before the Law was given, are instructive:

1. Abram tithes (Genesis 14:18–20 with Hebrews 7:1–10).
2. Jacob tithes (Genesis 28:20–22).

B. Tithing, therefore, is not a legal duty but a freewill delight. It demonstrates:

1. Our acknowledgement of God as our maker
2. Our worship of God as our God
3. Our dependence on God as our provider
4. Our faith in God as our protector
5. Our joy in God as the source of all our blessings

C. Tithes and Offerings provide the finances to build and maintain the local church.

III. Grace Giving From the Heart—Not the Wallet

Grace Giving provides the finances to support world evangelism. The money comes from the same people who provide the money to finance the local church. Some churches see this as expecting too much from their members. A lot of members agree. The answer is that God expects it! He has clearly given the local church the mandate to go into the whole world to preach the gospel (Mark 16:15 and Acts 1:8).

A. God does not need our help to spread the gospel—He could raise up the rocks to preach, if necessary. Yet we are His only chosen means to do so.

B. God does not need our money to spread the gospel—He could turn every rock into gold if He wanted to, yet He has chosen to use our money.

C. God's main interest is in the condition of the hearts of His people, so He chooses to work through His church and its members—you and me—to ensure that we learn through experience the great truth taught by Jesus:

1. "Give, and it shall be given unto you" (Luke 6:38).

2. He desires that we first give ourselves to Him (2 Corinthians 8:5 and Romans 12:1, 6:11–13).

IV. Grace Giving—How Much?

How do you discern an amount to give that is acceptable to God? The Bible does not indicate precise amounts for what we term "grace giving," but a clear pattern is revealed in 2 Corinthians 8:1–16. The apostle Paul's theme in this passage is:

A. The need is great.

B. The need is immediate.

C. The solution is to be generous.

    1. The example of the Macedonian Church (verse 2)

    2. The encouragement of Paul (verse 6–7)

    3. The motivation of sincere love (verse 8)

    4. The extravagant example of Jesus Christ (verse 9)

    5. The expedience of the test (verses 10–16)

        a. A reminder of former promises (verse 10).

        b. Give what you can out of what you have (verse 11).

        c. Give willingly (verse 12).

        d. Give, knowing that God balances the books. See verses 13–15 with 2 Corinthians 9:6–8.

So in answer to the question, "How much should we give?" we find that we must be generous, we must give as much as we can, and sometimes we must give more than we think we can!

TEST 8

[35 Points]

Note: Where no total point value is given for a question, each correct answer is worth one point.

1. List five reasons why many churches are not actively engaged in world evangelism. (10 points)
   a. *Many have never properly defined what the Great Commission means.*
   b. *Many have never taken it to heart.*
   c. *There is no passion for world evangelism.*
   d. *Churches are satisfied with the status quo.*
   e. *Churches believe that evangelizing the world is the responsibility of mission boards. Or most churches have never deliberately started another church.*

2. Complete this sentence: Every church should seek to be known by...
   its church planting program.

3. What is the only command in Matthew 28:19?
   Make disciples.

4. Explain the word "Go" at the beginning of verse 19. (4 points)
   It means "while you are going." It is assumed that Christians will be interacting with society and winning others to Christ in the normal course of their lives.

5. What is the meaning of the word "baptize"?
   To dip or immerse
6. To whom was the Great Commission given?
   To the church
7. Which Scripture verse indicates when the church was founded?
   Matthew 16:13–18
8. What is the only way in which the Great Commission can be achieved?
   Through soulwinning and church planting
9. Why do many local churches struggle to get started?
   Their vision is too limited.
10. What was God's unique way of getting the early church to spread the Gospel, according to Acts 8:1–4?
    Through persecution
11. What activity of the church must never be replaced by any other program, because it is not optional with God?
    Church planting
12. Complete this sentence: We may not all be called to go, but…
    we are all called to give.
13. True or False: Tithing in the church today is a continuation of Old Testament Law. Explain your answer. (4 points)
    False. It concerns our perception of who God is and our relationship with Him.
14. Mention three things that tithing demonstrates, from an individual standpoint.
    a. *Our acknowledgement of God as our maker*
    b. *Our worship of God as our God*
    c. *Our dependence on God as our provider*
       Our faith in God as our protector
       Our joy in God as the source of all our blessings

15. What is the great truth about giving that Jesus taught? Provide the Scripture reference. (2 points)
    "Give, and it shall be given unto you" (Luke 6:38).
16. With regard to how much we should give, the apostle Paul taught:
    a. *The need is great.*
    b. *The solution is to be generous.*

Introduction To World Religions

- *Introduction*
- *Competing Religions*
- *Three Steps to Finding the True Religion*
- *Christianity and The Manifest Presence of God*

I. Introduction

In the next few lessons we will look at various religions, traditions, and belief systems. Our understanding of why they exist and how we should view them will be helped by the context provided in this general overview.

II. Competing Religions

The many religions in the world may be loosely categorized in two types: those that aggressively go out into the world with a message that theirs is the only right path, and those that are not really interested in the world but seek instead a personal inner peace. The first category includes Islam, Roman Catholicism, Mormonism, and Jehovah's Witnesses; the latter includes Buddhists, Hindus, and Shinto.

There is yet another "religion"—evolution—that is outside of these categories since it does not classify itself as a religion but contains the essential elements of religion—primarily commitment by faith to a dogma that provides a plausible worldview for its adherents and cannot be "proved" by science.

Christianity, that is, the Christianity of those who accept the Bible as their final authority, is different from all other belief systems or faith traditions. The Gospel of Jesus Christ is preached to the whole world by those who are called to die to self and meekly turn the other cheek to their enemies. Christians reject the world system and are sustained by the invisible power of an omnipotent, personal God, yet they focus on the needs of the world's spiritually oppressed and hungry all about them.

Catholics and Muslims seek to conquer and rule the world; Buddhists and Hindus seek to escape the world; Christians seek to transform one person at a time, by sacrificial love.

The biggest difference between religions and biblical Christianity lies in their concept of attaining their ultimate destiny. All religions teach a process of observances and works designed to achieve spiritual growth that may in turn result in reconciliation with God. Biblical Christianity teaches immediate salvation and reconciliation with God to establish a personal relationship that fuels a process of spiritual growth and transformation.

III. Three Steps to Finding the "True Religion"

A search for the "true religion" among all of the world's belief systems and faith traditions ultimately presents just three possibilities. Truth may be found by those who honestly trust their eyes and ears and common sense about the physical and spiritual world in which they live, and look also into their own hearts and acknowledge the defects found there. The possibilities are:

A. This world is the result of an accident. Humans are little individual accidents within the larger accident–brief sparks of life between two oblivions. Life is meaningless.

B. The world was created by god, or gods, or some form of impersonal higher power. Individuals must strive in various ways, obeying specific rules and following certain procedures, to be reconciled to or ultimately, hopefully become one with Him or Her or Them or It. The focus is on personal effort, personal merit, and personal achievement.

C. God created the world. He has a personality and a purpose. He can be personally known. Yet nothing I can do will impress Him or earn His favor. I must approach Him on the basis of His merit and what He has done for me, not my merit and what I can do for Him. My task is not to strive to reach Him but to yield to Him, receive His Life, and walk with Him.

IV. The Manifest Presence of God

Atheists and those who believe in evolution ultimately find emptiness, despair, immorality, and nihilism (the denial of reality, because nothing has meaning).

God is brought into view through religion, but religious philosophy, outward forms, rituals, and ceremonies only partially satisfy the human soul. This explains why so many different religions exist in the world, as each tries to address one or more aspects of man's spiritual need.

Christianity is the only "religion" teaching that God can be known by faith alone—that believing in God's finished work and yielding to Him makes His presence manifest in the human heart. This *believing* and *receiving* is essential. The apostle John declares that those who *receive* Him are given power to become His children (John 1:11). Moreover, when the Spirit of God enters, the human heart is completely satisfied.

So while religion tries to explain God to man, Christianity first explains that man is a sinner and then reveals God to him. Religion teaches how to succeed in the pursuit of God; Christianity teaches how to submit to the love of God.

Part I:
Hinduism, Buddhism

- *Hinduism*
- *Buddhism*

I. Hinduism

Hinduism is the main religion of India. Like Islam's impact on the Muslim world, Hinduism influences the whole Indian way of life.

It is a polytheistic religion, acknowledging thousands of gods (even Jesus Christ). Although all are worshipped, three gods are considered to be more important than the others—Brahma, the Creator; Shiva, the Destroyer; and Vishnu, the Preserver. However, these gods and all the others, along with humans, plants, animals, and everything else in the world are all believed to be part of the World Soul.

Hindus believe that during their earthly existence people are separated from the World Soul and their goal in life is to be reunited with it by following the Hindu religion and earning merit that will lead to salvation. This salvation differs radically from the Christian concept in that it is achieved by good works through a cycle of several lifetimes—a process called reincarnation (rebirth in a physical body). Progressively better works lead to reincarnation in progressively better circumstances, while bad works may result in rebirth as a person of low estate, or even as an animal or an insect. This is why Hindus are generally passive and fatalistic people, careful not to kill plants, insects, or animals. It also explains the fatalism of low-caste Hindus who believe they are doomed by bad deeds in a previous life to uncomplainingly work out their salvation through the adverse circumstances of this life. Of course, really bad people may experience the misfortune of reincarnation as a dog or even as a toad or a cockroach, which brings some comfort to those of the lowest caste for whom the least desirable occupations are reserved.

The different castes in descending order of purity are priests, rulers and warriors, merchants and traders, and servants. At the very bottom are those who are completely outside of the caste system, the so-called untouchables or outcasts, whose jobs may include grave digging or cleaning toilets. Other rules governing the members of each caste include directions on where they live, what they wear, who they may marry, and with whom they may eat.

Some Hindus believe they can hasten the purification of their souls by starving themselves or inflicting pain on themselves, but any Hindu who does more or less than his caste allows is disqualified from advancement to a higher level in his next life.

As may be expected from a religion with so many gods, Hinduism has many scriptures, the most important of which are known as the four Vedas. These include the Upanishads (in which the spiritual meaning of the Vedic texts are explained); the Bhagvad Gita; the Puranas (books of mythology); and the Ithihaas (books of legend).

A devastating consequence of the complex and multifaceted Hindu religion is that it is very difficult to lead Hindus to salvation in Christ: to them, Jesus is just another one of the thousands of gods. Their belief in everything ultimately means that they really believe in nothing!

Note: A peculiarly American version of Hinduism is known as Transcendental Meditation or TM. It is simply Hinduism repackaged in a high-tech form that sells well in the U.S.

II. Buddhism

Around 500 B.C. (about the same time as the biblical Daniel), Siddhartha Gautama rejected the teachings of Hinduism and went on to establish his own religion. He particularly disagreed with the idea that only members of the highest caste were ready to reunite with the World Soul, even though he was the son of a ruler and therefore a member of a high caste. He was troubled by the suffering he saw all around him and determined to seek answers that Hinduism could not provide to his satisfaction.

At the age of twenty-nine he left the wealth and ease of his home and set out on a spiritual journey to seek enlightenment and peace. First he tried living as a hermit, almost starving to death as he fasted and prayed. Then one day as he sat under a tree, he received a revelation about the meaning of life and would henceforth be known as Buddha, which means "Enlightened One."

He set out his enlightenment in Four Noble Truths:
- All life is suffering.
- Man's desires for the things of this world—pleasure, possessions, and power—is the cause of suffering.
- Man must destroy his desires to remove suffering from the world.
- Doing good works helps to overcome both desires and suffering.

Buddha went on to explain how one could do good works through what he called the Eightfold Path:
- Right Understanding
- Right Thought

- Right Speech
- Right Action
- Right Work
- Right Effort
- Right Awareness
- Right Meditation

The ultimate goal was to be good and kind to others and to think only good and happy thoughts so as to escape the wheel of reincarnation and go on to Nirvana, or heaven.

Buddhism spread rapidly through Asia, although Hindus for the most part did not accept the teachings, since they were seen to be critical of Hinduism. Different forms of Buddhism developed in different regions, the two most important of which offered different vehicles by which to achieve salvation—the one version was strict and available only to a few people, while the other was less demanding and offered a lesser salvation to many.

Japan developed its own form, Zen Buddhism, which placed special emphasis on the importance of meditating on unsolvable questions.

PART II:
ROMAN CATHOLICISM

- *Introduction*
- *History*
- *Additions to Scripture*

I. Introduction

In order to understand the religious movement known to its followers as the Catholic Church, it is helpful to understand its name. "Catholic" is a word from the Greek language: it means all-inclusive, universal. In other words, the Catholic Church sees itself as the whole Christian church, a universal church, the only true church. Protestants (those Christians who protest against the Catholic Church) and Baptists add the word "Roman" to the title to indicate that it is not the only, universal church, but a religious movement with its headquarters in Rome. Today, that movement has over one billion members worldwide, with over sixty million members in the United States. "Roman" also distinguishes this so-called "western orthodox" religion from "eastern orthodox" offshoots—Coptic, Greek, and Russian.

II. History

The entire authority of the Roman Catholic Church is derived from a single passage of Scripture found in Matthew 16:13–20. In this passage Jesus uses a play on words to make an important point about Himself and the power of divine revelation regarding His true identity (verses 16–17). He tells Peter that his name means little stone ("petros") but on the massive stone or bedrock ("petra") of Himself He will build His church (verse 18).

But the Roman Catholics claim that Jesus meant to build His church on Peter, therefore Peter was the first Father (Pope, from the Latin "Papa") of the Christian church, which he established in Rome. Apart from the fact that it is by no means clear from historical records that Peter ever went to Rome, the elevation of Peter to such a lofty position of leadership over all Christians simply does not agree with Scripture. However, this did not prevent Pope Boniface the Eighth from declaring in 1302 that "it is altogether necessary to salvation that [every human creature] be subject to the Roman Pontiff." Today, the Pope is known as the Bishop of Rome, the Vicar (personal representative on earth) of Christ, the Head of the Church. When he speaks from his throne, his words have the same weight as Scripture.

Notwithstanding this belief in the superiority and infallibility of the Roman Church, the current Pope, Benedict XVI, has issued a statement declaring that "the Catholic Church rejects nothing that is true and holy in these [other] religions. She [the Catholic Church] regards with sincere reverence those ways of conduct and life, those precepts and teachings which, though differing in many aspects from the ones she holds and sets forth, nonetheless often reflect a ray of that Truth which enlightens all men."

III. Additions to Scripture

The Roman Catholic Church has added so many doctrines, traditions, and human ideas to Scripture over the centuries that most Catholics can no longer see God's will or God's Word in their faith. In fact, they are discouraged from even reading Scripture but are rather to trust their priests to interpret it for them. The tragic result is that salvation has been removed far from them.

Here is what the Bible says about some of their beliefs:

- **The Universal Church**
The idea of a universal world church is not found in Scripture. The word "church" comes from the Greek "ekklesia." It means "called out" and always refers to a local group of Christians led by their own pastor, under Jesus Christ, the Head.

See Paul's letters to various churches and Christ's messages to seven distinct and different churches in Revelation 1:11, 20, and chapters 2 and 3 of Revelation.

- **The Eucharist**
The word means "giving of thanks" and is the Roman Catholic version of the Lord's Supper, or Communion. Catholics teach that the bread and wine become the actual body and blood of Jesus Christ as the priest prays over them (the doctrine of transubstantiation), and that Christ is sacrificed again each time the Eucharist is celebrated.

But this is a terrible blasphemy. See Hebrews 9:24–28 and 10:6–14, against the background of Exodus 17:5–6 and Numbers 20:7–12.

- **The Priesthood**
In the Old Testament a special class of people were set aside as priests, to stand between God and His people. In the New Testament we find that our great High Priest, Jesus Christ, has made a new and living way for each of us to enter boldly into the very presence of God.

See Hebrews 10:19–22. Also 1 Peter 2:5, 9; Revelation 1:6, 2:6, 5:10; Matthew 23:8–11 and 1 Timothy 2:5–6.

- **Statues, Ceremonies, Special Days**
The Bible urges us to not to obscure our relationship with Jesus Christ under a cloud of traditions and ceremonial worship.

See 2 Corinthians 11:3 and Exodus 20:1–5; 1 Timothy 4:1–3; Romans 14:1–8, 17; Ephesians 2:8–9.

• **_Worship of Mary_**

Mary was an exceptional young woman among all the women in Israel, among all the women in the whole world, for she was chosen by God to be the mother of Jesus. We should respect her for living a life that made her eligible to be chosen. But we should not worship her!

To Roman Catholics, however, Mary is the Mother of God and the Queen of Heaven, equal to Jesus in many ways and even superior to Him. They believe that just as Jesus was born sinless, because He was born of a virgin with God as His Father, so Mary herself was born without original sin—the "immaculate conception"—and never sinned. More than that, after giving birth to Jesus, she remained a virgin and never died, but was raised both body and soul into heaven, where she now reigns beside Jesus Christ. She is a Redeemer and a Mediator just like Jesus. In fact, no one can approach Christ except through the Mother. So in Catholic churches Jesus is portrayed as a dead man on a cross or as a helpless infant in the arms of Mary. If you want help, you need to look to Mary.

These teachings are blasphemous, detracting from the honor and worship due to Jesus Christ alone, and clearly at odds with Scripture. The fact that many sincere Catholics are not fully aware how anti-Christian some of these beliefs are does not excuse them. The Scriptures are very clear on the subject of Mary. See Luke 1:46–48, 11:27–28; Matthew 12:46–50.

In Acts 4:10, 12 we read: "By the name of Jesus Christ of Nazareth… whom God raised from the dead…Neither is there salvation in any other: for there is none other name under heaven given among men, whereby we must be saved."

PART III:
IDEOLOGY AS RELIGION

- *Introduction*
- *Evolution, the Great Hoax*
- *Marxism—Dead-end to Eden*

I. Introduction

Many factors shape the identity of the world we live in—technology, instant mass communication, pop culture, ease of travel, fearsome weapons, massive population growth—but the most significant impact comes in the realm of thoughts and ideas.

For the first time in human history, godless ideologies have captured the popular imagination on a wide scale. Marxism (God does not exist, and man has it in his own power to create heaven on earth), Freudianism (there is no sin), and moral relativism (there is no right or wrong), have wreaked havoc in society. Evolution as a theory of the beginning of life postulates the absence of God in creation and has become the official, state-approved, and publicly sponsored religion of the western world.

The essayist Robert Conquest, in his "Reflections on a Ravaged Century," argues that the main responsibility for the disasters of the last hundred years lies with "ideas that claimed to transcend all problems but were defective or delusive, devastating minds and movements and whole countries." In other words, when man trusts in himself as his own god, chaos follows.

II. Evolution—the Great Hoax

A major obstacle to faith in God is the unchecked rise during the past 150 years of the theory of evolution. Belief in evolution is as much a religion as belief in creation. Despite its claim to the contrary, evolution is not science: it is a dogma, a set of beliefs that seeks to explain the world in which we live—its origins, its present, and its future. It provides answers to the big questions: Who are we/where did we come from? (We are the result of chance chemical processes working over very long periods of time.); Why are we here? (There is no specific or guiding purpose.); Where do we go from here? (Back into the chemical dust of the earth).

Evolution sets the human mind in the place of God. The theory's flaws are not hard to find, but to see them, the doubter must look past the imposing edifices that have been raised everywhere in its name—the great museums of natural history found in every major western city, the courses taught in every secular university, the libraries full of impressive scientific books, the unquestioning reporting of evolution's claims by the world's media, the display everywhere of pictures tracing evolution's supposed progress, and last but not least, the mandatory imposition of evolution's certainty on every public school in every country that considers itself a part of the modern world.

But dig through this immense and imposing pile to the heart of the theory and its folly is exposed: evolution does not merely teach that man is descended from a monkey, but that man's earliest ancestor was a rock. And the rock begat an amoeba and the amoeba begat a monkey and the monkey begat man.

Add to this foolishness the fact that much of evolutionary theory is clearly at odds with empirical evidence (most notably the fossil record and also the second law of thermodynamics), and one is left wondering how such a hoax could become so universally accepted and so dogmatically sustained.

The simple answer is that the theory survives because it must. Either God created the world, or it happened by accident (and we humans are merely individual accidents within the larger accident). For a human race increasingly bent on worshipping itself, any possibility of the existence of God must be rejected at all costs.

III. Marxism—Dead-end to Eden

Just as Charles Darwin provided a "scientific" explanation for the natural world that excluded the necessity of a creator God, so Karl Marx provided a "scientific" framework for understanding and promoting the evolution of man in society.

The insidious ideology that brought the evils of communism to the world and caused the brutal death of more than one hundred million people in the twentieth century challenged the idea that God was central to the fulfillment of human destiny. Instead, by understanding and directing the force of man's economic need, which Marx said influences all social relationships and actions, it would be possible to establish a perfect society. Man has it in his own power to establish heaven on earth.

Unfortunately for Marxists, every socialist "paradise" created by them has inevitably degenerated into a ruinous hell. Yet they refuse to be convinced by the facts: Marxists see themselves as the enlightened guardians of a bright hope for tomorrow, with time and history on their side. Eventually they will get it right. Their fantastic vision will not be denied; Eden will be recaptured, and the Marxist visionary will, at last, be seen as Creator.

But the Christianized West is a major roadblock to the universal realization of this dream, the establishment of a communist new world order. The West must be conquered. As the richest and most powerful nation on earth, America is a special target, particularly since it acknowledges to a greater degree than anywhere else the one doctrine that offers a true alternative to Marxism's tantalizing promise—the Gospel of Jesus Christ. For Marxist Socialism to reign triumphant and unchallenged, this alternative message must be fully discredited and completely obliterated.

The biblical truth that states unequivocally, "In the beginning, God!" must be replaced by the Marxist call, "In the future, Man!"

Over the course of the last fifty years, the battle for the soul of America has raged with growing intensity, with Marxist philosophy on the ascendancy everywhere against the traditional family and churches, the educational system, the media, entertainment, literature, science, and history. This Cultural Marxism is now so entrenched in the thinking of many Americans that they view with increasing suspicion and hostility those raised in the traditions of God, family, patriotism, and free markets.

Whereas America was once proud to declare its allegiance to Jesus Christ, the new rallying cry of the elite, politically correct, "progressive" multiculturalists is: "I believe in nothing and am tolerant of everything."

PART IV:

ISLAM—A RELIGION SET ON WORLD RULE—PART ONE

- *Introduction*
- *Beliefs*
- *The Five Pillars of Islam*
- *The Qur'an*
- *Converting to Islam*

I. Introduction

The most aggressive and fastest-growing religion in the world today is Islam. It has spread from its seventh century tribal roots in Arabia, to dominate more than 50 countries in the Middle East, Africa, and Asia, while significant numbers of its 1.4 billion followers are found in almost every other nation. The largest number, 200 million, are in Indonesia. There are over 100 million Muslims each in India, China, Pakistan, and Bangladesh. Turkey and Iran have over 60 million each. The second largest religion in Europe today is Islam. America is home to about 4 million.

While Islam claims to be the "religion of peace," it is best known in recent times as the religion that spawns terror attacks, violent protests over cartoons, and aggressive confrontations with the established laws and cultures of the western countries in which it has taken root. Muslims are pushing to establish Islamic law ("Sharia") and Islamic courts in Europe and Canada and to silence free speech wherever Islam is criticized. It is determined to have its way and will sweep aside all who resist.

185

II. Beliefs

The word "Islam" (from the Arabic al-Islam) means "submission to the will of God." It is one of the world's three monotheistic religions, with Judaism, and Christianity.

The central faith of Islam is contained in the so-called two testimonies: There is no God but Allah, and Muhammad is the messenger (prophet) of Allah.

Muslims believe that Allah revealed His word through many prophets, including Adam, Noah, Abraham, Moses, and Jesus. But the last and greatest prophet, the Seal of the Prophets, is Muhammad, who was born 570 years after Jesus Christ and died in 632.

The Qur'an is accepted as the final written record of God's revelation to humanity, replacing the Jewish and Christian Scriptures which Muslims believe have been misinterpreted, distorted, or corrupted by their followers. Thus, the Qur'an is seen as a correction of Jewish and Christian Scriptures.

There are six basic beliefs shared by all Muslims:

1. Belief in one God. This God is so far above man in every way that he is virtually unknowable.
2. Belief in the Angels
3. Belief in the books sent by God
   a. The Scrolls of Abraham (Suhuf-i-Ibrahim)
   b. The Torah sent to Moses (Tawrat)
   c. The Psalms sent to David (Zabur)
   d. The Gospels sent to Jesus (Injil)
   e. The Qur'an sent to Muhammad
4. Belief in the prophets and messengers sent by God
5. Belief in the Day of Judgment and in life after death—heaven and hell
6. Belief in Fate

III. The Five Pillars of Islam

Muslims are split into various subgroups, the two largest of which are Sunni and Shia. The groups are split based on their belief concerning who was the rightful successor to Muhammad at his death. Eighty-five percent of the world's Muslims are Sunni. Majorities of Shia Muslims are found in Iran and Iraq, while Sunni Muslims dominate Saudi Arabia, Indonesia, and Pakistan. The two groups differ in some of their beliefs and practices, but all Muslims believe in five basic obligations:

1. *Shahadah:* Testifying that there is none worthy of worship but God and that Muhammad is his servant and messenger
2. *Salah:* Performing the five daily prayers
3. *Sawm:* Fasting from dawn to dusk in the month of Ramadan
4. *Zakat:* Giving to charity
5. *Hajj:* The Pilgrimage to Mecca, the Muslim holy city in Saudi Arabia, is compulsory once in a lifetime for one who has the ability to do it.

Some have added a sixth Pillar of Faith, the Holy War or "Jihad." The intent is the spread of Islam by force.

Shia and Sunni also agree on the following beliefs, although they classify them differently:

- The justice of God
- The Day of Resurrection
- Commanding what is good
- Forbidding what is evil
- Striving to seek God's approval

IV. The Qur'an

"Qur'an" means "recitation." Muslims believe the Qur'an was revealed to Muhammad by God through the Angel Gabriel on numerous occasions between the years 610 and 632, the year Muhammad died. In addition to memorizing his revelations, his followers wrote them down on parchments, leaves, and even stones.

The Qur'an is almost worshipped, being wrapped in a clean cloth when not in use and read only after hands have been washed. Most Muslims memorize parts of the book, and many memorize it all. It contains 114 chapters or Suras.

V. The Kaaba

A strange aspect of Islam centers on the worship of a sacred black stone, probably the remnant of an ancient meteorite. The stone is contained in the Kaaba, a large, black building, roughly the shape of a cube, located inside the mosque in Mecca.

This is the holiest site in Islam. Muslims throughout the world face the Kaaba during their prayers, and during the Hajj they perform a ceremony of walking round and round the Kaaba.

VI. Converting to Islam

The community of Muslim believers is known as the "Umnah" ("family"). To become a Muslim it is sufficient simply to accept the central beliefs of Islam (the "Shahadah") and recite them publicly. However, it is impossible to leave Islam, and the penalty for apostasy is death.

PART V:

ISLAM—A RELIGION SET ON WORLD RULE—PART TWO

- *Introduction*
- *The Muslim Way to Peace*
- *Islamic Law*
- *Distinctions between "Moderate" and "Radical" Islam.*

I. Introduction

Each local New Testament church is empowered by the "Great Commission" of Scripture to go into all the world and teach all nations about Jesus Christ (Matthew 28:18–20; Mark 16:15). Muslims seek to turn the whole human race into Muslims. The Qur'an declares (Sura 34:28): "We have sent you forth to all mankind." While the commission may sound the same, there is a vast difference in the approach of the two religions.

Jesus Christ declared: "My kingdom is not of this world: if my kingdom were of this world, then would my servants fight" (John 18:36). Jesus taught that His followers were to conquer unbelievers and enemies alike by loving them and presenting His truth to them so that they could freely choose to accept or reject Him. Those who follow Him are to be in the world but not focused on the world. The highest expression of Christian love is to give one's life, figuratively and sometimes literally, so that others may live.

Muslims, by contrast, are set on obtaining worldly power and establishing a worldwide, earthly kingdom—by brute force, if necessary. The highest expression of Muslim devotion is to kill those who stand in the way of Islam. Extra merit is obtained if the Muslim dies in the process.

II. The Muslim Way to Peace

Mankind is divided into two groups—Muslims and non-Muslims. The Muslims are part of the "umma"—the Muslim community—while all non-Muslims are people of the "Dar ul Harb," the Land of Warfare. They are destined to come under Islamic rule either by conversion or by war, for Muslims are obliged to wage Holy War against those who will not voluntarily submit to the Islamic religion.

However, expansion through war or violence is not seen as aggression by Muslims, since the end result will be to spread Islam as a way of peace. Peace, in turn, requires that non-Muslims either convert to Islam or submit to its rule by accepting the status of a religious minority, the *dhimmi,* who pay a special poll tax, wear special identifying clothing, and live as second class citizens.

III. Islamic Law

Islamic Law or "Sharia" is the law that applies in an ideal Muslim community. Here there is no "separation of church and state"—supreme authority resides in the Qur'an, and its teachers and all government and society submit to Sharia, which must be accepted without doubts or criticism. Sharia controls the entire life of the believer and the Islamic community. An individual living under Islamic Law is not free to think for himself.

Islam does not value the individual, and minorities are not tolerated. Women are second class humans, objects for the use of men. There is no freedom of opinion or freedom to change one's religion. Apostasy is punishable by death.

In all litigation between a Muslim and a dhimmi, the validity of the oath or testimony of the dhimmi is not recognized.

IV. Distinctions Between "Moderate" and "Radical" Islam

Islam is a totalitarian ideology that aims to control the religious, social, and political life of mankind. It teaches clearly and without apology that in order to advance Islam, Muslims must strive, fight, and kill in the name of Allah. This is the concept of Jihad. The only time Muslims are taught to mute their aggressive behavior is when their opponents are too powerful to be overthrown or subjugated by force.

Passages in the Qu'ran, like Sura 4:76; 8:12; 9:5–6; and 9:29 (among many others), speak unambiguously of fighting and killing and striking off heads. Those who believe fight in the cause of Allah. Thus, the terrorists who attacked America on 09/11/2001 were acting in accordance with the teachings of Islam. The only "moderate" or "tolerant" Muslim is one who is not acting in accordance with these teachings! Moderate Islam has never existed as a concrete social and religious reality.

Extremism and terrorism have characterized Islam for 1,400 years. History records the massacre and extermination of tens of millions of non-Muslims by those waging Jihad: Zoroastrians in Iran; Buddhists and Hindus in India; Jews in Fez, Morocco in 1033, Granada in 1066, Marrakesh in 1232, Morocco in 1790, and Baghdad in 1828; 1.5 million Armenians in Turkey at the beginning of the twentieth century; and 2 million Sudanese Christians and Animists at the close of the twentieth century. To these must be added the more recent and increasingly bold attacks of Islamic terrorists, hijackers, rioters, and suicide bombers in Israel, America, England, Scotland, Spain, Holland, Belgium, France, Lebanon, the Philippines, Iraq, Germany, Bali,

Kenya, Tanzania, Egypt, Russia, Chechnya, Pakistan, India, and Saudi Arabia.

These recent attacks are not in response to mistreatment of Muslims by western nations as apologists for Islam like to claim: they are instead evidence of a resurgent and triumphant Islam imposing its will on increasingly weak, vacillating, and corrupt societies.

THE UNIQUENESS OF CHRISTIANITY

- *All Religions Are Exclusive*
- *Religion and Christianity*
- *Christianity's Unique Claims for Itself*
- *Christianity's Unique Demands on its Followers*

I. All Religions Are Exclusive

Many people say they are offended by the claims of Christianity concerning exclusiveness of truth and salvation. It was Jesus Himself who declared, "I am the way, the truth, and the life: no man cometh unto the Father, but by me" (John 14:6). However, the fact is that all religions make exclusive claims concerning the truth of their teachings—it is precisely this that differentiates one from the other. To believe that *everything* is of equal truthfulness, value, and authority is to believe in *nothing*.

Yet Christianity is indeed exclusive in a way that other religions are not. All world religions offer sets of rules or guidelines or beliefs or practices that claim to equip their followers to draw closer to that religion's god, or gods. We call these "works-based" religions. That is, in each of these religions salvation is the result of good works outweighing bad acts. Christianity, on the other hand, is the only religion that has as its core belief the declaration of man's absolute inability to draw near to God based on his own efforts. In other words, no one is able to perform enough good works to earn salvation. Salvation is available equally to all as a free gift. It is *this* that makes Christianity offensive to some and a source of great good news to others.

Humanists (those who hold to a philosophy that has self at the center, rejecting the entire idea of God, or at least a God who is involved supernaturally in human affairs) are particularly offended by the idea that they might have inherent flaws that make them unacceptable to God. The open-mindedness that they preach as tolerance is, in reality, a requirement for the inclusiveness of all doctrines without making any qualitative judgment. Thus, they regard Christianity as the most bigoted of all religions, claiming that it engenders guilt and a poor self-image, and it conjures frightening myths of bloody sacrifices and eternal suffering.

What is really at issue, however, is that Christianity does not allow any person to claim acceptability to God except through belief in the death, burial, and resurrection of Jesus Christ. That, humanists say, is too narrow a philosophy.

II. Religion and Christianity

All religions attempt to establish a basis on which man can draw closer to God. As such, all religions have three common strands—but Christianity adds a unique fourth strand:

A. A sense of a world beyond this world; life beyond this life

B. A sense of morality and consciousness of guilt (or at least, insufficiency or imperfection)

C. Acknowledgement of a Higher Power or a Force ("God") beyond this world, who establishes moral standards

D. God left the world beyond this world and became a man, to provide through His work and His merit alone the only means whereby man may enter the next world with God (John 1:1–5, 10–14; Philippians 2:5ff).

This last point presents a unique truth that is so offensive to many because it takes the initiative away from man and gives it to God. It implies that man is incapable of saving himself. Indeed, Christianity goes so far as to say that all human works of righteousness are as filthy rags in God's sight (Isaiah 64:6).

III. Christianity's Unique Claims for Itself

A. *God came to earth as a Man*
Christians do not worship a prophet, a reformer, a great leader, or a wise and good teacher, but God Himself. Jesus Christ, God in human form, is unique in His:
1. Virgin Birth
2. Virtuous Character
3. Vicarious Death
4. Victorious Resurrection

B. *Jesus Christ taught as no man has ever taught*
1. He alone has the words of eternal life (John 6:68).
2. No man ever spoke like this man (John 7:46).

C. *Salvation through Jesus Christ is unlike any other*
1. Approved by God
2. Free
3. Fair
4 Certain
5. Complete
6. Eternal

IV. Christianity's Unique Demands on its Followers

With a great gift—salvation through Jesus Christ—comes a great responsibility! Jesus Himself outlined that responsibility when He told us to go into the whole world and tell everybody

the unique, good news about how to get to heaven (Matthew
4:14, 28:18–20; Acts 1:8).

TEST 9

[65 Points]

Note: Where no total point value is given for a question, each correct answer is worth one point.

1. Name two aggressive religions (a and b) and two mainly concerned with seeking inner peace (c and d).
   a. *Islam, Roman Catholicism, Mormonism, Jehovah's Witnesses*
   b.
   c. *Buddhists, Hindus, Shinto*
   d.

2. How would you categorize Christianity? (5 Points)
   Biblical Christianity rejects the world system, yet Christians focus on the needs of the world's spiritually oppressed all about them. Christians seek to transform one person at a time, by sacrificial love.

3. If nothing we can do will impress God, what is our task in this life? (2 points)
   Not to strive to impress Him, but to surrender to His Will.

4. What is the difference between a polytheistic and a monotheistic religion? (2 points)
   A polytheistic religion acknowledges many gods; a monotheistic religion acknowledges only one god.

5. Name   (a) a polytheistic religion
              (b) a monotheistic religion
  a. *Hinduism, Buddhism*
  b. *Christianity, Judaism, Islam*

6. What does "Buddha" mean?
   Enlightened One

7. How do Hindus view Jesus?
   As just another one of the thousands of gods

8. Buddha's plan for good works is known as:
   The Eightfold Path

9. Why do Protestants add the word "Roman" to the title, "Catholic Church"? (4 points)
   Catholic means "universal." Addition of the word "Roman" indicates that the Catholic Church is not the only, universal church, but a religious movement with its headquarters in Rome.

10. What is the "petra" to which Jesus referred in his discussion with Peter recorded in Matthew 16:16–17? (2 points)
    Himself

11. What is the meaning of "Pope"?
    Father

12. List Roman Catholic beliefs that run contrary to Scripture:
    a. *The Universal Church*
    b. *The Eucharist*
    c. *The Priesthood*
    d. *Statues, ceremonies, special days*
    e. *Worship of Mary*

13. Many factors shape the identity of the modern world. What makes the greatest impact?
    Thoughts and ideas

14. What is the official religion of the western world?
    Belief in evolution
15. In what way is the theory of evolution less like science and
    more like religion? (2 points)
    *It is a dogmatic set of beliefs that seeks to explain the world in
    which we live.*
16. What is evolution's greatest flaw? (2 points)
    The belief that man's earliest ancestor was a rock.
17. How do Marxists see themselves? (2 points)
    *As the enlightened guardians of a bright hope for tomorrow,
    with time and history on their side.*
18. What is the rallying cry of "progressive" multiculturalists?
    (2 points)
    I believe in nothing and am tolerant of everything.
19. Where does Islam rank among religions in Europe today?
    Second largest
20. What is the central faith of Islam? (4 points)
    *The two testimonies: There is no God but Allah, and Muham-
    mad is the messenger of Allah.*
21. What is name of the Muslim holy book?
    Qur'an
22. Describe a strange aspect of Islam. (4 points)
    *Worship of a sacred black stone, probably a meteorite, contained
    in the Kaaba, a large, black building, roughly the shape of a
    cube, located inside the mosque in Mecca*
23. Explain the differences between Muslims and Christians
    with regard to the way they seek to spread their beliefs to
    the whole world (5 points):
    *The highest expression of Christian love is to give one's life,
    figuratively and sometimes literally, so that others may live. The
    highest expression of Muslim devotion is to kill those who stand
    in the way of Islam. Extra merit is obtained if the Muslim kills
    himself in the process.*

24. True or False: Christianity alone makes exclusive claims for itself. Explain your answer. (4 points)
False. All religions have exclusive claims that differentiate them from each other. To believe that everything is equally true is to believe nothing!

25. Explain why the unique truth of the Gospel message is so offensive to many people. (3 points)
The Gospel takes the initiative away from man and gives it to God; it implies that man is unable to save himself.

26. List three unique claims of Christianity:
    a. *God came to earth as a man.*
    b. *Jesus Christ taught as no man has ever taught.*
    c. *Salvation through Jesus Christ is unlike any other.*

What Constitutes A Call To Christian Service?

- *All Christians are called to serve God*
- *Some Christians are called to full-time service*
- *Preparation to hear a specific call from God*

I. All Christians are called to serve God

All Christians have a general call as a consequence of their conversion. The Bible tells us we are called:

A. To be saints (Romans 1:7)
B. To be conformed to the image of Christ (Romans 8:30)
C. To be holy (1 Thessalonians 2:12)
D. To be soulwinners (Matthew 4:19, 28:19)

A problem that many Christians face is how to recognize a call from God to serve Him in a specific way.

II. Some Christians are called to full-time service

Some Christian men are specifically called by God to be pastors or missionary evangelists. These unique ministries of the local New Testament church are aided by other individuals who are completely yielded to the leading of God in their lives to be pastors' wives or teachers in Christian schools or church administrators or to work in some other avenue of service.

There is no set formula for a call to full-time Christian service: God calls whom He wills, how He wills, when He wills, to go where He wills—and since individuals have unique personalities and capabilities, no two calls are ever the same. Some Christians are not moved to serve God until they feel called in a clear and unmistakable way—others simply see a need and volunteer, asking God to stop them if He doesn't want them to serve!

Fortunately, there are clear principles set forth in the Scriptures that enable individuals to discern God's specific will for their lives.

III. Preparation to hear a specific call from God

God speaks most clearly to those who listen. This simple principle may be seen at work in those who have prepared their ears to hear by adopting certain scriptural attitudes:

A. *Submission*
  1. To the Lordship of Christ (Acts 9:6; 2 Corinthians 10:5)
  2. To the Will of God (Romans 12:1; John 7:17)
     * To know God's will, one must be ready to do God's will!
  3. To the local church (Acts 13:1–4)

B. *Separation*
  1. Not in love with this world or the things of this world (Romans 12:2; James 4:4; 1 John 2:15–17)
  2. Not in love with sin (Romans 6:6–13)
  3. Not unequally yoked with unbelievers (2 Corinthians 6:14)

C. *Sensitivity*

1. To the leading of the written Word of God, the Scriptures (Hebrews 4:12)

2. To the leading of the Holy Spirit (1 John 2:27; Isaiah 30:21)

3. A "hearing ear" is essential! That is, an ear sensitive to the voice of God, willing to follow His directions (Revelation 2:7,11, 17, 29; 3:6, 13, 22).

FOLLOWING GOD
ALL THE WAY

- *Introduction*
- *Scriptural Examples of those called by God*
- *Benefits of the call of God*
- *Problems surrounding the call of God*
- *Following God all the way!*

I. Introduction

An unfortunate aspect of Christian service is the number of individuals who respond to God's leading or call, only to turn from or abandon it after a time as they succumb to doubt, temptations, the allure of the world, or trials. Missionary evangelists are often most vulnerable, because they are isolated on a foreign field, far from much that is familiar in their lives. The best insurance against failure of this sort is to be certain about the leading or call of God and to understand at the same time that it does not automatically confer "Super Christian" status on anyone! Whoever we are, wherever we are, whatever we're doing, we all need the Holy Spirit's guidance and power to direct our steps every day.

II. Scriptural Examples of Those Called by God

Note that these examples are all of men called to the ministry. The general principles would apply in most respects to Christian men and women who may feel led to some other form of full-time service.

A. Moses (Exodus 3:10–4:17)
   1. The Call of God (3:10)
   2. The Excuses of Moses (3:11–4:13)
       a. I'm a nobody (v.11)
           • The answer: I will be with you! (v.12).
       b. Who are you? (How can I trust you?) (v. 13)
           • The answer: I am the ever-present God (v. 14).
       c. Nobody will believe me! (4:1).
           • The answer: I will confirm my word (4: 2–9).
       d. I'm not a good speaker (v. 10).
           • The answer: I will speak through you (4:11–12).
       e. I just don't want to do it! (v13).
           • The answer: I will equip you. You have no excuse! (4:14–17)

B. Isaiah (Isaiah 6:1–10)
   1. His perception of God (6:1–4)
   2. His perception of himself (v. 5)
   3. God's provision for his frailty (6:6–7)
   4. His humble submission to God's call (v. 8)

C. The Apostle Paul (Acts 13:1–4)
   1. Man doesn't do the calling. The church doesn't do the calling. God calls!
   2. Paul knew clearly who he was, what his purpose was, and who it was who called him (Romans 1:1; 1 Corinthians 1:1; etc.).

III. Benefits of the Call or Leading of God

A. Provides direction (Acts 16:6–10)

B. Provides determination (Acts 26:19; 2 Timothy 4:7)
Note that God doesn't need our help, just our obedience (Exodus 4:12).

C. Provides all our needs (Matthew 6:33)

IV. Problems Surrounding the Call or Leading of God

A. *Lack of Patience*

1. God is never late, never early, always on time. Beware the sin of Saul (1 Samuel 13:8–14).

2. Simply present yourself to the Lord and wait (Romans 12:1–2).

3. Worry not so much about when you go, or where you go, but about how live each day (Psalm 37:23).

B. *Lack of Priorities*
(Matthew 6:33)

C. *Lack of Prayer*
(Isaiah 40:28–31)

D. *Lack of Preparation in God's Word*
(Psalm 119:105; Proverbs 3:5–6)
Never put a question mark where God has put a period! Obey the clear commands of God in Scripture—99% of His will is contained there.

E. *Lack of Personal Counseling*
You are not alone. Seek help and counsel before making decisions (Proverbs 11:14, 12:15, 15:22, 20:5).

F. *Lack of Personal Separation*
You cannot serve God and the world!
(Psalm 1:1–3, 37:4; Hebrews 13:21).

G. *Lack of Perspective*
(1 Peter 1:3–8, 4:12–13)
But note the positive alternative (Hebrews 7:16).

V. Following God All the Way

Hebrews chapter 11 provides stirring examples of ordinary people who did extraordinary things when they decided to follow God all the way! Note some key statements in this chapter:

A. Without faith it is impossible to please God (v. 6).

B. Keep your eyes on God's kingdom (10, 13–14).

C. Don't look back (15–16)

D. See Him who is invisible (24–27)

1. Every giant of opposition or discouragement you face will shrink in proportion to how you view God.

2. Note that in the story of David and Goliath told in 1 Samuel 17, the real giant on the battlefield is not Goliath but God!

REVIEW AND SCRIPTURE TEST

- *Review*
- *Test Memorized Scripture Passage*

INFORMAL SURVEY AND TESTIMONIES

1. **Informal Survey**

   a. How many students feel called:
      - to be a pastor?
      - to be a missionary evangelist?
   b. How many students feel led:
      - to some other area of full-time Christian service?
   c. How many are not presently conscious of a call or leading from God but are willing to follow God wherever He may lead them?
   d. How many are hoping God will call or lead them into full-time Christian service in some capacity? For men, this might be a call as a pastor or missionary evangelist.

2. **Students Share Testimonies**

   a. What have they learned from this course?
   b. How has their newly acquired knowledge affected their view of their commitment to Jesus Christ?

Lesson By Pastor Or Visiting Missionary Evangelist

- *Lesson By Pastor Or Visiting Missionary Evangelist*
  ☆ May be inserted at any time this quarter.

SCOPE AND SEQUENCE

World Evangelism: First Quarter

Lesson One (Unit 1)

- ***Introduction To World Evangelism***
  - ☆ Present Outline of the Course.
  - ☆ Discuss: What Motivates Us?
  - ☆ Introduction to Foundational Concepts:
    - ← Personal Evangelism
    - ← World Evangelism
    - ← The two-fold Purpose of God for each Local Church
    - ← "Missionary" Defined
  - ☆ Informal Survey of Students:
    - ← How many are disposed to full-time Christian service?

Lesson Two (Unit 2)

- ***World Missions Demographics (Part One)***
  - ☆ The World—nations and populations
  - ☆ World Missions
  - ☆ World Religions
  - ☆ Bible Translations

215

☆   World Regions/Peoples

☆   The "10/40 Window"

Lesson Three (Unit 3)

- ***World Missions Demographics (Part Two)***
  ☆   Christian Outreach in Relation to Population
  ☆   The Fields Are White Unto Harvest!

1. Review and Test (Unit 4)

- Review Lessons 1–3
- Test

Lesson Four (Unit 5)

- ***God's Unfolding Purpose For Humanity***
  ☆   God's Purpose
  ☆   The Progressive Revelation of God to Man
  ☆   Carrying the Revelation of God to the Ends of the Earth

Lesson Five (Unit 6)

- ***The Local Church***
  ☆   What is the Local Church?
  ☆   Who "owns" it?
  ☆   What is its Purpose?

Lesson Six (Unit 7)

- ***What Is One Soul Worth?***
  ☆   A Challenge to Emulate Great Soulwinners

☆ Overcoming the God of This World
☆ The Reality of Hell
☆ Weighing Our Commitment

2. **Review and Test (Unit 8)**

• Review Lessons 4–7
• Test

Lesson Seven (Unit 9)

• *Missions And World Evangelism*
  ☆ The Meaning of Evangelism
  ☆ The Motivation for Evangelism
  ☆ The Message of Evangelism
  ☆ Missionary Evangelists

Lesson Eight (Unit 10)

• *A Personal Responsibility For A Great Commission*
  ☆ A Personal Responsibility for Souls
  ☆ A Great Commission for Soulwinners
      ← According to Matthew
      ← According to Mark
      ← According to Luke
      ← According to John
      ← According to Acts

3. **Review and Test (Unit 11)**

• Review Units 9–10
• Test

Lesson Nine (Unit 12)

- *The Link Between Personal Evangelism And World Evangelism*
  - ☆ The Meaning of "Personal Evangelism"
  - ☆ The Need for Personal Evangelism
  - ☆ Three Conditions
  - ☆ Prerequisites for Personal Evangelism

Lesson Ten (Unit 13)

- *The Importance Of A Personal Testimony*
  - ☆ The Power of a Personal Testimony
  - ☆ Three Reasons for a Personal Testimony
  - ☆ Key Elements of a Personal Testimony
  - ☆ Students Share their Personal Testimonies of Salvation

Lesson Eleven (Unit 14)

- *Presenting The Gospel*
  - ☆ Why We Present the Gospel
  - ☆ How We Present the Gospel
  - ☆ Steps In Presenting the Gospel

Lesson Twelve (Unit 15)

- *Introducing The Gospel—and Tying The Knot*
  - ☆ The Power of a Tract
  - ☆ Answering Questions by Asking Questions
  - ☆ More Questions
  - ☆ Tying the Knot
  - ☆ Next Steps

4. Review and Test (Unit 16)

- Review Units 12–15
- Test

Lesson Thirteen (Unit 17)

- *Lesson By Pastor or Visiting Missionary Evangelist*
  ☆ May be inserted at any time during this quarter

Lesson Fourteen (Unit 18)

- Review Quarter
- Test Memorized Scripture Passage

END OF FIRST QUARTER

World Evangelism: Second Quarter

Notes On This Quarter

The second quarter—18 Units—is devoted to a study of the lives of great missionary evangelists, to illustrate what can be achieved by those who will obey God's call to full-time Christian service.

1. *Giants of the Missionary Trail* by Eugene Myers Harrison is recommended as the textbook for this quarter.
   - The book recounts the struggles and achievements of eight missionary evangelists.
   - The end of each chapter provides a comprehensive list of useful questions.
2. In addition to this classroom study, each student will be required to do a book report on the life of a great missionary evangelist. See list, Unit 19, page 71.

Lesson Fifteen (Unit 19)

- *Introduce And Briefly Survey Giants of the Missionary Trail*
- *Review List Of Books For Book Reports*

Lesson Sixteen (Unit 20)

- Henry Nott—Tahiti
  - ☆ Summarize highlights of the story.
  - ☆ Set questions selected from the list at the end of the chapter as a homework assignment.

Lesson Seventeen (Unit 21)

- Test
- Discuss main lessons learned from Henry Nott story.
- Homework: read chapter on William Carey.

Lesson Eighteen (Unit 22)

- William Carey—India
  - ☆ Summarize highlights of the story.
  - ☆ Make special note of Carey's status as the "father" of modern missions.
  - ☆ Set questions selected from the list at the end of the chapter as a homework assignment.

Lesson Nineteen (Unit 23)

- Test
- Discuss main lessons learned from William Carey's story.
- Homework: read chapter on George Grenfell.

Lesson Twenty (Unit 24)

- George Grenfell—Congo
  - ☆ Summarize highlights of the story.
  - ☆ Set questions selected from the list at the end of the chapter as a homework assignment.

Lesson Twenty-one (Unit 25)

- Test
- Discuss main highlights from George Grenfell's story.
- Homework: read chapter on Adoniram Judson.

Lesson Twenty-two (Unit 26)

- Adoniram Judson—Burma
  - ☆ Summarize highlights of the story.
  - ☆ Set questions selected from the list at the end of the chapter as a homework assignment.

Lesson Twenty-three (Unit 27)

- Test
- Discuss main highlights from Adoniram Judson's story.
- Homework: read chapter on Samuel Marsden.

Lesson Twenty-four (Unit 28)

- Samuel Marsden—New Zealand
  - ☆ Summarize highlights of the story.
  - ☆ Set questions selected from the list at the end of the chapter as a homework assignment.

Lesson Twenty-five (Unit 29)

- Test

- Discuss main highlights from Samuel Marsden's story.
- Homework: read chapter on David Livingstone.

Lesson Twenty-six (Unit 30)

- David Livingstone—Southern Africa
  - ☆ Summarize highlights of the story.
  - ☆ Set questions selected from the list at the end of the chapter as a homework assignment.

Lesson Twenty-seven (Unit 31)

- Test
- Discuss main highlights from the David Livingstone story.
- Homework: read chapter on James Chalmers.

Lesson Twenty-eight (Unit 32)

- James Chalmers—New Guinea
  - ☆ Summarize highlights of the story.
  - ☆ Set questions selected from the list at the end of the chapter as a homework assignment.

Lesson Twenty-nine (Unit 33)

- Test
- Discuss main highlights from the James Chalmers story.
- Homework: read chapter on Jonathan Goforth.

Lesson Thirty (Unit 34)

- Jonathan Goforth—China
  - ☆ Summarize highlights of the story.

☆ Set questions selected from the list at the end of the chapter as a homework assignment.

Lesson Thirty-one (Unit 35)

- Test
- Discuss main highlights from the Jonathan Goforth story.

Lesson Thirty-two (Unit 36)

- *Lesson by Pastor or Visiting Missionary Evangelist*
  ☆ May be inserted at any time this quarter

END OF SECOND QUARTER

World Evangelism: Third Quarter

Lesson Thirty-three (Unit 37)

- *Review Second Quarter*
- *Test Memorized Scripture Passage*

Lesson Thirty-four (Unit 38)

- *Presentation by the Pastor or Missions Director/ Secretary*
  ☆ Details of Missions Outreach by your church and administration of the program
  ☆ Numbers and locations of missionary evangelists and church planters

Lesson Thirty-five (Unit 39)

- *Adopt A Missionary Evangelist*
  ☆ Purpose
  ☆ Details of the project
  ☆ Students are assigned contact names and addresses

Lesson Thiry-six (Unit 40)

- *So What In The World Is The World Like?*
  ☆ First World and Third World
  ☆ Civilized and Uncivilized
  ☆ Hygienic and Unhygienic
  ☆ Food and Hunger
  ☆ Personal Space and Other Problems
  ☆ Language

Lesson Thirty-seven (Unit 41)

- *God's Purpose And Our Response*
  ☆ God's Purpose Revealed in Scripture
  ☆ New Testament Soulwinning
  ☆ Our Commission and Response

Lesson Thirty-eight (Unit 42)

- *Great Missionary Movements Of The Bible*
  ☆ Part I: Jesus Christ, the Founder of Missions

Lesson Thirty-nine (Unit 43)

- *Great Missionary Movements Of The Bible*
  ☆ Part II: The Apostle Paul, Church Planter

Lesson Forty (Unit 44)

- *Great Missionary Movements Of The Bible*
  - ☆ Part III: The Apostle Paul, Church Planter

1. **Review and Test (Unit 45)**

- Review Units 41–44
- Test

Lesson Forty-one (Unit 46)

- *The Person Of The Missionary Evangelist—Part 1: Qualifications for the Ministry*
  - ☆ Spiritual Qualifications
  - ☆ Character Qualifications

Lesson Forty-two (Unit 47)

- *The Person Of The Missionary Evangelist—Part II: The Power Of Prayer*
  - ☆ Prayer is Talking to God
  - ☆ Prayer was Evident in the Life of Jesus Christ
  - ☆ Prayer was Evident in the Life of the Early Church
  - ☆ The Apostle Paul was a Man of Prayer
  - ☆ Prayer is the Key to Joy, Power, and Fruitfulness

Lesson Forty-three (Unit 48)

- *The Person Of The Missionary Evangelist—Part III: Hindrances*
  - ☆ The Command to "Teach!"
  - ☆ Hindrances to Going

2. **Review and Test (Unit 49)**
   - Review Units 46–48
   - Test

Lesson Forty-four (Unit 50)

- *The Mission Field, Part I—The World*
  - ✩ Introduction
  - ✩ Geography and Population
  - ✩ Peoples and Languages
  - ✩ Religions

Lesson Forty-five (Unit 51)

- *The Mission Field, Part II—Africa and Europe*
  - ✩ Geography and Population
  - ✩ Peoples and Languages
  - ✩ Religions

Lesson Forty-six (Unit 52)

- *The Mission Field, Part III—Asia and Pacific*
  - ✩ Geography and Population
  - ✩ Peoples and Languages
  - ✩ Religions

Lesson Forty-seven (Unit 53)

- *The Mission Field, Part IV—The Americas (North America, Latin America, Caribbean)*
  - ✩ Geography and Population
  - ✩ Peoples and Languages
  - ✩ Religions

3. **Review and Test (Unit 54)**

- Review Units 50–53
- Test

END OF THIRD QUARTER

World Evangelism: Fourth Quarter

Lesson Forty-eight (Unit 55)

- *Review Third Quarter*
- *Test Memorized Scripture Passage*

Lesson Forty-nine (Unit 56)

- *The Heart Of The Great Commission: Part I*
  - ☆ Church Planting is the Heart of the Great Commission
  - ☆ What the Great Commission is Not
  - ☆ A Better Understanding of Matthew 28
  - ☆ A Better Understanding of Acts 1:8

Lesson Fifty (Unit 57)

- *The Heart Of The Great Commission: Part II*
  - ☆ New Testament Church Planting
  - ☆ The Great Commission Today

Lesson Fifty-one (Unit 58)

- *"Grace Giving" In Support Of World Missions*
  - ☆ A Plan to Fulfill the Program
  - ☆ Grace Giving Goes Beyond the Tithe

    ☆   Grace Giving From the Heart

    ☆   Grace Giving: How Much?

1. Review and Test (Unit 59)

- Review Units 56–58
- Test

Lesson Fifty-two (Unit 60)

- ***Introduction To World Religions***
  - ☆ Competing Religions
  - ☆ Three Steps to Finding the True Religion
  - ☆ Christianity and the Manifest Presence of God

Lesson Fifty-three (Unit 61)

- ***World Religions—Part I***
  - ☆ Hinduism
  - ☆ Buddhism

Lesson Fifty-four (Unit 62)

- ***World Religions—Part II—Roman Catholicism***
  - ☆ Introduction
  - ☆ History
  - ☆ Additions to Scripture

Lesson Fifty-five (Unit 63)

- ***World Religions—Part III—Ideology as Religion***
  - ☆ Introduction
  - ☆ Evolution—the Great Hoax

☆ Marxism—Dead-end to Eden

Lesson Fifty-six (Unit 64)

- *World Religions—Part IV—Islam*
  - ☆ Introduction
  - ☆ Beliefs
  - ☆ The Five Pillars of Islam
  - ☆ The Qu'ran
  - ☆ Converting to Islam

Lesson Fifty-seven (Unit 65)

- *World Religions—Part V—Islam*
  - ☆ Introduction
  - ☆ The Muslim Way to Peace
  - ☆ Islamic Law
  - ☆ Distinctions Between "Moderate" and "Radical" Islam

Lesson Fifty-eight (Unit 66)

- *The Uniqueness Of Christianity*
  - ☆ All Religions Are Exclusive
  - ☆ Religion and Christianity
  - ☆ Christianity's Unique Claims for Itself
  - ☆ Christianity's Unique Demands On Its Followers

2. Review and Test (Unit 67)

- Review Units 59–65
- Test

Lesson Fifty-nine (Unit 68)

- ***What Constitutes A Call To Christian Service?***
  - ☆ All Christians Are Called to Serve God
  - ☆ Some Christians Are Called to Full-time Service
  - ☆ Preparation to Hear a Specific Call From God

Lesson Sixty (Unit 69)

- ***Following God All The Way***
  - ☆ Introduction
  - ☆ Scriptural Examples of Those Called By God
  - ☆ Benefits of the Call or Leading of God
  - ☆ Problems Surrounding the Call or Leading of God
  - ☆ Following God All the Way

Lesson Sixty-one (Unit 70)

- ***Review Fourth Quarter***
- ***Test Memorized Scripture Passage***

Lesson Sixty-two (Unit 71)

- ***Informal Survey***
- ***Students Share Testimonies***

Lesson Sixty-three (Unit 72)

- ***Lesson By Pastor Or Visiting Missionary Evangelist***
  - ☆ May be inserted at any time this quarter

END OF FOURTH QUARTER

An Outline for Guest Speakers

1. **The Purpose of This Course**

   * To introduce students entering high school to missions and world evangelism and to instill in them an appreciation for a key biblical doctrine and a core belief of our church.

   * To equip students with a framework of understanding about the importance and nature of world evangelism.

   * To prepare the hearts of students to be receptive to a possible call or leading by God.

2. **The Purpose of Guest Speakers**

   * To enhance the classroom experience by exposing students to speakers who are able to both educate and inspire.

   * Speakers will in some way be intimately involved with world evangelism, as sponsoring pastors or active missionaries or those about to be sent out by a local church.

3. **Suggested Themes for Speakers**

   * Why I feel passionately about world evangelism.
   * How God called me.
   * How I answered the call.

- The greatest challenges I have faced in answering the call.
- The greatest blessings I have experienced in answering the call.
- Triumphs and tragedies on the mission field.
  - ☆ Hilarious/frightening/sobering/heart-breaking/ heart-warming experiences
- Who was the first person you led to Jesus Christ on the mission field?
  - ☆ How long did it take to see the first person converted?
  - ☆ How did it happen?
  - ☆ Where is that person now?
- If you could live your life over again, would you choose to live it in God's service? Why?

Authority without Territory

Literatures and Cultures of the Islamic World

Edited by Hamid Dabashi

Hamid Dabashi is Hagop Kevorkian Professor of Iranian Studies and Comparative Literature at Columbia University. Hamid chaired the Department of Middle East and Asian Languages and Cultures from 2000 to 2005 and was a founding member of the Institute for Comparative Literature and Society. His most recent books include *Islamic Liberation Theology: Resisting the Empire*; *Makhmalbaf at Large: The Making of a Rebel Filmmaker*; *Iran: A People Interrupted*; and an edited volume, *Dreams of a Nation: On Palestinian Cinema*.

Published by Palgrave Macmillan:

Authority without Territory

The Aga Khan Development Network and the Ismaili Imamate

Daryoush Mohammad Poor

palgrave
macmillan

First published in 2014 by
PALGRAVE MACMILLAN®
in the United States—a division of St. Martin's Press LLC,
175 Fifth Avenue, New York, NY 10010.

Where this book is distributed in the UK, Europe and the rest of the world,
this is by Palgrave Macmillan, a division of Macmillan Publishers Limited,
registered in England, company number 785998, of Houndmills,
Basingstoke, Hampshire RG21 6XS.

Palgrave Macmillan is the global academic imprint of the above companies
and has companies and representatives throughout the world.

Palgrave® and Macmillan® are registered trademarks in the United States,
the United Kingdom, Europe and other countries.

ISBN: 978–1–137–42879–0

Library of Congress Cataloging-in-Publication Data

Mohammad Poor, Daryoush, 1975–
    Authority without territory : the Aga Khan Development Network and
    the Ismaili imamate / Daryoush Mohammad Poor.
        pages cm—(Literatures and cultures of the Islamic world)
    Includes bibliographical references and index.
    ISBN 978–1–137–42879–0 (hardback)
    1. Ismailites. 2. Aga Khan IV, 1936– 3. Aga Khan Development
    Network. I. Title.

BP195.I8M65 2014
297.8′22—dc23   2014013057

A catalogue record of the book is available from the British Library.

Design by Newgen Knowledge Works (P) Ltd., Chennai, India.

First edition: September 2014

10 9 8 7 6 5 4 3 2 1

كان أخي موسى عينه اليمنى عمياء و أخي عيسى عينه اليسرى عمياء و أنا ذوعينين

My brother Moses had a blind right eye and my brother Jesus had
a blind left eye, but I have sight in both eyes.

A *ḥadīth* attributed to Prophet Muḥammad

Contents

Figures

Note from the Editor

The Islamic world is home to a vast body of literary production in multiple languages over the last 1,400 years. To be sure, long before the advent of Islam, multiple sites of significant literary and cultural productions existed from India to Iran to the Fertile Crescent to North Africa. After the advent of Islam in the mid-seventh century CE, Arabic, Persian, Urdu, and Turkish authors in particular produced some of the most glorious manifestations of world literature. From prose to poetry, modern to medieval, elitist to popular, oral to literary, this body of literature is in much need of a wide range of renewed scholarly investigation and lucid presentation.

The purpose of this series is to take advantage of the most recent advances in literary studies, textual hermeneutics, critical theory, feminism, postcolonialism, and comparative literature to bring the spectrum of literatures and cultures of the Islamic world to a wider audience and appreciation. Usually the study of these literatures and cultures is divided between classical and modern periods. A central objective of this series is to cross over this artificial and inapplicable bifurcation and abandon the anxiety of periodization altogether. Much of what we understand today from this rich body of literary and cultural production is still under the influence of old-fashioned orientalism or post–World War II area studies perspectives. Our hope is to bring together a body of scholarship that connects the vast arena of literary and cultural production in the Islamic world without the prejudices of outmoded perspectives. Toward this end, we are committed to pathbreaking strategies of reading that collectively renew our awareness of the literary cosmopolitanism and cultural criticism in which these works of creative imagination were conceived in the first place.

—Hamid Dabashi

Preface

This book is a study of modern developments of the institutions of the Nizārī Ismaili imamate during the time of the present Ismaili Imam, Shāh Karīm al-Ḥusaynī, Aga Khan IV, as the forty-ninth hereditary living Imam of Shi'i Nizārī Ismaili Muslims, particularly addressing the formation of the Aga Khan Development Network (AKDN) and the functions of the Community institutions. Beginning with Weberian ideal types and evaluating them against classical and emerging models of authority, this research breaks away from dominant Eurocentric approaches to the study of the Muslim world. The case of the Ismaili imamate, and the AKDN, in the modern period is a fine example of how prevalent Orientalist methods fail to see the nuances and the epistemic shifts that have occurred in the encounter of a Shi'i Muslim community with modernity.

Using the case study of the AKDN and the Nizārī Ismaili imamate, this book demonstrates that the three ideal types of authority as proposed by Weber, namely the traditional, charismatic, and legal-bureaucratic types, are not sufficient to explain the dynamics of authority among Muslims. This is partly due to Weber's belief in the uniqueness of Western civilization, which is a product of his thesis on Protestant Ethics and partly because his ideal type system does not work in the case of the Muslim societies. The Ismaili imamate with its multifarious institutions in contemporary times is the most suitable counterexample by which to powerfully demonstrate that Weberian models of authority fail to explain this phenomenon, and it would indeed appear as a paradoxical institution if viewed with Weberian theses.

The Ismaili imamate in contemporary times represents a paradigm shift and a transmutation not only as regards the Weberian models but also when viewed from inside the tradition of Shi'i Muslim history. This evolutionary leap forward, which has been crystallized over the course of the past half a century in the Ismaili imamate, suggests the development of a new form of authority which is unprecedented. There are clearly

various elements in this form of authority which could be discerned as rooted in tradition and history; however the distinctive elements of this new form of authority give it a defining and exciting dimension.

There are several qualities which are peculiar to the contemporary condition of the Ismaili imamate and its style of leadership which are distinctive. Most importantly, while some central features, like succession by way of designation (*naṣṣ*) has not changed, there is one overarching quality which can best capture all these elements, and that is the transmutation of the Ismaili imamate from the person of the Imam into the office of imamate. Thus we are now facing the institutionalization of the imamate, and the office is the embodiment of the authority of the Imam. I have described this new development as "authority without territory" which marks a significant and unprecedented shift in how the concept of authority in the Shiʿi Ismaili Muslim tradition is understood and exercised. If we were to highlight three distinctive features of this shift, they would be: (a) the transcendence of the person of the Imam into the "office of imamate" and its unprecedented institutionalization; (b) bifocal leadership of the Ismaili Imam in maintaining a balance between religion and the world; and (c) the development of authority free from nationalistic and ideological boundaries of territorial nation-states.

Acknowledgments

This book is based on my PhD research, which would have never even started if it were not for the encouraging and indefatigable insistence of my wife, Elahe Kianpoor, who had to then endure my being constantly away on long hours of study and research. She has been a constant source of support and encouragement at times when it would have been otherwise impossible to proceed under the extremely difficult circumstances of our turbulent life. I finished the final revisions of this book after our daughter, Toranj, was born and my wife had to single-handedly care for her while I was completing my revisions.

This research was undertaken with the kind patronage and sponsorship of the Institute of Ismaili Studies in London. I am deeply indebted to the support and encouragement I have received from Professor Azim Nanji, former Director of the IIS, and Dr. Farhad Daftary, currently Co-Director, who made it possible for me to undertake my doctoral studies. Special thanks go to Mr. Shiraz Kabani, who never failed to give me advice and consultation on various detailed matters of this research. I am also grateful to all the individuals who agreed to the interviews I had for the purpose of this research including the late Professor Mohammed Arkoun, who was among the very first people sharing with me his thoughts on this area of research. I am also grateful to Dr. Aziz Esmail, a Governor of the IIS, with whom I had a number of conversations which always intellectually challenged me. I should also sincerely thank Professor Hamid Dabashi for the many fruitful conversations I have had with him in the concluding months of my work.

There have been various people at the leadership level within the Ismaili Community and the Ismaili imamate institutions, including my friends at the French Delegation of the Ismaili Imamat at Aiglemont in France, who have been supporting me throughout this research. I am grateful to all of them for their trust and confidence in my research.

I am also immensely grateful to my PhD supervisor, Professor John Keane, whom I have known and worked with since my postgraduate studies at the University of Westminster. His presence, advice, guidance, and brilliant hints have always been a source of inspiration to me, sometimes giving me the energy to work for days without ever noticing how time flies. I remain indebted to him for putting me in the right direction in my academic life. My second supervisor Dr. Ali Paya has also been an incredibly meticulous advisor particularly when it comes to nuanced philosophical matters; without his sharp eye, I would have missed many subtle and precious points. I am deeply grateful to him.

Also, in the period of the formation of the central question of this thesis, I have had the privilege of having many fruitful conversations with an erudite friend, Dr. Mohammad M Mojahedi, currently the KNAW Visiting Professor (of Comparative Political Theory) at Leiden University. His depth of knowledge, clarity of thought, and his input has been most valuable in polishing certain parts of this book. I am most grateful to him. I would also like to thank Dr. Jalal Badakhchani, who kindly agreed to read various drafts of the Introduction and made useful comments and suggestions to improve it. I would also like to express my sincere gratitude to Mehrdad Shoghi, who kindly agreed to produce the cover design for the book, with his imaginative style.

Finally, I would like to dedicate this book to my mother whose unwavering faith and many long years of struggle for the education of her children as a sacred task has shaped my entire life. And also, this is in loving memory of my late father, who passed away prematurely when I was too young, but left me a library and a legacy that remained with me for many years to come.

DARYOUSH MOHAMMAD POOR
London, March 2014

Note on Transliteration

The system used for transliteration of Arabic and Persian words and terms is the system used in the *Encyclopaedia Islamica* (Brill), as follows.

Consonants

ء ʾ	ر r	ف f
ب b	ز z	ق q
پ p	ژ zh	ک k
ت t	س s	گ g
ث th	ش sh	ل l
ج j	ص ṣ	م m
چ ch	ض ḍ	ن n
ح ḥ	ط ṭ	ه h
خ kh	ظ ẓ	و w
د d	ع ʿ	ی y
ذ dh	غ gh	

Short Vowels

◌َ a

◌ُ u

◌ِ i

Long Vowels

ا ā

و ū

ی ī

Diphthongs

◌َو aw

◌َی ay

ة a; at (construct state)

ال al- (article)

Abbreviations

AKAA   Aga Khan Award for Architecture
AKDN   Aga Khan Development Network
AKES   Aga Khan Education Services
AKFED   Aga Khan Fund for Economic Development
AKTC   Aga Khan Trust for Culture
AKU   Aga Khan University
EIs   Encyclopaedia Islamica
GCP   Global Centre for Pluralism
IIS   The Institute of Ismaili Studies
ITREB   Ismaili Tariqah and Religious Education Board
UCA   University of Central Asia

Introduction

This book aims at the study of Ismaili imamate in contemporary times with particular focus on the imamate of the present Aga Khan, the forty-ninth hereditary leader of the Shiʿa Imami Ismaili Muslims. The focal point of this research is how the Ismaili imamate, with its strong consolidated, traditional roots that go back some 1,400 years ago, has transformed into its present institutional apparatus and how the Aga Khan Development Network (AKDN), whose constituency is much wider than the Ismaili Community, is connected with the Ismaili imamate. The book also addresses the relationship of AKDN with internal Ismaili community institutions.

The transformation of the Ismaili imamate into its current institutional form will be examined by drawing on the concept of authority. The methodological tools and guiding principles will be based on a Weberian perspective. To avoid confusions and misperceptions, words, technical terms, and concepts of frequent usage in relation to the Ismaili Community will be explained and defined.

Who Are the Ismailis?

The word "Ismaili" in its present usage designates a religious community officially known as the *Shiʿa Imami Ismaili Muslims*. Ismailis are also known as the Nizārī Ismailis. Ismailism came into being as a result of a dispute over the succession of Jaʿfar al-Ṣādiq, the sixth Shiʿi Imam (d. AH 148/AD 765). The outcome of the dispute was the creation of two major Shiʿi groups—later on divided into many subgroups or sects—namely, the Twelvers (*Ithnā ʿasharī* or *Imāmiyya*)[1] and the Ismailis. The former maintained the succession right of Mūsā al-Kāẓim, the fourth and youngest son of Jaʿfar al-Ṣādiq, and considered him the rightful heir to the position of the imamate. This group continued the tradition of hereditary succession until the occultation of their twelfth Imam, known as the Expected Guide (*Mahdī-yi mawʿūd*), who is believed to be in hiding and expected to return at the end of time. The followers of Twelver Shiʿism are

scattered all over the world, with the largest concentration in Iran, where it is the official religion.

The other group, which is the subject of this book, is a group that came to be known as the Ismailis. They are also scattered all over the world, but Ismailism is not the official religion of any particular country. Ismailis believe in the legitimate authority of Ismāʿīl b. Jaʿfar al-Ṣādiq. Ismāʿīl was the latter's second son from his first wife, and his heir to the imamate. Ismailis maintain that Jaʿfar al-Ṣādiq had, during his lifetime, made an explicit designation (naṣṣ) as to the imamate of Ismāʿīl (d. after AH 136/ AD 754), a designation that cannot be revoked under any circumstances.

Phases of Ismaili History

Initial Stage and the First Period of Concealment

The history of the early Ismailis is clouded in ambiguity despite numerous scholarly works about them in recent years. The first phase of Ismaili history begins with the death of Ismāʿīl. This phase, lasting until the establishment of the Fatimid state, is generally known as the period of concealment (dawr al-satr) because the Imams after Muḥammad b. Ismāʿīl,[2] nicknamed the Hidden (al-Maktūm), continued their clandestine activities under severe precautionary measures, by practising taqiyya.

This period marks the beginning of widespread and intense intellectual activities of the Ismailis, which were taking place in the larger context of the intellectual movements in the Muslim world. Some scholars have argued that the Brethren of Purity, who compiled their encyclopedic epistles (Rasāʾil Ikhwān al-ṣafāʾ), had Ismaili affiliations (Daftary, 2007: 28, 235). It is also argued that by keeping their identity a secret, the Ismailis may have been collaborating in paving the way for the establishment of the Fatimid Caliphate (Hamdani, 1999: 73–82). It is during this period that we see the earliest appropriation of neo-Platonic ideas for the Ismaili mission.

The Fatimid Period

The second phase in Ismaili history begins with the establishment of the Fatimid state as a Shiʿi empire in North Africa between the fourth and the tenth centuries. The founder of the Fatimid state was ʿAbd Allāh al-Mahdī (d. AH 322/AD 934), the twelfth Ismaili Imam.[3] After the reign of al-Mahdī, the Fatimid state expanded throughout North Africa and captured territories beyond North Africa. It is during this phase of

the Ismaili history and the imamate of the eighth Fatimid Imam-Caliph al-Mustanṣir biʾllāh (d. AH 487/AD 1094) that the second major schism, the Nizārī-Mustaʿlawī schism, occurred over the issue of succession through designation (naṣṣ). Historical sources unanimously maintain the initial designation in favor of Nizār, the eldest son of al-Mustanṣir. This designation laid the foundation of Nizārī Ismailism, which was promoted and championed by Ḥasan-i Ṣabbāḥ.

During the Fatimid period, a complex administrative system came into being for running the affairs of the state. Various Ismaili scholars and dāʿīs contributed to the philosophical, theological, and legal conceptualization of Fatimid Ismaili thought during this period.

Alamūt Period and the Second Occurrence of Concealment

The defenders of the legitimacy of the imamate of Nizār (d. AH 488/ AD 1095) came to be known as the Nizārī Ismailis. Their main base was initially north of Persia, but it gradually extended to Syria and the highlands of Lebanon. The community was led by the famous Persian dāʿī Ḥasan-i Ṣabbāḥ (d. AH 518/AD 1124). In his campaigns in support of the imamate of Nizār and in order to organize the community in Persia, Ḥasan-i Ṣabbāḥ captured the Alamūt fortress, which became the main headquarters of the Ismaili state in Persia, a state within another state during the Seljuk rule in Persia. The phase beginning with the imamate of Nizār and the establishment of the Alamūt state is the third historical phase of the Ismaili movement. This period lasted until the fall of the Alamūt state at the hands of the Mongols in AH 654/AD 1256.

The record of the Ismaili Imams descended from Ismāʿīl b. Jaʿfar al-Ṣādiq down to the Fatimid times and the Alamūt period shows a second period of concealment (dawr al-satr) similar to the earlier period for which there is a lack of historiographical records after the death of Nizār. Non-Ismaili sources, quoting ambiguous Ismaili sources, maintain that either the son or the grandson of Nizār was secretly taken to Persia, where the followers of Nizār had established the Alamūt state. Throughout the early years of the Alamūt period, the governors of Alamūt used the title dāʿī and acted on behalf of the Imam, who was to return soon and take control of the affairs of the community. This return did not happen until the time of the fourth ruler of the Alamūt state, Ḥasan II (d. AH 561/AD 1166). Ḥasan II was known as the son of Muḥammad b. Buzurg Ummīd (d. AH 557/AD 1162). Initially Ḥasan II claimed to be the representative of the Imam, but later he claimed to be the Imam himself. The official genealogy of Ismaili Imams lists three Imams in between Nizār and Ḥasan II without

giving any historical details about their activities.[4] This period is generally known as the second period of concealment, which ends with the appearance of Ḥasan II in Alamūt and the beginning of his imamate in AH 557/ AD 1162.

The most important event in the Alamūt period that caused the marginalization or exclusion of the Ismailis from the rest of the Muslim community was the proclamation of the doctrine of Resurrection (*qiyāmat*) by Ḥasan II in AH 559/AD 1164. In the proclamation Ḥasan declared that for those who had reached the spiritual level of unity (*waḥdat*) with the Lord, observing the rituals of the Islamic canonical law (*sharīʿat*) was no longer obligatory. The domain of faith was, henceforth, absolutely spiritual, and people adhering to faith could only fall within one of the three ranks that caused their distinction from each other. These ranks were "remaining in the domain of the *sharīʿat*," "moving from *sharīʿat* to the *qiyāmat*," and "reaching the realm of *qiyāmat*." In other words they will be the denizens of the realm of discord (*taḍādd*) or hierarchical ascent (*tarattub*) or unity (*waḥdat*).

This proclamation meant a radical leap from the Fatimid period in which there was a balance between the exoteric aspect of faith (*ẓāhir*) and its esoteric aspect (*bāṭin*). What Ḥasan II termed as *qiyāmat* was in contrast to the *sharīʿat*. The binary representation of faith, which was quite dominant in earlier Ismaili theology (e.g. *tanzīl-taʾwīl*; or *ẓāhir-bāṭin*), was changed into a threefold representation that could also be found among the Sufis. The Sufis spoke of three different stages of reaching truth, namely the *sharīʿat*, *ṭarīqat*, and *ḥaqīqat*. The proclamation of *qiyāmat* by Ḥasan was a significant epistemic shift from the Fatimid period, which further enabled the Ismailis to engage in their hermeneutical and more esoteric approach to faith.

Post-Alamūt Period and the Continuation of Concealment

After the fall of Alamūt, contrary to the general remarks in historical records that claimed the complete annihilation of the Persian Ismailis, the community survived and went into a long period of concealment,[5] which lasted until the time of Aga Khan I (d. AH 1298/AD 1881) when Ismailis came back to the full light of history. Early on during this post-Alamūt revival period, right after the fall of Alamūt, there is mention of another schism over the issue of succession that happens at the time of Shams al-Dīn Muḥammad (d. ca. AH 710/AD 1310), the first Ismaili Imam of the post-Alamūt period. The dispute was between the two sons of Shams al-Dīn, namely Qāsim Shāh and Muʾmin Shāh. The lineage

of the present Ismaili Imam is traced back to Qāsim Shāh. As such, it is more accurate to call the Ismailis, which are the subject of the present study, the Nizārī Qāsimshāhī Ismailis. But since the Mu'minshāhī branch, in the absence of an Imam, gradually disintegrated, we might as well use the term Nizārī Ismaili to designate the followers of the present Ismaili Imam who is generally addressed as the Present Imam (*ḥāḍhir imām*) Shāh Karīm al-Ḥusaynī Aga Khan IV.

The post-Alamūt period is generally known as the period in which Ismailis are closely affiliated with Sufis to the extent that they are sometimes unrecognizable from Sufi orders. In later episodes of the post-Alamūt period, we can even see the names of Ismaili Imams appearing on the list of *pīr*s and the spiritual leaders of Sufi orders (Ivanow, 1938: 57–79). This strategy, which is often seen as a precautionary dissimulation measure (*taqiyya*),[6] has been easily adopted by Ismailis given their earlier affiliations with Sufis and Sufi ideas[7] during the Alamūt period.[8]

Modern Period

The modern period of the history of Nizārī Ismailis begins with Aga Khan I and his migration to the Indian subcontinent as a result of court rivalries among the Qājār dynasty in AH 1257/AD 1841.[9] This led to the permanent departure of the Ismaili imamate from Persia. Although the history of the life of each of the Aga Khans deserves full and detailed study, this research is not concerned with the first three Aga Khans and is only devoted to the developments of Ismaili institutions during the imamate of Shāh Karīm al-Ḥusaynī, Aga Khan IV. The Shiʿa Imami Ismaili Community with its elaborate institutional apparatus, and different degrees of activity, is now represented in 25 countries with significant populations in Tajikistan, Afghanistan, and Northern Pakistan. Similar to the Twelver Shiʿi Muslims, the Ismailis also live in almost every continent on earth, in Asia, Africa, Australia, North America, South America (no institution here), and Europe, and constitute the second largest Shiʿi Muslim community.

The modern period of the Ismaili history continues throughout the colonial period, extending to the early years of the imamate of Aga Khan IV. The imamate of the first two Aga Khans should be viewed as the period of consolidation when the imamate was confronted with legal battles, minor schisms, and the application of modern parameters of institutional authority. Despite the fact that some very early seeds of the current institutions are found during the imamate of Aga Khan II, the

major internal institutional shift of the Community happened during the time of Aga Khan III. Aga Khan II's period of imamate was brief and no major change is recorded during his imamate.

It is during the imamate of Aga Khan IV when major political changes across the globe lead to the dissolution of colonial powers and witness significant institutional shifts externally and internally within the Ismaili Community that particularly constitutes the focus of this research.

Key Words and Technical Terms

The Ismaili da'wa

During the Fatimid period, the religious, social, and political activities of the Fatimids, which generally revolved around spreading the cause of the Fatimid Imams and their legitimacy, were officially structured around a system of propaganda and recruitment, both internally and externally, which was known as the *da'wa*. The term *da'wa* literally means the mission or the call. This term and the term *dā'ī* both come from the same root. The job of a *dā'ī* was to defend the cause of the Ismaili Imam of his time and as such they acted as preachers and missionaries. Outstanding characteristic of the Ismaili *dā'īs* were their high level of knowledge and mastery of various skills of the time. They were particularly well versed in Ismaili theology and religious debates. It was during the Fatimid time that they came to be organized under a centralized system of *da'wa*, defined around the ideas of ranks in the world of religion (*ḥudūd-i dīn*), which orchestrated all the activities of different *dā'īs* in the vast territories of the Fatimids and beyond, in areas where Fatimids had no political influence or rule.

The term itself dates back to early Ismaili history when the term 'Ismaili' was not yet used to refer to the community. In the early phases of the Ismaili history, Ismaili *dā'īs*—before the Fatimid period, during and after it—referred to themselves as the *aṣḥāb al-da'wa al-hādiyya* or the people of the rightly guiding call or mission. The call was to the authority of the legitimate successor of the Prophet through his daughter Fāṭima and his son-in-law, 'Ali b. Abī Ṭālib, the first Shi'i Imam.

This system of *da'wa* was the first structured organization of the Ismaili missions in an institutional form. As such it could be called a prototype of later institutions of the Ismaili Community. However, this institution must not be confused with the state institutions in the Fatimid period and the Alamūt period, as they manifested themselves in administrative bodies that dealt with the affairs of the state.

It is also noteworthy here to mention that central themes of the Ismaili *daʿwa* changed in the different periods of the Ismaili history. During the Fatimid period, a coherent legal system was also in place with the efforts and contributions of al-Qāḍī al-Nuʿmān in his major legal work, the *Daʿāʾim al-Islām*, particularly after the consolidation of the Fatimid Empire when the city of Cairo (al-Qāhira) had become the capital of the state (Jamal, in Cotran, 2000–2001).[10]

The concept of *taʿlīm* or the authoritative instruction and teaching of the Ismaili Imam had always been central to the Ismailis—as to other Shiʿi groups; however, during the Fatimid period, the emphasis was mainly on maintaining a balance between the exoteric aspects of faith—the *sharīʿa* in broader terms—and the more spiritual or esoteric aspect of it, which is the *taʾwīl* (spiritual or esoteric exegesis).[11] This equilibrium radically changed during the Alamūt period, particularly after Ḥasan II, the fourth ruler and Lord of Alamūt, proclaimed the *qiyāmat* and was later recognized as the first Ismaili Imam, from the progeny of Nizār, ruling in Alamūt.

During the rule of the first three Lords of Alamūt, the concept of *taʿlīm* became a prominent theme to the extent that it brought about a new name, i.e. the *Taʿlīmiyya* for the Nizārī Ismailis. Contemporary heresiographers (al-Shahrastānī, 2001) describe this development as the *daʿwa al-jadīda* (or the new call/mission) as opposed to the *daʿwa al-qadīma* (which was the older *daʿwa* of the Fatimid era). The gist of this doctrine was that knowledge of God is impossible to attain by relying only on human reason, and mankind needs the instruction of a teacher. That teacher is the Ismaili Imam who is unique and is the only one on the face of the earth with such claim. Apart from the simplified theological content of the doctrine, which was at the same time critical, it served as an important platform to make the Nizārīs distinct from the Fatimids who followed the other son of al-Mustanṣir.[12]

The Authority of the Ismaili Imam

One of the central and key terms that frequently come up in this research is "authority." Although in a very classical sense, one may find the term coming up in many different contexts among other Shiʿi groups and Sufi orders, this term has its particular sense and implications in the Ismaili Community, especially in the modern period.

The term authority also has political implications, and its use is not restricted to religious communities alone. Therefore, apart from making clear what the term means within a Muslim—and Shiʿi Ismaili—context,

it is good to have a general working definition of the term. In this context, I draw on Max Weber's definition of authority, particularly because in later chapters I will further discuss the relevance of Max Weber to this research as it deals with bureaucratic authority, legitimate authority, and the relation between authority and power. Max Weber's approach is particularly relevant because we are looking at the authority of the Ismaili Imam in the modern period, where the effect of modernity in articulation and reformulation of this authority is palpable. Max Weber is also a key figure in discourses of modernity in the West, and his role and impact will be further studied in later chapters.

According to Max Weber, authority refers to "the likelihood that a demarcated command will find obedience among a specific circle of persons" (Weber, in Kahlberg, 2005: 175). Moreover, there is also a question of legitimacy—historically important for the Ismaili imamate—that is required for this authority. Therefore, this obedience is closely related to an emotional attachment to the authorities:

> In general, it should be kept clearly in mind that the basis of every authority, and correspondingly of every kind of willingness to obey, is a *belief*, a belief by virtue of which persons exercising authority are lent prestige. (Weber, in Kahlberg, 2005: 174)

In the Shi'i Ismaili tradition, the concept of authority has a history and a tradition behind it. The term authority for the Shi'i Ismaili Imam is closely connected with the event of Ghadīr-i Khumm. According to both Shi'i and Sunni sources, when the Prophet Muḥammad was returning from his "farewell pilgrimage" (*ḥijjat al-widā'*) on 18 Dhū al-Ḥijja 10/16 March 632, he asked the people to stop for a congregational prayer. He then took the hand of 'Alī, his cousin and son-in-law, and lifted him to his feet to stand next to him and said: 'O people, know that what Aaron was to Moses, 'Alī is to me, except that there shall be no prophet after me, and he is my *walī* to you after me. Therefore, he whose master (*mawlā*) I am, 'Alī is his master' (Mohammad Poor, in Daftary and Madelung, 2011: 518–19). The Shi'i interpretations of this *ḥadīth* and the event differ from that commonly found among Sunni scholars, but it serves as one of the foundations for Shi'i devotion to 'Alī.

This *ḥadīth* along with a number of verses from the Qur'ān serve to form the concept of authority attached to 'Alī and his descendants as Shi'i Imams—for Ismailis and other Shi'i groups. In particular, Shi'i Muslims interpret the following Qur'ānic verse to be connected with the event of Ghadīr-i Khumm: "O Messenger! Proclaim [the message] which

has been revealed to you from your Lord. If you do not do this, you will not have conveyed His message. And God will defend you against the people" (5:67). Shi'i interpretations of this verse consider it to be the revelation or declaration of the position of 'Alī as the rightful heir to the Prophet in his authority.

So, the term authority, in English, may be corresponded with the Arabic term *walāya* as used in the Ghadīr-i Khumm *ḥadīth* and the occurrences of the term in Qur'anic verses, which have been interpreted from a Shi'i perspective to refer to 'Alī. However, this term, referring to a number of instances of its usage in the Qur'ān in different forms, speaks of the political and spiritual authority of 'Alī. Moreover, it also refers to the love and devotion given to him by those who recognize his authority. Its references to the political authority of 'Alī are closely connected with disputes over the Prophet's succession and the rows over caliphate. Yet, the term *walāya* is also used by Shi'i groups and particularly by Ismailis in juxtaposition with the term *nubuwwa* (prophecy): the Prophet is responsible for the revelation or the *tanzīl*, and the Imams—'Alī and his descendants—are responsible for the esoteric and spiritual interpretation of the revelation, or the *ta'wīl*, at all times (Mohammad Poor, in EIs, 2010: 518–23).

As can be seen from the above descriptions, the concept of authority is a complex one with different facets. In the political dimension of it, there is clearly a reference to the legitimacy of the authority of 'Alī and Shi'i Imams in relation to their succession to the Prophet. It is here that there is an overlapping of legitimate authority with political power.

However, the legitimacy of the authority of Shi'i Ismaili Imams must not be conflated with their having legitimate political power. As we have seen in the earlier description of the different periods of Ismaili history, there have been episodes when Ismaili Imams did not have political power over a territory, as in the present time, but the spiritual authority of the Ismaili Imam that demanded the obedience of the faithful continued to be there. As can be discerned from Ismaili doctrines of the medieval periods, assuming political power, in and by itself, is not seen as an essential part or requirement for the imamate (even though, it appears from the text below that avoiding political power is seen as leading to difficulties for people):

He sometimes finds it advisable to occupy a throne, or possess dominion, wealth, an army and a great treasury. [At such times] he opens the door of his summons, which is the greatest mercy to all mankind, to all the world's inhabitants. He treats everyone with forbearance, kindness and tolerance,

and under his great reign everyone prospers and is happy. At other times, however, he avoids the outer paraphernalia and luxuries of royalty and power, leaving people to suffer the afflictions and perplexities of [divine] tribulation, thus subjecting them to severe torments and sparing no one. (Ṭūsī, 2005: 128)

The only significant shift occurs in the contemporary period when the Ismaili imamate, despite having no territorial rule, has a vast network of bureaucratic institutions at its disposal, over which the Imam presides both internally and externally. Here is where the boundaries between authority and power sometimes blur. However, it is a critical point to make a distinction between these two concepts, even in the case of the present institutions of the Ismaili imamate, in the AKDN and the Community institutions.

Authority and Power

Making a clear distinction between authority and power is particularly critical in the case of studying the Ismaili imamate—as in other cases— and it would help avoid many errors that may arise from the confusion of these two concepts.

To be more precise, we must distinguish between legitimate authority and power. Weber makes a distinction between the two in his classical formulation. He defines power as 'the likelihood that one person in a social relationship will be able, even despite resistance, to carry out his own will' (Weber, in Kahlberg, 2005: 174).

Although we have to make a distinction between authority and power, given Max Weber's definition of power, it extends to realms beyond simply the power of a state or political power. That is why Weber argues that all ruling powers, be they profane, religious, political, or apolitical, appeal to *rational-legal*, *traditional*, or *charismatic* principles of legitimation.

The three Weberian ideal types that deal with domination, are closely related to a discussion about authority, which will be covered in the chapter 1—and later on referred to on other occasions in this book—but it is nonetheless important to see the different functions of authority, in its different forms, and power.

One of the major focus areas of this research is to demonstrate that the authority of the Ismaili imamate has undergone a transmutation. While Weberian ideal types greatly serve to highlight some of the important aspects of this transmutation, it fails—as we shall see—to fully capture this transmutation.

Rationality

Another term which will be often used is rationality. By rationality we mean "goal-oriented conduct that is guided by the spirit of calculation and abstract-general rules, and that therefore reduces its fields of operation to objects of administration" (Keane, 1984: 31).

In the Weberian sense, rationalization refers to

> a uniquely progressive development of thought and action that entailed systematic self-control as well as methodical and systematic use of a variety of logical operations that clearly are intended to arrive at more accurate and more efficient outcomes. (Huff, in Huff and Schluchter, 1999: 11)

These rationalizations cover main areas including economic life, technique, scientific research, military training, law, and administration (Weber, in Huff and Schluchter, 1999: 12). Of these, in particular, Weber's typology is important for this research in classifying legal systems, which are, according to Weber, based on two criteria: "the degree of 'rationality' and the degree of 'formality'" (Huff, in Huff and Schluchter, 1999: 12). This rationality could be examined against the functions of the Ismaili Constitution which gives a legal framework for the Community and the imamate institutions. The legal rationality here, in Weberian terms, is to be assessed formally and substantively. However, in the case of the Muslim law, which is generally classified under jurisprudential law (*fiqh*), it is only motivated by substantive considerations.

In the case of Islam, Muslim jurists had considerations of a substantive nature, and Huff argues that "there is no good reason to apply the term 'rational' to Islamic law" (Huff, in Huff and Schluchter, 1999: 12). On the formulation of the problem of Western rationalism, Patricia Crone believes that it is a major mistake and it should be abandoned (Huff and Schluchter, 1999: 10) and considers Weber's typology of law based on these two types of rationality as inadequate. However, the case of the Ismaili Constitution is different from a typical legal formulation based on *fiqh*, and as such it deserves more careful attention (I will discuss the Ismaili Constitution at length in chapter 3).

Leadership

The other key term which is used here is leadership. This is the twin term that often appears with authority, and as I explain in a later chapter, sometimes in Muslim cultures, they are even seen as synonymous (see Chapter 2, section on etymology and issues of translation). To clarify

this point further, authority empowers some, and it is a formula for empowering some to make decisions. Thus, it is a solution to the problem of the leaders and the led. So, all forms of authority, all recorded forms of authority, as Max Weber shows, imply and functionally require leaders or leadership.

Going to the Weberian types, (a) in the case of tradition, it is the figure or the authoritative leader who reminds everybody of the fundamental importance of yesterday in preserving the customs that are a part of our forefathers' and foremothers' legacy; (b) the charismatic figure or leader is in effect asking the followers that he be given all the power on the basis of his magical or supernatural qualities; and (c) the bureaucratic leader is asking to have authority on the basis of his expertise and the files and the cabinets he holds. We can also add to the qualities of a good leader within the framework of Weber's typology of authority, which will be addressed in detail when reviewing the Ismaili doctrines on the qualities of the Imam (as *the* leader of the community).[13]

Charisma: The Ismailis and the Sufis

As it was mentioned above, the term authority, in at least one of its senses, corresponds to the term *walāya*. One of the references of *walāya* is the love and devotion of the followers of the Shiʿi Imams for them in the context of Prophetic traditions and the Qurʾānic verses, as they are interpreted by Shiʿi Muslims, in general.

The term *walāya* is also widely used by the Sufis as an important component of the spiritual authority of the *pīr* or the head of the Sufi order. Here, it is interesting to note that there are overlapping areas between the Ismaili perceptions of *walāya* and that of the Sufis. This overlap is a result of the close intermingling of the Ismailis with the Sufis in the post-Alamūt period, when they practiced the precautionary dissimulation (*taqiyya*) to protect themselves against hostilities.

There is evidence from the Alamūt period that suggests that the Ismailis of Alamūt were very close to the Sufis of their own time. The few extant fragments of the words of the Ismaili Imams of the late Alamūt period contain clear quotations from renowned Sufi figures of the time such as Sanāʾī Ghaznawī and Farīd al-Dīn ʿAṭṭār. Indeed, in a recent publication of the largest Ismaili poetry collection of the Alamūt period, the influence of Sanāʾī is quite explicitly recognized (Badakhchani, 2011: 287).

In a number of the writings of ʿAyn al-Quḍāt Hamadānī (d. AH 525/AD 1131), a Sufi-philosopher who lived during the Alamūt period of

the Ismaili history, there are implicit and explicit references to Ismaili doctrines, including the doctrine of *taʿlīm* on which he has written an extensive letter (letter 75 in his *Nāmahhā*). His quotations from Nāṣir-i Khusraw, an Ismaili *dāʿī* of the Fatimid period, indicate his familiarity and close connections with the Ismailis of his time. But the affinities between ʿAyn al-Quḍāt's views on eschatology and on resurrection further strengthen the hypothesis that interactions between the Sufis and Ismailis had started long before the downfall of the Alamūt state.

A critical point, which needs to be highlighted here, is that the proclamation of the *qiyāmat* by Ḥasan II and the greater emphasis on esoteric and spiritual aspects of faith paved the ground for the future association of Ismailis with the Sufis of their time. It also served as a liberating force that further allowed the Ismaili Imam to make amendments in the practice of *sharīʿa* drawing on his authority as the Imam who interprets the faith. Even if we set aside the claim of Ḥasan II to imamate, his passion for philosophy and Sufi ideas is certainly an element that should be taken into consideration when studying the context of his proclamation of *qiyāmat*.

Bearing in mind the common areas between Ismaili doctrines with those of Sufis, one can see how the concept of *walāya* gets reinforced using doctrinal elements from both the Ismaili and Sufi traditions. After all, Ismailis have always been open to appropriation and borrowings from other schools of thought and religious communities, the prime examples of which can be found in the Fatimid period when Ismaili *dāʿīs* extensively used neo-Platonic and Hellenistic ideas in their *daʿwa*.

Charisma: The Weberian Sense

Charisma refers to the supernatural and superhuman qualities of a leader, the abilities that a leader is endowed with, his demonstration of unusual powers, and a right to rule. The term charisma has been used in at least three senses: (a) the classical Weberian sense of charisma is the supernatural endowment and the divine gift possessed by the leader; (b) the sacred and awe-inspiring property of groups, positions, or objects, and this is where Weber mentions the routinization of charisma (*amtscharsima*), kinship (*gentilcharisma*), and blood lines (*erbscharisma*); and (c) in the popular sense of it, charisma refers to the personal qualities of a leader and his attributes as opposed to a divine gift (Spencer, 1973).

In the Shiʿi Ismaili tradition, the Imam is endowed with the divine light. He is the embodiment of the divine command (*amr*) and the manifestation of the divine word (*kalmia*) (Ṭūsī, 1998: 41; 2005: 120).[14] As

we can see, the sacred and awe-inspiriting element is quite strong here. Moreover, with regard to the process of succession and how an Imam is designated by the previous one, the Ismaili doctrine spells out that the Imam must be physically connected with the previous Imam by way of blood lineage and he should also have a spiritual connection with him by way of explicit designation (*naṣṣ*) (Ṭūsī, 1998: 43).

Charisma, in one of its senses, is also considered a divine gift. Max Weber owes the concept of charisma to Rudolph Sohm and it is derived from early Christian terminology (Haley, 1980), and as we can see in Haley's examination of the connection between Weber and Sohm, the concept is heavily influenced by Christian theology. The use of this term as the "gift of grace" is not entirely absent in the case of the Ismailis. However, the closest expression that one may find with a reference to mercy—which is not the same as grace—is in the seminal text of the Alamūt period regarding imamate:

> For the greatest expression of divine mercy to mankind is the appearance of the Imam of the age (*imām-i zamān*), as a man among others, so that through him man may know God in the true sense (*bi-ḥaqīqat*) of recognising Him, and obey God in the true sense of obeying Him. (Ṭūsī, 2005: 120)

To Weber, there are some belief systems in which a person of authority is considered to have a supernatural gift that is a source of awe.[15] Weber gives qualities for the charisma he defines that can depersonalize it:

> From a unique gift of grace charisma may be transformed into a quality that is either (a) transferable, or (b) personally acquirable, or (c) attached to the incumbent of an office or to an institutional structure regardless of the persons involved. (Weber, 1978: 1135)

And as a result of its becoming depersonalized—the way he justifies it—Weber argues that "It is for this very reason that charisma can fulfill its social function" (Weber, 1978: 1135).

As we can see in the Weberian description of charisma, it can be transferred or attached to the incumbent of an office, in this case the office of the Ismaili imamate. This idea is indeed embedded within classical Ismaili theology and doctrines, but we have to be careful in applying the Weberian terminology to the case of Ismaili imamate bearing in mind that his articulation comes out of a different context although similarities and affinities are unmistakable.

Max Weber's Three Pure Types of Domination

Weber uses three ideal types to describe different forms of legitimate domination, and these ideal types are often used to describe different forms of authority and styles of leadership.

The validity of claims to legitimacy, according to Weber, may be based on:

> 1. *Rational grounds*—resting on a belief in the legality of enacted orders [e.g., civil service rules] and the right of those elevated to authority under such orders to issue commands (*legal authority*). 2. *Traditional grounds*— resting on an established belief in the sanctity of immemorial traditions and the legitimacy of those exercising authority under them (*traditional authority*); or finally. 3. *Charismatic grounds*—resting on devotion to the exceptional sanctity, heroism or exemplary character of an individual person, and of the orders revealed or ordained by him (*charismatic authority*). (Weber, in Kahlberg, 2005: 192)

We can find manifestations of each of these three grounds, very broadly, in the case of the Ismaili imamate. Apart from the broad application of these types, there are certain new elements added to the settings of the Ismaili imamate in modern times, which require a more nuanced study. These elements include a pervasive "secularism" in the West, which is where the Office of the Ismaili imamate is located and where there is an influential populations of the Ismailis. However, the above types give us an appropriate working definition to consider the case of the Ismaili imamate.

A close study of the developments in the institutions of the Ismaili imamate indicates that with the inadequacy of Weberian ideal types, we may suggest minimally a fourth type, which can overcome some of the limitations of the Weberian articulation.

Modernity and Modernization

The turning point for the attachment of charisma to the office of imamate is the emergence of modernity or, to make it more precise, modernization. In the modern period of the Ismaili history it is important to take into account the role of modernity in the transmutations that have occurred.

In his article on the modernization of the Ismaili Community in East Africa, Azim Nanji gives a framework to describe the changes in the Ismaili Community (Nanji, 1974), and although his perspective

essentially involves the Community in East Africa, it is nonetheless applicable to the development of the current institutions of the Community. He makes a distinction between modernity and modernization (in a footnote) and then describes the conceptualization and development of the current institutions as an "Ismaili response" to modernization:

> Modernization needs to be seen as an ongoing process that generates a series of common and often similar problems, to which different responses are possible. The Ismaili response can be seen as an attempt to develop a society which, while creating a new system and generating continuous change, would also be able to absorb these changes without breaking at the center and assure at the same time the continuity of its essential identity and values. (Nanji, 1974: 124–25)

This response clearly has its roots at the critical stage of the migration of the Ismaili imamate to India, but it does not start taking off until the time of Aga Khan III when the Community begins to institutionalize itself. Even though at the time of Aga Khan II, there were attempts by him to promote "educational and philanthropic projects for the benefit of all Indian Muslims" (Daftary, 2007: 477), these projects did not take a more organized and coherent form until the time of Aga Khan III, particularly in the early years of the twentieth century.

Politics of Modernization

In almost all cases of the encounter of various Muslim communities with modernity, the question of whether tradition is compatible with modernity lies at the heart of their engagements with modernity. It is at the same time closely connected with politics. Modernization theories, as they are presented today, were not so clearly formulated and articulated during the time of the first two Aga Khans, but we can later see them reflected in the time of Aga Khan III. In his *Muslim Politics* (1996), Eickelman addresses some of the key issues regarding this encounter including the gap or discrepancy between political and religious authority. Moreover, he refers to what he calls the "sharp contrast between two artificial constructs, 'modernity' and 'tradition,' and the subsequent misunderstanding of the entrenched social functions of tradition" (Eickelman and Piscatori, 1996: 23).

Although some of the debates about modernization in Muslim societies may also be applicable to the Ismaili Community, there are a number of differences that need to be taken into account. The first and foremost

is the position of the Ismaili imamate toward politics. Following the departure of Aga Khan I from Persia (AH 1257/AD 1841), almost any claim to a political position of authority involving a national territory disappears from the function of the Ismaili Imam (except only briefly at the time of Aga Khan III that withers away very quickly).

Therefore, the idea of an "Islamic state"—or an Ismaili one—does not seem to be the concern of the Ismaili imamate any longer, while we constantly see the issue coming up in various Muslim communities (Eickelman and Piscatori, 1996: 47–79). Nonetheless, the issue is more delicate and involves issues more than just the desirability or the possibility of an "Islamic state" in theory or practice. Eickelman argues that

All Muslim leaders are conditioned by the modern world, and distinctions between "fundamentalists," "traditionalists," and "modernists" are misleading if they ignore the common ground on which they all stand. Very real differences in type of education, social position, and ideology exist among them, but none has remained unaffected by the normative and technological changes that have swept the world in this century. (Eickelman and Piscatori, 1996: 68–69)

This is quite true about the Ismaili imamate and its institutions today. They are still framed by modernity. However, the encounter of the Ismaili imamate with modernity cannot be easily categorized, as the Ismaili Community today is a widely dispersed one living in pockets all around the globe. Yet this much can be said about the Ismaili imamate that it does not fall in line with Eurocentric perceptions of modernity, particularly those championed and inspired by Max Weber's articulation of modernity. In fact, it is evident through the work of the Ismaili imamate's institutions and the AKDN that despite using modern technologies, it continues to draw on a perception of tradition in all its work, and it is particularly evident in the Aga Khan Award for Architecture and the Aga Khan Trust for Culture (which I will discuss in more detail in the chapters to come).

Economy of the Ismaili Imamate

One of the major aspects of the current institutions of the Ismaili imamate is their strong economic and financial capacity. With the migration of the Ismaili imamate to India, the Aga Khan found direct access to the vast financial resources of the Community, which were significantly larger than those available among his Persian followers.

Apart from the Ismaili Khojas who lived in India at the time of the Aga Khan's arrival, there were communities of Ismailis in East Africa living there as businessmen.

The role of the commercial and entrepreneurial segment of the Ismaili Community in the development of the present institutions is significant, both economically and institutionally. Nile Green (2011) has studied some aspects of the religious economy of the Ismaili Community in India, but a more focused and detailed study of the economic activity of the Community is done by Jean-Claude Penrad (in Aubin and Lombard, 1999) tracing the economic development of the Community in East Africa.

Although the availability of financial resources at the time of the first two Aga Khans significantly helped with the consolidation of the Ismaili imamate's activities and the organization of the Community, it is with the leadership of the next two Aga Khans that the economic status of the Community and the Ismaili imamate gets further established and takes a more institutional form.

In the early years of the twentieth century, the Ismaili imamate introduced a series of constitutions (and rules and regulations) for the Community which gave a governance framework for the Ismaili Community. These constitutions became the legal foundations for the institutions that were later created. Therefore, as we reach the period of the imamate of Aga Khan IV, one can see the strong traditional aspect of the Ismaili Community alongside its legal-bureaucratic organization. The Imam who leads the Community and sits at the head of its organizations is believed to be endowed with divine qualities, as briefly mentioned in the section on charisma, and it appears that there is an element of charisma in the leadership of the Imam. All these elements justify using a Weberian methodological tool to assess how relevant Max Weber's articulation could be in the case of the Ismaili imamate.

Problematizing Authority

The greater bulk of literature on leadership and authority is heavily Eurocentric, and there is a parochial approach to the study of the issue, claiming that the roots of these deliberations lie mainly in Roman perceptions of authority.[16] European scholarship considers modernity a threat to the existence of authority. Authority, as Arendt describes it, "resting on foundations in the past as its cornerstone" is held to have been radically shaken by the modern world. In the legacy of scholars like Arendt,

the modern world, by means of change, threatens the "permanence and durability which human beings need" (Arendt, 1961: 95).

One can get the same impressions from the works of Max Weber, as Turner has described it:

> The debate about religious asceticism and the modern ethic, the bureaucratization of life and its standardization, the contrasts between hedonism and discipline, the disappearance of the autonomous liberal individual in the iron cage of state regulation, the emergence of science out of the irrational religious quest, the decline of charismatic authority with the spread of the administrative machine, the erosion of the intimate in the face of large-scale administrative structures, the death of God and the pluralization of the life-world. (Turner, 1993: vii)

The impact of modern representative democracy on authority/leadership in the Atlantic region has further diversified the debates on the issue, but nonetheless it fails to acknowledge important contributors to the area, that is to say the Muslim civilizations.

The Muslim civilizations have traditions rich in their understanding of authority that are of great historical significance but have been poorly investigated in the legacy of Western scholarship. The Shi'i Ismaili community, as a minority in the Muslim world, is even far less studied in terms of its contribution to theories of authority and the models of leadership that have developed in this community. In the references that I have made to modern sources in Ismaili studies in the literature section, there is not a single comprehensive work that addresses in a theoretical and critical way how the Ismaili Community has developed as whole. Case studies and specific papers have addressed only some aspects of these developments, but an overall intellectual narrative of these developments with a coherent theoretical framework is missing.

The case of the Ismaili imamate and its institutions today represents a distinctive and multifaceted narrative of a novel and strange perception of authority. This book aims to explore this richness with a particular emphasis on the institution of the Ismaili imamate, focusing mainly on the imamate of the incumbent Ismaili Imam, Aga Khan IV.

The Ismaili imamate has shown a degree of resilience and a propensity to experiment with new forms of leadership, building on an authority rooted in the past. This is a peculiar case. I have struggled to find a proper name for this new form of authority because of the many diverse qualities that are now embedded in it. I propose to, minimally, use the

term "kaleidoscopic leadership," because of the different roles that the Ismaili Imam plays as the head of the AKDN and as the incumbent Imam. This is a leadership with a corporate dimension dominant in it; yet it carries the weight of authority too, seeing the Imam as both the "Chairman of the Board" and the "Ismaili Imam" (holder of religious authority).

As it can be sensed here, there is also a very strong entrepreneurial dimension to this leadership, which has often confused Western viewers as to how it can be reconciled with the role of a Muslim leader (and we see this in the responses of the Aga Khan himself). This is an integral point in the vision of the Ismaili imamate, which has now, more than ever, established its conviction that there is no dichotomy between the faith and the world. This point is further explored in the section on the Ismaili Imam's vision.

This book attempts to show that during the imamate of the present Ismaili Imam, Aga Khan IV, the institution of the Ismaili imamate (with its associated institutions) has been increasingly represented by the work of the AKDN. This is the first comprehensive study of this network, with a theoretical approach. This network of institutions, I argue in this book, represents a shift in models of leadership and a mutation in the understanding of authority. This mutation is demonstrated by way of comparing the present period of the Ismaili imamate with previous periods.

The institution of the Ismaili imamate (or "the office of Imamat"[17] as the present Ismaili Imam often tends to call it) is different in many ways from other institutions of authority in the Muslim world.[18] The form this authority takes and the kind of leadership that is exercised by the Ismaili imamate today is radically different from that which can be found in other communities (despite certain similarities that clearly exist).

This change and radical shift has not only occurred in the *form* of this authority, but, as I show, it is also deeply reflected in the thinking processes which occur in the Ismaili imamate. We are witnesses to a change not only in *form* but also in *content*, in the Ismaili imamate, and it is precisely for this reason that I referred to it as "transmutation"; the Ismaili imamate has moved from the notion of the leader being the "personification of authority" (as reflected in earlier classical Ismaili doctrines) to the "institutionalization of authority" (the AKDN being the best example of it).

This change, when compared with similar institutions of leadership in the Muslim world, shows more than just a comparatively rapid pace

of adaptation to the changing circumstances of the world, where other communities and leaders have either not adapted at all or have been slow in keeping pace with change. A move beyond theological dialectics and polemic discourses, replacing dense theological perceptions with a more humanistic, civilizational, and developmental approach, has now become one of the prevalent themes in the vision of the present Ismaili Imam.

I argue that the decision to adopt these changes is an unprecedented development with far-reaching implications and consequences for the organization of the Ismaili community and its leadership. This research demonstrates that perceptions of leadership, and of the authority of a religious leader, have changed under the reign of the present Ismaili Imam, Aga Khan IV. My contention is that the AKDN is now, as I have chosen to describe it, an embodiment of the *transmutation of the authority* of the Ismaili Imam. This network of institutions has had a dynamic interaction with the leadership he represents. Using the term "transmutation," I explain that the form of this authority has radically changed; the underlying perceptions in the vision of the person who is currently the Ismaili Imam have changed, and we now face a thoroughly different leadership.

This change is very well represented in the vision of the present Ismaili Imam (and the legacy of the previous Imam, Aga Khan III[19]). Through historical references and contemporary evidence, it can be seen that there is a visible shift in the realm of authority for a Muslim community, with profound implications for its leadership. This leadership is neither political nor bureaucratic (in a strict Weberian sense) nor civic; it is not subject to periodic elections. Yet this model of leadership has left its lasting impression on all these three areas in regions where the AKDN has been active. I argue in this book that the AKDN is an embodiment of a "hybrid leadership" which is not eroded by modernity, but it has even become more powerful through it.

There has been a constant redefinition of authority throughout the history of the Ismaili community. This constant reinvention and continuous adaptation is particularly interesting because, in the case of the Ismaili community, it reflects certain paradoxes at the same time as opening new pathways and new challenges for this leadership.

The Ismaili imamate is faced with the difficult position of combining the past, present, and future; reconciling the faith with the world; maintaining a balance between reason and revelation; and bridging citizenship and identity. The authority of the Ismaili Imam comes from the past, and the transmutation that is occurring now is future-oriented,

taking the institution through the tensions of past, present, and future. The metaphysics or the theology to support this shift does not seem to exist, except may be in a very minimal form the likes of which we may see in the AKDN ethical framework, unlike earlier periods. This unusual mix of tradition, modernity, "the East and the West" has now resulted, I argue, in the transmutation of authority, or in a far clearer description, in "authority without territory," which is the central thesis of this book.

Research Methodology and Methods

This research is founded on an in-depth analysis of both the existing literature about authority and leadership in a Western context and that which is found in Muslim communities. In this work, my attempt is to move beyond a simply historical approach to the Ismaili community and its leadership. To this date, nobody has done any theoretical and philosophical evaluation of the developments of the Ismaili imamate in the past century, and this research will be the first critical analysis of the Ismaili imamate institutions.

The topic of the authority without territory requires a historical understanding, and certain historical introductions are inevitable in order to show the link between the past and the present, but my research is also based on an in-depth theoretical and philosophical engagement with contemporary developments in the leadership of the Ismaili community and the formation of a new perception of authority, which did not exist in the past. So, this is a particular kind of interpretation where I am engaging with the past as a point of comparison in order to understand and interpret what is happening at the present time and how this present situation points for the future.

This is a narrative about how the AKDN came into being, and it explains how a particular action on the part of the leadership of the Ismaili community has shaped the concept of authority and the way we encounter this new form today (and what it can become in the future). The gist of my hermeneutical approach is summed up in the words of Bevir and Rhodes, "we account for actions, practises and institutions by telling a story about how they came to be as they are and perhaps also about how they are preserved" (Bevir and Rhodes, in Marsh and Stoker, 2002: 134).

Here, it is essential to say a few words about the background against which I have done this work. This also sheds light on the methodology

that I have adopted to carry out this research. I was born and raised in an Ismaili family, and as such I have had direct and immediate experience of and exposure to the community. I have also been working with the Institute of Ismaili Studies since 2002. From a critical point of view, it is imperative to demonstrate that my approach is not positively prejudiced. In the methodology which informs my critical approach to the collected data and information and guides my epistemological discussions, I have chosen a Gadamerian approach to the issue, which I explain below under the rubric of "critical intimacy."

A Gadamerian Approach: Prejudice Methodologically Justified

By adopting a hermeneutical approach to the central question of this research and the study of the Ismaili community, I have had to remain sensitive to any interference that could influence the outcome of this research in a negative way. However, this sensitivity, as Gadamer puts it, "involves neither 'neutrality' with respect to content nor the extinction of one's self, but the foregrounding and appropriation of one's own fore-meanings and prejudices" (Gadamer, 2004: 271).

Here, the central issue that I had to remain aware of was my own bias such that it would not prevent me from seeing the subject of research in all its otherness. Here, Gadamer refers to Heidegger who gives a concrete form in the question of being to the hermeneutical problem (Gadamer, 2004: 272). As such,

> It is not at all a matter of securing ourselves against the tradition that speaks out of the text then, but, on the contrary, of excluding everything that could hinder us from understanding it in terms of the subject matter. It is the tyranny of hidden prejudices that makes us deaf to what speaks to us in tradition. (Gadamer, 2004: 272)

Therefore, the hermeneutical approach in this research works like corrective lenses enabling the reader or researcher to see the dynamics of this authority in sharper focus rather than distorting what the text is telling us. Thus, the fact of the researcher's background need not have any adverse effect, disadvantage or harm for the outcome of the research. As Gadamer explains, this "prejudice" does not necessarily entail a false judgment. It is all dependent upon the positive or negative value which comes with it. In this research, I have been intimately involved with the subject of research, and therefore I have been able to see some nuances that outsiders could hardly discern.

Critical Intimacy

Gadamer takes on the Enlightenment's prejudice against prejudice itself which has ignored the methodological value of prejudice. He then suggests:

> The only thing that gives a judgment dignity is its having a basis, a methodological justification (and not the fact that it may actually be correct). For the Enlightenment the absence of such a basis does not mean that there might be other kinds of certainty, but rather that the judgment has no foundation in the things themselves—i.e., that it is "unfounded." (Gadamer, 2004: 273)

Therefore, instead of discrediting prejudice, it is positively used to methodologically enhance the approach to the subject. In the methodological narrative of his book on ʿAyn al-Quḍāt Hamadānī (1999), Dabashi employs the same hermeneutical approach and explains:

> The task of a critical intimacy with a culture begins with the detection of that overwhelming sacred imagination that informs and animates the terms of enchantment constitutional to these enduring justifications of an otherwise unjustifiable world. Central to all acts of enduring enchantments are rejuvenative forces of the charismatic that periodically resignify the world with ever more convincing illusions of self-re-invention. (Dabashi, 1999: 27)

Critical intimacy in this sense unpacks, undoes, and deconstructs self-legitimizing master-narratives "in the particular historicity of their self-realizations" (Dabashi, 1999: 27). In the case of the Ismaili imamate, there is a strong link between the sacred and the very office of imamate. This link and every interpretation of it anticipate its self-realization and self-legitimation. This kind of critical intimacy stands in sharp contrast with dominant Orientalist approaches and as Dabashi expounds,

> detailed and particular attention to specific texts, individuals, institutions, or symbolics of authority is the most immediate way to oppose and end the de-facing, de-personalizing, and totally de-historicizing language of "Orientalism" as attribution of abstract thoughts to de-faced individuals, to fabricated races. (Dabashi, 1999: 28)

Being an Ismaili, as the person who engages in this research is both difficult and rewarding. It is difficult because there is always a potential of falling into the trap of justification and apologetics. It is rewarding

and indeed a privileged position because I have not only had access to the Community internally, thus overcoming many of the obstacles that outsiders face, but I have also been in constant battle with myself trying to deconstruct and reinterpret these developments, from a homocentric perspective. This critical intimacy allows for the articulation of ideas and hearing voices which may otherwise remain unheard or unuttered regarding how these institutions develop and the challenges and tensions they face.

Method of Research

There is a huge bulk of literature mainly produced after the 1930s following the works of Ivanow and in particular the original sources that have, over the years, been published by the Institute of Ismaili Studies (IIS). These sources have been instrumental in exploring the roots of the issue with more up-to-date information that have helped in clearing many misunderstandings that had existed due to the lack of primary sources from within the community.

Apart from the existing material on the Ismaili community's history and the ideas that shape it, another part of the present research rests on interviews and dialogues with senior members of the community and those who have been at the center of its work for many years. One of the components of the research is interviews with key figures who have played a role in the conceptualization of the current institutions of the Ismaili imamate and those who make intellectual and administrative contributions to its functions. These interviews, complemented by the hermeneutical approach that I have adopted, will help to develop the core of the book, as presented above.

CHAPTER 1

Max Weber, Authority, and Leadership

The influence of Max Weber (1864–1920) on political and sociological analysts and theorists is an undeniable fact, and there is no dispute about his impact on twentieth-century European thought. Although his ideas have been heavily criticized and assessed, after over a century now, they still seem to dominate the field of social sciences, particularly in the area of the study of authority and leadership.

In the greater narrative of trying to respond to some specific events in the Muslim world, there is still a visibly Weberian approach to the understanding of Muslim societies and communities around the globe among Muslims and non-Muslims alike. This is particularly evident in the way modernity is understood among the Muslims.

The purpose of this work is to demonstrate that a transmutation or an epistemic shift has occurred in the Ismaili imamate through its institutionalization in the form of the Aga Khan Development Network (AKDN) and its Community institutions, which I describe under the rubric of *authority without territory*. By adopting a Weberian framework, I also show that the methodological and conceptual tools of Weber and his model of ideal types are inapplicable for understanding the Muslim world.

The life work of Weber is his reinterpretation of the Christianization of Europe. Weber's assessment of modernity, his belief in the uniqueness of the West, and his models for understanding authority and leadership have long persisted in social sciences, and they have also been widely used as methodological tools for research about the Muslim world.

The Muslim world of our time has been constantly confronted with the question of how it encounters modernity, democracy, civil society, human rights, and all that is historically assumed to be the achievement

of the West. There is often a tendency in the Muslim world and among both its religious and secular intellectuals who try to respond to these questions to identify the concepts of modernity, democracy, human rights, and a host of other ideas with the Enlightenment period in Europe and consider these concepts to be inextricably a part and product of the European legacy of the Enlightenment (see Eickelman and Piscatori, 1996: 22–45 for a wide range of responses to this position)

As a consequence, often when dealing with issues such as democracy, human rights, and freedom of speech, it appears that the mentality of many religious or secular intellectuals who deal with the Muslim world is conditioned by the Enlightenment period making all their references to an ideal concept from that period. Any hint at a postcolonial or post-orientalist approach to refresh our understanding of such concepts vis-à-vis the Muslim world usually faces stiff resistance or vehement opposition.

To all of this one must add the Orientalist attitude which—as Edward Said describes it—"connotes the high-handed executive attitude of nineteenth-century and early-twentieth-century European colonialism" (Said, 2003: 2). This approach or style of thought is "based upon an ontological and epistemological distinction made between 'the Orient' and (most of the time) 'the Occident'" (Said, 2003: 2). Said captures this Eurocentric attitude in scholarly work as follows:

> To speak of Orientalism therefore is to speak mainly, although not exclusively, of a British and French cultural enterprise, a project whose dimensions take in such disparate realms as the imagination itself, the whole of India and the Levant, the Biblical texts and the Biblical lands, the spice trade, colonial armies and a long tradition of colonial administrators, a formidable scholarly corpus, innumerable Oriental "experts" and "hands," an Oriental professorate, a complex array of "Oriental" ideas (Oriental despotism, Oriental splendor, cruelty, sensuality), many Eastern sects, philosophies, and wisdoms domesticated for local European use—the list can be extended more or less indefinitely. (Said, 2003: 4)

In the bigger picture of the Eurocentric academic (and popular) approaches to the West, Max Weber holds a unique place. To Max Weber, modernity equals the rise of capitalist markets, bureaucratic territorial states, the rule of law, and the disenchantment of the world, and Western development is characterized by increasing rationality, bureaucratization, and modernization. And, according to him, these are all peculiar to the West and could never be achieved in the Orient or by Oriental societies, which includes the Muslim world, mainly concentrated in areas that are

now called the developing world and not quite long ago were called the "third world."

This Eurocentric approach, which is quite palpable in Weber, based on his interpretation of the Christianization of Europe and the rise of capitalism as a result of Protestantism, is widely present in academic writings about the Muslim world. In his sociology of religion, Weber "attempted to understand the values which created secular modernity" (Turner, 1998). Therefore, his sociology of religion also greatly contributes to at least one of the interpretations of secularism, too: building the Western secular modernity upon the unique qualities of the West and the Protestant movement, although he is quite pessimistic of the future of this development too, when he considers it an "iron cage."

In this book, I refer to the main positions of Max Weber vis-à-vis authority and the forms of leadership which accordingly follow it, drawing on his ideal types. At this point, this work is minimally a critique of Weber's stance on modernity and then there is a transition to his theory of authority. Then, I adopt two ways to show that his model is inapplicable for dealing with issues of authority in the Muslim world. One way is to show that his methodological tool is just not comprehensive enough to be able to deal with the complexities of the Muslim world. The other approach would be simpler and, yet, more critical. I will assume that Weber's model could, in fact, be applied to our case. Therefore, given the validity of his model, it should be a good "working hypothesis" to explain every phenomenon in the Muslim world. Then, as I proceed to examine a specific example, I demonstrate that the Weberian model fails to explain Muslim institutions of authority, and in particular the AKDN.

The AKDN and the institutions of the Ismaili imamate is the case study of this work. The Ismaili imamate, with all its institutions, is an antithesis to the methodological tool of Weber, and it represents a transmutation in authority which cannot be explained by any Weberian model; as such the Weberian ideal types are inapplicable and inadequate, despite its rich insights.

The earliest take on the inapplicability of Weber's ideal types in the case of Shi'ism was done in the groundbreaking work of Hamid Dabashi, *Authority in Islam* (1989), where he argues that we must posit the possibility of the perpetuation of charisma, which he develops in detail in his work.

The key questions of this book revolve around the Weberian models of authority and leadership. Weber's study of Islam, as part of his

research on the sociology of religion, did not actually bear fruit, and it remained simply in the form of scattered comments in his monographs in law, religion, and economic organization (Huff, in Huff and Schluchter, 1999: 2). However, Weber's comparative study of Islam has remained a driving framework for many scholars, engaging them to look at Islam from this perspective (and criticize the Weberian outlook too). The volume edited by Huff and Schluchter (1999) bears testimony to this influence.

Max Weber is also relevant in the context of this book, particularly in terms of his articulations of the ideal types of authority and leadership. As it was briefly mentioned in the Introduction, in the Ismaili Community, we have a strong sense of tradition giving weight to traditional authority as understood by the Shi'i Nizārī Ismaili Muslims. The Ismaili Community has developed a legal-bureaucratic structure for its organizations and institutions, and even though traces of a legal background for it may exist in the past, at first glance, the institutions appear to be structured like bureaucratic corporations in the West, with its internal and external financial checks and balances and their recruitment policies. The third aspect of it is the existence of a sort of charismatic quality attributed to the Imam that is rooted in Ismaili doctrines and theology.

These aspects make the case of the Ismaili imamate a suitable candidate to be checked against Weberian ideal types. The raison d'être for Weber, however, extends beyond these elements. The Ismaili Community is also highly modernized, and even though one should speak with caution about its being modern, the economic status of the Ismaili Community is also another issue that may justify the use of Weber in this context. This being said, we must note that the highly successful economic and entrepreneurial enterprises of the Ismaili Community is mainly restricted to the Ismailis of East African origin—or Khojas— and the rest of the Community still lags behind in this respect.

The most important and particularly critical work written so far about Weber and Islam has been Hamid Dabashi's work in which he gives a hermeneutical explication of the idea of charismatic authority.[1] Dabashi devotes a full chapter to articulating the idea of Muhammadan messengership (al-risāla al-Muḥammadiyya) (1989: 47–70; also, 2008: 70). Following Phillip Rieff's work, Dabashi also traces the idea of charisma back to its Christian origin of *gift of grace* (1989: 36–53 and 101–16) to pave the way for an Islamic version of it, being acutely aware that charisma is a Christian concept and it is only through hermeneutics that he could bring in this comparative study (Dabashi, 1989: 33).

Here, I have tried to find parallels of charisma in the Ismaili doctrines as well drawing on original sources with their distinctively Ismaili dimension, examples of which are given in the Introduction. Other works regarding Weber's ideas about Islam are published about a decade earlier (originally published in 1974, reprinted in 1998) by Bryan Turner, whose work is referenced here. However, Turner's work does not touch upon the topics that are dealt with in this book, namely, authority and leadership in the context of the Muslim world today, and although he gives a very good overview of the Ismaili history in his work (Turner, 1998: 87–91), it comes to an abrupt termination when he speaks about the Mongol invasion and so assumes the Ismailis to be out of the picture for good. I carry on the disrupted scholarly work about Ismailis up to the present time. The edited volume of articles published a year later (Huff and Schluchter, 1999) is even poorer in terms of attention to the diversity of the Muslim world and only in passing refers to the Shiʿi Muslims.

Turner's article about Islam and capitalism is one of the finest examples of a critique of Weber. Dabashi's work, which was his PhD thesis supervised by Rieff, is far more developed in this sense. His work, however, remains focused on the early stages of Islam following the death of Muhammad, and he tries to use the methodological tools of Weber and his ideal types to explain the schisms following the death of the founder of Islam. Since the time of Dabashi, only a few people have written extensively about Weber and his interpretation and understanding of the Muslim world, but the few who have positively and approvingly used his methodology have almost consistently failed to point out that Weber's model is practically inapplicable and does not prove helpful in *solving* our problems—with the exception of Dabashi, of course, who has sought to overcome Weber's limitation by introducing Shiʿism as the perpetuation of charisma. What they have almost invariably done with the Weberian model is merely an explanation of what the situation is when viewed with a Weberian lens, but they usually fail to address a specific problem and try to suggest a solution.[2] In the case of Shiʿism, the charismatic leadership of the Imams knew no specific limitations—and as we will see in the case of the Ismailis, it works as a liberating factor, which can pave the way for even epistemic shifts, and as Dabashi has noted:

> This theological necessity of the Imams is the foundation upon which their charismatic authority is sought to be institutionalized. The Qurʾan and the Imams' unique "knowledge" of interpreting it, after the death of Muhammad, became an integral part of one another and together constituted the sole source of authority (Dabashi, 1989:106)[3].

The twentieth century has witnessed the rise and return of Islam and the Muslim world to the public consciousness, through extensive media coverage and representations, and to the academic circles beyond the hitherto established Orientalist approaches to Islam. One of the reasons I have chosen authority for this research is that, in one way or another, every acute problem of the Muslim world, particularly in terms of its politics and development, is closely related to the issue of authority. Authority being the center point of all the critical issues of the Muslim world is not something that has emerged recently or in modern times; it goes back to the very early days of Islam following the death of the Prophet Muḥammad and the dispute over his succession.

The dispute over succession is essentially a dispute over authority. Therefore, the problem of authority reveals itself right at the outset in the form of a dispute over succession, but for sure it took other forms at the later stages of the history of Muslim civilizations and societies. It is here that authority has become connected and interrelated with legitimacy, power, and leadership in Muslim history up until now. Hence, the burning issue remains to be that of authority, and Max Weber is the first and foremost thinker who has touched upon this matter in a defining manner.

Looking back at what Weber has written about Muslim societies and about authority, power, legitimacy, politics, religion, charisma, culture, and a variety of other themes with his insight and his theories, we may very well see many considerations missing, particularly as our knowledge of Muslim societies has hugely expanded, but not yet to the extent that we can confidently say that nuances and subtleties of the subject are now clearly recognized and understood.

We must note that as regards Weber's sociology of authority, his model is a carefully and powerfully crafted one whereas his poor knowledge of Muslim societies—and his death before he could do some serious research about them—does not allow for the incorporation of a complementary element to his model.

A Methodological Point of Departure: Islamic or Muslim?

This brings me to an important note which must be made at the outset about certain terms which are consistently used throughout this book. In almost all cases, except where there are quotations or in cases where it is technically not possible to use a different term, I have referred to the Muslim world, Muslim societies, and Muslim civilizations (plural) instead of the Islamic world and the Islamic society and the Islamic

civilization (singular). This is because when we talk about Islam, we are indeed talking about an array of interpretations of Islam that are the products of the history of Islam as a faith. As such, we do not deal with a faith that has a single legitimate and valid interpretation excluding all other interpretations, except the one claiming to have access to the absolute truth, as illegitimate or less valid.

From a methodological point of view and also as a normative measure, throughout this work, I will be referring to Muslims and Muslim societies to highlight the diversity of interpretations and the actual pluralism that exists in the Muslim world. Also, I have made reference to Muslim civilizations in the plural rather than what is customarily used in singular. This is because the variety of interpretations made by Muslims throughout history of the sacred text or of Islam itself has paved the way for different civilizations in different parts of the Muslim world and as such it would be inaccurate to refer to just one single monumental Muslim civilization or even to a single Islamic civilization. However, in cases where I have directly quoted others or where there has been no other way to highlight this plurality and also the human agency in interpreting faith, I have had to use the more common terms.

In justifying the use of Muslims as opposed to Islam in this context, Bayat argues that

> The terms "Islamic world" and "Islamic society," used in singular abstract forms, may indeed imply that Islam is the central factor that shapes the dynamics of these societies. "Islamic society" becomes a generality constructed by others to describe Muslims and their cultures. It tells how others imagine what Muslims are and even how they should be. (Bayat, 2007: 2)

And he continues that adopting the descriptive term of Muslim serves as a liberating designation that "allows a self-conscious Muslim majority to define their own reality in an inevitably contested, differentiated, and dynamic fashion" (2007: 2). By doing this, Bayat is shifting the emphasis on the agency of Muslims: "the emphasis is not on Islam but on Muslims as *agents* of their societies and cultures, even if not of their own making" (2007: 2, emphasis mine). Bayat is particularly aware that the opposite leads to an exclusivist representation that is shared by both skeptics and apologists:

> Both "skeptics" and "apologists" share an exclusive commitment to texts, drawing their arguments from the literal reading of sacred scriptures (the

Qur'ān and *ḥadīth*), and pay astonishingly little attention to what these texts mean to the fragmented Muslim citizenry in their day-to-day lives. What is more, rarely is there discussion of how these meanings change over time. (2007: 4)

This designation is particularly important when we address issues of democracy and modernity where the question of compatibility with Islam is posed. Bayat addresses the question from another perspective, which is a corollary of his reference to Muslims rather than Islam: "The question is not whether Islam is or is not compatible with democracy or, by extension, modernity, but rather under what conditions Muslims can make them compatible" (2007: 4). He, thus, argues that asking whether Islam and democracy are compatible is asking the wrong question and it ignores the agency of Muslims by referring to Islamic society in singular form.

Dabashi (2013: 29–36) also engages with the designation of "Islamic societies" in the context of the Islam/West binary and charges against the essentialism which is deeply embedded in such binaries: "All our (substantive and strategic) critical work must be entirely targeted against both the epistemological and the political assumptions of essentialism—'Islam' and 'the West' chief among them" (Dabashi, 2013: 32). Challenging such binaries and avoiding essentialism is not only a methodological observation of this book but, as we shall see, it will also emerge on the radar of the Ismaili imamate's approach to the issues of the Muslim world.

Literature: Ismaili Studies and Authority

Modern scholarship on the Ismaili community began with the efforts of the late Wladimir Ivanow (1886–1970). Before Ivanow, major works relating to the study of the Ismaili community mainly remained in the form of heresiographies, which depicted an outcast community. The pioneering efforts of Ivanow and the recent scholarly works of Farhad Daftary have now provided an opportunity for a more substantial and better analysis of the role of this community and its weight in Muslim history.

Despite the richness of all the historiographic work, which has been done about the Ismailis, they largely remain focused on earlier periods, rather than the modern period. The first three periods of the Ismaili history, the early period, the Fatimid period, and the Alamūt period are the ones that have received extensive attention, both in terms of historiography and theological doctrines.

To date, a substantial and coherent assessment of the history and doctrines of the Ismailis in the modern period is not available. Daftary's work (2007), which is the most comprehensive history of the Ismailis, contains very little information about the modern period in comparison with earlier periods. Even though he gives a very good account of the period of the first two Aga Khans, there is still a lot to be done in the late modern period of the Ismaili history.

The following literature review, which is not in a chronological order, covers the most important literature available on the modern period of the Ismaili history, relevant to the subject of this book.

The Ismaili Imamate and Its Institutions: Contemporary Literature

Although a comprehensive work has not yet been done on the late modern period—by which I mean the period of Aga Khan IV—there are many scattered articles available, which can help construct this part of the history and fill the gap.

It is interesting that among the earliest papers that were published about the contemporary Ismaili Community, there is an article by Robert J. Bocock in *The British Journal of Sociology* with a heavily Weberian overtone: *The Ismailis in Tanzania: A Weberian Analysis*. This is probably the first paper[4] that draws on Weber's theories to make sense of the Ismaili Community and the institutions of the Ismaili imamate. Very early on in the paper, the author uses the term "charisma" with regard to the Ismaili imamate and equates it with "light or 'nass'" which is "passed from the Imam to his appointee" (Bocock, 1971: 366), thus ignoring its fundamental differences with its original Christian context.[5] The rest of this article is replete with Weberian terms, and it is not at all surprising that it is quite Eurocentric and fails to see the nuances of the Ismaili Muslim context of it.

Apart from the theoretical framework of the article, which is a misappropriation of Weber, the rest of the article gives some valuable historical information regarding the early development of the institutions of the Ismaili Community, particularly in the colonial period in East Africa. Even in his description of the Ismailis, he does not fail to employ different terms and categories provided by Weber:

> The Ismailis are a status group acting to preserve and improve their economic, political, and social position in various societies in the world, and also, equally importantly, trying to preserve their Ismaili identity and

way of life based on their religious beliefs, values and rituals. They are an important empirical test case for examining the inter-relations of ideal and material interests. (Bocock, 1971: 368)

He continues further down to compare the Ismailis with Calvinists, and it is no wonder that he tries to explain every development in the Ismaili community with the same framework that he has adopted in his article.

I have briefly mentioned earlier on—in references to "gift of grace"—that theories which have been articulated in a different political imaginative context and are used and applied to explain the situation cannot sufficiently help us in understanding the situation with the Ismailis and particularly—in the case of this book—the nature of the Ismaili Imam's authority and his leadership. Moreover, Bocock's concern is not leadership at all. However, it contains fragments of valuable information, although he repeatedly draws parallels, in an excessive manner, with Weberian concepts and terms.

The fact that among the literature about the Ismailis we come across a research with such references to Weber can explain why and how it is always tempting for researchers to take up the easy but deceiving task of explaining this leadership in a Weberian sense, without realizing how profoundly different it is from a Weberian test subject.

Another work, which was published by Peter B. Clarke, a few years later in the same journal in 1976 moves a little ahead in time, and instead of putting too much emphasis on the Ismailis in East Africa and the early institutions of the Community, it mainly deals with contemporary institutions that have been established by Aga Khan IV.

This article does not in any way, whatsoever, try to study the Ismaili Community by employing Weberian terms and methods. More than anything else, it is a historical account of the doctrines and history of the Community with a particular emphasis on the life of the Ismailis in London. The scope of the research remains very limited. However, it begins to touch on an area that is of interest to this book: the idea of leadership and how the community has prospered under this leadership forms a significant part of the article.

Toward the end of his work, Clarke gives an example, which is one of the significant events of the imamate of Aga Khan IV:

The recent history of Ismailism—the expulsion from Uganda, the insecurity of their position in Uganda generally—has made a successful leader critically important to his people. During a situation of crisis and in times

of insecurity a people tend to make a one-to-one identification between their survival and the person of their representative.

And he ends on an admiring note:

Since the community is considered to be more than the sum of its parts (whether one bases this on ethnic criteria or in terms of economic interest), the leader has become more than ever the objective embodiment of the Ismaili community's being and existence. The Imam's attributes of "big man" are emphasized more now: his authority is moral, representing the virtue residing in the community, his power extraordinary since he is the living embodiment of the reality and importance of the community. Consequently, recent fate and history have emphasized for Ismailis the central tenet of their faith and its importance and strengthened the spirit of community, and dependence upon the Imam. He is the link with tradition, with Islam, the present "political" leader, the manifestation of God, the synthesis of the "sacred" and the "profane." (Clarke, 1976: 493–94)

The first most detailed study of a part of the modern institutions of the Ismaili imamate appears in the work of Paul J. Kaiser, which is published in 1996. The book is titled *Culture, Transnationalism and Civil Society*, and its focus of study is the Ismaili imamate's social services initiatives in Tanzania. The scope of this work is limited and it does not go into the Ismaili imamate's institutions as a whole, but at the center of his focus, we see his constant references to the transnational nature of these institutions.

The work is focused on Tanzania, where he has conducted his research. The general framework of the book is heavily under the influence of the discourses of transnational corporations and the Civil Society. It responds to the concerns of his time and the dominant questions that were in the consciousness of the academia of his time. The main emphasis of the book is on the education and health initiatives of the Ismaili imamate's institutions.

Somewhere toward the end of the book, Kaiser has a paragraph that can, in a nutshell, describe the overall approach of his research:

Ismailis live in over twenty countries throughout the world, and they are a minority in every setting. This transnational community developed sophisticated communal and non-communal international organizations headquartered in Geneva and Aiglemont under the leadership of Aga Khan IV. Their health facilities and schools reflect a balance between the

local and international concerns of the community. International financial, material, and labor resources enhanced the effectiveness of Aga Khan
facilities. In addition, the corporate ethos perpetuated by Aga Khan IV
affected the degree to which Ismaili facilities were able to achieve financial self-sufficiency in terms of daily operation and limited infrastructure
development. (Kaiser, 1996: 104)

What Kaiser refers to as the "corporate ethos perpetuated by Aga
Khan IV" is probably one of the important aspects of the institutions
as they are led today by the Ismaili imamate. This corporate element
is something that again tempts some scholars to see the AKDN in a
Weberian framework by drawing a parallel to the bureaucratic leadership
that might be easily ascribed to the AKDN and the Ismaili imamate's
institutions.

As the AKDN further expanded, scholarly material regarding its work
becomes slightly richer in content, although the size of the materials
is still scarce. The focus on the nature of the work of the AKDN is
greatly sharpened in Tazim R. Kassam's article titled "The Aga Khan
Development Network: An Ethic of Sustainable Development and Social
Conscience" (Kassam, in Foltz, 2003: 477–96). This short article is one
of the few in capturing the theoretical and ethical content of the AKDN
as a whole, as reflected in the Ismaili imamate's policies. What is duly
and properly highlighted in this article is the "development" aspect of
these institutions as the Aga Khan has brought to his work. As such, this
article can properly contextualize the network's activities in the right
social context as it is related to the Ismaili imamate. Kassam's article does
not focus on authority or leadership but helps in a general way to get a
clear picture of how the network functions within the ethical ideals of
Islam.

With regard to the current institutional developments of the community, there are a number of articles that are very important for
understanding the genesis of these institutions. Arif Jamal's article on
the development of the Ismaili law (Jamal, in Cotran, 2000–2001) is
an important one that explains the developments in the formation of
the current Ismaili Constitution drawing on the history of the Ismaili
Community in medieval times and in the modern period. It demonstrates how from an Ismaili legal document like al-Qāḍī al-Nuʿmān's
Daʿāʾim al-Islām in the Fatimid period to the Ismaili Constitutions of
the modern period, significant changes have occurred. Jamal shows the
relevance of East African Ismaili Communities for the development of
these constitutions.

Another important work, which Jamal and Kaiser reference in their works, is Shirin Walji's PhD thesis (1974), which is about the history of the Ismaili Community in Tanzania. Although her work is focused on Tanzania—and East African Ismaili Communities in general—it gives us interesting and detailed information about the functions of the constitutions and the gradual shifts that happen in it as a result of the changes in the socioeconomic conditions of the Community during and after the colonial period. Her assessment of the constitutions and hierarchies of the Community from 1900 through the 1950s gives us a defining framework for understanding the intricacies of this legal development, which is critical in the institutions of the Community and the imamate. Her work is written at a time when the existing modern institutions of the Ismaili imamate—and the AKDN—were not yet in place, but it can give us backgrounds as to how things have unfolded within the East African Ismaili Communities.

Of particular relevance to this research is Jean-Claude Penrad's article (in Aubin and Lombard, 1999) that gives a commercial history of the Ismaili Community in East Africa. The presence of Ismailis in East Africa, which goes back to the time of Aga Khan I, is particularly important for the economic developments in the Community and helps us better understand how the Ismaili imamate managed to transform the life of the Community into an entrepreneurial entity, which is the economic backbone of its institutions today. He gives a very good account of the trading empires of the Ismailis, like Sewa Haji Paroo, Tharia Topan, and Allidina Visram, who were leading members of the community during the colonial period.

The article by Malise Ruthven titled "Aga Khan III and the Ismaili Renaissance" (in Clarke, 1998) is mainly focused on Aga Khan III and his modernization of the Community. Ruthven gives examples of the specific instructions that Aga Khan III gave to the Community on issues as diverse as education, business practices, religious tolerance, the imamate itself, women's emancipation (which is one of the most significant developments during the time of Aga Khan III in the Ismaili Community), avoiding alcohol and tobacco, diet, dress, and spiritual matters. While describing these instructions, Ruthven gives precedents and references to the Alamūt and Fatimid period highlighting Aga Khan III's stress on the esoteric aspects of faith. The imamate of Aga Khan III is marked by changes that he introduces in the areas of rituals drawing on his authority as the Ismaili Imam to make these changes.

Ruthven, thus, gives a very appropriate context for the genesis of the current institutions of the Ismaili imamate and how the authority of the

Imam transformed into a figure with humanist concerns. The interesting point about Ruthven's narrative is that it is clearly influenced by Weber in the way he understands the Ismaili imamate in modern times. His concluding paragraphs have some special resonance with the topic of this book.

On the role of the AKDN as an NGO, there is practically very little written, with Kaiser's work being the only exception that is still limited to a certain area in an East African country. Nejima Susumu's article titled "The Ismaili Imam and NGOs: A Case Study of Islamic Civil Society" (2000) focuses on the NGO aspect of the AKDN institutions. As Kaiser has done in his work about Tanzania, Susumu does a similar job—albeit more limited—in the case of Pakistan, which is one of the major areas where AKDN institutions are active. In the conclusion, Susumu evaluates the AKDN and the Ismaili imamate among "Islamic Revival Movements" and considers it an important part of Islamic civil society.

Alongside Jamal, Penrad, and Walji, it is also noteworthy to see Nile Green's chapter titled "The Making of a Neo-Ismāʿilism" in his *Bombay Islam: The Religious Economy of the Western Indian Ocean, 1840–1915* (2011). The style, perspective, and methodology of Green serves a different purpose as he is looking at the Ismailis in a wider framework in which Sufi orders, the Parsi Zoroastrians, and a host of other communities are studied for their economic life. His chapter is primarily focused on Aga Khan I and the beginning of the modern period of the Ismaili history, but in terms of shedding light on the economic life of the community, it is still not as rich as Walji and Penrad.

With regard to the modern history of the Ismailis, there are two other works: one by Hamid Algar and one by Marc van Grondelle. Hamid Algar's article (1969) is focused only on Aga Khan I and his dispute with the Qājār rulers, demonstrating how the migration of the Ismaili Imam was rather a result of court rivalries, which were so dominant in the entire Qājār period, than some conspiracy on the side of Aga Khan I with the aid of the British. Van Grondelle's work is particularly interesting in this regard in reinforcing Algar's argument, as van Grondelle indicates that he has found that Aga Khan I is barely mentioned in colonial and government archives—and this is even more so in the period that Aga Khan I was in Iran and had a dispute with his Qājār relatives who were in power. The rest of van Grondelle's work is mostly devoted to exploring the relations between Aga Khan III and the British Empire during the colonial period. His assessment is mainly concentrated on the documents he has found in the government archives, and there is rarely a balanced

account of the Aga Khan's involvement with the British drawing on other sources. A recent study of the Ismaili imamate in colonial India is Teena Purohit's (2012) research into the Aga Khan case, which is primarily written from an anticolonial perspective but attempts to analyze and dissect the devotional literature of the Ismailis (the *ginān*s) while trying to argue that the Ismaili imamate was an accomplice of the British colonialists. Purohit's work suffers from a historical and methodological lack of accuracy (with obvious historical errors in some instances).

An important element, which would provide insights into the current institutions of the Ismaili imamate, is the biography of the Aga Khans. Willi Frischauer's *The Aga Khans* (1970) is a very detailed biographical account of the life of the Aga Khans, particularly the last two Aga Khans. It can give us an idea of the complexities and the contingencies of the Community and the imamate in issues of succession and the day-to day-life of the Aga Khans. Even though the book is not written in an academic and critical way, it nonetheless provides some valuable details when it comes to issues of authority and the leadership of the Community. The strength of Frischauer's book, which is now about half-a-century old, is that he has had access to the family of the Aga Khans, and his references and quotations seem to be accurate in many cases.

Among the most recent works published with the dominant themes of the contemporary Ismaili imamate is *A Modern History of the Ismailis: Continuity and Change in a Muslim Community* edited by Farhad Daftary in 2011. Out of the articles in this volume, there are two that are particularly important. Zulfikar Hirji's "The Socio-Legal Formation of the Nizari Ismailis of East Africa, 1800–1950" is quite informing in understanding the development of the Ismaili institutions in Africa and the genesis of the Ismaili Constitution in its early forms. A lengthy descriptive article by Malise Ruthven on "The Aga Khan Development Network and Institutions" gives a detailed account of the entire range of the institutions in the network. Other articles in the book, altogether, serve as a very informative compendium to better understand the different dynamics of how the Ismaili Community and the Ismaili imamate function in our times. The book, however, does not touch on issues of leadership or authority in particular. As such, it is, more than anything else, a historiograghical account.

A more recent study is the work of Jonah Steinberg titled *Isma'ili Modern: Globalization and Identity in a Muslim Community* (2011). Steinberg identifies the role of leadership and succession right in the beginning of his work, and although in his later chapters he generally focuses on the Ismaili Community in Central Asia, the political-science

perspective of the work is quite palpable. Steinberg captures the core of the issue by highlighting authority and leadership:

> The role of leadership, succession, and schism in the history of Islam warrants careful (albeit brief) consideration here. It is only through an understanding of these processes that the story of Isma'ilism can be fully explained. At almost every historical moment, how the Isma'ili community defined and redefined itself revolved around questions of succession and rightful authority. (Steinberg, 2011: 33)

Later on, Steinberg notes the role of Aga Khan IV's leadership, saying that "certainly under his leadership the delicate relationship between Isma'ilis and individual states has been refined and redefined," and when making reference to the Ismaili Constitution, he concludes that it "reinstitutionalized" the authority of the Aga Khan over his subjects (Steinberg, 2011: 56).

The final section of the second chapter of his work is titled "Aga Khan IV: A Corporate Globality," chosen intelligently to reflect a very significant aspect of the Ismaili Imam's leadership having a corporate and a global dimension to it.

A most recent chapter by Karim (in Cherry, 2014) is a brief overview of the AKDN with more rigorous methodology. Curiously enough, Karim uses the term "metamorphosis" (Karim, in Cherry, 2014: 147–48) when he tries to explain the trajectory of the development of the Ismaili imamate institutions from what they were at the time of Aga Khan III until the establishment of the AKDN. I had originally used this term while trying to explain the shifts in the notions of authority but later on relinquished it because of its very thick biological similes. However, Karim uses the term in relation with the Community rather than authority itself. Karim's article is one of the most detailed and up to date mostly descriptive pieces written on the AKDN.

The above are some of the most important sources that can help see different perspectives that shape the current outlook of the AKDN. Almost all of these works contain an introductory section speaking about the Ismaili imamate itself with various degrees of details and nuances. Out of these articles, Ruthven's article is a very concise and informative one, giving the wider context and perspective of the Ismaili imamate.

The following section is an effort to see how Max Weber's legacy often gets employed in the context of Muslim leadership and how it does not work, despite its intriguing qualities, to explain the case of the Ismaili imamate and the AKDN.

Strengths and Inadequacies of Weber

It is a key methodological tool of this book that the Weberian model is used initially to make sense of what one example of a Muslim institution of authority is and then based upon a critical assessment of the capacities of the Weberian model to explain this phenomenon, which is the Ismaili imamate and its institutions. The final conclusion of this theoretical exercise is that the Weberian ideal typical model, as it is, proves to be inapplicable.

In order to make this framework functional with regard to the Ismaili imamate and the AKDN, I am proposing a hybrid model with certain other features added to what is found in the Weberian model and other features removed from it to propose a new model, which is the working pattern of the AKDN.

In the course of this critical assessment, which is employing the case study of the AKDN and the Ismaili imamate, I am indeed highlighting the fact that Weber is stressing the wrong questions about Muslim communities, and our case study helps us go back to a corrected or more accurate question of what the problems are about.

The crucial distinction that has to be made here is that Weber's typology is rich while his remarks about Islam are poor. We must not confuse criticizing the latter with a negation of the former. Weber's typology of authority should not be conflated with his superficial remarks about Islam.

Bryan Turner has pointed out this acute problem in his assessment of Weber's theses about capitalism, "Although Weber's analysis of Islam was not particularly successful, it is ironic that when Muslim reformers came to explain the decay of Islam, they employed implicitly Weberian arguments" (Turner, 1993:42). Turner's description of this issue is expressed in even stronger terms in his later work on Weber:

> While one can make these criticisms of Weber, it is ironic that when Islamic reformers in the nineteenth century came to define a new set of motives for Islam in the modern age, their analysis of the problem of social change was almost entirely Weberian. (1998: 144)

Here, we have to note that however Weber's ideas about Islam remains limited, his theory of authority remains pregnant of fresh ideas for the Muslim world. Turner then acknowledges that there are parallels between the Islamic Reform and the Protestant Ethics but then also warns that this is a deceptive parallel and "should not be treated as any

direct confirmation of the Protestant Ethic thesis" (Turner, 1998: 144).[6] However, notwithstanding Turner's remark, we should note—once again—that a critical revision of Weber's sociology would give us rich possibilities for reading Muslim societies.

Working with the Weberian model to begin with and critically assess it in this research, I draw upon the case of the Ismaili imamate and the AKDN trying to fill a gap in scholarship, which is often filled with Weberian explanations but should be dealt with otherwise. Using this method, more than saying what the Ismaili imamate is about, this book will show what the Ismaili imamate and its institutions are *not*.

The Weberian ideal types, briefly described earlier, are the ones that lead Weber to the question of the universality of bureaucracy. Weber thinks that we are in danger of having a world run by bureaucrats, which not only does not appeal to him but is something that seems to end up in nihilism, and it becomes a dead end in itself. So he considers two options. One would be a charismatic authority, so it ends in charismatic politics. Weber points out the problem with charismatic authority: it burns out. It fades away and it cannot become permanent. The other option for him is to revive tradition, but it seems too late as the world has now become increasingly scientific-technical-bureaucratic.

Finding a means to get out of this trap is at the heart of Max Weber's political anxiety. Therefore, what he proposes is a new form of leadership, or new forms of leadership, which have shades of charisma in them and have all the great features of parliamentary democracy with elections and parliaments that produce leaders in the process. So, we have his plebiscitarian leader-democracy. However, he has done all of this with trepidation. When he speaks of the "iron cage," he seems to be quite pessimistic of the future of this model. The experience of the Nazi Germany proved that his pessimism had a strong element of truth in it.

But can bureaucratic states produce people with authority?

Rationality, Bureaucratization, and Modernity

These terms frequently come back in a web of statements made by Weber in the methodological tools that he adopts. To begin having a rough sketch of Weber with regard to modernity, rationality, and bureaucratization, I refer to his approach to modernity and what he thinks of Oriental societies.

Weber's three ideal types of legitimate domination, the traditional, charismatic, and legal-rational types, are not specifically linked to each other. Yet, when Weber refers to the third type of legitimate domination

or authority, he proposes that this third legal-rational type is a characteristic of modern, developed Western societies. In this third type of legitimate domination, what preoccupies Weber is the presence or absence of rationalization in different societies and the impact of this factor on development (Curtis, 2009: 265). Weber, however, believed that modern societies are perfectly capable of charismatic outbursts, and this is what frightened him.

Weber believes in the peculiarity of the rationalism of Western cultures. He considers them unique and asks, "Why did not the scientific, the artistic, the political, or the economic development" in Oriental societies, "enter upon that path of rationalization which is peculiar to the Occident?" (Weber, 2001: xxxviii). Weber is very clear on this: this legal-rational development could not happen in the Orient because they did not follow this path of modernity like the West. To him, the dominance of magic in Oriental societies is the most important impediment of the rationalization of economic life. Here, Weber conflates and confuses capitalism with the West. The element of disenchantment is one of the elements that are missing in the Oriental societies, according to Weber (Weber, 1949: 339, 341–2, 361; 2001: 16).

The passage below is a vivid description of how Weber perceives the Western world as unique.

> Only the Occident knows the state in the modern sense, with a constitution [*gesatzter Verfassung*], specialized officialdom, and the concept of citizenship. Beginnings of this institution in antiquity and in the Orient were never able to develop fully. Only the Occident knows rational law, made by jurists and rationally interpreted and applied, and only in the Occident is found the concept of citizen (*civis Romanus, citoyen, bourgeois*) because only in the Occident does the city exist in the specific sense of the word. Furthermore, only the Occident possesses science in the present-day sense of the word. Theology, philosophy, and reflection on the ultimate problems of life were known to the Chinese and Hindu, perhaps even of a depth not reached by the European; but a rational science and in connection with it a rational technology remained unknown to those civilizations. Finally, Western civilization is further distinguished from every other by the presence of men with a rational ethos for the conduct of life.

This is where Weber conflates modern Capitalism with the West again and ahistorically expands it. He continues to say that

> magic and religion are found everywhere; but *a religious basis for conduct that, when consistently followed, had to lead to a specific form of rationalism*

is again peculiar to Western civilization alone. (Weber, 1961: 232–3, the emphasis in the last sentence is mine)

This is a revealing passage that gives us the Weberian view of modernity and the uniqueness of the Western civilization in a nutshell.

Also, for Weber, the idea of a modern capitalist state is closely related to this legal-bureaucratic system that is characterized by certain features: a constitution and written documents, regular elections, separation of powers, limits on exercise of power, monopoly of the legitimate use of force and coercion, protection of rights, autonomous cities able to legislate for themselves, impartial judiciary, and "specialised officialdom" (Curtis, 2009: 267).

Weber recognizes at least four elements that are common to modern bureaucratic institutions. (1) Bureaucratic organizations suspend all personal criticism, and the one ideal life of the people in such organizations is to conform; (2) there is a complex division of tasks or offices and the rules specifying these tasks are typically calculated through empirical observation and guided by such considerations as the minimum of cost and spelled out in written documents; (3) there is a depersonalized rationality flowing through these institutions, and the watchword for the bureaucratic nature of these organizations is "without regard to *particular* persons or situations." Weber finds that this "impersonalism" indicates the neutrality of these institutions making them available to any power which claims their business services; (4) under modern— capitalist—conditions, the predomination of bureaucratic institutions is by virtue of their *technical* superiority, and it is precisely due to this technical competence that Weber believes these institutions can tackle the complexities of this world (Keane, 1984: 32–33).

Weber insists that it is under these modern conditions, as he demonstrates with the above characteristics, that bureaucratic capitalist enterprises come into existence that deploy fixed capital and "free" labor power (Keane, 1984: 34).

Therefore, the explanation of the situation from a Weberian point of view runs along these lines: the Christianization of Europe and the influence of the Protestant ethic led as its unanticipated consequence to the cultivation of a "capitalist spirit" and capitalist modernity was born; as in Europe all the other obstacles, which he identifies in the Orient, do not persist to the extent that they were present in the Orient. Also, the religious spirit that he identifies in Europe is something that leads to a specific form of rationalism that he finds characteristic of Western civilization in its capitalist mode alone.

The spirit of so-called Orientalism is quite palpable in the Weberian approach. Many critics of such perceptions, from Edward Said onward, have shown that many analyses "undertaken by Western and Western-inspired scholarship have imposed concepts and categories rooted in the cultural program of modernity that developed in the West" (Eisenstadt, Hoexter, and Nehemia, 2002:142).

As opposed to the notion of a unique modernity, which is at the center of the Weberian model, we now have the idea of multiple modernities and Muslim modernities (see Sajoo, 2008: 1–23), which increasingly show that conceptions viewing the modern nation state as the epitome of progress and development are not entirely true. Moreover, there is also a sense of patronization and parochialism embedded in this seemingly academic exercise with deep roots in the Orientalist tradition, which can also be part of the problem when dealing with the issues of the Muslim world.

Protestant Ethics and the Foundations of a Capitalist Modern Bureaucratic State

According to Weber's analysis of the development of the modern legal-bureaucratic state, the self-rationalizing activities of the Protestant movements were guided by a religious evaluation of the faithfuls' duty in respect of worldly affairs, as an unanticipated consequence. Engagement in worldly affairs was described as the highest form of ethical activity and a response to the divine call in which labor is one approved divine calling. In the Protestant ethic,

> living acceptably to God was not to be equated with the suppression of worldly morality in monastic asceticism...Restless, continuous, and systematic labor thereby became in itself the prime end of earthly life, the ascetic means of future salvation, the most certain sign of rebirth and genuine faith. (Keane, 1984: 49)

The religious asceticism as prescribed by the Protestants led the workers, with low wages and earthly frugality, to identify with the bureaucratized work life considering it to be the will of God. However, this Protestant asceticism does not remain at this stage and leads to unintended consequences. In the words of John Keane,

> Gradually, the intensity of the ascetic search for the kingdom of God eroded, giving way (among the rising propertied strata, at least) to

comfortable and disciplined bourgeois lives, marked by a utilitarian worldliness supplemented only by a "good conscience." The labors of the Protestant reformers produced unforeseen, and even unwished-for, effects. In this unintended development, there is a deep irony. Under pressure from the temptations of wealth—temptations that it had itself stimulated— Protestant asceticism succumbed increasingly to a secular consumerism and attempted self-renewals (such as the great revival of Methodism prior to the English Industrial Revolution). Under the "iron cage" conditions of contemporary capitalism, Weber argues, the spirit of religious asceticism has almost completely faded. The relentless pursuit of wealth through formal rationalization has become uncoupled from the old religious supports in whose name it once proceeded. (Keane, 1984: 50)

Secularism, Its contingencies and Complexities

As it was briefly noted in the Introduction, the institutions of the Ismaili Community and how the Ismaili imamate has developed, in terms of its institutional engagements, are seen as an "Ismaili response" to modernization (Nanji, 1974). While there may be arguments suggesting that the Ismaili Community has emerged as an increasingly "secular" Community, it is important to know, first of all, what we mean by secularism.

A secular society is understood to be a society in which one can engage in public activities without encountering God, as opposed to few centuries back in Western and Muslim civilization in which "religion was 'everywhere,' was interwoven with everything else, and in no sense constitute[d] a separate 'sphere' of its own" (Taylor, 2007: 2). As such, one understanding of secularity is in terms of public space: in a secular age or society, religion is absent from the public space.

This perception of secularism is closely interconnected with modernity and all the concepts that come with it, including rationality. In a secular society, according to Taylor,

> the norms and principles we follow, the deliberations we engage in, generally don't refer us to God or to any religious beliefs; the considerations we act on are internal to the "rationality" of each sphere—maximum gain within the economy, the greatest benefit to the greatest number in the political area, and so on. (Taylor, 2007: 2)

The absence of religion from the public space signifies the *first* meaning of secularity, as Taylor puts it. He identifies a *second* meaning for secularity which is "the falling off of religious belief and practice, in

people turning away from God, and no longer going to Church" (Taylor, 2007: 2). In this sense, Taylor believes that among Western European countries "even those who retain the vestigial public reference to God in public space" have become mainly secular.

Taylor provides a *third* meaning of secularity in which people experience a kind of belief or commitment, religious or spiritual, which is considered "one option among others, and frequently not the easiest to embrace" (Taylor, 2007: 3). This third meaning of secularity opens up options for religious belief even in an age in which there are restrictions for the kind of encounter you have with God in the public space; belief in God is no longer axiomatic, and the hallmark of this secularity is providing alternatives to remain religious, nonetheless.

According to Taylor, all the three modes of secularity he describes make reference to "religion":

> As that which is re-treating in public space (1), or as a type of belief and practice which is or is not in regression (2), and as a certain kind of belief or commitment whose conditions in this age are being examined (3). (Taylor, 2007: 15)

However, he proceeds to claim that the coming of modern secularity "has been coterminous with the rise of a society in which for the first time in history a purely self-sufficient humanism came to be a widely available option" (Taylor, 2007: 18). And by humanism, he means one that accepts "no final goals beyond human flourishing, nor any allegiance to anything else beyond this flourishing." Out of the three modes of secularism that Taylor identifies, he maintains that the third secularity is one which comes along "with the possibility of exclusive humanism, which thus for the first time widened the range of possible options, ending the era of 'naïve' religious faith" (Taylor, 2007: 19).

As we can see in Taylor's third meaning of secularity, a sense of spiritual quest and individuality is attached to it. We may find some affinities between this meaning of secularity and what emerged in the Alamūt period of the Ismaili history during the *qiyāmat*. This perception is further strengthened during the time of Aga Khan III. This is a point that Ruthven touches upon when studying the teachings of Aga Khan III: "To his followers the Aga Khan preached the essentially secular humanist doctrine that humans find their destiny in the here-and-now, rather than the hereafter" (Ruthven, in Clarke, 1998: 382). Reiterating a point from Boivin, he concludes that "there are echoes of the Grand Resurrection, with the here and now becoming the fundamental dimension of existence

and the hereafter relegated to the background" (Ruthven, in Clarke, 1998: 382).

In this sense, one might claim that this process of secularity had started in the Ismaili Community long before the coming of the modern age, but again such a claim has to be made with great caution as during the Alamūt period, after it, and even during the time of Aga Khan III, an Ismaili's "encounter with God" was never absent in any sphere of life. As I shall explain in later chapters on the AKDN, even in the most "secular" activities of the AKDN, there is an ethical dimension that connects it in one way or another to the divine and the sacred. This connection may be mild and not too thick or ideological, but it is certainly there; it has not retreated to a private sphere.

There is, however, another dimension to our understanding of secularism that Taylor has described in a public lecture in the University of Westminster in 2010. In his lecture, Taylor introduced two types of secularism. The *first* type is the one that bears the three meanings that he covers in *A Secular Age*. He speaks of a "secular regime" as one whose focus of attention is on the position it takes toward religion, its presence or participation in the public sphere and in politics and seeks to restrict this presence and participation (see also Taylor, 2004: 93). The mottos of this approach to secularism can be summarized in (a) the separation of church from state; (b) the impartiality or neutrality of state (in the issue of religion); and (c) the distinction between the private and public spheres (as it regards religion to belong to the private sphere, not the public sphere).

Taylor argues that the interpretation of the separation of church and state as the separation of religion from politics is a sloppy application of the original idea.

In the *second* type of secularism that Taylor provides, the focus is not on a position toward the role of religion in society; it is rather concentrated on the issue of diversity and pluralism, and it is concerned with the fair management of this diversity. As such, this second approach to secularism is concerned about the management of multiculturalism. The second type of secularism seeks to establish these three goals: (a) freedom of belief or conscience; (b) basic equality of people in society, be they religious or non-religious; and (c) ensuring that people's different voices are heard equally (thus highlighting the importance of listening to minorities).

Taylor believes that this second type of secularism can be summarized in these three mottos: liberty, equality, and fraternity.[7]

As we can see above, there are some affinities between Taylor's third meaning of secularism and the second type that he introduces, as it embraces pluralism and multiculturalism, but his second type opens up the space for religion in an increasingly secular society, allowing for all voices to be heard equally. As such, it is a response to a kind of prejudice which disenfranchises religious people and discriminates against them in the name of secularism.

Apart from the philosophical and theoretical articulations described above, the terms "secularism" and "secular" themselves have come to find somewhat derogatory meanings in Muslim countries. The term "secular" is sometimes used to denote someone who has no religion—used as opposed to religion—and someone who has no moral or ethical values. This is clearly not the definition we are concerned with. It does not apply to the Ismaili Community either, because there is a very strong sense of ethical commitment in the Ismaili Community. For the Ismaili imamate, secularity is not tantamount to abandoning ethical or religious values.

This overview sheds some light on how we can possibly consider the Ismaili Community and the Ismaili imamate as secular. There are certainly elements that may fit well with one meaning of secularity, but they are not necessarily peculiar to the Ismailis, and such trends may also be found among other Muslim communities.

In a sense, we are facing similar problems in the case of the Ismaili imamate and the AKDN in terms of its being secular, as well as a model to which Weberian ideal types could be applied. The Ismaili imamate falls somewhere in between, but does not go to extreme ends: it is a religious institution, but there are increasingly some elements in it that have a secular tone—in at least one of the meanings that Taylor has in mind. It is likewise very close to the Weberian ideal types, which explains why so many people have actually drawn on Weber to make sense of it, but there are still elements of it that makes this applicability problematic or, as I explain below, paradoxical.

The AKDN and the Ismaili Imamate: A Weberian Paradox

The features that I have so far covered delineating the Weberian model are closely interconnected with how they will be used in the case study of the AKDN for the assessment of this model and suggesting an alternative model that does not suffer from the chronic problems of the Weberian system.

The AKDN and the Ismaili imamate are prone to be uncritically assessed in this theoretical effort for various reasons, while the Weberian methodology certainly sheds light on some aspects of its development. The main and overarching point that has to be made at the outset and as a form of methodological statement is that the AKDN and the Ismaili imamate seem to be the institutions most likely to be compatible with Weberian models. The paradoxical nature of this assumption only reveals itself when we go into further details of the Ismaili imamate and the AKDN and place them in the appropriate context of their development in history.

In a very general and sweeping assessment, the Ismaili imamate bears elements of tradition, with a hereditary leader whose authority is deeply rooted in the past. It also bears a form of charismatic element: the followers of the Ismaili faith view their Imam with such love, affection, dedication, and submission that it is very difficult to reconcile this particular form of charisma with other aspects of his leadership. It is also highly bureaucratic, and there is a huge network of institutions and organizations that operate on a basis for which we cannot find any other appropriate description than rational-bureaucracy.

The particularly unique or rare, to say the least, approach of the present Ismaili Imam to earthly life and the balance between the faith and the world may also seem to be strikingly similar to the Weberian description of the Protestant ethics (Ruthven, in Clark, 1998: 391–92), but in fact the numerous nuances, which are part of the Ismaili imamate's interpretation of faith, are so radically different that it does not allow for simple, formal comparisons. The case of the Ismaili imamate may also to some degree be explained by Dabashi's idea of the perpetuation of charisma in the case of Shi'ism, and it can better be seen in the postcolonial context of the Ismaili Community.

The most significant elements that make the Ismaili imamate an appropriate example for our work follow below, not in any order.[8]

1. In the Ismaili imamate, blood lineage is important: the imamate, the position of authority, is hereditary, and every Imam is chosen by the sole authority and decision of the previous Imam from among one of his male descendants. Here there is a solution to the succession problem, although it is not completely resolved, but the solution lies in the fact that as death approaches, there is nothing to threaten this institution as the next Imam is appointed using the unfettered choice of the previous Imam

with the hereditary condition. However, this fact alone does not preclude the occurrence of disputes over succession.

2. Building on the earlier point, there is a lesser chance of the charisma losing its vigor when the previous Imam passes because this charisma finds its embodiment in the new Imam. The Ismaili Community is built around the idea of a present living Imam, and the term they use for every Imam of the Time (*Ḥāḍir Imām*) reflects this theological doctrine.[9] Therefore, the continuity of the imamate is an essential tenet for the Ismailis. Yet, we have charisma having different expressions in different Imams. In this regard, one can compare Aga Khan III and Aga Khan IV.

3. There is a system of revenue-raising: the Ismaili Community contributes to the running of the affairs of the community through its voluntary donations, which is historically part of a Muslim culture of service to the community, and it has come under the rubric of concepts such as *zakāt*.

4. There is a strong sense of the transcendent: this world is not identical with a higher world, but this is not a straightforward "religious" belief, as we see a strong sense of interdependence between this world and the other world (as seen in the Aga Khan's exposition of *dīn* and *dunyā*, the faith and the world). A careless outsider view might simply see the Ismaili Community very secular and the Ismaili imamate to have become increasingly secular, while this is far from the reality of this institution.[10]

5. There is a quality to the Ismaili imamate's institutions that resembles the ideals of a semi-democratic system in it, partly because the community is made of highly educated and successful members and above all as a result of the non-state formation of the Community. It is true that the imamate itself is an unelected authority and democratic rules do not apply to it, but it can still function with a democratic sense attached to it. This quality is more clearly displayed in the appointments that are made to the leadership of the community where you have a rotation of power, and the entire institutions are designed in such a way that they bear a clearly democratic quality.

6. The Ismaili imamate is acutely aware of the complexity of the world. Institutions and leaders are not overburdened in the AKDN. This is best explained in the wide array of leaders who serve in various voluntary positions in running the affairs of the community.

7. There is an interconnection and interdependence between the leader and the led in the Community—which is very well a charismatic community (*gemeinde*) in a Weberian sense.[11] The simplest form of it is embodied in the oath of allegiance or the *bay'a*, which is a voluntary but binding act. Nonetheless, the individual's choice is respected in this relation between the leader and the led.

8. The Ismaili imamate is very media savvy. It is true that for historical reasons the Ismaili imamate has been cautious of media publicity, but the bulk of images, interviews, public speeches, and appearances of the Ismaili imamate gives it a highly media-savvy dimension. The phenomenon of the Jubilees, which are the celebrations of the Ismaili imamate on the 25th and 50th anniversaries of the imamate, in the case of the present Aga Khan, is one of the examples of its media dimension.

9. There is a strong commitment to the welfare of the community and humanity at large, which can be seen as a sort of solidarity between people. This strong commitment to the welfare of people has a common phrase in the language of the Aga Khan: improving the quality of life.

10. There is a kaleidoscopic quality to the Ismaili imamate: the Imam takes on various roles at the same time. He is the spiritual leader of the community, the chairman of the board of the IIS, the chairman of many other agencies within the AKDN, which deal with various areas of life such as education, health, architecture, economy, civil society, humanitarian relief, etc. The Ismaili imamate has the resilience and flexibility to function in different situations with high standards.

11. The Ismaili Imamate gives a Constitution to its community that works as a unifying legal framework—a semi-rational-legal framework in conformity with modernity—bringing under one umbrella all the scattered Ismaili communities around the globe. The Shia Imami Ismaili Constitution (as reads the title of the document) is not just a set of rules and regulations with detailed measures as to how the community institutions should function; it is also something like a contract, but in a stronger sense than a contract: it is a *covenant* that regulates the relations between the leader and the led. This document is, however, the product of human efforts, and it is not any divine revelation. It is not carved in stone, and since the beginning of the twentieth century, when its most primitive copies were prepared, it has undergone many changes.

12. The Ismaili imamate has been decoupled from both nation and state. As such we neither have an Ismaili state nor an Ismaili nation. There are territories defined in the Ismaili constitution with the same nation-state divisions of the political systems of the world, but such divisions do not divide the Ismailis. The Ismaili imamate is a form of authority that is no longer tied to the territorial state or empire.

13. The language used by the Ismaili imamate is not one with polemic divisions or theological biases. In a world where religious authority is often marked by its theological or polemical positions, the Ismaili imamate has moved beyond polemics or narrow-minded theological divisions and instead presents a humanistic-developmental quality in its authority.

14. The expansion of the institutions and the way this authority has developed gives the Ismaili imamate the ability to cultivate other Aga Khans. So, faced with the question of what will come in the next generations, this institution of authority can now be more confident in the sustainability of its institutions, even though it does not completely obviate the possibility of future schisms

15. The Ismaili imamate cultivates leaders: it produces leaders from inside the community. The leadership and authority of the Imam does not stand in sharp contradiction with the authority of other leaders who can undertake work in the community. The community institutions of the Ismaili *Jamā'at* are examples of this tradition of cultivating leaders.

16. The Ismaili imamate has transformed itself from a personalized and individual authority to the "office of the imamate." Now, more than any time in the history of the Ismaili imamate, the authority of the Imam is increasingly embodied in the institutions that he has created rather than being concentrated in his own person. The office of the imamate is the personification of the authority. This institutionalization, in effect, leads to the routinization of charisma (as Ruthven argues in the case of Aga Khan III).

The Legacy of an "Office" and Its Future

To use a biological simile, whether it is a genetic modification or a mutation that has happened in the course of this evolution, the institution of the Ismaili imamate is now different in form and in content from what it was a hundred years ago. Yet, it is still defining itself with a Shi'i Muslim

identity that sets itself within ethical frameworks of a distinctively Shi'i tradition.

The chapters which follow undertake to give a detailed and more critical examination of what has been briefly discussed here. This opening chapter acts as a kind of road map for this book, and the rest of this work rolls out in further detail on what has been touched upon here.

The AKDN and the institutions of the Ismaili imamate provide us with a valuable example to test the hitherto generally accepted theories about authority and explore the possibility of proposing other models that are more conducive to formulating better theories capable of responding to the needs of our times. Considering the paradigm shift, which is represented in this institution in contemporary times, some deeper philosophical questions are also posed as to what will be the fate of this institution and how this legacy will be continued.

The bigger question lies in the sustainability of this form of authority, which has transcended the person of the Imam into the office of the imamate. The imamate is now exercising its authority in multiple ways through its network of institutions. The way the Ismaili imamate is represented in its community institutions and the manner in which its development organizations function suggest that there is an interconnected vision in all of them. This vision is now seen in the institutions rather than in what a particular individual Imam decides for the community.

The paradoxical aspect of this transcendence or transmutation is that the Ismaili doctrines and the very text of the Ismaili Constitution do give the Imam (or the imamate) the unfettered choice to decide about the worldly and religious affairs of his followers. As such, the final decision always rests in the hands of the Imam himself who may choose to go down a different path than that which his ancestors have gone. There is historical precedent for this that one Imam goes in a totally different direction than his predecessor, and the Ismaili history is full of such examples.

The fact that it is difficult to make a distinction between the person of the Imam and his symbolic presence had become clear even during the time of Aga Khan III, as Ruthven describes it:

> The this-worldly thrust of Aga Khan III's teachings is also implicit from the style of his discourse. Although the Imam was sometimes presented as being symbolically distinct from the person of the Aga Khan, there appeared to be no distinction in practice between his religious and secular statements. (Ruthven, in Clarke, 1998: 348)

Ruthven also highlights the charismatic quality of Aga Khan III and argues that by introducing constitutions, which by extension meant the setting up of institutions, "into what had been an unfettered spiritual autocracy, he was in a sense responsible for 'routinizing' this charisma himself" (Ruthven, in Clarke, 1998: 391). He then explains that as a result of this shift,

> his successor inherited not only a spiritual office, but a functioning institution oriented towards secular goals; the improvement of the health, welfare and education of the Isma'ilis and their adjacent communities. The age-old Isma'ili project of the universal *da'wa*—"the call" to Islam and the Imam—having long been suspended, the movement's evangelical thrust found a new outlet in twentieth century humanitarianism. (Ruthven, in Clarke, 1998: 392)

The doctrinal and theological solution for this contradiction was that it is the Imam who is the center of truth and the ultimate source of distinguishing what is right and what is wrong in any given age. However, given the expansion of the Ismaili imamate institutions, one cannot say with certainty whether at any given point in the future any single Imam might be able to arbitrarily and with reference to his endowed traditional authority, undo whatever has been achieved by his predecessors.[12] As such, these institutional developments and the transcendence of the person of the Imam into the office of the imamate may suggest something more than a mere accident or a contingent matter; it may be something of an irreversible move, for which there is, of course, explanation and rational justifications.

As such, the Ismaili imamate in our times is indeed engendering a model of leadership to be sustained and it is in fact a legacy that is for continuation rather than disruption. This development can be in part explained by the increasing stability of the community, which was, in a not too distant past, constantly threatened by various forces to the extent of complete elimination.

CHAPTER 2

Imamate and the Question of Authority in the Muslim and Shi'i Contexts

The question of authority is a key question and indeed the key to many of the problems that the Muslim world is grappling with today. Understanding authority in this context is not an easy task. The issue becomes further complicated when theories that have been articulated in a different political imaginative context are used and applied to explain the situation. To this, one must add the predominant perceptions, which are not only promoted heavily by the media, but are also part of the knowledge production, that prevails in the European and even non-European academic thinking.

Before going into specific issues and questions of authority among Muslims, it is important to see the context in which modern scholarship on these issues has developed. This is particularly imperative because without having this context in mind, we will fail to see the complexities involving a critical study of the Muslim world. Part of this context is political. This political context has often shaped how Muslims are portrayed in the public consciousness and in the media. The following sections precede the parts that deal with the historical backgrounds of the issue.

Problematizing the Muslim World: Construction of a New Other

Recent events in the world have thrown the Muslim world to the forefront of heated debates regarding the way in which Muslims relate to the modern world. Issues of the relationship between "Islam and democracy,"

"Islam and human rights," gender issues, and a wide range of dominant themes have cast their shadow on the bulk of academic writings. These concepts are, of course, relatively new.

Prior to the 1979 revolution in Iran, the range of issues that were highlighted regarding the Muslim world differed. Following the end of the Cold War and the West's urgent need for creating a new "other," Islam was pushed once again to the forefront of the international concern. It is not new to view the Muslim "East" on such terms: the East-West binary (itself a problematic construct) has its origins in Eurocentric discourses. And polemical discourses of even the Middle Ages presents us with this polarized view of the long wars between the "Saracens" and the Christians[1] (Karim, 2000: 1–3).

However, with the end of the Cold War resulting in a "threat vacuum," this polarizing and monolith-constructing machine gained momentum and "faced with the loss of their *raison d'être*, some of the military and intelligence gathering establishments began searching for new enemies" (Karim, 2000: 3), and it is in this context that a number of ideologies began representing Islam as the new Other.

Re-interpreting the Muslim World

However, this question has not remained only within the context of a Eurocentric approach to the Muslim world. It has also left its impression on the Muslim communities and countries as well. There is already a lot of debate going on about the compatibility of Islam and democracy, whereas there are many unexplored areas that are equally important and can even shed light on some of the ambiguous issues that seem to be puzzling in the way Muslims have approached or dealt with democracy. The question is if there is at all any other way of approaching the Muslim world? As it was mentioned earlier in chapter 1, referring to Bayat (2007), moving from homogenizing the Muslim world and giving due weight to the agency of a diversity of Muslim societies overcomes this issue to some extent.

Bayat's exposition mainly dealt with the issue of democracy. However, there are other issues that deserve a more critical assessment in this regard. I suggest bringing a new dimension to the issue of leadership/authority that can play a key role in responding to the questions with which the Muslim world is now grappling. These debates started much earlier by a generation of Muslims like Jamāl al-Dān al-Afghānī in the late nineteenth century and a number of other Muslim thinkers, followed up by the efforts of Muhammad Iqbal in *The Reconstruction of Religious*

Thought in Islam (1934). However, to this date, there are few scholars who have focused on the issue of authority per se (the exceptions being scholars like Madelung, Dabashi, Watt, and Amir Arjomand), although all of these debates are in one way or another principally debates on authority: they all deal with the issue of interpreting faith, and it is closely connected with authority.

In order to better grasp the gravity of the issue in question, one can read the following paragraphs from Mohammed Arkoun on the issue of authority and power (italics are mine), which corroborate my line of research:

> Islam as a religious experience and an historical force...still remains a prisoner in the anthropological triangle traced by **Violence**, **Sacred**, **Truth** (*dīn al-ḥaqq*). This theological statement is reinforced by *sociologists and political scientists who focus their interest on the fundamentalist expressions of political Islam, neglecting or undermining other expressions less visible, often silenced, but significant in the present context. While political scientists provide a wider audience for an arbitrary selected manifestation of what is presented globally as "Islam," they do not offer any positive intellectual contribution to enhance the interpretation of the religious phenomenon and its functions in all contemporary societies...It is vital to show that contemporary sociological and political Islam ignores and dismantles what classical Islamic schools of thought have achieved and bequeathed concerning authority and power.* Consequently, the so-called "*ulamā*," who claim to be the reliable spiritual authorities for contemporary believers, are unable—even in terms of classical *ijtihād* and *taqlīd*—to point to the intrinsic limitations of the whole legacy on the subject we are examining here. (Arkoun, 2002: 206–07)

Historical Background

As it was briefly explained in the Introduction, the question of authority in Shi'i contexts is significantly different from its wider Sunnī Muslim context as it refers predominantly to the question of the legitimacy of the Shi'i Imams.

For Sunnī Muslims, after the death of Prophet Muḥammad, there is no continuation of prophetic authority. The general area of dispute after the death of the Prophet was over his succession and the question of who should lead the Muslim community after him. One of the problems about studying the roots of the Shi'i-Sunnī schism lies in the "orthodoxy-heterodoxy" dichotomies, for which mainly Muslim heresiographers were responsible (Dabashi, 1989: 71–72). These false dichotomies are polemical terms, rather than hermeneutical and help little for understanding the complexities of the Muslim community.

The daily life of Muslims was very much determined by the Qur'ān and the *sunna* of the Prophet during his life time. As Dabashi points out, contrary to Weberian characterization, Muḥammad himself was the "ultimate source of authority, as the messenger of Allah" (Dabashi, 1998: 73). The particular social relationships after the migration of the Prophet to Medina necessitated the presence of charismatic personal qualities, and the death of the Prophet posed serious challenges to a community that relied on the charisma of the Prophet. The immediate reaction to this appears in the issue of the succession.

Shi'i Muslims, unlike the Sunnīs, believed in the continuation of the authority, which rested in the Prophet, even though they did not claim the same position as a messenger of Allah for their Imams through 'Alī. The earliest roots of the dispute were found in the event of Ghadīr-i Khumm, to which I have referred earlier, but theological articulations of it did not happen until a much later time.

After the death of 'Alī, his two sons by Fāṭima became "the focus of devotion for those who supported the claim of the House of the Prophet to leadership of the Muslim community." And, "after the death of these two, the son of Ḥusayn, 'Alī Zayn al-'Ābidīn, came to be recognized by most of the community as the head of the Prophet's House" (Modarresi, 1993: 5).

With the issue of succession, the common belief among the Imāmiyya—and the Ismailis—was that "each Imam designated his successor from among his male descendants through testament (*waṣiyya*), sometimes also called explicit designation (*naṣṣ*)" (Modarresi, 1993: 5), as we see it articulated in exactly the same terms in the Ismaili Constitution today.

The question of the role of the Imam and his function seems to have been established from very early on in Shi'i doctrines, but Modarresi puts it in a larger framework:

> Islamic legal and theological works describe the office of imāmate as the supreme leadership over the affairs of religion (*dīn*) and mundane life (*dunyā*). The *imām* was, thus, the head of the Muslim community, the successor to the Prophet, and the guardian of all Muslim religious and social affairs. (Modarresi, 1993: 6)

This articulation obviously had political implications too, to the extent that

> the Shī'ites believed that when the time came, the true Imam would take up arms, expel the usurpers, and regain his proper place. Many Shī'ites

hoped that when this occurred, they would be the reigning party and would finally be free from the persecution they had so long endured. (Modarresi, 1993: 6)

What further strengthened this position was that already by the late first to the early eighth century, it was well established in the Muslim community that at some point in the future, someone from the House of the Prophet would rise in a revolution to overthrow the usurpers and establish the rule of justice and truth (Modarresi, 1993: 6). This figure was known among the Shiʿites to be the *qāʾim* who became not only the center point of Imāmī doctrine before and after the occultation of the twelfth Imam, but also an essential ingredient of Ismaili theology in at least two significant junctures in their history: (a) with the establishment of the Fatimid state; and (b) with the proclamation of the *qiyāmat* by Ḥasan II (which, of course, had a more esoteric dimension to it and its political aspect was somewhat different).

Politicization of the Imamate: Competing Narratives

Some of the scholarly narratives, which give a particularly political drive to the imamate, are somewhat under the influence of political events of modern times in countries that have a Shiʿi base for their political movements, but as Amir-Moezzi notes:

> There is neglect of the fact that the politicization of Imamism, even if it has its roots in the theological-juridical-rational tradition, is the result of a long doctrinal and historical process lasting several centuries, a process that did not begin to concretize until the sixteenth century and the declaration of Imamism as the state religion in Iran by the Safavids. (Amir-Moezzi, 1994: 61–62)

Amir-Moezzi finds "methodological incoherencies" in such articulations that reduced "the historical existence of the imams to the theological and political roles that they played" (Amir-Moezzi, 1994: 62). He then divides the political life of Shiʿi Imams (and his focus is on the Imāmiyya) into four categories:

> a) Those who were directly and positively involved with politics; b) those to whom no political activity has been attributed; c) the particular case of the third imam, al-Ḥusayn b. ʿAlī; and d) the particular case of the twelfth imam, the Mahdī. (Amir-Moezzi, 1994: 62)

In the first category, we have the case of ʿAlī and his son Ḥasan. In the case of ʿAlī, his "caliphate began in one of the most troubled periods in the early history of the Muslim community. His two predecessors had met with violent deaths, and the ephemeral coalition that brought him to power was a quite heterogeneous group" (Amir-Moezzi, 1994: 63), to which I will presently come back in the section of caliphate below. At this time, Amir-Moezzi notes that

> The ascetic spirit of ʿAlī and some of his companions like ʿAmmār b. Yāsir, Abū Dharr al-Ghifārī, Ḥudhayfa, and others, with the religious politics of the Prophet as a model, clashed violently with the new Umayyad aristocracy formed in a society that was beginning to taste the advantages of riches and urbanization. (Amir-Moezzi, 1994: 63)

The political engagements of Ḥasan b. ʿAlī led to his abdication from power under certain conditions: "that the Umayyad religious authorities cease their public cursing of ʿAlī, that Muʿāwiya abstain from mistreating the Shiʿites, and that al-Ḥasan be given a subvention from the public treasury," and Amir-Moezzi notes that "none of these conditions was either particularly political or very demanding (receiving a subvention from the public treasury was a legitimate right of any Muslim, and especially of a close relative of the Prophet)" (Amir-Moezzi, 1994: 63).

On the case of Ḥusayn b. ʿAlī and his murder in Karbalā (in AH 61/AD 680), Amir-Moezzi warns that "great methodological care must be taken in a truly objective study of the historical circumstances that led to the tragedy at Karbalā" (Amir-Moezzi, 1994: 64), but despite all nuances and various interpretations that can put the event in a more historical context,[2] the tragedy turned into a driving force for the Shiʿi communities of later centuries in which mythology and revolutionary ideas were combined.

This overtly political scenario, however, underwent a number of shifts, among both the Imāmiyya and the Ismailis. The earliest expressions of these shifts were during the imamate of ʿAlī Zayn al-ʿĀbidīn, his son Muḥammad al-Bāqir, and his grandson Jaʿfar al-Ṣādiq. In the wider political momentum, which was present during the Umayyad period and the early years of the establishment of the ʿAbbāsid rule, some groups had political expectations from the Imam, while others only "viewed him as the most learned man from among the descendants of the Prophet who was to teach people what was lawful and what was not and to exhort them to turn toward God" (Modarresi, 1993: 8). But for those who had a political aspiration attached to the imamate, Jaʿfar al-Ṣādiq's failure to

assume a political position "resulted in a major reconsideration of the institution of imamate" (Modarresi, 1993: 8). With the occultation of the twelfth Imam of the Imāmiyya, we have both ends of the extremes, from a radically apolitical position of the Shiʿites to overtly political messianic movements, which emerged at later stages among them; to avoid digressions, I have to focus back on the Ismailis. Later developments of such movements are studied by Amir Arjomand (1984).

These early political shifts gradually led to the articulation and formulation of the theological doctrines about the imamate itself to which Jaʿfar al-Ṣādiq himself contributed greatly and it is a common theme among both Ismailis and the Imāmīs that most of the constituent traditions on the qualities and the role of the Imam are attributed to him.

Traditions: Shiʿi and Sunnī Perspectives

There is a common area between the Shiʿites and the Sunnīs in that they both regard the Qurʾān and the tradition to be the authority to which Muslims should refer, but there are significant differences between how the Sunnīs and the Shiʿa understand this.

First, by tradition, we mean terms such as *sunna*, *ḥadīth*, *khabar*, *athar*, and *riwāya* (all of which can be roughly translated as tradition, but must not be confused with how tradition itself is understood in English). Second, as Amir-Moezzi points out, 'According to the early writings of the imams, the Qurʾān and the *ḥadīth* (i.e., the prophetic traditions reported by the imams as well as the traditions of the imams themselves) constitute the only two authorities, absolute and complementary, to which the faithful should refer for all matters regarding their religion" (Amir-Moezzi, 1994: 23).

The significant difference here is that for the Shiʿites—the Imāmīs and the Ismailis alike—tradition is founded on the words of the Imams, and the entire Imāmī doctrine revolves around Imamology, to the extent that a famous *ḥadīth* "warns against the danger of perdition for those who do not know their Divine Guide: 'He who dies without an Imam [or "without having known his Imam"] dies the death of "ignorant pagans"'" (Amir-Moezzi, 1994: 123). Here is the fault line that clearly distinguishes the Imāmīs and the Ismailis from the rest of the Muslim community. As Amir-Moezzi suggests, "contradicting the Sunni tradition appears to constitute another criterion for the degree of credibility of the traditions that the imams alluded to" (Amir-Moezzi, 1994: 25), which indicates that from early on, the Shiʿi imamate with the central figure of Jaʿfar al-Ṣādiq had chosen a different path. He then quotes

passages from a dialogue between Ja'far al-Ṣādiq and one of his disciples, which clearly delineates this approach:

> Choose the tradition that is in accord with the Qur'ān and the Sunna, and not in accord with the "mass" [al-'āmma, i.e., the Sunnites; the Shī'ites are referred to as the "elite," al-khāṣṣā], and leave aside the one that is not in accord with the Qur'ān and the Sunna, and which the "mass" agrees with (meaning, the Sunnites run counter to the Qur'ān and the Sunna)...The right direction is found in the tradition that contradicts the "mass" (wa ma khalafa al-'āmma fa-fihi al-rashād). (Amir-Moezzi, 1994: 25)

Therefore, giving primacy to the authority of the Imam is indeed pushing into the shadows other criteria like "chains of transmission, authority, or even the formal expression of the tradition (matn)" (Amir-Moezzi, 1994: 26).

The period culminating at the time of Ja'far al-Ṣādiq, which was a politically turbulent time, also witnessed the extensive documentation and writing of Shi'i doctrines, with Ja'far al-Ṣādiq urging his followers to write and communicate their knowledge:

> Ja'far's alarmist tone exhorting the faithful to put traditions into writing is evidence of the unrest fomented by these violent tensions: "Write [our traditions] and communicate your knowledge to your brothers [the Imamites]; at the time of your death, leave your books to your sons, for the time of calamities (zamān harj) will fall upon those men who have no other companions but their books. (Amir-Moezzi, 1994: 27)

The absolute doctrinal necessity of the Imam is central to Shi'i theology, as opposed to the Sunni position that finds no need for an Imam in the sense that Shi'i Muslims understand it.

The Shi'i Imamology among the Imāmiyya is articulated differently than what we see among the Ismailis, particularly after the occultation of the twelfth Imam. In the case of the Ismailis, in some branches like the Must'alawīs, the concept of an Imam in occultation returns very much like the Imāmīyya, but for the Nizārī Ismailis, the presence and accessibility of the Imam and his authority is essential, and it is articulated differently. Another major difference between the Ismailis and the Imāmiyya is that theological doctrines were articulated in the presence of the Imam himself, while in the case of the latter, it was consolidated after the occultation. Each of these theologies had their own political implications that were all connected to the issue of succession after the Prophet, which led to the establishment of the early caliphate.

Caliphate or Monarchy: What Was the Prophet's Form of Governance?

The Muslim world was very much "political" in a very broad sense. And this "political scheme" reportedly started during the lifetime of the founder of Islam, Prophet Muḥammad. The events following his death resulted in a very stormy and complex setting in which Muslims were to decide about who would be the successor to the Prophet, in other words who should have the "authority" and "leadership" after the Prophet (a quintessential political issue: who gets what, when and how?).

The first four Caliphs were part of this stormy and bloody atmosphere, and the events surrounding the death of the Prophet proved that monarchy (or for that matter any other form of governance) was not an essential part of Muslim history, and there seemed to be an agreement that no one would support it.[3]

If we look at the early Muslim history, in the Arabia of the time of the Prophet of Islam, there was neither any monarchy in place nor was there any form of political establishment to encourage it. ʿAlī ʿAbd al-Rāziq, the Egyptian scholar, wrote a book, which was first published in 1925, exploring the issue of caliphate in Islam.[4] His main proposal was that the Muslims could agree on any form of government, and that establishing a political order was not a necessary part of the Prophet's mission.

In his book, ʿAbd al-Rāziq proposes that the caliphate, which developed later as a result of the consultation process that happened following the death of the Prophet, later on led to the establishment of a form of monarchy, or pseudo-monarchy that was totally alien to Islamic teachings (ʿAbd al-Rāziq, 2000: 48).

This point is also noted by Amir Arjomand:

> Faced with the problem of administering a vast conquered empire, the Umayyads (661–750) increasingly concentrated their efforts on the political aspects of leadership at the expense of the religious ones, and were accused of "secularizing" the hitherto theocratic Islamic government, of turning the caliphate into kingship (*mulk*). (Amir Arjomand, 1984: 33)

The basis of this criticism of the Ummayads was how they had separated their temporal rule from religious dimensions that gave legitimacy to it. This was not the case for the Imāmīs. For them,

> there was no explicit recognition of the separation of temporal and religious authority, and, *de jure*, the Imam was considered the supreme political and

religious leader of the community. However, *de facto*, the conception of imamate was drastically depoliticized. (Amir Arjomand, 1984: 34)

ʿAbd al-Rāziq's main arguments start with the sources of authority for the rulers of the Muslim community, and he examines the two competing theories on authority: one in which the caliph derives his authority from God and the other in which the caliph derives his authority and power from the community only. He concludes that Muslims do not need this caliphate either for their worldly affairs or for their religious affairs and even goes further to claim that this caliphate has always been harmful to Islam and Muslims and the source of evil and corruption (al-Hamidi, 1991: 76).[5] He then claims that he could not find any clear evidence concerning the form of the prophet's government (al-Hamidi, 1991: 77).

ʿAbd al-Rāziq's approach to the issue in the early twentieth century can give us a flavor of the nature of debates that have been going on in the Muslim world for centuries. However, later developments both in terms of new scholarship and massive political sea changes, particularly in the late twentieth and early twenty-first centuries give us a different perspective now.

Monarchy in Shiʿi Context: The Problem of Legitimacy

The particular case of Persian Muslims' engagement with politics in medieval times, especially after the establishment of the Safavid state when Shiʿism became the official religion of the state, reflects some interconnections between monarchy and the legitimacy of the ruler. This is influenced by pre-Islamic Persian cosmologies regarding kingship or monarchy, which maintained that the king is endowed with a divine gift of *farrah*. This pre-Islamic cosmological perception is reiterated in the great poetical masterpiece of Firdawsī, the *Shāhnāmah* (Book of the Kings).

At the time of the Arab conquest of Persia, the Sassanian kings were assumed to have divine charisma, which reflected the influence of Aryan theories of kingship (Amir Arjomand, 1984: 90).[6]

However, Amir Arjomand notes that "the definitive separation of religious authority from the political during the formative period of the development of Imāmī Shiʿism entailed the secularization of kingship" (Amir Arjomand, 1984: 89). Yet, we can see the return of the idea of this divine gift for kings, after the establishment of the Safavid state,

and it lasted until the last dynasty of kings in Iran—during the Pahlavi era—was ousted following the 1979 revolution. Even though Shiʿi clerics were closely affiliated with the Safavid rulers and lent them some degree of legitimacy,[7] their kingship was still considered to be restricted to temporal sphere:

> Doctrinal indifference to the principles of legitimacy of temporal rule— which was thus relegated to the realm of the profane, "the world"— amounted to granting autonomy to pre-Islamic theory of sacral kingship and at the same time restricting its relevance to the temporal sphere. (Amir Arjomand, 1984: 89)

The Ismailis and Temporal Rule

Issues of legitimacy and authority for temporal rule have had a different fate among the Ismailis, in contrast with that of the Imāmiyya mainly due to the accessibility of the Ismaili Imams, with the exception of periods of concealment in which the $dāʿīs$ still claimed connection with the Imams. Therefore, whenever Ismaili Imams had political power, as in the case of the Fatimids and during the Alamūt period, the legitimacy of their rule was closely connected with their authority as Shiʿi Ismaili Imams.

There have been instances after the fall of Alamūt when some Ismaili Imams were assigned to positions of governorship, but in all those cases, this position was never based on their authority as Shiʿi Imams; they were simply ruling on behalf of the sovereign power of their own time. Discussions about the legitimacy of these rulers, on whose behalf the Ismaili Imams sometimes ruled, does not seem to be reflected in any Ismaili document; so we have no such example like the case of ʿAlī al-Riḍā (the eighth Imam of the Imāmiyya) who was named as a successor to the ʿAbbāsid caliph al-Maʿmūn.

The Ismaili Community became increasingly apolitical in the post-Alamūt period moving into the modern period. The involvement of the Aga Khan family, after the time of Aga Khan III, in international service, does not bear any claims to political positions based on territorial states or even any form of grand messianic movement. So, in general, one can see similar shifts like the ones that occurred during the formative period of Shiʿism to have occurred in the history of the Ismaili Community, currently placing the Ismaili Communities around the globe, and the office of the Ismaili imamate, in a position of political neutrality.

Authority and Leadership: Etymology and Issues of Translation

In Chapter 2 of his *Authority and Reason*, Carl Friedrich gives a rather long paragraph on the etymology of the term "authority," which is to some extent useful in understanding authority in a Western context. However, it requires further clarifications to see how this works in the case of the Ismaili imamate. Friedrich gives an account of the etymology of the term "authority" in English:

> It is obviously a Roman term. What were the historical phenomena to which *auctoritas* refers? There has been some learned controversy over the answer to this question. According to the great Mommsen, *auctoritas* is not readily definable in its original meaning. He thought that it had predominantly a sense related to a verb from which it is derived, *augere*, to augment, to enlarge. This derivation has been questioned and can no longer be accepted, but that does not basically affect Mommsen's argument which is to the effect that *auctoritas* implements a mere act of the will by adding reasons to it. Such augmentation and confirmation are the result of deliberation by the old ones. *Auctoritas* was what the *senatus* composed of the *senes* possessed, as contrasted with the *potestas* of the people. (Friedrich, 1972: 47)

This *auctoritas* finds a stronger sense in that it goes beyond simply a command of the leader for the led and also finds a religious sense connected with "scared tradition":

> The *auctoritas patrum* is more than advice, yet less than command. It is advice which cannot be safely disregarded, such as the expert gives to the layman, or a leader in parliament and party to his followers. This augmentation, implementation, and confirmation had religious significance, in ancient Rome as elsewhere. While it was not intended to set limits to the free decision of the people, it was meant to prevent a violation of what was sacred tradition In the established order of things, the assumption being that the people themselves would want to avoid such violation. (Friedrich, 1972: 47).

Friedrich's attempt at defining and describing authority, in this context, relies to some extent on the term and the vocabulary itself giving the lexicological aspects of it. A similar observation can be made in the context of Oriental languages to highlight the values attached to the term.

Etymologically, in the English language, such terms as author, authorization, and authority are derived from this Latin root. This notion or

concept of *auctoritas* was often used by the papacy in the Middle Ages for deposing kings as well. However, the case is different in a Muslim context. There would inevitably be some similarities between the Greek discourses on authority and the concepts that Muslims, particularly the Shiʿi Muslims, later developed.

With the terms used for "authority" in Arabic, we do not come up with such etymological similarities as we find in Latin and English for obvious reasons. In my research, the focus is not on the terms or the words used to describe authority, but the thoughts and the ideas that drive it. However, it is also important to see what the term implies in the Muslim context rather than a European or Greek context, even though we may come up with some interesting parallels too.

In the following sections, which contain references to the Ismaili concepts of authority, I have chosen to quote from Naṣīr al-Dīn Ṭūsī and Ḥamīd al-Dīn al-Kirmānī. The latter is an Ismaili *dāʿī* from the Fatimid period and the former is the author/compiler of almost all of the critical theological doctrinal Ismaili texts of the Alamūt period. The reason for choosing these two among others is that, first of all, in the case of al-Kirmānī, he joins the service of the Fatimid caliph at a time when the Fatimid *daʿwa* is in crisis and its structure needs considerable reshaping. Second, the period when the al-Kirmānī writes also coincides with the emergence of the Druze, who promoted the idea of al-Ḥākim bi-ʾAmr Allāh's (d. AH 411/AD 1021) divinity. Al-Kirmānī was commissioned to organize the *daʿwa* and to respond to these extremist views (see Walker, 1993).

The importance of Ṭūsī is self-explanatory because almost the entire corpus of Ismaili writings from the Alamūt period is produced either by him or under his supervision. It is also important as Ṭūsī joins the Ithnā ʿasharīs after the downfall of Alamūt and produces a number of significant theological works with a philosophical bent for the Ithnā ʿasharīs. Both these figures are writing during periods of crisis or extreme theological significance in the Ismaili history. The doctrinal articulations of the theories of *qiyāmat* and new perceptions of the doctrine of the imamate in the Alamūt period are owed to Ṭūsī.

Naṣīr al-Dīn Ṭūsī, a famous Muslim philosopher, theologian, mathematician, and astronomer of the thirteenth century, who is also regarded as one of the most revered and important figures in the Ismaili history, has important contributions to issues of authority. He wrote a number of books and treatises during his affiliation with the Ismailis of Alamūt, one of which is his magnum opus on ethics called the *Nasirean Ethics* (*Akhlāq-i Nāṣirī*).

In this book, there are passages that shed light on the historical background for understanding authority in the Ismaili community then and now. In the discourse "On Politics," he has a section titled "on the reason of man's need for civilized life, and an exposition of the nature and virtue of this branch of science." He gives an account of the imamate among Shi'i Muslims in the following terms[8]:

> Now in determining judgments, there is need (also) for a person who is distinguished from others by divine support[9] (ilhām-i ilāhī), so that he may be able to accomplish their perfection. Such a person, in the terminology of the Ancients, was called an Absolute King (malik-i 'alā al-iṭlāq), and his judgment the Craft of Kingship (ṣinā'at-i mulk); the Moderns[10] refer to him as the Imam, and to his functions as the imamate. Plato calls him Regulator of the World, while Aristotle uses the term Civic Man, i.e. that man, and his like, by whose existence the ordering of civilized life is affected.

From here, he proceeds to refer to specifically Ismaili terminology:

> In the terminology of some, the first of these persons is called the Speaker (nāṭiq) and the second the Foundation (asās).
> It must be established that the sense of the term "king" in this place is not that of someone possessing a cavalcade, a retinue or a realm: what is meant, rather, is one truly deserving of kingship, even though outwardly no one pays him any attention. If someone other than he be carrying on the management of affairs, tyranny and disorder become widespread.

The following section contains parallels with the doctrine of qiyāmat in which the Imam has the authority to make amendments to rituals:

> In short, not every age and generation has need of a Professor of the Law, for one enactment suffices for the people of many periods; but the world does require a Regulator in every age, for if management ceases, order is taken away likewise, and the survival of the species in the most perfect manner cannot be realized. The Regulator undertakes to preserve the Law and obliges men to uphold its prescriptions; his is the authority of jurisdiction (walāyat-i taṣarruf)[11] over the particulars of the Law in accordance with the best interest of every day and age (bar ḥasab-i maṣlaḥat-i har waqt wa rūzigār). (Ṭūsī, 1964: 192)[12]

There are a number of relevant and important points here. First, these passages contain the core idea of the Ismaili theory of the imamate in the

classical age (they are later fully developed in Ṭūsī's other works, some of which are quoted later here), but presented in philosophical language that does not at first glance resemble plain Ismaili philosophy.

We must remember that this text was written in a period of the Ismaili history very close to the Fatimid age. During the Fatimid times, Ismaili theology was heavily influenced by or presented through the use of Greek or Hellenistic terms, although we have to remember that the most prominent figures in the Ismaili mission (da'wa) who presented Ismaili doctrines retained their criticisms and comments on Greek ideas, and they were not just mechanically reproducing Greek views.[13]

A very good example of this is the case of Ḥamīd al-Dīn al-Kirmānī, whom I shall quote a little later when it comes to the qualities of the Imam. This was, of course, the general trend of most philosophers in the Muslim world and was not peculiar to the Ismailis.

Second, in the second paragraph Ṭūsī refers to the Speaker and the Foundation.[14] These are two specifically Ismaili terms referring respectively to the Prophet and the Imam (specifically to the first Imam, ʿAlī b. Abī Ṭālib). Further on, the closest match to a "Regulator," in Ṭūsī's sentence, is the Ismaili Imam. The implications are very clear, if stripped of all the abstractions. He is plainly saying that at all times, there needs to be a "Regulator" (Imam) who is following the example of the Speaker and the Foundation. Also, we can see echoes of the Civic Man and civilized life as mentioned in Ṭūsī's text in our present times.[15]

In order to explore the etymology of authority in a Muslim and particularly in a Shiʿi context, we cannot simply replace all other terms with authority, expecting the term to suggest the same meaning as it does in Latin and in English. There is an issue of translation here as well.

In the context of this research, we should know what we mean by authority and/or leadership here. Also, we must be aware the person possessing this authority. Above all, we have to clearly explain how authority and leadership are related. A part of this clarification has to be made in translation. If we are lost in translation at the outset, we will often face misrepresentations in the future.

In the Arabic (and Persian) language, we have a number of terms that correspond to authority in the English language. Some of these terms are very close to the original *auctoritas* described earlier in Friedrich's terms. A working definition on which we can build our discussion of the matter is the one which was provided earlier (in the Introduction and in chapter 1). For authority as "the right or legitimate claim to obedience" as its

essential component (Amir Arjomand, 1988: 1),[16] we usually come up with the following terms, definitions, or usages in the Muslim world.

1. One of the earliest terms, which is the most straightforward one is used in the Qur'ān. This term is "*ulu al-'amr*," which could be literally translated as someone "possessing command." This is the entire verse in the Qur'ān as translated by Arthur J. Arberry:

> O believers, obey God, and obey the Messenger and *those in authority* among you. If you should quarrel on anything, refer it to God and the Messenger, if you believe in God and the Last Day; that is better, and fairer in the issue (Qur'ān, 4:59).

   The equivalent of this term in English is "command"; we later see the term "commander of the faithful" (*amīr al-mu'minīn*) used for Muslim caliphs. In the very beginning of a section of his *Da'ā'im al-Islām*, al-Qāḍī al-Nu'mān, the opening paragraph of the book of *walāya* starts with the above verse followed by a quotation from Ja'far al-Ṣādiq explaining that they are "the people meant by God in this matter" (al-Nu'mān, 2002: 28) referring to "*ulu al-'amr*" and gives a number of other verses from the Qur'ān to support this argument.

2. The most common term closely related to the concept of authority is *Imam*. This is also a word that is often found in the canonical scripture, the Qur'ān, and has very strong Shi'i connotations as well. There are numerous verses in the Qur'ān that use the term Imam and they are particularly used by the Shi'i Muslims in support of the concept of the imamate, the right of the Prophet's household through his daughter and son-in-law to the leadership of the Muslim community (even this description should be read with sensitivity).

3. The term "*walāyat*" could be the closest translation for the word "authority" in Persian at least. This term has the root *wāw-lām-yā* (ولي), from which many other words are derived such as *walī*, *mawlā*, *tawallā*, etc. "*Walī*" or "*mawlā*" is a term that is frequently used among the Shi'a for the first Imam, 'Alī and by the Sufis for their masters. The term has also been used for God, as there are numerous references to it in the Qur'an (e.g., 2:257). '*Mawlā*' has also a different meaning of "a freed slave" and does not have much connection with the issue at hand. The term "*tawallā*" is also one with strong Shi'i connotations. It literally means showing friendship or

loyalty to someone. In the specific sense, it means remaining faithful and loyal to the oath of allegiance to the Imam.[17] Al-Nuʿmān again quotes Jaʿfar al-Ṣādiq on this verse repeating what he had said about "*ulu al-ʾamr*": "We are the people meant by God in this verse." (al-Nuʿmān, 2002: 29)

4. One of the other terms that sometimes come up in the translated texts in Persian is "*iqtidār*" that is a very close word to "authoritarianism" meaning someone whose authority must not be disobeyed. Contrary to the other rather subtle terms explained above, this one is more solemn and is even loaded with force and power. This equivalent, unlike the previous ones which were more or less rooted in religious scriptures, has a more political and secular genealogy.

5. There is also another equivalent that is sometimes used in Arabic for authority: *ḥukm* or *ḥākimiyya*. This translation is also reminiscent of "command" or "decree" as such.[18]

6. Another term that is closely related to the abstract notion of authority, in the Muslim context, is *sulṭān*. This term is used in connection with political authority (Amir Arjomand, 1988: 18), but it is not exclusive to political power. Nonetheless, we have to be conscious that the authority of the political ruler (*sulṭān*) does not always overlap or correlate with the authority of the Shiʿi Imam. This distinction is more than clear in the doctrinal and theological texts that talk about the imamate.

As we can see from the terms used in Arabic or Persian in translating authority, we have a number of terms that are mostly wrapped in a religious package filled with theological perceptions. The equivalents for the term "leadership" turn out to be more neutral and less religiously inclined (e.g., "*rahbarī*," as the standard translation for leadership, or a more Arabic version of it in "*zaʿāmat*"; there is another equivalent for it: "*riyāsat*").

However, as explained above, the term *sulṭān* also corresponds, in one of it senses, to political authority. This term can be approximated with the term leadership too, although it is often translated to refer to authority. Of the same root in Arabic, there is the term *salṭanat*, which has also been used frequently in Persian to refer to political authority of the kings and specifically to monarchy.

As regards the imamate, in the Ismaili Community, even though the Imam does not hold any political position, it does not preclude the leadership of the Imam in matters regarding the community's religious and

worldly affairs. This is embedded within the constitutional framework of the Community, which is not in conflict with the laws of the followers' place of abode (this point is further explained in the section on the Ismaili Constitution).

It is crucial to acknowledge the role of language and the different vocabularies used in describing and defining authority. This becomes even more sensitive in the case of the Ismaili Community and the AKDN, because in our times the *lingua franca* of the Ismaili imamate and its institutions is English. Thus, in one way or another, a translation process inevitably does occur, not only in understanding the faith, its history, and sociological developments but also in the discourses it creates in its leadership styles.

Here we have to note that language, despite its importance in facilitating communication, cannot act as the proxy for reality. Even in the realm of social interactions where language helps us create collective intentionalities, it is the reality of the social relations or the social entities that, in the final analysis, shape our understanding of terms, and not vice versa. In this context the experience of the Ismaili community with the English language is an interesting one, since all those Ismailis whose first language is English would come to comprehend the Arabic/Persian terms I have introduced above, either through real interactions in their communities (which are by definition informed by modern measures) or through modern English words used as their equivalents.

In linguistic terms, although there appears to be a conscious effort to keep the terms used for authority and leadership distinct, there is still some sort of organic relationship between authority and leadership. This much is sufficient for an initial, but determining, look at the etymologies of the terms in the context of this research. It will be briefly touched upon in later sections of this book, however.

Moving past the etymological and translation issues, there are some conceptualizations and methodological issues with regard to authority. Mohammed Arkoun calls for a fresh understanding of the issue, and unlike Arendt he does not seem to be speaking about the vanishing of authority and the complete degradation of religion, tradition, and authority. He sees things differently:

> My philosophical contention is that the epistemological posture, the conceptualisations and the methodologies used so far under the authority of the reason of enlightenment, which replaced the *auctoritas* of the theological legalistic reason that prevailed for centuries in Christianity and Islam, this whole cognitive system is obsolete and irrelevant to the emerging

multicultural, multi-ethnic societies. An emerging reasoning is following up these contexts in which a leader assisted by a group of disciples, succeeds in gaining the emotional adhesion of masses to a politics of hope. (Arkoun, 2002: 224–25).

Arkoun also tries to capture the new emerging meanings that are being assigned to the term "authority" through real-life practices and not by means of linguistic/genealogical explorations. He finds the "authority of the reason of enlightenment" obsolete and irrelevant to the needs of the "emerging multi-cultural, multi-ethnic societies." He is speaking of an "emerging reasoning," and he obviously sees an interaction between this "reason" and authority.[19]

Here, we should note that Arkoun's claim is based on the assumption of the plurality of models of rationality. This is something that all postmodern writers and most sociologists of knowledge and many other relativist writers such as Alasdair Macintyre uphold.[20] But realist philosophers, especially critical rationalists, argue against this relativism.

One of the central concerns of this book is the dynamic interaction between authority and leadership in the Ismaili imamate. The current example of leadership in the Ismaili Community and especially the way it is displayed by the present Imam, Aga Khan IV, has some peculiarities that make it distinct from its predecessors. These peculiarities are all too obvious. The Ismaili Imam, who is seen as head of the AKDN, does not resemble any other Muslim leader in the world who is in a position of authority (in any sense). In his eyes, the Ismaili Imam is not merely responsible for the interpretation of faith or simply giving religious instructions to his followers. He does not exclude involvement in mundane affairs of the world from his role as the Imam: being the Imam requires him to pay attention to all aspects of human life.

On the same day that one can see him performing religious ceremonies and rituals of his followers, you might find him sitting at a table dealing with serious economic issues like a market entrepreneur. He speaks about pluralism and civil society like a social scientist[21] or a politician, and at the same time he is concerned about sustainable development, restoration of historic cities, and the degradation of the architecture of the Muslim world. His style of leadership has a kaleidoscopic quality that makes it distinct from any other leader in the world. And yet, he is in a position of authority.

There is also a strong link between the sacred and the imamate, and the position he occupies is somehow "authorized" by the words of the Prophet (see the lengthy list of traditions and sayings of the Prophet and

the verses quoted from the Qur'ān to legitimize the position of the Shi'i Imam used equally by all the Shi'i Muslims and by the Ismailis with much more emphasis). This in itself is a quality of leadership: *the ability to function in different capacities and contribute in a meaningful way to one's role as the "leader" of a community.*

The present Imam seems to have had this clarity of vision from the very early days of his imamate. In his presidential address to the Seerat Conference in Karachi Pakistan on March 12, 1967, he has made the following remarks:

> The Holy Prophet's life gives us every fundamental guideline that we require to resolve the problem as successfully as our human minds and intellects can visualise. His example of integrity, loyalty, honesty, generosity both of means and of time, his solicitude for the poor, the weak and the sick, his steadfastness in friendship, his humility in success, his magnanimity in victory, his simplicity, *his wisdom in conceiving new solutions for problems which could not be solved by traditional methods, without affecting the fundamental concepts of Islam,* surely all these are foundations which, correctly understood and sincerely interpreted, must enable us to conceive what should be a *truly modern and dynamic Islamic Society* in the years ahead. [Emphases are mine.][22]

Whereas, given earlier examples, here with the present Aga Khan we see the capacity of synthetic or synergetic combination of different qualities or abilities, we also have a new capacity for reason that fits within that kaleidoscopic perception of leadership. The "wisdom to conceive new solutions for problems which could not be solved by traditional methods" would not be something we hear very often among Muslim leaders. There is a very strong voice of reason here.[23] This voice of reason is displayed both in leadership and in authority. Friedrich rightly raises this point about authority (and its relation to reason) that authority was "a matter of adding wisdom to will, reason to force and want, that is to say, a knowledge of values shared and traditions hallowed to whatever the people wished to do" (Friedrich, 1972: 48).

Nonetheless, the implications of this application of reason in the case of the Ismaili imamate are far reaching. The Ismailis have been known to be patrons and defendants of reason and intellect throughout their eventful history in the Muslim world. No matter how perceptions of reason have changed through time, whenever there has been a chance for this community to develop its own institutions, we have witnessed

the flourishing of reason and an approach to faith in which the role of intellect is crucially highlighted.

Transmutation of Authority and Institutional Shifts

The form of authority and leadership has changed in the Ismaili community. There has been a transmutation or a transcendence of the person of the Imam into the office of the imamate. The means of exercising this authority has changed. Conceptualizations are gradually beginning to show themselves more openly: the heavily theological crust is becoming increasingly thinner and replaced with a more developmental outlook. Does authority disappear? Does it vanish in the Ismaili community? These are some of the questions that will be addressed in further detail in later chapters of this book.

The first and the most visible aspect of this change is the shift of emphasis from the "person of the Imam" or the individuality of the Imam to the "office of imamate."[24] This does not, however, mean that the person of the Imam becomes unimportant or irrelevant. It is rather to suggest that the visibility of the institutions and the agencies that are available to the imamate has become such that it increasingly reduces the need for the Imam to be personally involved in every single matter of the community. The office of the imamate is not the Imam himself. It is rather the transcendence of the person of the Imam to the office of the imamate. The link between the person of the Imam and the office cannot be broken. The office of the imamate would become meaningless in the absence of the Imam. Conversely, the Imam himself without having an "office" and the agencies or institutions which facilitate his work would not be able to reach out to his community as easy as he would wish.

It is perhaps interesting to see how the Ismaili doctrines and the background of a theology can be seen in reverse in this instance. To further clarify this point, the following passage from Tūsī's *Rawḍa-yi taslīm* can help us better understand the context of this development:

> The intellect (*'aql*), too, is an abstract, mental concept, and as such it has no external existence, and when they wish to speak about it concretely, they can only do so [by pointing] to an intelligent person. Knowledge (*'ilm*) is also an abstract, mental concept, without any external existence, and when they want to speak about it concretely, they can only do so [by pointing] to a knowledgeable person. This is because, just as the truthful master (*muḥiqq*) is the soul and the form (*jān wa ṣūrat*) of truth, so the man of intelligence (*'āqil*) is the soul and form of intellect, and the man

of knowledge (*ʿālim*) is the soul and form of knowledge. Thus, the truth (*ḥaqq*), is like the body and the truthful master like the soul. (Ṭūsī, 2005: 159).

In the above passage, the Imam (*muḥiqq*—the term used by the Ismailis of the Alamūt period to refer to the Imam) is the embodiment of truth (*ḥaqq*). Here, truth is embodied in the very person (*shakhṣ*) of the Imam, and the Imam of the Time is the personification (*tashakhkhuṣ*) of truth and the embodiment of the word of God (*maẓhar-i kalima*) (Ṭūsī, 1998: 35–36). What has happened in the contemporary times, with the institutionalization of the imamate, is the transmutation of the earlier theology.

The person of the Imam is transcended into the institutions and his authority is the very source giving legitimacy to the organizations that function to ensure that the Imam has the necessary means available to perform his job. Thus, these institutions, the built environment and the Delegations of the Ismaili Imamat, serve as a symbolic reference to the presence of the Imam. The thick layer of theological and doctrinal perceptions drawing on truth and the Imam as the truthful master is replaced with a more earthly and easily intelligible symbolism without making any direct intervention to provide an alternative perception of truth—or making any radical changes to the doctrines themselves—as it was understood in earlier periods. In the absence of solid and functioning institutions, that theological or—more specifically—highly esoteric interpretation of truth continues to gain significance.

In contemporary times, it is the institutions of the Ismaili imamate and the office of the imamate itself that serve this purpose.

Here, the very shift from the personification of truth (*ḥaqq*) in the Imam's words and deeds toward institutionalization of it as embodied in the institutional, intersubjective relations of the Community should be precisely or concisely described: a shift that requires, but is not based on a prior, doctrinal review at a theological level.

Perhaps one can legitimately argue that—as an effect of this shift—theology and doctrinal opinions have already lost the status they used to enjoy in the past. Hence, this marks another dimension of the shift under scrutiny, i.e. the marginalization of the process of theological fixation.

In order to explain this shift in the theological approaches of the present institutions of the Ismaili imamate, we should be able to make sense of the theology itself and of the space that this theology allows the very person of the Imam in order to provide his interpretation of faith. What a superficial interpretation might suggest is a form of abrogation as if the

entire theology and doctrines of the Ismailis have been replaced with an entrepreneurial spirit. Such kind of a supposed abrogation—be it practical or doctrinal—has not happened in this case.

Even if we can—with a degree of caution and reservation—use the term abrogation, it is more or less a form of dialectical abrogation. The bedrock of this shift has to be seen in the relation that theology has with the life of the faithful in a religious community in general and in the Ismaili community in particular. What takes priority is not a solid or rigid set of theological or metaphysical doctrines. It is the actual condition and life of the faithful that takes precedence.

The role of the Ismaili Imam is fundamental in the relation between this theology and the life of his followers. In the Ismaili context, it is the Imam himself who is the source of legitimacy for any kind of theological shift—and there is massive historical and doctrinal evidence to support this.[25]

In order to legitimize any shift in the outlook of a religious community—in this case the Ismailis—either the leader himself could issue decrees or make theological amendments in the doctrines of a community, as we have seen on a number of occasions in the history of the Ismaili community, the Alamūt period being its most prominent example, or the very actions and policies of the Imam could signal this shift without any explicit theological amendments.

The core of the matter is that it is the Imam himself who has always been the legitimizing source of doctrines and the authority to give prominence to the theology and not the other way around. In terms of legitimacy, a direct theological amendment is as valid and as legitimate in the Ismaili community as the very act of the Imam and his policies. Therefore, it would be an error to ignore the shift or the transmutation that can take place as a result of the practical measures of the Imam through his initiatives and go back to the earlier existing theological doctrines and give prominence or priority to them as the source of legitimacy or authority.

This shift is delicately embedded in the preamble to the Ismaili Constitution, and the grounds for it have been already available in the substantial theological doctrines of the community in which the Imam himself is the source of authority. Therefore, it is a defendable position to say that this transmutation—what I have termed as development of authority without territory—has occurred as a result of the practical initiatives of the present Imam. This of course requires an elaboration of the doctrines that support this shift. Some of these are explored in the chapter that deals with the vision of the Aga Khan.

This in itself is a huge task, which is beyond the scope of this book, but I have made indications in various places in this book that this shift and its formulation, conceptualization, and elaboration have been in the making for the past 50 years, and its focus is becoming increasingly sharper and much clearer as time goes by.

The second aspect, which is interconnected with the transcendence of the person of Imam into the office of the imamate, is in a sense the dispersing of power. This leadership, this authority is being delegated in an unprecedented way. Previously the Imam was far more visible and took on further direct responsibility in all sorts of matters. A visible shift that has happened in the recent history of the Ismaili imamate pertains to how the authority of the Imam is exercised.

In our times, the mandate of the Ismaili imamate is not to establish a state, and the idea of the Imam being the head of a state has increasingly lost its meaning; while it has become even more vividly established that the Imam is the head of a network of institutions that are expressions of his role as the Ismaili Imam or, even better, as a Muslim leader. This new development is a direct consequence of the transmutation of authority.

It is important here to explain how this situation is different from that of other Ismaili Imams in the past, particularly that of the Fatimid period. During the Fatimid period, when an entire Muslim empire was at the disposal of the Ismaili Imam-Caliph, there were institutions and various administrative and political bodies that regulated the affairs of the state and the inner matters of the Ismaili community (which was part of the larger community led by the Fatimids). The difference of the current period and the Fatimid period is not in the existence or absence of institutions, but in the shift of paradigm, which has occurred in the vision that prevails in these institutions.

It is true that minimally the core of some ideas such as tolerance did exist in the Fatimid times, but when we speak of pluralism, which is so highly cherished by the Ismaili imamate today, we cannot just reduce it to the kind of tolerance that existed in the Fatimid period. Moreover, we must not forget that both in the Fatimid period and in the Alamūt period, the Ismaili Imams were also heads of a state. This situation has drastically changed.

One cannot disregard the role of the previous chapters of Ismaili history in the genesis of the present period. Nonetheless, this shift has occurred, which makes it unique and not comparable with other periods of Ismaili history.[26]

Unlike certain interpretations of the role of a Muslim leader and authority in a Muslim and Shi'i context, in the case of the Ismaili imamate, this institution of leadership has developed in such a manner that it works beyond divisions of nation-state, and it has come to a point that it would not be able to seriously consider working in the boundaries of territorial state limitations and at the same time promote its cause the way it is embedded within its institutions. The Ismaili imamate is now beyond ideological or political divisions and rivalries that are now part of territorial nation-states.

The key to understanding this shift is the fundamental role of pluralism which is an integral part of the institutions of the Ismaili imamate. Pluralism, which is now predominant in actions of the Ismaili imamate's institutions, has paved the way for the development of an increasingly cosmopolitan dimension to the authority of the Ismaili Imam and as such it cannot go back to being restricted or defined by nation-state considerations. It is as if pluralism is hardwired into the institutional framework of the Ismaili imamate, and the role of pluralism becomes even more critical when we look at the cosmopolitan dimension of the imamate institutions. Cosmopolitanism itself is at the risk of becoming an ideology but the presence of pluralism guarantees its continuation without becoming an intolerant system.

One could describe this process as removing some burdens off the shoulders of leadership, making it leaner and giving it more freedom to act. In other words, in more abstract terms, authority tends to be transformed into "authorization," that is everything that happens only happens with the authorization of the Imam; it becomes the entitlement of others to make decisions with the blessing, authorization, or sanctification of the Imam. However, it allows the world to play a role in the defining of authority itself. There are, of course, in practice, limits to this. These limitations are clearly spelled out in the preamble to the Ismaili Constitution.

To put it in plainer terms, it is a move from a traditional perception of authority to a more flexible authority, which is highly adaptable to change, within its broad ethical framework. However, this is done with a measure of reflexivity and awareness. And this reflexive quality is something that is embedded within the Ismaili Constitutions. This in itself is no small achievement. Such developments do not easily occur painlessly without any bloodshed or violent encounters. All these developments have occurred in the Ismaili community in a highly peaceful way, while keeping the core of this authority relatively intact.

Dynamic Interaction of Leadership and Authority

As mentioned a number of times earlier, the two concepts of authority and leadership are inextricably connected with one another. There are many things that could be said about leadership and the same things could be said about authority and vice versa. This becomes even more critical in the case of the Ismaili Community and its models of leadership displayed in an institution like the AKDN.

The reason it is important to recognize this interaction between leadership and authority is not too difficult to see. There are certain qualities that are shared between leadership and authority. A good leader and someone who is in a position of authority share certain qualities that are important to their leadership and authorizing position. If we look at leadership styles today and quickly glance at the Harvard Business School, we come up with certain ideas and qualities for leaders, which are incidentally central to the leadership of the Ismaili Imam (the *authority*).

Good leadership today is concerned about employing "best practices," and again these are the terms frequently heard in the words of the present Ismaili Imam. If we look at the literature of cutting-edge companies or businesses, we can see that good leadership involves recognizing limits of leadership (one can also speak of recognizing the limits of jurisdiction). This recognition of the limits of leadership is something that could be seen in the work of the present Ismaili Imam. It may not have been spelled out in words as a "limitation" (for which there might not even be a need), but it is certainly there. It is there in the personal style of the imamate of Aga Khan IV, making him incredibly different from his grandfather.

The practical living example of the life and leadership of the present Ismaili Imam is speaking of the interdependence of the leader and the led, not only in his words but also in his actions. This also leaves a legacy and a mark on his future descendants. So, given these few examples, it is crucial to recognize the dynamic link and interaction between leadership and authority. This emphasis will remain vibrant and alive throughout this book. There are clearly some nuances that make the case of the Ismaili imamate different from just about any business leadership. These nuances drastically change the scenario.

In business leadership, a venture capitalist simply thinks in terms of profit-making. Sometimes, the survival of the company and its reputation may trump profit rates. But what is the source of authorization of a company? And even beyond this, what is the source of authorization of

the president of a nation? How can they be compared to the source of authorization of an Imam in a Shi'i context?

When you have the sacred on your side, this is a force that no army could conquer and no profit rate could ever trump. And this is a very great asset. Thus, we have another quality in this "transmutation." It is the act or the art of balancing or striking proportionalities between this-worldly leadership and other-worldly authorization of authority, which is a permanent theme in the institutions of the Ismaili imamate and the AKDN.

An Antithesis to Max Weber?

In this book, we would not be able understand this shift without understanding the nexus between authority and leadership. This is, by the way, a response to Weber too. It is a very basic Weber thesis that the very problem of authority is that it has to deal with the world, and once it starts interacting and dealing with the world the authority is lost. This is empirically disproven in our case study. Paradoxically, the AKDN is a fine example for showing the contrary.

Here is an Imam authorized by the sacred but behaving in the world by encouraging the distribution of power,[27] the cultivation of leadership, and yet he is able to keep this dialectic between leadership and authority going on. By way of example, the very structure of the institutions of the Ismaili community, the way leaders of the community get appointed for limited terms to take charge of the social and religious affairs of the community, provides a fine example of how leadership is cultivated inside the community.

The long-standing tradition of voluntary service in the community is the overarching idea above the way members of the community take up positions of leadership: they do not have remunerations for the services they provide to their community and yet they have to provide good quality and high performance in their leadership roles. There are measures to check these performances. Some of these measures can be seen in the way budgets for these institutions are approved by the Imam and through the complex network of institutions. Some aspects of these examples are further explained later when we look at the structure of these institutions as they exist today.

The case of the Ismaili imamate *appears* to be the demystification, demythologization, bureaucratization, or secularization of religious authority (leading to its loss or dilution). There is no law for this to necessarily happen. In other words, we can say that this-worldly leadership

requires the support of spiritual authority and the spiritual authority can be strengthened, become more effective and more plausible, when it has a this-worldly component; and thus the dialectic continues here.

This also helps to explain the return of the sacred on a global scale in all sorts of contexts. It seems that effective administration and action so often, at governmental and non-governmental levels, depends upon receiving authorization by sacred criteria.

The chapters to come will demonstrate the above points at greater length with further details to backup the claims made above. In order to show the key thesis of this research, different historical aspects of the development of the community, particularly in modern times, will have to be carefully studied. One of the most important sections will be the process of the promulgation and consolidation of the Ismaili Constitution.

There are some theoretical and theological issues that would also be discussed as the debate about the transmutation of authority takes shape.

The leadership of the Ismaili Imam is in essence hereditary, and a great bulk of justifications for this hereditary nature of authority can be found in the Qur'ān. Wilferd Madelung gives a very concise account of these (Madelung, 1997: 2–6). I have also touched upon the most important aspects of it earlier.

At the same time when the Safavids represented a Shi'i model for authority and leadership in Iran (let us not forget that the Safavid sovereign was the king and claimed his legitimacy on the account of Shi'i doctrines), the rival Ottomans (reigning from AD 1299 to 1922) had their own system of a Sunni caliphate, which lasted until after World War I when it was dissolved. So we still see a system of monarchy (a Sultanate in the Ottoman case) in their authority—even though doctrinally it is not the monarchy itself that has legitimacy (Madelung, 1997: 5) [28] The two competing Safavid and Ottoman states ruled at a time when the Umayyad (r. AD 660–750), Abbasid (r. AD 750–1258), and Fatimid empires were long gone.

Were these forms of governance religious or secular? Were they any different from secular monarchies in the West? Mohammed Arkoun has an interesting theory about the Umayyads and the Abbasids:

> The Umayyad-Abbasid state is secularist in its sociological and anthropological basis, its military genesis and expansion, its administrative practice, its ideological discourse of legitimacy. The theological and jurisprudential endeavour developed by the *'ulamā* contributed to concealing

behind a religious vocabulary and sacralizing conceptualization, literary devices, the secularist, ideological basis of the so-called "Islamic" polity and governance.

Arkoun then argues that in Islam, there has been a "confiscation of spiritual autonomy" by the top and the bottom:

> All those scholars, Muslims and non-Muslims, who contend today that Islam confuses politics and religion, or Islam does not need to address the issue of secularism because—unlike Christianity—it never developed a clerical regime under the leadership of the Church, neglect the two major historical and sociological facts. These are the confiscation of the spiritual autonomy by the top (the state) and by the bottom (lay believers mobilized by "saints" in brotherhoods) that began in 661 and has lasted until today.

And he draws attention to the role of military power:

> Very early in the history of the state, military power played a pre-eminent role in the caliphate, the imamate, the sultanate and all later forms of governing institutions in Islamic contexts. (Arkoun, 2002: 248–49)

Therefore, in essence the Umayyad-Abbasid state is a secularist state concealing behind a façade of religiosity. The Umayyad-Abbasid rulers did have their own authority, but were they the major sources of authority in the Muslim world?

In the past, theologian jurists sometimes gave their blessings to the state and the head of the state was given the title of "Caliph" ("*khalīfat Allāh*" or "*khalīfa rasūl Allāh*"). None of these states ever claimed their legitimacy *on the basis of their genealogy* with the exception of the Ismaili Imams, whose most significant argument for their legitimacy has always been and still is their direct lineal descent from the Prophet's family and the first Shiʿi Imam, ʿAlī b. Abī Ṭālib.[29] In fact, the Abbasids did their best to challenge the authority of the Ismaili Imam-Caliphs by trying to undermine the most essential cornerstone of their legitimacy.[30]

This unique position is claimed by Ismaili Imams who argue for an unbroken chain of authority since the time of the Prophet himself. And here is where the paradox appears: we see a form of leadership and authority that at times is accompanied with political power; it is based on hereditary leadership and yet it does not exactly resemble any familiar form of monarchy. We see the role of blood-lineage taking the upper hand. It resembles monarchy, but it is not monarchy, and this is the core of its paradox.

We must also note the role of *military power* (as mentioned by Arkoun, above) during the Fatimid period and the Alamūt period in establishing the legitimacy of the state (as in the case of Qarmatians and the Druze) however, there are no similar instances of crushing opposition in Alamūt period (see Hodgson, 1955).

The Ismaili Doctrines and the Qualities of the Imam

Ṭūsī: The Qualities of the Imam

Ṭūsī (AH 597–672/AD 1201–74) elaborates on the basic concepts and ideas of leadership and authority in the following words:

> The formula of the profession of Divine Unity (*kalmia-yi tawḥīd*) is the [exclusive] heritage to be transmitted and inherited through his sacred progeny and holy descendants, in one line of descent and essence— "*offspring one after the other*" (3:34)—[a lineage] which will never be ruptured, even unto the end of time... Know that the imamate is a reality [which] will never cease, change or be altered. It will continue forever to be transmitted through the progeny of our lords (*mawālīnā*). It will never leave them, whether in form, meaning or reality.

He then proceeds to explain different forms of the relationships to the Imam, which sheds light on how some schisms are articulated:

> With regard to the situation of others [from the Imam's family], each of them enjoys a connection to our lord in a different fashion. One of them, like Salmān, is related [to the Imam] in his interior reality (*ma'nā*) rather than his external appearance (*shakl*), [i.e. their kinship is purely spiritual not physical]. [Thus, the Prophet said of him], "Salmān is one of us [our family]." Another, such as Mustʿalī, is connected to him merely in his external appearance without any relation to his interior reality. Another is connected to him both in external appearance and interior reality, like our lord Ḥasan. Still another takes after him in external appearance [and] in interior reality, while being in his proper reality actually him, like our lords Ḥusayn and ʿAlī. (Ṭūsī, 2005: 121–22)

Ṭūsī then emphasizes the necessity of the accessibility of the Imams at all times and formulates the idea of designation (*naṣṣ*):

> It is also necessary that the people should have access to the lights of his guidance; otherwise they would be deprived of attaining perfection, and the usefulness of the manifestation would be rendered futile. Since it is

necessary in the world of similitude that human beings should succeed one another through a recognized relationship (*'alāqa*), once this relationship which indicates continuity and succession (*ittiṣāl wa ta'āqub*) is disregarded, the means of knowing him will also be closed to people. The relationship can only be of two kinds, spiritual and physical. The spiritual relationship is the clear appointment (*naṣṣ*) of one by the other, and the physical relationship is that of the child to father by way of succession. Through these two relationships, the close affinity between these individuals becomes known, and [the meaning of the revealed] evidence (*athar*) "He made it a word enduring among his posterity" (43:28), and of the decree (*ḥukm*) "the offspring, one of the other" (3:34), becomes clear. By testifying to these two proofs of birth and clear appointment, all the inhabitants of the world have access to the individual who is the locus of the manifestation of that light. (Ṭūsī, 1998: 43).

The above doctrinal articulations have remained unchanged in the Ismaili Community. They generally describe how the issue of succession is resolved.

Al-Kirmānī: Qualities of the Imam

If we go back to an earlier classical Ismaili text written during the Fatimid period by Ḥamīd al-Dīn al-Kirmānī, a prominent Ismaili missionary (*dā'ī*) during the reign of the Fatimid Caliph-Imam al-Ḥākim (AD 996–1021), we can see similar lines of argument, but with further indications of how one can recognize this authority as the legitimate Imam of the age. In his book *al-Maṣābīḥ fī Ithbāt al-Imāma*, Kirmānī provides some tables in which he describes

> the traits that prevent [one] being worthy of the imamate in the form of an aide-memoire in order to understand from it the invalidity of the imamate of those who claim it and the necessity of its belonging to the one among them who truly has the right to it. (al-Kirmānī, 2007: 118)[31]

In his classical attempt to eliminate all other rivals of his time, he mentions the following:

> Being not among the lineal descendants of al-Ḥusayn precludes the imamate; being impure in body and soul precludes the imamate; thoughtlessness in the exercise of legal authority based on ignorance and utilization of resources for reprehensible purposes precludes the imamate; being devoid of religious knowledge, which consists of understanding what is permitted and what is forbidden and the revelation and the interpretation, precludes

the imamate; contempt for the regulations of God and for commanding good and prohibiting the bad and for maintaining the appeal (*da'wa*) precludes the imamate; not having the nobility confirmed by the designation and the appointment to the place of the Apostle precludes the imamate. (al-Kirmānī, 2007: 118–19).

Al-Kirmānī: Infallibility

As briefly mentioned earlier, the treatises and books written by al-Kirmānī on the issues of authority and the imamate, were all produced at a stage when the Fatimid empire faced challenges in terms of the understanding of the imamate. These challenges were sometimes of a political nature. The Qaramtians had separated from the Fatimids at an early stage, and later the Druze, who believed in the divinity of al-Ḥakim bi-ʾAmr Allāh, the Fatimid Imam-Caliph, seceded. These books were written mainly in response to these challenges, and one must note the context of the production of these works.

The approach taken up by al-Kirmānī is no doubt tainted and painted by his particular Ismaili interpretation (part of which is promoting the hegemony of the Fatimid state). Yet, he continues to emphasize the two main traits that are required of the Imam as the authority for the community that is a direct descendant of the Prophet through Imam ʿAli, who was appointed by the Imam before him. This position pretty much defines the Ismaili imamate as a whole. In al-Kirmānī's work, we see a definition of infallibility or divine protection against sin and error (*iṣma*), which is a product of history. In the chapter where he speaks about the necessity of the infallibility of the Imam, he does not speak about how one can ascertain that the Imam is infallible. He provides reasons to move the reader to a direction where he would accept that if he has acknowledged the imamate of a particular Imam, he would necessarily have to consider him infallible as well.

The ʿiṣma of the Imam: Contrasting Narratives

We have two contrasting pieces of information that might clarify our discussion and shed light on some ambiguous areas in regards with the infallibility of the Imam. Modarresi, in his *Crisis and Consolidation* gives a detailed background that the idea of infallibility or any theological doctrines elaborating on it (Modarresi, 1993: 46–47) did not exist in the Shiʿi discourse before the time of the Imam Jaʿfar al-Ṣadiq (who is accepted as an Imam by both the Ismailis and the Ithnā ʿasharīs).

He mentions the name of Hishām bin al-Ḥakam, the Imam's compan-ion, as the one who had initially introduced the idea of *'iṣma*: "Hishām b. Al-Ḥakam's theory of the Imām's divine protection against sin and error (*'iṣma*) was a major contribution to further accommodate the shift" (Modarresi, 1993: 9). Now given this background, when we move fur-ther ahead to the Alamūt period of the Ismaili history (by which time another split had occurred in the Ismaili community over the issue of succession and authority), we can clearly see a shift in understanding infallibility. Let us read a paragraph from Ṭūsī about infallibility (the translator has used "chaste purity" instead of infallibility for *'iṣma*; words in brackets and italicized are mine):

> Regarding the asceticism and chaste purity of the Imam, if one were to measure this on the scale proper to ordinary mortals, it would appear as if he had neither asceticism nor chastity [*quite in contrast to what al-Kirmānī says*]. This is because the relation of ordinary people to the Imam is like that of a wretched ant to a perfect man. Nay, they are more than a thou-sand degrees inferior to that. Now, just as no man bothers to avoid or be wary of an ant or any other animal in his actions, why should the Imam, who sees nothing [of substance] outside himself, bother to be wary of or take precautions for anything or anyone? How many learned persons there have been who considered themselves to be supreme justices (*qāḍī al-quḍāt*) or leading missionaries (*dāʿī al-duʿāt*), yet were unable to com-prehend the secret of this matter? The saw the Imam, heard his words and observed his actions, but adopted a perverse and hostile attitude [toward him], and by doing so have been humiliated and confused. We seek refuge from this in God, (Ṭūsī, 2005: 130–31).

This is a fascinating, yet revealing, paragraph when compared to the dif-ferent approaches to the issue of infallibility among the Ismailis.

We can clearly see a historical development or shift in the under-standing of the imamate and its traits. In other words, apart from the two major qualities (i.e., direct blood descent and clear appointment), all other traits seem to be somehow volatile, in the sense that they are always subject to interpretation and reformulation.[32] The reason for this, among the Ismailis, has probably been the fact that they have had liv-ing Imams and these Imams were living in real conditions with all the contingencies of a worldly life among ordinary people while maintaining their sacred, spiritual role.

If we take into account the contingencies and circumstances in which these authorities lived, and if we set aside the doctrinal and theological beliefs of believers, there would be every chance that if the other branch

had a living leader, they would also revisit this idea of infallibility. We can see these developments among Sufis too, although the Sufis do not maintain the same qualities of infallibility as developed by the Imāmiyya to be true for their *pīr*s too. Examples of this can be found in the works of Rumi and ʿAyn al-Quaḍāt Hamadānī. ʿAyn al-Quaḍāt goes so far to say that the *pīr* (the authoritative guide) can even commit sins while still being able to perform his role as the spiritual guide (Hamadānī, 1983: 2/119).

The entire literature produced about the qualities and traits of the Imam, who is considered the authority for Shiʿi Muslims, is very much a product of the contingencies of the time, rather than being a fixed notion not subject to change. The only two things that have remained unchanged in the Ismaili community are (a) blood lineage and (b) clear appointment or designation of an Imam by the previous one by way of *naṣṣ*.

However, it is not correct to say that the qualities which are mentioned by al-Kirmānī during the Fatimid era suddenly disappear for good. We often see a recurrence of these qualities at later times, but with interpretations that are bound by the circumstances of the time. In other words, there seems to be a dynamic mechanism of rejuvenating and revitalizing the imamate and bringing newer dimensions to it at all times. Nonetheless, the core concepts and qualities of the imamate as the legitimate authority have remained the same.

Weber writes: "In a purely empirical and value-free sense, charisma is indeed the specifically creative revolutionary force in history" (Weber, 1978: 1117).

Many have argued that Weber's idea of charisma as a supernatural gift, in a disenchanted world where we face a demythologization and demystification of religious or metaphysical ideas, is not possible (Spencer, 1973). However, despite all the developments of the modern world and the culture of globalization, we not only do not witness the decline of charisma, but we can even see a rebirth of charisma. It seems that charisma has a life of its own and it reproduces itself in different forms. However, this is not to say that charisma is understood and utilized in exactly the same way as was in the past.

If we look at the Ismaili doctrines, particularly in the Alamūt period, we see some striking similarities between what Weber and what Ṭūsī say regarding the imamate:

> If mankind knew what the imamate is, no one would have entertained doubts such as these. If only they had realized that mutability cannot

exist without some immutable [central] point, just as the circumference [cannot exist] without a centre point. For everything that rotates or moves requires a cause for its rotation and movement, and the moving force in relation to the object which rotates or moves must be stable and perfect, in order to be able to spin or move it. This is why it has been said [in the Gospels]: 'Heaven and earth will change, but the commandment of the Sabbath will never be altered' [Matthews 5:18; Luke 16:17]. This means that while the Prophets and the *ḥujjat* may change – at one time this one, at another time that one, at one time in this community, at another time in that—the Imam will never change: "We are the people of eternity." [The essential nature of the Imam will never change], even when he is a drop of sperm in the loins of his father, or [a foetus] in the womb of his mother. It is a total impossibility to suppose that the true Imam could cease to exist and the case of the acting (*mustawda*ʿ) Imam such as our lord Ḥasan [b. ʿAlī], could be any different.

He speaks about the unique and unchangeable quality of the imamate, giving each and every Imam the same rank; none is higher or lower than the other:

In reality, it is impossible for any past or future Imam to be better or more powerful than another, or to be better at one time than at another time. For example, it is wrong to suppose that he should be better when he reaches maturity than when he was a drop of sperm, or better when the designation (*naṣṣ*) was made than before it was made. The designation which is made is not in order to *make* him an Imam; it is only made so that people should recognize him as such—otherwise, from his standpoint and perspective, all such different states are one and the same.

His elaboration continues to cover the gist of what the Ismailis preached on the doctrine of *taʿlīm*:

Such is the case because a perfect man (*kāmilī*) must always exist amongst God's creatures in order to raise those who are incomplete and deficient to a state of perfection. Even if you assume that he is not that person [the perfect man], there would still have to be someone else. For, if each imperfect soul needs a more perfect soul [to perfect it], and the more perfect soul, [it is turn], needs an even more perfect one, and in the final case, [the chain] must terminate with the perfect man who does not need anybody else, and through whose instruction [all others] may reach perfection. Such a perfect man is a logical necessity and the matter must ultimately finish there [with him]. (Ṭūsī, 2005: 123).[33]

The paragraphs above are very rich containing a lot of significant pointers for our research, particularly when we compare it with Weber's idea of charisma.

First, in the Ismaili doctrines of the Alamūt period, authority is something permanent and inherent in its esoteric and supernatural sense; it is not something to be achieved or acquired. According to the Nizārī doctrines of the Alamūt period, the act of explicit designation for the Imam does not *make* him the Imam. This designation is understood to be only intended to introduce him to the people.[34] Therefore, he is essentially referring to spiritual or esoteric authority in the person of the Imam, which can be distinguished by knowing that he is from the descendants of an Imam and that he has been designated by the previous Imam.

In the Ismaili doctrines the existence of such an authority at all times is a "necessity" and the obligatory task of the Imam, and he cannot choose to be absent or leave his community without his guidance. As such he is the defender and protector of the faith of his predecessors.

The kind of charismatic leadership that Weber has in mind is ideal-typical, as opposed to the "necessity" of its existence for the Ismailis. In the Ismaili doctrines, this person of authority, or the Imam, who sometimes takes on a "revolutionary" role, must inevitably be present.

Weber speaks about a "creative revolutionary force." If we look at the classical period of the Ismaili history, we can see this "revolutionary force" in a number of cases. The most remarkable one of them occurs at the time of the twenty-third Ismaili Imam (of the Nizari branch, who is the ancestor of the present Aga Khan).[35] Ḥasan II, ʿAlā Dhikrihi al-Salām (d. AH 561/AD 1166), who is better known among the Ismailis as the *qāʾim al-qiyāma* (the Resurrector), declared an era of resurrection in which the Ismailis were considered to be the people of unity (*waḥdat*) and they are constantly united with the Lord and therefore they have witnessed paradise on earth. In his declaration, he announced that whosoever is part of this "people of unity" (*ahl-i waḥdat*) would no longer have to observe the exoteric rituals of faith, since they are spiritually united with the Lord (for a detailed account see Daftary, 2007: 358–66; Hodgson, 1955: 148–59). The Ismailis call this Imam the *qāʾim* or the Resurrector. In explaining the difference between Qāʾim and Imam, Ṭūsī writes:

> The meaning of the terms "*imām*" and "*qāʾim*" (Resurrector) are the same, but people use the name Qāʾim to refer to that Imam who introduces some great change in the religious law (*sharīʿat*). When the Qāʾim manifests himself in physical form, that is, when he propagates his mission by way of deeds but not [yet] in words, he is called the "lord of the necks"

(*mālik al-riqāb*); and when he manifests himself spiritually, that is, when he spreads his mission through both word and deed, he is called the "lord of hearts and necks" (*mālik al-qulūb wa al-riqāb*). (Ṭūsī, 2005: 127–28)

First of all, the *qā'im* is a revolutionary figure (he introduces great changes in the religious law). Then, Ṭūsī goes further to explain the role of institutions in authority. When the *qā'im*—and potentially each Imam is a *qā'im*—does not have any institutions or any power of any sort (be it political or otherwise), his mission is only through words. However, when he is in a position of implementing these through institutions, his mission would be expressed and implemented both in words and in deeds.

We can see a very close connection between the role of the authority, his charisma, and the institutions that are created to guarantee the implementation of his will. This is very close to the gift of grace that Weber refers to as "attached to the incumbent of an office or to an institutional structure regardless of the persons involved" (Weber, 1978: 1135).

What is significant about this model of authority is that it is not subject to the will and election of ordinary people. It is not a democracy where people can decide who would rule them. The people are subject to the lifelong leadership and guidance of an authority who *cannot* even abdicate. The authority and power of this Imam cannot be limited or restricted by the followers, as opposed to the relation between citizens of a democracy and the rulers or office bearers in a political regime.

This may look like an essentialist approach to the idea of the imamate, but if we look at the different periods of this institution of authority, we can see how the leaders and people of authority have adapted themselves to new situations wherever their conditions are altered. There is also an important observation to be made here. In order to see what the limits of this flexibility has been and how much the Imam and the institution of the imamate—in the case of the Ismailis—can adapt themselves to changing environments, we must note that—historically and at least to the present time—this adaptation has not been anything more than a family resemblance. There is a link—a historical and traditional connection—between the Ismaili Imams. The fact that the Ismaili doctrines give an unfettered authority to the Imam does not mean—and has not meant—an absolutist and arbitrary approach.

The present Imam, Aga Khan IV, spells out his role as responding to the spiritual and temporal needs of the community—what he describes as improving the quality of life. There are ethical considerations as well.

Even in the most radical stages of the Ismaili history, where a highly esoteric interpretation of Islam has been the dominant feature—like the Alamūt period, there has never been an abandonment of the basic Islamic doctrines.

This commitment has been beyond just a mere affirmation of the *shahāda* (belief in the unity of God and that Muḥammad was his last prophet). Even when it came to the interpretation of the religious law, there was never a complete and absolute abrogation of religious law—contrary to hostile reports of Sunni historians of the Alamūt period. Rather a highly spiritual dimension gained significance.

In reference to the proclamation of the *qiyāma* in the Alamūt period:

> This proclamation involved an emphasis on the *bāṭin,* though it should be remembered that the notion of the *bāṭin* along with its counterpart, the *ẓāhir,* was present in Ismāʿīlism from the earliest times. However, the current view among some historians that the proclamation involved an abrogation of the *sharīʿa* has never been substantiated. (Esmail and Nanji, in Nasr, 1977: 249)

If we look at the issue from an epistemological point of view, we can see that although the core idea of the qualities of the Imam remains the same among all Shiʿi Muslims, at different times certain modifications and revisions are introduced to accommodate the leadership of those who are the bearers of authority. In the case of the Ismailis, doctrines are revised and rendered in a fashion that enables the Imam to bring about the changes he deems necessary, albeit supported by the very idea of the undisputed authority of a designated descendant of the Imam. In a later section, I will address the issue of charisma and authority in the Ismaili community, and in particular with its reference to the present time.

Succession: The Key Issue of Authority

Given that monarchy was ruled out after the Prophet's death (even though it did not exist before the Prophet of Islam in Arabia), there remained a permanent issue of "succession," which afterward led to most of the schisms in the Muslim world. Disputes over the issue of succession, which have been in essence disputes over authority, were always been at the center of the discourses about authority and leadership. Meanwhile, in Europe, new concepts of leadership developed (the idea of "good leadership" and the works of Max Weber), which I will address in further detail later.

Leadership Revisited

The issue of leadership and how it was understood in early stages of Muslim history and how this understanding developed over time and history has been at the heart of many complex dilemmas in the Muslim world. As Mohammed Arkoun has pointed out, we must be aware and distinguish between "two irreducible frames of analysis, conceptualization and theorization, the one known as political theology and the other emerging in the context of European modernity under the name of political philosophy" (Arkoun, 2002: 205).

The idea of leadership has been a constant point of debate in both of these frameworks.[36] One of the purposes of this book is to investigate the legacy of what counts as leadership in the Muslim world and the multifarious dimensions of it. Furthermore, it investigates new developments and the consolidation of new perceptions of leadership, particularly in how it is reflected in the model of the AKDN.

It is important to read Weber again with regard to leadership, because as we move along to describe the qualities of a good leader, we will have to compare it against the ideal-typical Weberian leader.

Weber suggests that the ideal-typical leader must possess at least three decisive qualities. First, it is necessary for a genuine leader to have a passionate devotion to a cause and this devotion must be an unconditional one, which bears "a will to make history, to set new values for others," and it has to be "nourished from feeling" (Keane, 1984: 56).

Second, authentic leaders must "cultivate a sense of their objective responsibilities," and for the fulfillment of a definite goal, its realization, effects, and unintended consequences, they are the ones solely responsible (Keane, 1984: 57).

Third, genuine leaders must be able to give due weight to realities and "measure up to them inwardly." As such "effective leadership is synonymous with neither mere demagoguery nor the worship of power for its own sake. Passionate and responsible leaders will shun any uncompromising ethic of ultimate ends" (Keane, 1984: 57).

If we sum up these three qualities, we can see the Weberian ideal-typical leader as an ethically responsible leader. Weber integrated this view of leadership within the fabric of bureaucratic domination, though. Therefore, the solution he saw to the substantive irrationalism of bureaucratic domination was plebiscitarian leader democracy. Weber suggests this new form of leadership to compensate for what he considers the "iron cage" in which you have "specialists without spirit, sensualists without heart; this nullity imagines that it has attained a level of civilization never before achieved" (Weber, 2001: 124).

It is right here that the failure of Weber reveals itself. His political theory fails to distinguish between responsible democratic leadership and the charismatic domination of ruthless demagogues, such as Hitler, Mussolini, or Stalin. Incidentally, they all rose to power after Weber's death.

It is true that Weber's account of modern bureaucratic organization and its irrational effects is ideal-typical and as such the descriptive analysis of its elements can never be exhaustive. However, having Weber in mind, it is important to note that, first, his description of the qualities of authentic leaders can serve as a guiding principle in our case, and second, while giving due weight to Weber, we must be able to see beyond his formulation of the qualities of good leaders.

The case study of the AKDN very well serves our purpose in terms of the type of authority it represents, in terms of the leadership it cultivates and the model it has produced over the past 50 years.

Emerging Signs of a Paradigm Shift

We have witnessed a sort of degradation and disintegration of the concept of authority both in the West and among Muslims. The AKDN seems to be presenting a model of leadership and authority that stands quite distinct from all other models.

In the AKDN, the holder of authority is neither a civil or military servant, nor a president or a prime minister, who could be removed by election. They are not even subject to threats of removal by authoritarian powers in non-democratic states. Yet, the AKDN as an embodiment of the Ismaili imamate represents a kind of transmutation in the very concept of the imamate so that we are witnessing a subversive role on the part of the AKDN (note the use of vocabularies used in its discourse changing the linguistic constructs) and a sublimation of the person of the Imam into "the institution of imamate" or "the office of imamate." As such, these developments can be put under the rubric of a paradigm shift.

In speaking about a "paradigm shift," I have borrowed the term from Thomas Kuhn. Kuhn attempted to explain the shift from the Ptolemaic astronomy to Copernican astronomy, for example, or from the Aristotelian dynamics to Newtonian dynamics, using the term "paradigm." By choosing this term, Kuhn meant to

suggest that some accepted examples of actual scientific practice—examples which include law, theory, application, and instrumentation together

provide models from which spring particular coherent traditions of scientific research. (Kuhn, 1966: 10)

As such, we can speak of two distinct periods: the one before the imamate of Aga Khan IV and the one beginning with his imamate. It is true that these pre- and post-paradigm periods can coexist with each other, under certain circumstances, but the present period bears some characteristics that make it fit to be explained under the rubric of a new paradigm.

This research builds on the historical developments of the concepts of leadership with a specific reference to how this leadership was understood among the Shiʻi branch of Islam. However, instead of looking at the wider spectrum of the Muslim world, I have narrowed down the research to the particular case of the AKDN among various "networks" that exist in the Muslim world.

Some of the reasons that make the AKDN a good model for investigating this "paradigm shift" are outlined: (a) the AKDN has had a wide and deep impact in different regions of the world—going beyond nation-states and borders; (b) the AKDN has been indiscriminately promoting development whereas "discrimination" seems to persist in some other models; (c) the AKDN represents a sort of "mutation" in leadership given the history of the Ismaili imamate (these "mutations" have occurred a number of times in the past too); and (d) the network is increasingly becoming an embodiment of a "cosmopolitan" form of leadership, establishing itself on the foundation of pluralism, not just as a mere strategy but as a very essential and vital part of its existence.

We also have to take into account the historicity of leadership and the elements that form and shape the concepts of leadership and authority (here it does not make any sense to simply talk about leadership among only the Ithnā ʻasharīs or among only the Ismailis or other Muslims; there has been a constant interaction among all these branches on issues of leadership, and a great bulk of literature already exists on this). There are inherited patterns that are very well reflected in Shiʻi doctrines of leadership.

Throughout history, we have seen changes and differences in understanding leadership. But in our times, we are witnessing a sudden leap in these notions. The signs of this leap, particularly in the Ismaili Community, and even among the rest of the Shiʻi community in general, can hardly be overlooked.

We do have a broadening repertoire of conflicting models, but there are certain signs that mark a change of paradigm:

1. In the modern era, Muslim leadership has decided or learned to use the media in all its new forms (newspapers, radio, television,

internet, blogs, and very recently Web 2.0 social networks) to promote its cause;

2. The English language has increasingly become a dominant means of transmitting ideas instead of purely relying on traditional (non-Western) means of communication;

3. The emerging paradigm of leadership has defied the standard scholarly Weberian model in that it works across borders of nation-states but still remains within the boundaries of particular states without breaking any laws;

4. A new language seems to have developed: new terminologies and vocabularies are being increasingly used, which either did not at all exist in the Muslim leadership language or did not ever represent themselves in such a manner. These new vocabularies include Civil Society, democracy, pluralism, meritocracy, enabling environment, sustainable development, cosmopolitanism, constitution, and other terms that are vividly part of a modern set of terminologies that deal with leadership. However, the use of these terms are not within the Eurocentric discourses and models, and in the case of the Ismaili imamate, there are some nuances in the way these terms are used that make them sharply distinct from a Eurocentric model;

5. Muslim views about ethics have undergone significant changes, and I am particularly emphasizing "views" to indicate that this change of views is not a widespread practical issue. The degree of change in each case is different among different Muslim groups, but in the particular case of the Ismailis, this is something quite clear. These changes are reflected, for example, in how Muslims have dealt with medical issues, and specific examples can be seen in the Ismaili Community as well with how the leadership has tried to cast away traditional views on diseases. To be more precise, these changes may contribute to a science of ethics that can stand independent of religion;

6. The Muslim leadership has started using networks as an important factor in working with institutions, and this is reflected in the activities of the AKDN; this use of networks is not based on the traditional networks, which existed in the past; it draws on modern concepts of networks.

The central question of this book is connected to the impact of a particular interpretation of leadership, authority, justice, and ethics embodied and reflected in the activities of the AKDN that has impacted the

dynamics of civil society in certain regions in the Muslim world where the AKDN has been active.

The AKDN: An Unconventional Actor

As explained earlier, the model of the AKDN has turned out to be a vividly novel example of leadership and authority. The following paragraphs are introductory statements about the AKDN in its official website, which reflect some of the ideas in question:

> AKDN is a contemporary endeavour of the Ismaili Imamat to realise the social conscience of Islam through institutional action. AKDN agencies conduct their programmes without regard to the faith, origin or gender.
>
> The AKDN agencies, therefore, make a long-term commitment to the areas in which they work, guided by the philosophy that a humane, sustainable environment must reflect the choices made by people themselves of how they live and wish to improve their prospects in harmony with their environment. Sustainability is, thus, a central consideration from the outset.
>
> The AKDN itself is an independent self-governing system of agencies, institutions, and programmes under the leadership of the Ismaili Imamat. Their main sources of support are the Ismaili community with its tradition of philanthropy, voluntary service and self-reliance, and the leadership and material underwriting of the hereditary Imam and Imamat resources. (The AKDN Website)[37]

The AKDN is one among many NGOs and civil society organizations. It is governed by the leadership of the Ismaili Imam, which in itself does not make it distinct from similar NGOs with religious backgrounds. There are differences, however, that make the AKDN distinct from other networks. Some of these have to do with the overall approach of the AKDN to development. The commitment of the AKDN to sustainable development and long-term investments places it among a smaller number of NGOs with this vision. Moreover, the ethical dimension of it, which is the product of one interpretation of Islam, with Ismaili elements in it, is another aspect that makes it different. The Aga Khan's approach to education is often cited by him to be in line with the policies of his Fatimid ancestors in establishing the Al-Azhar University. Such articulations lie behind the rationale of the Aga Khan University (AKU), while it is clearly a highly bureaucratic institution based on Western models.

I will address further details of this unconventionality of the AKDN in later chapters, but the above examples give us an idea that we are dealing with a different sort of an NGO in the civil society.

The AKDN as an NGO in Civil Society

The AKDN is a non-governmental organization, by its very nature. It is neither run by any state nor is it controlled or influenced by state policymaking in a direct way. In a very broad sense, then, the AKDN is a network of NGOs.

Noting the complexity of the organization and the wide range of its activities, Ruthven argues that

> The AKDN eludes familiar definitions based on normal organizational categories. It is neither a non-government organization (NGO) concerned with international development nor a faith-based charity (although it has some characteristics of both). (Ruthven, in Daftary, 2011: 190)

Ruthven's point is helpful in making us aware of the complexities involved in attributing an NGO character to the AKDN. Nonetheless, the AKDN is generally categorized as an NGO that "organizes Ismaili cultural, economic, and social service institutions in a way similar to a transnational corporation" (Kaiser, 1996: 2).

There is a diversity of NGOs working nationally and internationally, and the AKDN shares many qualities with other NGOs. There are NGOs in the Muslim world whose agendas are radically different from the AKDN, and as Mandaville points out, among the diverse transnational expressions of Islam

> in global communications forums on the Internet, and in the activities of a growing number of Muslim NGOs, we find evidence of a transnational Islam whose agenda is organized instead around themes such as education, human rights, and gender equality (Mandaville, in Hefner, 2005: 302).[38]

There are transnational Muslim networks that are defined by militancy and revolution. Yet, "the boundaries between these two categories of Muslim transnationalism are not always clearly delineated" (Mandaville, in Hefner, 2005: 302). This is not the situation with the AKDN though, as its mandate is clear and easily distinguishable from networks from the other end of the spectrum. Since the AKDN itself is funded by the

imamate, the Ismaili Community, and international agencies, it is comparable with other NGOs in this sense. As Kaiser points out:

> This international context is not unique to Ismaili social service initiatives; many organizations in civil society are part of larger transnational enterprises or receive substantial support from such international donors as United Nations-related agencies, foreign governments, and private nongovernmental organizations in industrialized countries. (Kaiser, 1996: 2)

The AKDN has similarities with transnational corporations and civil society NGOs, in terms of international links and its integration with local communities where it is active (Kaiser, 1996: 2). What must be noted here is that the AKDN is not a local NGO; it has an international/transnational character, which is a product of the history of the development of the Community.

An awareness of this NGO quality of the AKDN is also present in the language of the Aga Khan himself, highlighting the role of the NGOs as balancers between local autonomy and effective oversight of foreign and national leaders, who have a global vision for organizations:

> Successful NGOs have effective boards to work with management on defining the mission, strategic directions and objectives. Management is held accountable for results. The right balance seems to have been struck between local autonomy and effective oversight. Risks are consciously evaluated, and a prudent equilibrium established between the need for social innovation and the danger of failure. (Aga Khan IV, in Kaiser, 1996: 9)

The AKDN as an NGO is distinguished from Community organizations even though the network is reliant on the voluntary input of the members of the Community. It is for this reason that Susumu evaluates the AKDN as part of the "Islamic civil society" (Susumu, 2000: 149) and further reiterates the point that Ruthven makes by referring to how the Ismailis themselves understand the relation between the AKDN, Community institutions, and the imamate:

> The NGOs are distinguished from the Ismaili religious organizations that are exclusively for jamaat—the Ismaili community. For the Ismailis, however, religious organizations and the NGOs are properly integrated into community life, since both come from the office of Imam: imamat. (Susumu, 2000: 150)

Susumu understands the role of the Aga Khan as a "balancer" between state and society. Assuming this role implies, according to Susumu, a "reconstruction" of the Community and the imamate (Susumu, 2000: 152). He refers to the traditional Islamic society as having a dynamic interaction between the society and the state whereby the ʿulamā function as balancers,[39] and he continues to compare the role of the Aga Khan with that of the ʿulamā:

> It is clear that Aga Khan IV is playing the role of a balancer in line with this model. In Ismailism, Imam is the sole interpreter of the inner, hidden meaning of the Quran. Thus the function of ulama in this model converges in the imamat. But in a country in which the Ismailis are a minority and the question of "which Islam?" is a crucial matter, claiming a peculiar form of Islam is not beneficial. (Susumu, 2000: 157)

Therefore, the idea of the AKDN as a new instrument for playing the role of a balancer becomes crucial, in which the institution is neither religious nor political but acts in the context of a global civil society and within the discourse of social development.

While the AKDN is not unique in terms of its NGO qualities, Susumu argues that it has to be seen within the context of Islamic civil society and takes one step further to claim that

> it gives us an occasion to reconsider our perceptions of "Islam as a threat." While NGOs based on Christian or Buddhist ideas are evaluated in their own terms, the Islamic ones are not. Understanding Islamic Revival Movements as a quest for public benefit through autonomous Islamic institutions will diversify and enrich our perception of civil society. (Susumu, 2000: 159)

However, there is one aspect about the AKDN that makes it unique among other models. The AKDN is headed by the Ismaili Imam, who is the present living hereditary leader of the Ismaili Community. I know of no other network claiming a similar quality for its head.[40]

The AKDN is an NGO and also a form of bureaucratic organization, which employs a certain degree of rationalism for achieving its goals. A Weberian approach to a bureaucratic-rational organization requires impersonalism as a guide to rational decision-making. For Weber, the more bureaucracy is dehumanized, the more successful it will be in eliminating personal emotions and purely personal, irrational, or emotional elements. As regards the AKDN, the case of this NGO is far more

complex than simply being a bureaucratic machine, although there are oscillations and centrifugal forces working to bring into harmony this bureaucratic character with its Community-based drive.

The AKDN Strengthening Civil society

The goal of the AKDN has also been described as trying to make the countries where they work countries of opportunity for their people. This goal has been explained by the Aga Khan in close connection with the civil society:

> The goal is clear: the aim is to create or strengthen civil society in developing countries. This single goal, when it is achieved, is in fact necessary and sufficient to ensure peaceful and stable development over the long term, even when governance is problematic. (Aga Khan, 2009)[41]

And it is right here that the Aga Khan highlights a significant point about these agencies: "The network ... is statutorily secular." (Aga Khan, 2009). The statutory aspect that the Aga Khan adds to this "secular" definition may dampen the effect of a secular attribute to it, but as I earlier explained about secularity, we must note that, first, the Aga Khan is not using it in a radical secular sense (as we can see it in his conduct and his vision). Second, this secularity deals only with the legal aspect of it, which does not bear a radical secularizing effect on the content and nature of the AKDN.

There is something peculiar about the AKDN. If we look back at history and study the formation of the Ismaili community, whose spiritual leader heads the AKDN, it sometimes seems like a paradoxical phenomenon. For example, if we look at the discourse used by the present Aga Khan (ideas such as pluralism, Civil Society, etc.), we can immediately see the difference of approach with that of his predecessor. However, this is something that the present head of the AKDN and the forty-ninth "hereditary" Imam of the Shi'a Ismaili Muslims claims is a continuation of the same tradition of his ancestors, i.e., the Prophet of Islam and his son-in-law, 'Alī, the fourth Caliph after the Prophet.

There are, of course, a wide range of issues that could be brought up regarding this "development network," but I have only restricted myself to the issues of authority/leadership.

The AKDN has a bureaucratic administration model, which grounds itself on the ethical principles of Islam. The ethical dimension of the network is the foundation of the activity of these institutions giving it

a distinctively Muslim character, reflected in the vision of the Ismaili imamate (which I will write about in detail in the section on the Imam's vision). The complexity of the issues at stake and the diversity of the constituencies of the AKDN (although it does continue to serve its primary constituency, which is the Ismaili community) make it an interesting case study.

The AKDN is carrying an element of "charisma" in it that is not properly studied and explored in light of these recent developments in the bureaucratic administration of the affairs of the institution of the imamate. Moreover, the mechanisms of how this charisma works in the Ismaili community is either not properly explained/understood or remain trapped within a traditionally Weberian perception of it.

CHAPTER 3

The Aga Khan: A Visionary Leader

Introduction

Aga Khan III, the forty-eighth Ismaili Imam, who had played a critical role in the modernization of the Ismaili Community and starting the engine of institutional proliferation, died in 1957. His grandson Karim succeeded to the office of the imamate on July 11, 1957. This appointment was the beginning of a new phase in the history of the Ismaili Community. Looking at the achievements of Aga Khan IV in 2011, Steinberg says,

> He has intensified and expanded, moreover, the institutional scope of the imamate, to the degree that it reaches into the lives (in different ways in different places) of most every Isma'ili subject. But it was his predecessor that set, in an earlier moment, the tone and timbre for contemporary Isma'ili institutional globality. (Steinberg, 2011: 55)

In a paragraph in his published memoirs when he speaks about his son Aly, Aga Khan III mentions his two grandsons:

> These boys are now at school, and in due course they will go to universities in America—the elder, Karim, who shows promise in mathematics, to M.I.T., we hope, and the other Amyn, probably to the Harvard Law School. (Aga Khan, 1954: 312)

Karim, who later became Aga Khan IV, eventually went to Harvard and studied Islamic History. A few years later, we read in the Aga Khan's will the following pronouncement regarding the issue of succession, in which he designates his grandson Karim as the forty-ninth Imam of the Ismaili Community:

> Ever since the time of my ancestor Ali, the first Imam, that is to say over a period of thirteen hundred years, it has always been the tradition of our

family that each Imam chooses his successor at his absolute and unfettered discretion from amongst any of his descendants, whether they be sons or remote male issue.

The above section is an articulation of the general Shi'i doctrine on the imamate and succession. The Aga Khan continues to give an explanation and justification for his choice.[1]

And in these circumstances and in view of the fundamentally altered conditions in the world in very recent years due to the great changes which have taken place including the discoveries of atomic science, I am convinced that it is in the best interest of the Shia Muslim Ismailia Community that I should be succeeded by a young man who has been brought up and developed during recent years and in the midst of the new age and who brings a new outlook on life to his office as Imam. For these reasons, I appoint my grandson Karim, the son of my own son, Aly Salomone Khan to succeed to the title of Aga Khan and to the Imam and Pir of all Shia Ismailian followers and should my said grandson, KARIM, predecease me, then I appoint his brother Amyn Mohammed, the second son of my son Aly Salomone Khan, as my successor to the Imamat.

This section of the will clearly gives an indication of Aga Khan III's awareness of the complexities of the modern world. Besides, there is the issue of longevity: a younger successor has a higher chance of living longer. He then adds a consultative measure to the institution for the benefit of his successor, and even though the new Imam has his own unfettered authority, the outgoing Imam suggests that the new Imam should be guided by his wife:

I desire that my successor shall, during the first seven years of his Imamat, be guided on questions of general Imamat Policy, by my said wife, Yvette called Yve Blanche Labrousse, the Begum Aga Khan, who has been familiar for many years with the problems facing my followers, and in whose wise judgment, I place the greatest confidence. I warn my successor to the Imamat, never to do anything during his Imamat that would reduce the responsibility of the Imam for the maintenance of the true Shia Imami Ismaili faith, as developed historically from the time of my ancestor Ali, the founder until my own. (Frischauer, 1970: 208)[2]

Signs of these shifts had begun to emerge before the appointment of the new Imam. The Aga Khan's will captures some of these in the way he articulates his will. It can be argued that this is a legal document, and this is what it is expected to be, but this argument disregards the position

of the Ismaili Imam and the theology behind his status. Here, we find seeds of a dormant rationalism embedded in the will. This is one of the rare occasions, if not the only case, when an Ismaili Imam explains *why* he is appointing someone as his successor; in the earlier times, the Imam would just pronounce and the community would be expected to abide by it. Even though the essential element of the authority of the Imam remains the same here, there is a prominent rational element in this approach. Once you open the gates for rational engagement, it would not be easy to roll back its effects. This is probably one of the effects of modernity and engaging with the modern world: the imamate would no longer wish to establish its authority without a modern appeal merely relying on pre-modern criteria.

The Aga Khan's Vision in Retrospect[3]

What we see today in the achievements of the present Ismaili Imam, his institutions, and the model of leadership he represents is nothing but a realization and an embodiment of the vision he has had in the beginning of his accession to the imamate of the Ismaili Community and that which has developed over the course of the years. Over the years, many changes have occurred in the world, and these changes have impacted the Ismaili Community around the globe in many ways. Hence, the vision of the Ismaili imamate has been adapting to the new circumstances and readjusting itself.

The main purpose of this chapter is to enumerate and investigate some of the most central elements and dominant themes in the vision of the present Ismaili Imam in a way that they can describe and explain the transmutation and readjustment of authority in the Ismaili Community. In order to put these elements in the right context, we have to address certain historical backgrounds of the Ismaili community.

Justice and the "Social Conscience of Islam"

One of the issues that has been in the memory of the Shi'i faith for centuries has been the concern for justice. The idea of justice has found many different expressions in other Shi'i communities. These expressions are sometimes common among all Shi'i groups. There is a historical understanding of justice among the Shi'i Muslims, which has given a political dimension to it, that remains until the present day and gets tied to its political—sometimes radical—expressions in our time. When we look at how the idea of justice is understood by the Ismaili imamate

and how it is pursued, it is important to go back and check the common ground and where the Ismaili imamate has chosen a very different path with far less political engagement when compared to other Shiʿi groups: one seeks justice through political action in the form of establishing a state, and the other one (the Ismailis) directs its pursuit of justice to areas where this justice can be achieved through development work.

In order to better address the issue of justice, I am going back in history to find parallels between what seems to be today a divergent path of the Ismaili imamate as compared to the other Shiʿi groups. If we look at one of the key issues at the heart of the present Ithnā ʿAsharī community (best expressed in the modern-day Iranian society), we can find a similar tone but with very different content in the Ismaili history, which can help us make sense of this idea of the pursuit of justice today: messianic religion and politics.

Messianism in Ismaili Thought

The concept of a messianic figure is a common theme in many religious traditions (specifically in the Abrahamic faiths). This idea has been prevalent particularly when making references to the appearance/reappearance of a savior in the future that would bring justice to all people and turn the earth into paradise. In the Islamic tradition, as Henry Corbin speaks of it (Corbin, 1962: 73), we find that apart from the prophecies of the appearance of a figure/leader/Imam in the Muslim context, we have a similar idea in the Zoroastrian tradition, which refers to the *Saoshyant* as the figurehead for the messianic person.[4]

In contemporary Iran, which is now a Shiʿi Muslim state following the Twelver branch of Shiʿism, the idea of the appearance of a savior has become much stronger. Speaking on the original contexts of the formation and development of the idea of the "absent Imam," Soroush says,

If we look at the political theories of Shiʿi jurists, the issue of the absence of the Imam is clearly reflected in them. For a while after the demise of the eleventh Imam, the Shiʿi [imami] community was in a state of bewilderment. Their theory of imamate was telling them that the Imam must always be physically present and accessible in the community and the raison d'être of the Imam was administration of the affairs of society and leading people to the right path. Therefore, an "absent Imam" was an unknown and undefined idea to them. For the same reason, for about a century after this, the Shiʿi community was in a state that was described by Shiʿi and Muslim historians as a "period of bewilderment" (*dawra-yi*

ḥayrat). It was during this same period of bewilderment that gradually a new meaning of the theory of imamate takes root in the Shiʿi community. The major content and prevalent theme of this new theory was that there is no necessity that the Imam should be present among people with his physical body. It suffices that he pays this attention and supervision on the people. Thus, the idea of the "absent Imam" (*imām-i ghāʾib*) was born. The absent Imam is in fact an absent authority (*walī*) who is among people and with the people. He has a real presence in the hearts and minds of the faithful. He is the medium of divine blessings without showing himself to them and he would one day appear. (Soroush, 2001: 60)

The same idea of the appearance of a "resurrector" (a *qāʾim*) (to use a specifically Ismaili term) has been dominant at different stages of the Ismaili history. The earliest references can be found in the initial stages of the Ismaili history when the Ismaili community had just begun identifying itself as a distinct religious community of Shiʿi leanings.[5]

In the Nizārī branch of the Ismaili faith (that is, followers of the present Aga Khan), there has been at least five instances when this idea has become dominant in one way or another. The first two instances are at the time of the formative period of the Ismaili community. And the figures in question were two Ismaili Imams, namely, Imam Ismāʿīl b. Jaʿfar al-Ṣādiq and his son Imam Muḥammad b. Ismāʿīl. During this period, the idea was still in its infancy and we often see the idea of a re-emergence after death (*rajʿat*), rather than prediction of the appearance of an Imam in the future.[6] After these two Imams, during a period that is called the first period of concealment (*dawr al-satr al-awwal*), there are some references to the appearance of an Imam called the Mahdi (Esmail and Nanji in Nasr, 1977: 234). This prediction coincided or, to quote Ismaili sources, was fulfilled with the military campaigns and expeditions of the eleventh Ismaili Imam (twelfth if we count Ḥasan b. ʿAlī b. Abī Ṭālib).[7]. Imam Muḥammad al-Mahdī became the founder of the Fatimid empire and the first Ismaili Fatimid Caliph-Imam. Wilferd Madelung's brief paragraph in the EI[2] article captures this idea:

In pre-Fāṭimid Ismāʿīlism, the terms Mahdī and Ḳāʾim were both used, as in Imāmī Shīʿism, for the expected messianic *Imām*. After the rise of the Fāṭimids, some of the predictions concerning the Mahdī were held to have been realised by the Fāṭimid caliph Mahdī, the founder of the dynasty, while others would be fulfilled by his successors. This theory was elaborated by the Ḳāḍī al-Nuʿmān (d. 363/974) in his K. *Sharḥ al-akhbār* where he quoted numerous traditions about the Mahdī from Sunnī, Imāmī, and Zaydī sources and applied them to Mahdī and his successors, partially

by interpreting them figuratively...The name Mahdī was henceforth reserved to the first Fāṭimid caliph, while the eschatological *Imām* and Seventh Apostle still expected for the future was only called the Ḳā'im. (Madelung, "al-Mahdī", in EI², Brill Online)[8]

The emergence of different narratives or traditions referring to his campaign and the establishment of a Muslim dynasty (whose claim was clearly the consolidation of justice in contrast with the Abbasid state) was nothing unusual. However, this idea did not disappear with the establishment of the Fatimid state. It continues in different forms, and as Madelung mentions, it continues to be referred to with the term *qā'im* (Ḳā'im).

Is it true to say that this flame continues to burn as long as there is a deep yearning for a justice that never seems to be completely established for good? We will have to trace this idea through history up until contemporary times.

In this context, Daftary speaks of the *ghulāt* (extremists):

The more radical Shīʿīs, especially the *ghulāt* theorists who had already established the tradition of *conferring superhuman qualities on their imams*, began to think even more freely about the person and authority of the imam. Simultaneously, they found themselves speculating on wider issues of religious importance, such as the nature of God, the soul and the afterlife. The speculations of the *ghulāt* soon brought about many more doctrinal innovations. As a result, *the earlier eschatological doctrines of ghayba, rajʿa and Mahdism, which in any case were to become accepted Shīʿī views, in themselves no longer represented ghuluww.* (Daftary, 2007: 87).[9]

In later stages of the Fatimid empire, the fourth case occurs. We can see the invocation of this idea during the time of the Fatimid Caliph-Imam al-Ḥākim bi 'Amr Allāh, the fifth Fatimid Caliph. With his disappearance and apparent death of the Caliph, a group of the subjects of the Fatimid states, who were extremist Ismailis, declared that the Caliph was not dead and he shall return to the world. This group had already got into clashes with the state, and the Fatimid Caliph had given explicit orders for suppressing them. The Ismaili *dāʿī* al-Kirmānī (earlier mentioned in chapter 2) was commissioned to write a book in refutation of their extremist views attributing divine qualities to the Imam (Daftary, 2007: 188). This group came to be known as the Druze and their remnants can still be found in present-day Lebanon and Syria. Daftary suggests that, "contrary to the claims of some later Sunni authors, there is

no evidence suggesting that al-Ḥākim himself had in any way encouraged or supported the extremist ideas upheld by the founders of the Druze movement" (Daftary, 2007: 187). As al-Kirmānī continues his refutation, Daftary argues,

> Recognizing that the Druze "heresy" was essentially rooted in the hopes for the advent of the *qāʾim* with its eschatological implications raised by earlier Ismāʿīlī teaching, al-Kirmānī repudiated the ideas that the resurrection (*qiyāma*) had occurred with the appearance of al-Hākim and that the era of Islam had ended. The era of Islam and the validity of its *sharīʿa* would, he argued, continue under al-Hākim's numerous prospective successors as imams. (Daftary, 2007: 188)

This era is the most controversial chapter in the Fatimid history, and later views of the Ismaili scholars continue to follow on the line of al-Kirmānī's views, such that even in the Persian writings of Nāṣir-i Khusraw, the Persian Ismaili *dāʿī* and poet-philosopher, there are explicit references to the idea of a the appearance of a "resurrector" (a *qāʾim*). In his Persian treatise titled *Khʷān al-Ikhwān*, he uses some terminologies and words that bring this idea of the resurrector (*qāʾim*) and his functions closer to what was about to happen, as the fifth case of the Ismaili messianism, in the Ismaili history of Iran a short while after his death.

The reason for studying this messianic aspect in the context of this book, which is about the transmutations of the Ismaili imamate, is twofold. First is the critical event in Alamūt, in the proclamation of the *qiyāmat,* which transformed the Ismaili Community, theologically and socially, in such a way that it paved the way for later developments. Rethinking the balance between the *ẓāhir* and the *bāṭin* left its impression on the Ismaili Community in terms of its later strategies of survival disguised among Sufis and the wider community of Muslims. It also continued until the modern period when Aga Khan III's teachings have a resonance of similar themes.

The second reason is to demonstrate that the kind of messianism, or apocalyptic attitude, has disappeared in the context of these transformations. The only element of that messianism that has survived is the theological consequences of the doctrine of *qiyāmat* in the Alamūt period.

In its very pure form, messianic modes act as a kind of "social imaginary," to use Charles Taylor's terms. And this social imaginary "is that common understanding that makes possible common practices and a widely shared sense of legitimacy" (Taylor, 2004: 23). In this sense, messianic modes with charismatic figures help devise concepts of political

leadership. The example of justice is helpful here because when there is an institution for justice, the concept of justice does not come into being *after* the establishment of an institution for it. You cannot accidentally stumble upon a court and then think that the court should dispense justice. There is already a shared vision about what justice is. The preconception is already there. And this depends more on practice than theory.

This is not about elite theory nor is it about academics. It is simply the way ordinary people understand it and relate to it, and it is out of these the institutions emerge (Taylor, 2004: 23). So, we may find the preconceptions of justice in the messianic mode. But what remains in the case of the Ismaili imamate today is that, first, the Imam is considered to have a link to the transcendental, and he has a message (which is the Shiʻi ideal of a fair and just society). Second, the Imam is not only the conveyer of this message, but he is also responsible for delivering and sustaining that message. So, the Imam has a dual role: one that is the transcendent one tracing his origins back to previous Imams all the way to the Prophet, and the other one is that he is pragmatic.

We can see that readjusting the balance between the *ẓāhir* and the *bāṭin* does not eliminate the need for justice or for institutions to realize them, and the core idea of a messianic mode keeps coming back even though not in a revolutionary sense.

The Ismailis of Alamūt and the Concept of Paradise on Earth

The era of the declaration of the resurrection (*iʻlām-i qiyāmat*) by the twenty-third Ismaili Ḥasan II, better known for his nickname ʻAlā dhikrihiʼl salām is perhaps the most controversial era of the Ismaili faith. The core of his teaching was that for those who have reached the core and inner meaning of the *sharīʻa*, there is no need to observe the exoteric aspects of the faith. Although, later in the Ismaili theology there are explicit and tough conditions as to what amounts to knowing and recognizing the esoteric and inner meanings of the faith, the general idea is that "those who belong to the realm of unity" (*ahl-i waḥdat*) are the ones who are exempt from observing the rituals of faith, and these are the people for whom paradise is fulfilled on earth.

This highly spiritual and esoteric interpretation of faith, which was so radically declared by the Ismailis of Alamūt, who were already a quasi-independent state within the majority Sunnī establishment of Iran, caused a great deal of difficulties for them. There were already Sufi

interpretations of faith in existence with such implications but they were never so boldly expressed in a religious setting by a recognized religious leader who was in the position of authority as well (see for example ʿAyn al-Quaḍāt Hamadānī, 1998: 266).[10]

ʿAlā dhikrihi'l salām came to be known as the "resurrector" or the qāʾim from that point on. It seems that this is the climax of apocalyptic and messianic ideas in the Ismaili faith. If there are ever any such references in the Ismaili doctrines to a messianic figure, it is merely in the context of their precautionary measures of concealment (taqiyya) in the guise of Sufis or Ithnā ʿasharīs. It is as if with the culmination of the idea of the resurrector in a figure whose revolutionary act of interpreting the faith in such a highly esoteric way completely brings to an end political ambitions based on the appearance of a savior.[11]

When the Ismaili Imam at Alamūt speaks about paradise on earth, he does not mean it in a literal sense. There were no doubt misunderstandings. Their contemporaries had assumed that he meant something like an apocalypse and the end of the world. The world did not end with his declaration of this resurrection nor in his sermons did he ever say this would happen.

Later developments in the history of the Ismailis reveal how significant that moment had been: subverting this equilibrium of the exoteric and the esoteric in the interest of the esoteric. It did not, however, necessitate a complete abrogation of the exoteric rituals from that point onward. These rituals do come back in different forms very frequently, but they still maintain that kind of spiritual ethos that transcends the boundaries of time and space in the practice of faith. They even return as early as a couple of decades in the time of ʿAlā dhikrihi'l salām's grandson, Jalāl al-Dīn Ḥasan.[12]

Beyond the End of History and Scripturalism

Whatever has happened so far in the Ismaili history, one thing has definitely disappeared from the official doctrinal thought of the present-day Ismailis (and it even makes more sense after the event in Alamūt). The determinist views of history are emphatically driven into the shadows in light of the current strategies of the Aga Khans in leading the community. It is as if there was no longer a need for this doctrine (see my notes earlier in chapter 2 where I have explained the dialectical abrogation). The Imam is already present among his followers. He is working for the improvement of their worldly quality of life without feeling the need for a subversive political revolution of reshaping the world order by means

of political power. Also, a few centuries before, a spiritual revolution had paved the ground for the easier modification of rituals in light of new interpretations of the role of the Imam.

In a rather different context, Ernest Gellner says:

> Just as the extreme cult-of-personality of the Ismailis gave the Aga Khan great freedom in choosing paths of modernisation for his community—for it caused him to be unhampered by either scripture or scholars—so a very narrow scripturalism could have a similar effect, at the opposite end of the religious spectrum (Gellner, 1981: 62–63).[13]

While his reference to the "cult-of-personality" is rather crude, the main argument is clear. The Aga Khan as the Imam has had the freedom and the "unfettered" authority to interpret the faith, while others did not and do not have this authority so simply to interpret the faith to this extent. However, it is important to realize that the Ismaili imamate has always been adamant that this interpretation of faith happens within the faith of Islam and it is not tantamount to denying the basic tenets of the faith (this point shall be elaborated separately and in greater detail when we discuss the Ismaili Constitution).

Developments in the practices of the Ismaili community and the decisions of the Ismaili imamate and particularly the Aga Khans have never occurred abruptly and without a context. Examples of these changes can be seen in the tensions that occurred during the imamate of Aga Khan I and led to a court case, which was eventually resolved in favor of the Aga Khan. Later, similar changes occurred in the time of Aga Khan III over a dispute with some of his relatives and a certain representative of his in Persia at that time.

The Ismaili Constitution: Cornerstone for Institutional Change

Following the migration of the Ismaili imamate to the subcontinent at the time of Aga Khan I after a conflict that had arisen between the Ismaili Imam of the time, Aga Khan I, and the Qājār monarch in Persia,[14] some years later, in the beginning of the twentieth century, we witness the genesis of a document that was initially called "Rules and Regulations" but was later labeled as the "Constitution."

In the very early copies of this document, the title reads: "*The Khoja Shia Imami Ismaili Council Rules and Regulations...Authorized by Mawlana Sarkar His Highness Aga Sir Sultan Mohamed Shah, Aghakhan.*" When we turn the page (in the 1913 copy for Poona), we come upon

a registration detail too: *Registered under the Government of India's Act XXV of 1867 AD.*

These rules and regulations that developed through time and finally culminated into what is known today as *The Constitution of the Shia Imami Ismaili Muslims* marks the beginning of an unprecedented era in the history of the Ismaili leadership.

Before we go into any further details of the implications of the coming into existence of such a document and its role in defining authority and power for the Ismaili community (and hence the role of its present-day institutions), one needs a proper historical background on why these documents came into existence in the first place and what was the context in which they were developed.

Like any religious community, the Ismaili community had its own traditions of funding and economy: the tithes, *zakāt* or the part of one's property or income that is believed to belong to the Imam. By tradition, every Ismaili was expected to give a proportion of his income (one tenth or one eighth) to the Ismaili Imam of his time.

The issue would be simple in cases where the Imam was physically available and people had easier access to him, as when he used to live in Persia, and his Persian followers did not have to go through a very complicated and lengthy process for submitting their dues, although even then there occurred certain conflicts between local leaders and the Imams, but these incidents could practically be ignored in the presence of the Imam.

In the case of the subcontinent where the Imam finally moved, the local leaders, or *Pīrs*, used to collect the funds and then send them to Persia to the Imam's headquarters. In any event, the point was that these local leaders had direct control and access to the funds that were, by tradition, to be submitted to the Imam.

As the Imam moved to India, new tensions began to surface between the Ismaili Imam and the local leaders, who were practically the elite of the Ismaili community, which was known as the *Khoja* community. During a dispute over the leadership of the Imam, the Khojas split into two groups: one that accepted the leadership and authority of the Aga Khan as their rightful Imam and the heir to the imamate of Ismaili Imams, and the other that did not accept the Aga Khan as the Imam and claimed that they had never been Ismailis. This latter group divided into two groups: a group that declared itself as Sunni (belonging to the bigger mainstream group of Muslims) and another that declared itself as Twelvers (like the majority of Shi'i Muslims in Persia).

The biggest change occurs at exactly this point. These schisms were nothing new in the history of a Muslim community (and the Ismaili Community too), but the way the issue was dealt with on the side of the Ismaili Imam was a method that had never been tried before. The Ismaili Imam accepted the court's decision to resolve the issue.[15]

This is a unique incident in the entire history of this community. No one had ever before, taken an issue of conflict and dispute inside this minority community to an outside court. The Aga Khan took the lawsuit to the British Raj of India. There are two major and important lawsuits by the Ismaili Imams in India: one at the time of Aga Khan I—the first Ismaili Imam who lived the later part of his life in India—and the other at the time of Aga Khan III. Both these cases were somehow linked to the way properties and funds were managed by the Imam and the extent of the authority of the heir to the Ismaili imamate. This may appear at first glance to be a purely financial issue, but the implications were far greater than a simple financial dispute.

These legal disputes occurred during the lifetime of two Ismaili Imams, Aga Khan I and Aga Khan III. The clashes were in essence a challenge to the authority of the Ismaili Imam. The struggles and challenges had in fact begun to surface just before the Imam migrated to India. Daftary gives an account of the backgrounds to the conflict:

> Under the circumstances, the first Āghā Khān established his religious authority in India only after some difficulty. He did, in fact, face periodical troubles from certain dissident members of the Khoja community. In 1829, while he was still in Persia, some Nizārī Khojas of Bombay had refused to pay the customary *dassondh* to him. As a result, he sent to Bombay a special representative, accompanied by his maternal grandmother, who filed a suit against the dissidents in the Bombay High Court. The suit was withdrawn in 1830. (Daftary, 2007: 474)

Another legal case was later filed in 1847 in which the Aga Khan's brother represented him and the case was about an inheritance issue of two Khoja sisters:

> In this litigation, the Āghā Khān, then represented in court by his brother Muhammad Bāqir Khān (d. 1296/1879), upheld the rules of female inheritance as laid down in Islamic law, while his Barbhai opponents supported the Khoja custom that essentially deprived the females from such inheritance. In the resulting judgement, Sir Erskine Perry, the presiding judge, ruled that the custom of the Khojas should prevail even though it might be in conflict with the provisions of Islamic law.

This judgement in effect recognized the Khojas as a distinct community. (Daftary, 2007: 475)

It is at this point that the issue of authority is taken very seriously by the Aga Khan, and he attempts to take measures in order to define the identity of his followers and the confines of his own authority. Daftary explains these steps as follows:

> It was under such circumstances that the Āghā Khān launched a widespread campaign for defining and delineating the specific religious identity of his Khoja followers. In 1861, the imam circulated a document in the Bombay *jamā'at* summarizing the religious beliefs and practices of the Nizārī Ismā'īlīs, especially regarding marriage, ablution and funeral rites, and requesting every Khoja family to sign it. The signatories were, in effect, asked to pledge their loyalty to the imam and to their Ismā'īlī Shī'ī Muslim faith as interpreted by him. (Daftary, 2007: 475)

The tensions did not come to an end and continued further. Dissident Khojas filed a lawsuit against the Aga Khan emphasizing that they had been Sunnīs (Daftary, 2007: 475).[16] The climax of these legal cases was a case that later came to be known as the Agha Khan Case, and in the course of this lawsuit the matter was finally resolved, and Aga Khan I overcame the challenge he had faced against his authority by some dissident Khojas:

> This case, generally known as the Aga Khan Case, was heard by Sir Joseph Arnould. After a hearing of several weeks, in the course of which the Āghā Khān himself testified and the history of the Khoja community was fully reviewed, in November 1866 Justice Arnould rendered a detailed judgement against the plaintiffs and in favour of the Nizārī imam and other defendants on all points. This judgement legally established the status of the Nizārī Khojas as a community of "Shia Imami Ismailis," and of the Āghā Khān as the *murshid* or spiritual head of that community and heir in lineal descent to the imams of the Alamūt period. It also established, for the first time in a British court, the rights of the Āghā Khān to all the customary dues collected from the Khojas, and placed all the community property of the Nizārī Ismā'īlīs in his name and under his absolute control. *The first Āghā Khān's authority was never seriously challenged again.* (Daftary, 2007: 476, emphasis mine)

Another instance of such legal disputes occurred at the time of Aga Khan III but the nature of the grievance was more specifically financial, and it came from inside the family of the Imam himself, although it also had some

implications as to the authority of the person of the Imam. The date of this case is around the same time when the first constitution for the Ismaili community was developed. Daftary summarizes the issue as follows:

> While the Aga Khan was in East Africa, a suit was filed against him in the Bombay High Court by certain discontented members of his family led by Ḥājjī Bībī, a cousin and another daughter of Āqā Jangī Shāh, and her son Ṣamad Shāh. The litigants had certain financial grievances regarding their shares in the estate of Āghā Khān I, and they also raised claims to the current imam's income and status. After lengthy hearings, in 1908 Justice Coram Russell, the presiding judge, ruled against the plaintiffs, confirming the Aga Khan's rights to the estate of his grandfather and to the offerings made to him by the Nizārīs. This ruling also established that *the Nizārī Khojas were distinct from the Shīʿīs of the Ithnāʿasharī school*, since the plaintiffs had claimed adherence to Twelver Shīʿism. (Daftary, 2007: 481, emphasis mine)

It is from this point onward that constitutions begin to appear in the administrative and legal affairs of the Ismaili community. In other words, they also become an apparatus of the authority and power of the Ismaili Imam and it is in this era that we see the consolidation of the authority of the Ismaili Imam but "after the earliest challenges to his status, Aga Khan III's leadership was accepted unquestioningly by his followers" (Daftary, 2007: 486).[17]

These accounts give the historical background to the consolidation of the authority of the Ismaili imamate and the development of an elaborate system of institutions to manage the affairs of the community. This is where and why the role of the constitutions in the Ismaili community becomes important to the subject of this book. Without the framework of the constitutions, it would not have been easy to envisage the development of the existing institutions of the Ismaili imamate that have practically spilled over to outside communities and now broadly cover many areas of society, which are now beyond the Ismaili community.

As Jamal has noted, "It may seem unusual for a community without any territorial jurisdiction to adopt the form of constitutions" (in Cotran, 2000–2001: 122), but these constitutions paved the way for a legal framework of a system of alternative dispute resolution:

> These eventually developed into the introduction of novel institutional structures for what we might call, in today's parlance, community-based alternative dispute resolution. The constitutions also outlined matters of personal law, particularly surrounding rites of passage namely, birth, marriage and death. (Jamal, in Cotran, 2000–2001: 122)

As Jamal has pointed out, some of the early roots of the more legal and theological aspects of these constitutions can be found in the Fatimid period in al-Qāḍī al-Nuʿmān's *Daʿāʾim al-Islam*, but:

> anyone looking at developments in the form of Ismaili law for the Shia Imami Nizari Ismaili community would see very different articulation of the law over time. The *Daʿāʾim al-Islam*, the major legal work of the Fatimid period during which time the Ismaili *madhab per se* was established, is in a very different form from the current Constitution of the Shia Imami Ismailis. (Jamal, in Cotran, 2000–2001: 125)

The basic features of the constitution in terms of its theological content are pretty much the same as earlier periods (as we will see below in a quotation from the Constitution). There are, however, two major elements that are worthy of attention here. First, it is a matter of the flexibility of Ismaili law in its form(s): "not only are the texts differently constructed but they have incorporated different institutional structures in an effort to meet needs of the community" (Jamal, in Cotran, 2000–2001: 125–6). The second important aspect is practically a consequence of the changed realities of the Ismaili Community and that is "the distinction between the allegiance of Ismailis to their place of abode and to their religious authority" and the benefits of this approach in practice was that "on the one hand, this is a framework that should not impinge upon an Ismaili's obligations to the laws of her or his land of abode" and on the other hand, "there is a framework for a community operating internationally, and resident in many different states" (Jamal, in Cotran, 2000–2001: 125).

The idea of the constitution, as Jamal also notes, was a novel and different idea but now it represented a distinctive form of law for this Muslim community, developing a language for its engagement in the modern world while retaining the principles and traditions stemming from the Shiʿi doctrine of the imamate and his authority.

While Jamal gives a larger context for these constitutions, as they have a global remit now, Hirji (in Daftary, 2011), has focused more on the role of these constitutions in the legal developments of Ismaili Communities in East Africa and finds it a kind of response by the Ismaili imamate that

> at the very least took into consideration the British colonial socio-legal systems which were in force on both sides of the western-Indian Ocean— systems that were subsequently used by many modern nation-states as the basis of their own post-colonial formation. (Hirji, in Daftary, 2011: 153)

While this assessment is certainly correct to a great extent, we must note that there is also an element of modernity here. The fact that the Aga Khan works with the British legal system—it could have been any other legal system—simply suggests the importance of a modern institution of justice that the Ismaili imamate started taking seriously. Therefore, it should not be seen only in light of postcolonial formations alone; this response to legal modernity is also critical. One can see a different expression of it in the arrangements for the declaration of a successor by the Ismaili Imam: Aga Khan III had left his will with a lawyer; it was not simply traditionally communicated to the followers. This is a modern development, which eases the transition period of succession, thus avoiding some schisms.

Ernest Gellner notes a different aspect of how the Ismaili imamate has gained this new prominent position although in some cases he reduces many of the dynamics of this shift to a mere financial status and the role of the British Empire. His overall description of the new phase of the Ismaili history follows on these lines:

> The sect which, presumably by the hazard of history, has survived with a concrete, tangible Imam is the Shia Imami Ismailia which, thanks to the activities of recent Aga Khans, its leaders, is well known and incorporated into popular English (and perhaps now international) folklore. The modern history of the movement begins in 1840 when "the first Aga Khan ... fled from Persia after an unsuccessful rebellion against the throne." Nothing unusual or interesting about this: this is the normal stuff of Muslim history. A leader endowed with a religious aura and some tribal support tries his hand at challenging the central power. Normally such efforts fail. If the leader is unfortunate, his severed head is displayed on the city gate by way of demonstration of the inefficacy of his charisma. If he is fortunate, he manages to escape. This one did. to British India. There he rendered some valuable service to the British Raj, and was awarded a pension and the title of Aga Khan. In due course, he settled among some of his followers located in Bombay. (Gellner, 1981: 105)

Gellner's account fails to see the nuances and sometimes makes obvious mistakes (e.g., the title of Aga Khan was awarded to the Ismaili Imam by the Qājār monarch not the British Raj, and he was the monarch's son-in-law). However, he spots some of the major areas of interest:

> A trading population, operating under a centralised colonial regime, had every motive for following a leader who could, through his political contacts, do so very much for them, and who was ideologically legitimated

for doing this. They did not need to be compelled. If Paris is worth a Mass, then the trading opportunities of the British Empire were surely well worth the Shi'a principles of incarnation, succession, and divine leadership, all the more so if you are already nominally committed to them anyway. And so it was. *The Ismailis prospered famously, displaying entrepreneurial virtues and an ideology which is virtually an inverse Weberian paradigm.* (Gellner, 1981: 109, emphasis mine)

One could disagree with Gellner in many ways. To him, the way the authority of the Aga Khan is recognized by his followers is no more than a "cult-of-personality," which is an over-simplification of history and tradition in the case of the Ismaili community. I will discuss this point in a different section when it comes to authority and charisma. Nonetheless, the point at stake here is simple and plain. For the first time in the Ismaili history, the Ismaili Imam takes his complaint to the legal decision of an external arbiter and he wins the case. Both parties were in a position to present their own case and it was not a unilateral decision on the side of the Ismaili imamate to decide to excommunicate a group of dissidents from his community.

There remain several questions here. Why would the Aga Khan go to the court and not try to resolve the issue within the community? Why did he feel compelled to resolve the case in a court? This situation would not or could not have arisen five hundred years earlier. This could not have happened at the time of the Prophet. A similar institution for justice did not exist in any other setting before in the Ismaili history. In feudal or monarchical systems under which the Ismaili Imam used to operate in the past, a similar issue had never been raised. Such debates or conflicts would be somehow resolved within the community and even then the context in which they lived did not accommodate such institutions as the modern judiciary. But this new turn of events has the signs of moving toward modern legal systems, which is a significant move.

This is the story of the beginnings of the formation of a constitution as a document to regulate the affairs of the Ismaili community. However, we do not see a significant change in the way the constitution develops until the time of the present Imam. The general framework of the constitutions laid the ground for consolidating the authority of the Ismaili Imam to be able to deal with any possible future challenges. When there is a degree of peacefulness, the process of institution building starts.

Here, there are certain questions to be asked. What is the role of the constitution at this stage in accommodating institutions? Is it the constitutions that facilitate the development of institutions or is it the personal

authority of the Imam (Aga Khan III)? The constitutions do not seem to have become a solid reference point as such, but even at their inception they had begun to define and regulate the affairs of the community while the authority of the Imam did have its own role to play. Hirji explains this development as part of the process of change and adaptation to new circumstances, in which the Ismailis lived in the colonial era first and then in independent countries after the colonial era:

> Part of the process of adaptation and change undertaken by the successive Imams in modern times involved establishing for the Ismailis in different parts of the world a framework of governance by which they could manage their communal affairs according to the tenets of Ismaili Islam and in tandem with the socio-political systems established in their regions of residence. (Hirji, in Daftary, 2011: 131)

However, as I explained earlier, one must note first of all the modern context of these developments. Also, as Jamal notes, the important shifts that happened in terms of the Ismailis remaining loyal to the laws of their land of abode and the constitution allowing for the international operation of the community must be taken into account.

Among the first radical moves made by Aga Khan III was support for education, placing particular emphasis on the education of women. This in itself was a radical move at that point in history where other Muslim communities not only did not allow their women to enjoy education so freely as the followers of the Aga Khan would, but they would hardly even encourage education outside the traditional teaching of religious literature.[18] One can hardly overlook the modernist aspect of such reforms.

Then there is the Ismaili imamate's institutional support in health care. It is here that the Aga Khan Schools and the Aga Khan Hospitals begin to flourish in East Africa (see Kaiser, 1996). These early institutions lay the foundation for future institutions. Nonetheless, a rapid proliferation and expansion of these institutions to the other realms of human activity do not appear until recent times during the imamate of the present Imam, Aga Khan IV.

The Constitution appears to have these institutions incorporated in it in the context of an ethical framework and part of the mandate of the Ismaili imamate. However, another significant step is also taken with the formulation and formalization of the constitutions. They delineate the identity of the Ismaili community. But as what? Is it simply as Ismailis?

Figure 3.1 Aga Khan IV, signing the Ismaili Constitution (Courtesy of AKDN: Ian Charles Stewart).

Asserting a Shiʻi Muslim Identity and an Inclusive Attitude

The very title of the current constitution is very assertive in this sense. It does not show the secluded life a minority community, which is constantly harassed and persecuted by other Muslim communities. It is no longer the identity of a population that would have to defend its "Muslim" identity or dismiss any accusation of "heterodoxy" by simply describing them as others who have gone astray from the straight path (which is the presumed "orthodoxy" of other Muslims).

The title of the current constitution reads: "The Constitution of the Shia Imami Muslims." Here, there is an emphasis on the point of identity. The Ismailis are not only "*Shiʻas*" by acknowledging the imamate and authority of ʻAlī as the legitimate heir to the Prophet after his death, but they are also "*Imamis*" (like the bigger sister branch of the

Twelvers), and they believe in a line of descendants of ʿAlī and Fāṭima's children (and here, once again, we see the "perpetuation of authority," if we use Dabashi's term). Most important of all, they are "*Muslims.*" This Constitution seems like a deliberate attempt at asserting the Muslim identity of the Ismaili community (a *gemeinschaft*).

The Preamble to the Constitution, quoted below, which covers the most strategic statements about the identity of the Ismaili community, explains and expands this ontological position claimed by the Constitution for the community.

> (A) The Shia Imami Ismaili Muslims affirm the *Shahādah* "*lā ilāha illa-llāh, Muḥammadur Rasūlu-llāh,*" the *Tawḥīd* therein and that the Holy Prophet Muhammad (*Ṣalla-llāhu ʿalayhi wa-sallam*) is the last and final Prophet of Allah. Islam, as revealed in the Holy Qurʾān, is the final message of Allah to mankind, and is universal and eternal. The Holy Prophet (S.A.S.) through the divine revelation from Allah prescribed rules governing spiritual and temporal matters.
>
> (B) In accordance with Shia doctrine, tradition, and interpretation of history, the Holy Prophet (S.A.S.) designated and appointed his cousin and son-in-law Hazrat Mawlana Ali (*Amīru-l-Muʾminīn ʿAlayhi-s-salām*), to be the first Imam to continue the *Taʾwil* and *Taʿlim* of Allah's final message and to guide the murids, and proclaimed that the Imamat should continue by heredity through Hazrat Mawlana Ali (A.S.) and his daughter Hazrat Bibi Fatimat-az-Zahra, Khātun-i-Jannat (*ʿAlayhā-s-salām*).
>
> (C) Succession to Imamat is by way of *Naṣṣ*, It being the absolute prerogative of the Imam of the time to appoint his successor from amongst any of his male descendants whether they be sons or remoter issue.

These first three articles in the preamble clearly define the identity of the Ismaili community. This ontological position has its own social and political consequences: this community can no longer be dismissed and suppressed as "non-Muslims" or "heretics." The significance of this position is that there is a deliberate attempt in upholding this identity. The Ismaili imamate does not find any shame in it, nor is it afraid that this position may be challenged. The institutions, which have been created, appear as a response to any possible challenge: this response is not in words (or in a polemical or theological layout); it is a response in the form of institutional action.

The Ismaili imamate attempts to show that its endeavors move toward the realization of the ideals of the Muslim community, the *Ummah*. And this is precisely where theoretical debates begin: one person's ideal may be another person's deviation. The approach of the Ismaili imamate seems to be a minimalistic or, to be more precise, a more inclusive rendering of theological precepts of Shiʿi Islam in the Ismaili Constitution's preamble. As we can see in this preamble, there is also no mention of the word ʿiṣma or the infallibility of the Imam and as such theological articulations claiming a position of infallibility seem secondary or nonexistent in the Constitution.

The skeleton of Ismaili leadership today seems to be quite minimalistic in terms of theological assertions. This shapes the bones of this body but not the entire corpus of this community or rather its leadership.[19] It is the institutions that form the flesh and blood of this community. To be more precise, the role of a maximalist, grand theological design is increasingly diminished (at least at an institutional and public level). There does not seem to be any polemical confrontation between the Ismaili imamate and other Muslim communities. To the Ismaili Imam of our time, that is Aga Khan IV, the rest of the Muslims constitute the *Ummah*; they are simply non-Ismaili Muslims who share the same ethical values with Ismailis.

Such ontological positions inevitably contain some epistemological reflections too. A couple of generation earlier, a son of Aga Khan II, and a brother of the forty-eighth Imam, called Shihāb al-Dīn Shāh al-Ḥusaynī (born around 1851–52), did not share similar ideas. His approach to other Muslims, i.e., to non-Ismailis, was no less harsh than the way the rest of the Muslim communities treated the Ismailis. Shihāb al-Dīn Shāh, who died prematurely, in his father's lifetime, in his youth (December 1884), has two published treatises in Persian: *Khiṭābāt-i ʿāliya* (1963) and *Risāla dar ḥaqīqat-i Dīn* (1947). The second one deals more with Sufi approaches to faith and does not contain direct attacks on other communities, but in the first one he is quite outspoken and does not hesitate to condemn some other Muslim communities (1963: 50).

Shihāb al-Dīn Shāh "was expected to succeed to the imamate" (Daftary, 2007: 480), but he died during his father's lifetime, a year before his father passed away. It is important to note the contingencies of the succession here. The Ismaili imamate did not continue in the descendants of Shihāb al-Dīn Shāh whose vision is very well seen in the two treatises left of him. It is true that at his time, the idea of pluralism did not make much sense in the community, but the least we can say here

is that it does make a difference when there is a different vision behind the imamate.

Today, one can hardly find the ideas of the Shihāb al-Dīn Shāh forming the mainstream thinking of the Ismaili community when dealing with non-Ismailis. In other words, a pluralistic and cosmopolitan Ismaili community could not have emerged out of such a vision with so little tolerance of non-Ismailis.

The earliest seeds of a pluralistic approach to communicating with other Muslims, although not very nuanced and not articulated philosophically, are more specifically highlighted during the Aga Khan's Silver Jubilee, in which he sent a strong message to his Community to remove walls and build bridges. The very basic precondition of this message was to abandon polemical demarcations and to move toward a more inclusive and pluralistic ethos. The Community received this message as one to bring Ismailis closer to other Muslims, and the expressions of it were found in the institutions that were open to Ismailis and non-Ismailis alike.

It is, nonetheless, important to take note of the context in which Shihāb al-Dīn Shāh, as the potential successor to his father, wrote. Regardless of judging or explaining why such reactions used to take shape not only among other Muslim communities but also among some Ismailis too, the approach remained very much polemical and theology-laden.

There are a number of points to be considered here. Shihāb al-Dīn Shāh was not the Imam but son of the Imam, so his ideas might be dismissed as he was not in the position of the Imam. But the fact remains that the atmosphere in which he lived carried this air of polemic and theology-laden statements. In contemporary or modern times, this approach seems to have vanished from public and most visible positions of the Ismaili imamate.

At a time when certain other Muslim groups barely tolerate one another, the Ismaili Imam seems to be much more tolerant of others despite the fact that the Ismaili community still suffers attacks on its very Muslim identity. This point will be further explained in a section dealing with the language and terminology used by the present Ismaili Imam.

Ismaili Constitutions: Contract or Covenant?

There is a significant difference between what is termed as the Ismaili Constitution and what is understood as a constitution in the political

literature of democratic institutions. The Ismaili Constitution is a legal document, which was born in the modern period and was a result of the modernization of the Ismaili Community. The earliest forms of the Constitution were produced under conditions of colonial rule, and it took into account how the Community could coexist with the legal framework around them.

There is, however, a big difference between the Ismaili Constitution and a secular constitution. While a secular constitution is subject to the will of the people of a country or a polity, the Ismaili Constitution cannot be modified in a similar way, nor is it a contract between the leader and the led. The preamble to the Constitution, even though very minimal, bears strong elements of religious belief and doctrinal precepts, which cannot be changed. The identity of the Community revolves around these central principles.

It is true that details of Ismaili law are subject to change, as we have seen in Jamal's assessment of the development of Ismaili law over history, but there are two important parameters for this change: first, it is bound by the authority of the Imam (unlike a secular constitution or contract), and second, it responds to the needs of the Community, some of which may come from the Community itself. These requirements are all met in light of the Imam's authority, rather than how people demand them to change.

The Ismaili Constitution came into existence under modern conditions, but the underlying principles for its formulation were not modern in nature. There is a very strong sense of the divine and the sacred attached to it, which makes it distinct from a constitution as a contract, so the best term that can characterize this Constitution is "covenant" rather than "contract."

In a constitution, the element of restricting the powers of the rulers is an integral part. Citizens' relationship with the rulers is not that of a subject before a monarch who assumes to have God-given rights. In the Ismaili Constitution, we have the *murīd* in place of the *citizen* and the *Imām* or the *pīr* instead of the *ruler* (president or prime minister in a democratic setting). Moreover, there is no polity. The Imam does not govern a nation-state; he is not even an Imam-Caliph like the Fatimid times. There is no element of restriction of power; the Imam's authority in religious and spiritual terms is unfettered, but when it comes to political matters, Ismailis are bound by the laws of their land of abode. Therefore, it is important not to confuse this constitution with a political contract.

The Ismaili Imamate and Institution Building

Further to what was mentioned so far, the leadership of the Ismaili imamate does not appear to be making references to any future promise of the consolidation of justice in an apocalyptic manner: the Ismaili imamate is fully engaged in establishing this justice through institutional work at the present time. The messianic and apocalyptic politics of the other Shiʿi communities tend to be in sharp contrast to the establishment of these institutions.

The Ismaili imamate has been on a determined journey of proliferating and expanding institutions. These institutions necessarily had to be in a position that could be internationally recognized and at the same time well defined within the ethical context of an Islamic community.

What does this mean for the leadership? What implications did this institutional pursuit have for the imamate itself? The immediate answer is that this institutionalization was also implemented with regard to the imamate itself. The person of the Imam was transcended into "the office of imamate." So we have an institution of imamate whose raw material was already available in the history and tradition of this particular Muslim community.

Concern for Justice: The Inherent Concept in Messianic Ideas

There are two ways of approaching this messianic idea among the Shiʿi Muslims. One perspective is the idea of the end of the world and a collapse of the societal order of human beings, which would be followed by the establishment of a just order. Another way of reading into this idea is to identify the core element embedded in this messianism. This core idea is justice.

From the very early days of the formulation of a Shiʿi theology in general, the idea of justice has received considerable attention. Justice is not only considered a necessary quality of God, but it has also been mentioned as an essential characteristic for the leader of the Muslim community, and in this case the Shiʿi Imam.[20] The same idea can also be seen among the Muʿtazilī Sunnis who are theologically closer to the Shiʿa.

The affinity of the Muʿtazila and the Shiʿa needs some explanation. The influence of Muʿtazilī thought was more often felt among the Zaydīs and the Imāmīs (Atamaj, Martin, and Woodward, 1997: 18). Their rigorous devotion to rational understanding of divine unity and justice

remained very strong. The early Muʿtazila had five basic doctrines, namely, (1) divine unity (*tawḥīd*); (2) divine justice or theodicity (*ʿadl*); (3) the promise and the threat of reward and punishment in the hereafter (*al-waʿd wa al-waʿīd*); (4) the intermediate position of who is a true Muslim (*al-manzila bayn al-manzilatayn*); and (5) the commanding of good and prohibiting evil (*al-amr bi al-maʿrūf wa al-nahy ʿan al-mukar*) (Atamaj, Martin, and Woodward, 1997: 64).

These affinities were not, however, always stable and recognized and at times refutations were written by Muʿtazilī figures, like al-Qāḍī ʿAbd al-Jabbār (Atamaj, Martin, and Woodward, 1997: 37) against the Imāmiyya. Another instance of these conflicts is in Ḥamīd al-Dīn al-Kirmānī's severe criticism of the belief of Muʿtazila in the unity of God, who conflates their belief in unity of God with that of heretics (*al-mulḥidīn*) (al-Kirmānī, 1953:53). So, even though the Muʿtazila were closer to Shiʿi communities, significant differences remained between them.

If we move forward in history, we are in a position to rethink this idea of justice vis-à-vis the Ismaili imamate and its institutions. As it was mentioned earlier, we do not see any trace of a messianic theological idea in the Ismaili thought of today. At least, this idea is never mentioned in any form in the institutions of the Ismaili imamate.

However, there is a theme that is common to both messianic ideas and that of the institutions of the Ismaili imamate (including the AKDN in particular). We see the idea of justice constantly circulating in different forms. The only difference is that it does not follow the classic messianic template anymore: there is no political rebellion anymore and there is no sign of attempts to establish justice by violent or aggressive means (nor is there any idea of awaiting the appearance of a savior, as the Imam is present and accessible for Ismailis). It seems that it is justice that comes first not the messianic idea. If the idea of a savior gains prominence throughout history, it is because there it is a theological necessity. There is a need for erecting this utopia in which justice is the cornerstone of the society. This requires power. The minority Shiʿi community, which has always been lacking this political power, could never be in a position to start building institutions that would serve the cause of justice and ethics. Hence, there is the ever-increasing need for the recurrence of a messianic theology.

What happens to this theological necessity of the Shiʿi thinking in the Ismaili community?

The Ismaili imamate expands its institutions whose seeds have been planted by the previous Imam in schools, hospitals, and economic

institutions. However, there is one theme that is re-presented or re-enacted in a different form. This theme appears in the AKDN mandate:

> The Aga Khan Development Network is a contemporary endeavour of the Ismaili Imamat to realise the social conscience of Islam through institutional action. It brings together, under one coherent aegis, institutions and programmes whose combined mandate is to help relieve society of ignorance, disease and deprivation without regard to the faiths or national origins of people whom they serve. (IIS Website, *AKDN Ethical Framework*).[21]

The above paragraph covers nothing but the very ideals that were sought by the other Shi'i groups in pursuit of justice that is to "*relieve society of ignorance, disease and deprivation without regard to the faiths or national origins of people.*" This is the ethical framework of the AKDN. And this is exactly where the idea of a messianic figure undergoes a thorough shift and the radical, revolutionary idea is redressed in the form of a peaceful, civil institution but still retains its ideals.

In this sense, we can clearly see that the Ismaili imamate and the AKDN do not break away from the overall Shi'i ethos. This mandate of the AKDN is also the mandate of the Imam. It is as if we read a description of the role and responsibility of the Imam at the same time. A prominent characteristic of the leader becomes his endeavor to 'realize the social conscience of Islam'. How is it realized? The AKDN and the Ismaili imamate attempts to realize this "through institutional action."

This is what the present Aga Khan, as the forty-ninth hereditary Imam and the leader of the Ismaili community, publicly declares:

> The Imamat is a Muslim institution with a history going back over 1400 years. As Imam of the Ismaili Muslims, I am to be concerned with the quality of life of the community and those amongst whom it lives. Over many centuries and decades, that responsibility of the Imamat has entailed the creation of institutions to address issues of the quality of life of the time, and it today includes a number of non-governmental organisations, foundations and economic development agencies.[22]

"Improving the Quality of Life"

The concern for the quality of life is a topic which is often touched upon in the words of the Aga Khan and it is a defining framework for all his development activities. This theme is a recurring theme in the

ethical framework of the AKDN (which is like a working document and a guideline for institutional activity). Whichever area of the vision of the Aga Khan we highlight, we see that it bears some relevance to his concern for the quality of life of his followers and the people amongst whom they live. The phrase "improving the quality of life" is the watchword in the language of the Ismaili imamate today.

One of the mandates of his imamate, which has often been mentioned by him and clearly demonstrated in the institutional endeavors of Imamt, has been the safety and security of his *jamāʿat*. This sounds like a very broad framework but if we bear it in mind, many of the efforts of the Aga Khan can be easily decoded. It is not just a haphazard or philanthropic decision by the Aga Khan to include others and the people among whom his followers live. It is also a strategic decision to minimize any possible threat to the security and safety of his community. Therefore, within this context, recognizing pluralism, which is so central to his discourse today, has its advantages too: it also guarantees the safety of his own community.

This is by no means to reduce the value of the efforts of the Aga Khan in promoting pluralism, but we should also realize the context in which the Ismaili Imam is taking the decision to move in this direction.

The question that immediately comes to mind is if the conditions were different, how would the Ismaili Imam behave? If the Ismaili community was not a minority community and enjoyed greater power than what it has today, how would it position itself toward ideas like democracy, pluralism, and free market economy? A part of the answer to this question is not difficult as we have historical evidence from the past like the case of the Fatimid empire in which Ismailis and non-Ismailis alike were protected by the empire, but one can argue that precedents cannot be a defining vector for the future decisions of the leadership of the Ismaili community. However, personal characteristics of the Ismaili Imam and the irreversible facts of the diversity of the Ismaili community, which is scattered around the globe, makes this conjecture almost impossible.

Consultation

One of the most important elements in the transmutation of authority in the case of the Ismaili imamate is the personal characteristics of the Imam. Apart from the structural changes, which have occurred in the past 50 years as a result of the leadership style of the present Imam and because of his own individual vision, the personal characteristics have also contributed to this shift.

I will give a number of examples as to how these personal characteristics reveal themselves in different layers and through a narrative of what takes place in the public display of these characteristics, I will try to explain in this section how this shift can be discerned in these turning points.

Mohammed Arkoun, who has been quoted in this book a number of times and who was interviewed specifically for this book right at the outset, was a Muslim intellectual who has left a lasting impression on scholarship about Muslim communities. He served a number of times on the jury for the Aga Khan Award for Architecture and he was a governor of the IIS for many years until he passed away. These were of course his official capacities in the institutions of the Ismaili imamate. Beside all this, he was engaged in debates and discussions on various occasions with the Ismaili Imam.

Mohammed Arkoun was a scholar, a non-Ismaili one, whose thought often stands in sharp contrast with the position of the Ismaili Imam or at least with the orthodox perception of the role and position of the Imam. The Imam is usually obeyed. A Shi'i Imam rarely gets into a position where he would or could be reasoned with. Yet, the Aga Khan, who carries the heavy weight of tradition behind him, came face-to-face with a character like Mohammed Arkoun, whose life and academic work put him in the position of deconstruction of tradition as such. The Ismaili Imam not only did not shy away from such encounters, but he also encourages and embraces such interactions. Moreover, he puts these same very people in positions of decision-making and judgment in his institutions.

These interactions leave their impressions on the interlocutors of the Imam. In describing the Imam, when I interviewed him, Arkoun says: "He is a man with judgment, a man with culture, a man with consideration, a man who reasons."[23] These descriptions bring out some important elements for someone who takes consultation seriously.

There is also another dimension to this spirit of consultation. In the modern developments in the function of the Imam, one can hardly see the Imam making theological pronouncements. These are the job of experts, professionals, and scholars who are active in the field. This is the raison d'être of the IIS. When there are matters of concern that need theological, philosophical, or religious investigations, they are referred to the IIS and then the feedback goes to the Imam for his final decision. Therefore, prima facie, such tasks are not undertaken by the Imam himself, at least not directly. The function of the Imam has changed as a result of institutional transformations.

If we think about this example, one cannot help rethinking how the doctrine of *ta'līm* is to be understood in this context. This doctrine certainly does not resemble its earliest articulations as in the Alamūt period. The institutionalization of the imamate has now given it a vehicle to exercise his role as the authoritative and truthful instructor (*mu'allim-i ṣādiq* as it was termed during the Alamūt period), but in a different context. A hierarchical system has been introduced in the institutions, but the consultation process does not simply happen in a vertical way. There is also a horizontal process of consultation where people can sit face-to-face with the Imam.

Even though to some extent this consultation process seems to have been institutionalized, Arkoun has his doubts and serious objections in that he does not see the Community as active as it should be:

> The community has to ask itself. It has not to wait for the Imam to transform its mentality, or its culture or its language to understand this. Why are they always focussing on the Imam? The Imam has to do everything like my mother.[24]

Arkoun finds that the function, the language, and the role of the Imam have changed, but there is still a discrepancy between where the Imam stands and how the Community responds to this new function:

> The responsibility of the community has to be assessed, before assessing the responsibility of the Imam, because there should be a communication between the two. There should be an exchange. But the exchange cannot occur.[25]

According to Arkoun, the reason for this deficiency is that the Community is too dependent on the Imam in all its day-to-day matters. But for the Imam, this process of consultation, at all levels, has become so central to his leadership that shapes his entire approach to the issue of embracing different opinions. This is what he calls the humility to listen to others.

I have been thinking long how this characteristic could have become so central to his leadership. Could it be some special sort of training in the family of the Aga Khan or the dynasty of the Ismaili Imams? This does not fit into the whole idea that accession to the imamate is by designation and it is only known by the previous Imam who does not reveal it until the last moment. In other words, I cannot see any reason why we should attribute this to a predetermined blueprint of what would happen in the future.

My contention is that these characteristics are developed by the very person of the Imam independent of his role as the Imam. It is true that his role as the Imam has put him in a position to act differently and to make different decisions. Yet, it has massively helped him carve his own role out of what has been already been made available to him, or, as Arkoun describes it, the Imam has defined new functions for himself.

The Jubilees

As explored earlier, one of the interesting characteristics of the Ismaili imamate is its patience and long-term vision. We can see this in the many projects now undertaken, which were once inconceivable in the Ismaili community. The initial phase of the institutional work of the Ismaili imamate remained more or less within the community itself and it took years until it came to the cruising level and started stabilizing itself, so to speak.

There are two visible historical landmarks in the history of the Ismaili imamate, which are in the Jubilees of the present Aga Khan. His first Jubilee, which was his Silver Jubilee, the commemoration of 25 years of his imamate, witnessed the completion of certain projects, including the Ismaili Center in London and the Aga Khan University in Pakistan. The 25 years of the imamate of Aga Khan IV marked some important milestones in the expansion of the institutions of the Ismaili imamate. It took some other 25 years for the Ismaili imamate to reach a level that its institutions become increasingly recognized internationally. The projects that were completed during his Silver Jubilee are:

- The Ismaili Centre, London, United Kingdom
- The Ismaili Centre, Burnaby, Canada
- Aga Khan University, Karachi, Pakistan
- Aga Khan Girls Academy and Hostel, Karimabad, Pakistan
- Aga Khan Primary School, Sherqilla, Pakistan
- Aga Khan Medical Centre, Singal, Pakistan
- Aga Khan Rural Support Programme, Gujarat, India
- Rural Medical Centre, Gujarat, India
- Aga Khan Medical Centre, Kisumu, Kenya
- Aga Khan Hospital, Dar-es-Salam, Tanzania
- Immunization Clinics, Dacca, Bangladesh

All the above projects are either in the area of education or health care. The Ismaili Centres are of course the core buildings, which are called the

"high-profile" buildings or, as the Aga Khan likes to call them, "ambassadorial" buildings. This is the first phase of the institutional development of the Ismaili imamate, with a visible architectural expression. It is very much a continuation, expansion, and elaboration of what was started at the time of Aga Khan III.

From this point onward, the cruising of the Ismaili imamate institutions begins, the culmination of which is later seen in the Golden Jubilee of the Aga Khan in 2007. The celebrations of 50 years of his imamate during his Golden Jubilee involved the expansion of other institutions that brought greater visibility to the imamte around the globe and addressed some of the emerging issues that were not earlier on the agenda of the Ismaili imamate (such as pluralism, civil society, meritocracy, etc.) or at least not articulated in the form in which they were now expressed in the language of the Ismaili Imam.

The Aga Khan sees the role of institutions as the foundation and the most important platform for change. If leadership is to survive, it needs strong institutions that keep pace with the circumstances of their time. In other words, when he speaks of an "enabling environment," one of the things that inevitably surfaces here is the issue of strong institutions. In a speech in Kenya, in 1982, during his Silver Jubilee year, he touches upon the issue of an enabling environment as follows:

> Both the development of the economy and the success of social institutions depend on the creation of the right environment for progress, an environment which enables both businesses and people to realise their full potential.
>
> This enabling environment is created by various things. Confidence in the future. Reliance on the rule of law and a system of laws which itself encourages enterprise and initiative. Democratic institutions. Protection of the rights of citizens. These are what encourage investment, encourage good managers to remain, encourage doctors and nurses and teachers to want to serve their country rather than to emigrate as soon as they are skilled. *The creation and extension to all areas of the nation's life of this enabling environment is the single most important factor in Third World development. It is as critical to national growth as sunlight is to the growth of plants.* [Emphasis mine][26]

This vision has been with him all along, and strong institutions make a big contribution to this enabling environment. Some of these institutions came into being during his jubilees (as the earlier institutions were created following the glamorous jubilees of his grandfather).[27]

The financial contribution of the community, its voluntary service, and the dedication of the Ismailis to their Imam, their offerings to him were all managed in a most efficient way for the creation of institutions, which have now brought a different dimension to the Ismaili imamate and the Ismaili Community. The role of voluntary service in this Community has been extremely crucial for the success of these institutions. This tradition has been encouraged and strongly supported by the Aga Khan. The Aga Khan even publicly declared and acknowledged recently in a generous gesture of appreciation the importance of this service, when he received the Carnegie Medal for Philanthropy in 2005:

> The achievements of the AKDN would not be possible without the tireless contributions of the global community of Ismailis that I lead, residing in Central and Southern Asia, the Middle East, Africa, Europe and North America. Our volunteers and contributors also include many thousands of others from multiple cultures and faiths around the world. They are united with us in our mission to help build capacity and dignity for individuals, to enable them to take control of their own development. *It is on behalf of these many thousands of selfless and dedicated men and women of multiple languages, cultures, faiths and nationalities, urban and rural, that I accept this award today.* [Emphasis mine][28]

One significant shift in the Jubilees is how services and contributions of the Community are channeled into institutional activity. During the Jubilees of Aga Khan III, the celebrations reflected the unconditional offerings of the Community to the Imam in financial terms and the funds were used to build and enhance the institutions. In 2007, the Ismaili Imam introduced the idea of "Time and Knowledge Nazrana" (TKN), which went beyond financial contribution[29]. It was no longer like the glamorous Jubilees of his grandfather in which he was physically weighed in gold of diamond. Now, members of the Community offer their time and knowledge to the service of the Community and the imamate to further enhance these institutions. It is no longer measured just in terms of financial donations.

The Aga Khan's Bifocal Leadership: *dīn* and *dunyā*

The terms *dīn* and *dunyā* are literally translated as "religion" and "the world" immediately bringing to mind the separation of the temporal from religious, as understood by certain people around the world. The Aga Khan, from the very early days of his imamate, has been vocal in

stressing what could be described as the false dichotomy between the faith and the world. He did not see his role as purely a religious role that only concentrates on matters of faith. To him, the faith and the world are intertwined.

In a speech in the Swiss-American Chamber of Commerce in Zurich in January, 1976, he unveiled very clearly how he understands matters of the world to be related to his role and function as the Imam of a Muslim community (and in fact as a Muslim):

> Seen against the background of Christian religious tradition, it might appear incongruous that a Muslim religious leader should be so involved in material and mundane matters of this world. It is not an Islamic belief, however, that spiritual life should be totally isolated from our more material everyday activities. The nature of the religious office which I hold neither requires nor is expected by the members of my Community, to be an institution whose existence is restricted to spiritual leadership. On the contrary, history and the correct interpretation of the Imamat require that the Imam, while caring first of all for the spiritual well-being of his people, should also be continuously concerned with their safety and their material progress. (Aga Khan IV, 1985)

This idea has often resonated in the life and work of the present Ismaili Imam as he repeatedly comes across it. The above passage is part of a speech made after about 25 years of his imamate, published in a collection of his lectures marking his Silver Jubilee. Twenty years later, we see the same idea repeated in a lengthier form than before (which implies that this reconciliation of the faith and the world is not easily grasped by the people who look at his work).

One of the important points to be considered here is that in the context of what the Ismaili Imam mentions regarding the misinterpretation of the relation of the faith and the world, we have two aspects for understanding the issue. In Muslim religious texts, the world (or *dunyā*) has two connotations: the world as the nature and the world as greed for the material world. Rūmī describes his position regarding the faith and the world in the following words:

> What is "the world?" Being ignorant and unmindful of God; the world (as it has been despised) does not mean owning properties, having money, possessing estates and beautiful women;
>
> If you possess these properties for the sake of faith (as your faith dictates you to do so), then the Prophet calls this the most decent and the best property. (Rūmī, 1935: 1/61)

On the first level, this is precisely what the Ismaili Imam is referring to. However, the point is that in Sufi tradition, this material world is generally despised and thus to many it does not appear to be worthy of any attention. At least, historically this seems to be true in Sufi doctrines. However, the concept of taking the world seriously may not actually make much sense if we want to project it to the past. For the present, though, we can only compare what the Ismaili Imam does with what others do in dealing with the material world. He makes it clear that as the Imam, and the spiritual leader of this community, he is responsible for both the religious and the material well-being of his followers and he cannot ignore the realm of the material without going beyond and outside his responsibility.

Here is what the Ismaili Imam has to say about why and how he takes the world seriously:

> One of the central elements of the Islamic faith is the inseparable nature of faith and world. The two are so deeply intertwined that one cannot imagine their separation. They constitute a "Way of Life." The role and responsibility of an Imam, therefore, is both to interpret the faith to the community, and also to do all within his means to improve the quality, and security, of their daily lives.

He continues to show his dissatisfaction at how his role is misunderstood in the West:

> I am fascinated and somewhat frustrated when representatives of the western world—especially the western media—try to describe the work of our Aga Khan Development Network in fields like education, health, the economy, media, and the building of social infrastructure.

And he highlights the sharp separation between the religious and the secular in the West, showing his own position at the other end of the spectrum:

> Reflecting a certain historical tendency of the West to separate the secular from the religious, they often describe it either as philanthropy or entrepreneurship. What is not understood is that this work is for us a part of our institutional responsibility—it flows from the mandate of the office of Imam to improve the quality of worldly life for the concerned communities.

This is where he ties his own role and function as the Imam to keep a balance between the secular and the religious. He goes on to contex-

tualize this position in his own understanding of the Qur'ān and the tradition:

> Our spiritual understandings...are rooted, of course, in ancient teachings. In the case of Islam, there are two touchstones which I have long treasured and sought to apply. The first affirms the unity of the human race, as expressed in the Holy Qu'ran where God, as revealed through the Holy Prophet Muhammad, may peace be upon him, says the following:
> "O mankind! Be careful of your duty to your Lord, Who created you from a single soul and from it created its mate and from the twain hath spread abroad a multitude of men and women." (4:1)
> This remarkable verse speaks both of the inherent diversity of mankind—the "multitude"—and of the unity of mankind—the "single soul created by a single Creator"—a spiritual legacy which distinguishes the human race from all other forms of life.

Next, he brings another element of this tradition, which directly relates to his own role and function as a Shiʿi Imam descended from ʿAlī:

> The second passage I would cite today is from the first hereditary Imam of the Shi'a community Hazrat Ali. As you know, the Shi'a divided from the Sunni after the death of the Prophet Muhammad. Hazrat Ali, the cousin and son-in-law of the Prophet, was, in Shi'a belief, named by the Prophet to be the Legitimate Authority for the interpretation of the faith. For the Shi'a today, all over the world, he is regarded as the first Imam.
> I cite Hazrat Ali's words so that you may understand the spirit in which I have attempted to fulfill the mandate left to me as the 49th hereditary [Ismaili] Imam after the death of my grandfather. I quote:
> "No belief is like modesty and patience, no attainment is like humility, no honour is like knowledge, no power is like forbearance, and no support is more reliable than consultation."
> Hazrat Ali's regard for knowledge reinforces the compatibility of faith and the world. And his respect for consultation is, in my view, a commitment to tolerant and open-hearted democratic processes.[30]

The above passages describe how he interprets both his role as the Imam and the example that people should follow for consultation and he ties it to tolerant and democratic processes. So, in a sense, he is also, minimally, interpreting tolerance and democracy here.

The emphasis of the Aga Khan on keeping a balance between *dīn* and *dunyā* reminds us of another predominant binary: *dīn* and *dawla* which lies at the heart of all contemporary political debates in the

Muslim world. Here, *dunyā* has replaced *dawla* for the Aga Khan. Part of the reason for this replacement is simple and straightforward: the Aga Khan does not have a political position and he is not the head of a state. His institutions do not fall under the category of state organizations (in the *dawla*), but they are better termed as secular (*dunyawī*). In highlighting this new balance, he is in a sense subverting the dominant *dīn/dawla* (or religion/politics) binary and replacing it with *dīn/dunyā*.

This approach to the faith and the world in the leadership of the Aga Khan could be called a bifocal approach, which is an integral part of his authority. Maintaining this balance between the faith and the world is one of the most prominent elements of his leadership. As such, one could label his leadership as "bifocal leadership."

The Role of Language

The English language has been the lingua franca of the Ismaili community for the past century. The engagements of the last four Ismaili Imams, i.e., the Aga Khans, give an initial explanation of the emergence of English as a mode of communication. However, the first two Aga Khans, were still mainly in the cultural atmosphere of Qājār princes[31] and their communication language was still Persian. It was with the imamate of Aga Khan III that English started playing an important role in the Ismaili community.

If we put the role of the English language in the right context, we should definitely see it in light of the enthusiastic support and encouragement of education by the Aga Khans, as well as understanding of the necessity of learning the language of science and technology of the modern world. Also, a great population of the followers of the Aga Khan lived under colonial rule and understandably learning the language would be one of the essential elements to the development of the community.

After the time of Aga Khan III, when English gained its initial importance in the Ismaili community, during the imamate of Aga Khan IV, the English language still remained on the agenda and it has continued to gain an importance to such a degree that English is now the international language of the Ismaili community. The instructions of the Ismaili Imam, his edicts (*farmān*s) and messages are all issued in the English language. The Ismaili Constitution is written in the English language and all the academic institutions, organizations, and agencies of the AKDN use English as their first language.

The religious *farman*s of the Imam and his speeches are translated in the languages of the areas where English is not the main language or the majority of the community does not speak English. Nonetheless, the importance of the English language is never diminished and the Aga Khan continues to emphasize the importance of English on the occasions when he speaks to his community directly.

To summarize the point I have raised here, this is now an established fact that the Ismaili Imam wants a community fluent in English as part of their educational training and beside their national language. This is an issue of linguistics, but it is important to note how concepts developed in the English language and in the context of Western and European cultures get translated to the languages of the Ismaili communities around the globe and vice versa. There are theological and historical ideas which are translated from Arabic, Persian, and Indic languages into English. I have given examples of this change when it comes to the translation of the term authority.

Conversely, this linguistic shift occurs when classical texts of Muslim and specifically Shiʿi Ismaili traditions are translated into the English language. It is a process that happens both ways. Not only concepts and ideas in the English language find their way in the consciousness of those members of the Ismaili community, who do not speak the language, but also concepts of the original languages of Ismaili Muslims get translated into English.

The semantics of the terms which are translated include certain civilizational dimensions which do not exist in the English language and one has to know the contexts of these terms or concepts to fully grasp the weight of what one reads. It is a challenge for the Ismailis, too. However, the very fact of it strongly encourages and signifies openness to change and a readiness to let new ideas of other cultures and civilizations in the consciousness of the Ismailis.

The difference is much better felt when we look at communities of Muslim groups who are not that comfortable with the English language or learn it simply as a defensive mechanism rather than embracing it as part of a learning process. It is true that there are many Muslim communities that are fluent in English, but it does not seem to have become part and parcel of their religious following as such, whereas in the case of the Ismailis, following the edicts of the Imam is considered a sacred obligation of a faithful.

There is also a more delicate aspect here in terms of the language of the Community. The Ismaili Community is diverse and spread all around the globe. While in the tradition of the Ismailis from the subcontinent,

the devotional literature of the Community has been in the form of *ginān*s, poetical writings that convey the main themes of the faith, the new generations are beginning to lose their contact with the original language as they no longer learn the Indian languages directly. The same thing is true about the Qur'ān. With the exception of the countries where Arabic language is part of the national curriculum, Arabic is not part of the language of the Community. Therefore, any understanding of these texts happens through translations in the process of which a part of the meaning is lost.

While the predominance of the English language has certainly strengthened the position of the Community in many ways, the risk of losing touch with national and local languages of the Community is a serious matter for those members who live in countries with English as their national language.

Architecture: A Passion for the Aga Khan

A very important body of institutions, which are operative in the AKDN, is the one that deals with architecture and the built environment. The explanation for the genesis of these agencies, which fall under the culture section of the AKDN, is the fact that the Ismaili Imam was himself a client of architectural projects. This need was simply arising from the fact that a large number of schools, hospitals and different buildings were inherited and they needed restoration. Apart from this, congregational spaces for prayers (known among the Ismailis as *jamāʿatkhāna*s) either needed to be built or required restoration. However, the fact is that architecture was more than just a situation which needed attention; it became more than anything else a passion for the Ismaili Imam.

In an interview with Phillip Jodidio, he responds to the question of how he was drawn to architecture:

> I travelled extensively, meeting with various communities in different parts of the world. I came into contact with visible forms of poverty that I had not known before. I had been educated in Switzerland and the United States. Anyone who visited the slums of Karachi in 1957, or who visited the high mountain areas in the Karakoram, or who simply visited the periphery of Bombay or Calcutta, came into direct physical contact with levels of poverty which were absolutely indescribable, and which were very much evidenced by the physical environment in which the people lived.

The Aga Khan here touches on the issue of the quality of life and how poverty is reflected in the physical environment:

The first indicator of a community's poverty, what you see, is the physical context in which they live. Therefore, my interest in architecture was driven at that time by the question of *what to do to improve the quality of life of the ultra-poor*. That brought into focus a very serious question that impacted my thinking on architecture. It was apparent that the material needs to change this process were so enormous that the idea that these parts of the world could ever enter the domain of the consumer society was simply unrealistic.

He then puts this concern in the context of the existing institutions of his Community, where there were schools, hospitals, and housing projects underway:

What you were doing at the time was to look at every way possible to obtain the highest return on any investment, whether it was for a school or a hospital, or housing. It was not possible to think in terms of the useful life of a building. The useful life of a building was quite simply as long as it was going to stand up. That completely changed my attitude to building programmes.

And he notes the gap between Western societies and the ultra-poor societies in terms of the built environment:

Whereas in the consumer societies of the West you can build and then pull things down, in these ultra-poor societies you cannot afford to do that. What you have to do is to modify buildings or adjust them; therefore, the flexibility of the plan that you put in place has to be conceived with a different view of time than it would be in other parts of the world. (Jodidio, 2007: 36–37; emphasis mine)

In his response, we can clearly see his preoccupation with improving the quality of life, and this is where his vision of architecture and this passion for him meets his perception of the world and the faith (with his bifocal leadership and his belief that this dichotomy is a false one). Further on, he comes to describe architecture in very eloquent terms where it relates to his work and his position:

Architecture is the only art that is a direct reflector of poverty. Music does not reflect poverty in a tactile way, nor does literature. In architecture there is an inherent and unavoidable demonstration of the quality of life, or its absence. (Jodidio, 2007: 37)

Here, it is interesting to note that the Aga Khan's approach to architecture and music is quite nuanced in terms of practical issues of the

Muslim world. Max Weber's study of the social and rational foundations of music reflects that the art and music are highly influenced by scientific and technological principles, representing progressive developments. In assessing Weber's study of music and art in the context of rational and scientific developments, Schluchter notes: "developments of modern scientific rationalism demonstrates connections not only with economics but also with aesthetic developments, especially with the Western development of music" (Schuchter, in Huff and Schluchter, 1999: 57)

For the Aga Khan, the quality of architecture is an indicator for the quality of life; something that cannot be reflected in music or literature.

Thus, we can clearly see how architecture becomes part of his outlook on development. Moreover, his involvement with architecture goes beyond simply being a client; it has also become a "search." This component of search has transformed some of the programs which were later added to his architectural institutions (details of these institutions will be covered in the chapter 4) and it became more than a matter just of awards and projects; there was also a learning process involved, both for the clients and for the architects.

Elsewhere, he has expressed another reason for his preoccupation with architecture in terms of how he interprets Islam:

> Muslims believe in an all-encompassing unit of man and nature. To them there is no fundamental division between the spiritual and the material, while the whole world, whether it be the earth, sea or air, or the living creatures that inhabit them, is an expression of God's creation. The aesthetics of the environment we build and the quality of the social interactions that take place within those environments reverberate on our spiritual life, and there has always been a very definite ethos guiding the best Islamic architecture. (Aga Khan IV, 1985)[32]

Therefore, the quality of the built environment for him reflects the way a Muslim practices his faith. It does not simply remain at a personal level of engagement with the issue. Yet, his knowledge of issues of architecture is such that most architects and those involved in building are amazed. With his personal interest in the issue and the inspiration he draws from faith, he gives an unprecedented dimension to his efforts in promoting Islamic architecture:

> What happens to the built environment is highly visible. You notice decay and change in it immediately. But it was not only architecture which went

into eclipse for a long period, the other arts were also affected: literature, music and painting.

Furthermore, when I speak about Muslims' concern for the built environment in the Islamic world, I am talking about the majority of the world's 800 million Muslims... my awareness that there might be a case for seeking to re-invigorate and perhaps re-orient the built environment of the Islamic World was awakened by the needs of my own Ismaili community. But I decided very early on that to attempt to tackle my own constituency alone could be interpreted as self-serving, and might even isolate us from other Muslims if they did not genuinely share our concerns. The problem appeared generic to the whole Islamic world and if this was confirmed, as indeed it was, it had to be approached in the widest context. (Ibid.)

The above paragraphs also show a concern for identity. The decay of architecture, to him, is also a sign of the decay of "literature, music and painting." Architecture becomes interrelated with other domains of life and in his view of the world and the faith, they cannot be separated. Therefore, we continue to see a constant and unwavering support for architecture in his style of leadership that led to setting up some very prestigious and long-lasting agencies that are not only of international importance for the AKDN as a Muslim development agency, but also critically important to the architectural heritage of the Muslim world.

"Venture Capitalist" or "Adventurist Capitalist?"

In an article in the Forbes magazine (Gupte, May 1999), the Aga Khan (the present Ismaili Imam) is described as a "venture capitalist." This article was written at a time when the work of the AKDN had gained momentum and had become one of the most important development networks around the world. When we speak of venture capitalist, we have someone in mind that goes into a business or an activity, resurrects a company, and after having gained the profit leaves it. The history of the AKDN and the Aga Khan's vision shows the contrary. This description of his work does not seem accurate. Tom Kessinger, the General Manager of the Aga Khan Foundation, who has been working with the Aga Khan for years, describes him as an "adventurist capitalist":

He is not a "venture capitalist" investing for the short term and then moving on, he is an "adventurist capitalist" because he will go into places where others won't and he is a patient capitalist. And again, most capital flies. You take a couple of events in a country like Kenya and the impact

on the tourist industry and everybody all of a sudden is saying, we need to pull back and maybe get out. Or all of AKDN's activities in Afghanistan. He is not going to give up on them, because he really believes in the mission and his commitments.[33].

The Aga Khan's vision in development is one based on seeking opportunities and managing them. He has invested in areas where most development agencies normally avoid going. The case of Afghanistan is a very good example. Despite the instability of the country and the regular threats to the AKDN institutions, he has remained there and continued his work. With him, it is a matter of "risk tolerance" that makes him unique among other people who are involved in the field and in this area of work. This story from Tom Kessinger is a good example of how he views things:

> He and I had an exchange in a meeting in front of some other people. And he thought I was being very negative about one of the things he was suggesting. And he said, "Why are you being so negative?" And I said, "Well, I think I am trying to manage risks." And he said something like—I am not sure if they are the exact words—"I think you are mismanaging opportunity." So, there you are. And everybody's risk level and risk tolerance is different at different situations.[34]

Deliberative Forms of Leadership

During the time of the present Imam, there has been a visible shift in the form of leadership provided by the Ismaili Imam. This shift may be better explained, as elaborated earlier in this thesis, by speaking of a shift from "personal leadership" to "institutional leadership"; during the time of the previous Aga Khan, the role of the Imam's individual decision making was far greater than what we see today. This institutionalization of the imamate has resulted in making it more deliberative.

What I mean by deliberative is the situation in which decisions are not taken unilaterally by the Imam alone. Rather, the Imam draws on the expertise of various scholars, even in matters of the interpretation of faith, where there is need for a pool of knowledge and professional expertise to be tapped into. So, this ethos of deliberative leadership is quite palpable here. The amount of consultation which happens in different levels is incredibly greater than it was in the past.

While we do not have any specific historical evidence as to whether this practice used to exist during the time of previous Imams to this extent, we can at least judge from the absence of this huge network

of institutions, both for the community and for the general public (as in the form of the AKDN), that this level of sophistication for deliberative leadership, which attaches significance to consultation, was not there. And this is all to be expected of course, because the sheer size and number of institutions and agencies required much more effort and expertise.

Some might argue that during the time of the Fatimids, there were academic institutions, administrative institutions and other forms of organization necessary for running the state. Still, even during the time of the Fatimids, the role of the individual Imam was so great that it cannot be compared with what we have today. The amount of consultation which exists today has been unprecedented.

Pluralism and Tolerance

The Aga Khan has been speaking of the importance of pluralism for over two decades now. This emphasis has been both inside his own community and outside for the wider public. As far as it regards the community itself, it arises from the fact that within the Ismaili community there is a diversity of ethnic, geographic and cultural backgrounds. The Ismaili community is made of people who speak different languages and have different cultures. Hence, we have this emphasis on pluralism by the Imam.

Following the collapse of the Soviet Union and the emergence of Ismailis from central Asia (specifically Tajikistan), a large population of Ismailis openly joined the wider Ismaili community around the globe. The same happened after the collapse of the Taliban regime in Afghanistan allowing large populations of Afghan Ismailis to come into contact with the wider Ismaili community and the institutions of Ismaili imamate.

Tajikstan, Afghanistan, and Iran were the three Farsi-speaking countries with their own unique heritage, which was different from that of the Ismailis from the Indian subcontinent. There is a term often used to describe Ismailis from the subcontinent background: the Khojas.[35] The diversity of the Ismailis goes beyond these regions where, historically, the Ismailis lived. There are Ismailis in parts of China and Syria too. This enormous diversity required some sort of a strategy to ease the tensions that could emerge when these different cultures met.

This was immediately touched upon by the Aga Khan. The concept of pluralism, spoken by the Ismaili Imam, bears an ethical dimension, too, rooted in the Muslim tradition. The Imam often quotes a verse from the

Qur'ān describing the differences in the Muslim *Ummah*. By contextualizing the term in the background of Muslim tradition, the Imam has actually given it a familiar aspect without creating too much theoretical debate about the concept itself. Yet, the term being used there is constantly defined and explained and it has become an invariable part of the institutional culture of the Ismaili community around the globe.

Pluralism and tolerance has worked both ways, inside and outside the community. The Aga Khan had insisted from the early days of his imamate on the necessity of building bridges with other communities. A precondition for building bridges was clearly a more epistemological position to the effect that Ismailis were not the sole bearers of truth. And here comes in the idea of tolerance. No Ismaili is in a position to judge the faith of another Muslim.

They can clearly make a distinction between Ismailis and the non-Ismailis as the conditions for being an Ismaili are crystal clear. From the Imam's perspective, there are some basic conditions for being a Muslim, and these conditions are so minimal that one does not fail to see the resemblance of this position to the original references in the Qur'ān and the tradition.

His support for pluralism is itself a form of political statement too. With the image that the media projects of the Muslims around the world as well as the radical and fundamentalists interpretations of Islam, his position also draws a line as to what can be done and what cannot be done in the name of Islam. Therefore, his support for pluralism is not something that would work only inside his own community to harness existing differences in a positive manner, but it also has a more global dimension to it in how to deal with the larger communities among whom the greater Muslim population lives.

His position on pluralism has become something more than just a mere choice. To him, it is now an inevitable and necessary part of the existence of human societies:

Tolerance, openness and understanding towards other peoples' cultures, social structures, values and faiths are now essential to the very survival of an interdependent world... Pluralism is no longer simply an asset or a prerequisite for progress and development, it is vital to our existence. (Aga Khan IV, April 2005)[36]

The Aga Khan's concern about pluralism goes beyond simply the dynamics of his own Community. This is reflected in an institutional form in the creation of the Global Center for Pluralism in Canada. The

Center, created under the leadership of the Aga Khan, a secular facility located within the Delegation of the Ismaili Imamat in Canada, is an institution to "advance global understanding of pluralism as an ethic of respect that values diversity as a public good and enables every person—irrespective of ethno-cultural differences—to realize his or her full potential as a citizen."[37]

The more nuanced and theoretical articulations of the kind of pluralism that the Aga Khan promotes are best described in a paper published by the Global Centre for Pluralism. According to this paper, pluralism is understood as rejecting "division as a necessary outcome of diversity, seeking instead to identify the qualities and experiences that unite rather than divide us as people and to forge a shared stake in the public good" (Global Centre for Pluralism (GCP), 2012: 1). The paper distinguishes between pluralism and multiculturalism in that pluralism "emphasizes individual choices as well as collective compromise and mutual obligation as routes to peace, stability and human development" (GCP, 2012: 2).

Pluralism is also given an ethical foundation; it is considered an "ethic of respect" that values human diversity:

Fairness and respect are thus the cornerstones of a pluralistic ethic, as well as mechanisms of balance between the sometimes competing claims of group rights and human rights and the obligations and/or choices implied. Respecting difference depends on a capacity and willingness to acknowledge, negotiate and accommodate alternative points of view. (GCP, 2012: 2)

There is an interconnection between pluralism and active citizenship, and as such pluralism is seen as part of the mutual civic obligations of citizens:

To support pluralism, citizens must enjoy the freedom to meet their civic obligations as well as exercise their rights. Reciprocity—a sense of shared experience and mutual obligation—is the foundation for understanding between people, groups and nations. Compromise requires identification with the greater good. Active citizenship grounded in reciprocity is a vital "bottom-up" support to pluralism. (GCP, 2012: 11)

The very foundation of this approach to pluralism is to recognize that within every society conflicts exist. Thus pluralism is seen as a way not to "eliminate differences" but to "foster the mechanisms of compromise

and accommodation that lead to peace and prevent violence in at risk societies" (GCP, 2012: 14).

Here, in the Aga Khan's vision pluralism is expressed both within his own community and in the outside world at national and global levels. As regards the Community, tensions do exist, particularly with the modern developments and the expansion of the institutions. Part of these tensions and conflicts has cultural reasons as Ismailis come from different backgrounds. The dominant elite who run these institutions are mostly of the East African background and belong to the entrepreneurial and executive strata running these institutions on a daily basis. However, even though theoretically and at a global level, such articulations of pluralism seem to have valid points and could be negotiated, it is not clear whether and to what extent this pluralism can be reflected in the institutions of the Community.

Cosmopolitanism and Cosmopolitan Ethic

Earlier when I had made reference to the terminologies that frequently come up in the language of Aga Khan IV, I had mentioned that these terms bear the Aga Khan's own brand and his own take on these concepts. In the previous section, where I had described the Aga Khan's views about pluralism and how it gets embedded in his institutional and Community work, I mentioned that he finds pluralism essential for cosmopolitanism.

The Aga Khan, however, approaches cosmopolitanism in a critical way. He believes that although the world has become more pluralist, it has not been keeping pace in spirit and he brings this up in connection with cosmopolitanism: "'Cosmopolitan' social patterns have not yet been matched by what I would call 'a cosmopolitan ethic.'"[38] He picks up the theme that he had left in his Evora speech in the Tutzing Evangelical Academy upon receiving the Tolerance Award on May 20, 2006: "Societies which have grown more pluralistic in makeup, are not always growing more pluralistic in spirit. What is needed—all across the world—is a new 'cosmopolitan ethic'—rooted in a strong culture of tolerance."[39]

For him, pluralism is not something you just take up once and then tick it away. It is a matter which requires "constant re-adaptation" because "identities are not fixed in stone."[40] Hence, he believes that "we should be open to the fact that there may be a variety of 'best practices,' a 'diversity of diversities,' and a 'pluralism of pluralisms.'" (Ibid.)

It is here that he tries to outline, with a further degree of clarity, what he means by a cosmopolitan ethic: "A readiness to accept the complexity of human society. It is an ethic which balances rights and duties. It is an ethic for all peoples," and he further embeds a religious element into it as well:

Such an ethic can grow with enormous power out of the spiritual dimensions of our lives. In acknowledging the immensity of The Divine, *we will also come to acknowledge our human limitations, the incomplete nature of human understanding.* (Ibid.)[41]

So, we can see that even when it comes to cosmopolitanism, which he receives warmly but with caution, he gives his own interpretation of it, just as he does so with pluralism.

It is interesting to note that when the controversy of Danish cartoons arises, his immediate reaction is two-fold. First, he expresses his concern that freedom of expression is abused and it is reduced to license. Second, he takes the opportunity to criticize the famous theory of Huntington and says this is more than anything else a "clash of ignorance" rather than a "clash of civilisations."[42] The Aga Khan has spoken about this on a number of occasions to the extent that the phrase "clash of ignorance" has found its own brand now:

Take as an example the phrase "clash of civilisations" which has travelled far and wide. I have said many times previously, and I would like to reconfirm today my conviction that what we have been observing in recent decades is not a clash of civilisations but a clash of ignorance. This ignorance is both historic and of our time. This is not the occasion to analyse the historic causes of the deep ignorance that exists between the Judeo-Christian and Muslim worlds. But I am convinced that many of today's problems could have been avoided if there had been better understanding and more serious dialogue between the two.[43]

As regards the cosmopolitan ethics, Ulrich Beck expresses similar concerns at a more theoretical level:

If we want to develop a cosmopolitan ethics and politics we must first ask what ideological misuses a well-meaning cosmopolitanism makes possible: ideological self-criticism is the criterion of validity of the new cosmopolitanism. On this criterion there is no way to avoid assessing the necessity and the radicality of the distinction between emancipatory and despotic cosmopolitanism. (Beck, 2006: 45)

To Beck, this self-criticism of cosmopolitanism is important to avoid confusing it with a despotic version of it, which he finds possible. Further on, he says that

> only a devil's advocate who questions well-meaning cosmopolitanism as to its emancipatory function and its misuse can open the debate over the ethics and politics of cosmopolitanism. (Beck, 2006: 47)

It seems that Beck can somehow find his "devil's advocate" in the concerns echoed by the Aga Khan. However, it is also true that once we speak of the cosmopolitanism that the Aga Khan refers to, we are not facing a substantive and sophisticated theory for it in his words. We can find seeds of what could become a theory, but with reservation and caution.

When the Aga Khan is referring to ethics in this context, we can only guess from the context that he means an open and tolerant ethics, which is unmistakably Muslim in his words. There is still room for legal ethics and this is an imperative matter as with the vast network of the institutions of the Ismaili imamate—whether within his Community or outside—the issue of a "cosmopolitan legal ethics" is bound to come up. And this is what Beck draws our attention to:

> A cosmopolitan legal ethics completely inverts relations of priority, so that the principles of cosmopolitan law trump national law. Crimes against humanity can neither be legitimated by appeal to national laws nor tried and condemned within the nation-state. In sum, the historically novel category 'crimes against humanity' abrogates the principles of national legislation and adjudication. (Beck, 2006: 170)

As such, we can see that there is still much room for further elaboration of these themes, but the crucial point here is that in the language of the Aga Khan the term is used so carefully and as time passes by, it becomes sharper in focus. It is also important to note how various aspects of cosmopolitanism inevitably become important in the Aga Khan's vision through his preoccupation with architecture which is so central in the work of his institutions.[44] As such, one can also argue how the development of different institutions and agencies within the AKDN pose new questions that provide the ground for further philosophical and theoretical considerations as they grow within the ethical framework of the AKDN.

Cosmopolitanism is branching off the idea of pluralism but pluralism itself is much wider, whereas cosmopolitanism, in the way the

Aga Khan sees it, is a kind of ethical field in which you argue about pluralism because it is connected to both identity and citizenship. It provides an opportunity to create a bridge between the religious and the civil. The ethical content of it comes from a religious background but its application in terms of social identity connects us to citizenship.

The AKDN is very much interested in promoting both local citizenship and the ideal of global citizenship, which the AKDN itself signifies. In all the projects of the AKDN, there is one common thread running and that is a refusal to allow narrow local identities to define the character of its projects. A classic example of this is the Al-Azhar Park Project. The Al-Azhar Park project was the collaboration between the UNDP, the Aga Khan Trust for Culture (AKTC), and the Egyptian government. The model of the park is neither a modern park as we see in London or in New York, nor a traditional Islamic one like the Shalimar Gardens. The collaboration to create the park was a cosmopolitan venture, but it was not just the cosmopolitan nature of the actors. The image of the park was also important.

The park is anchored in history; it is not a mixture of international identities or a patchwork of different elements. The idea was that it should be in the middle of Cairo, cutting across class lines and that people in the neighborhood should have privileged access to it. It is also a tourist attraction, but people also get culture in it, not just nature. Examples like this abound in the work of the AKDN, reaching back to history but also reaching forward. The key to understanding the work of the AKTC is cosmopolitan aesthetics, ethics and identity. Describing it simply under the rubric of modernity is too weak.

The AKDN is creating a bridge between cosmopolitan identities and cosmopolitan citizenship. In order to explain this, it is not sufficient to argue that the imamate advocates loyal citizenship. We need something more than this. We should ask what the cosmopolitan aspirations of the AKDN are. And how do they reflect and require the kind of leadership that can draw upon ethical integrity and not just political integrity?

This ethical cosmopolitanism is not achieved only by sound human resource management. The question is how you bring together people with ideas completely different from yours. I asked Amyn Sajoo[45] how we could address this question in this context. His response was:

> This was a vital challenge for John Rawls. And his response was to say that we require an "overlapping consensus." In my view, the Imam takes

it one step further. He says in effect, "Well, if you want your overlapping consensus, what is it that there will be a consensus on? Just tactics and strategy, or on principles?" If it is only about the former, then this is strictly a pragmatic game to quarrel over. But if it is about principles, then you would require a thick description.[46]

This "thick description" according to Sajoo, requires first agreeing on principles. Then in order to see how the AKDN serves cosmopolitan civil ends and therefore promotes a citizenship that is responsible and accountable, both locally and internationally, we should ask "How the leadership required to steer AKDN into those cosmopolitan waters must demonstrate ethical credibility and integrity."[47] And therefore, it requires someone like this Imam and not just a politician.

In order to achieve this, we should then ask how does it require an evolution of his own authority and what kinds of transitions are required from a traditional pure type of charismatic religious authority to a more civil one.

In response to these questions, Sajoo believes that we must make a distinction between ethical cosmopolitanism and mainstream liberal cosmopolitanism. The latter merely requires managerial skills. This kind of governance essentially demands "technocrats," while the former "requires familiarity with cultural read-outs, with the way people actually behave in situations that test their identity and so on."[48]

The most important distinction that Sajoo makes about the secular (or liberal) cosmopolitanism is that "no vision is required"; there is no ultimate and higher transcendent truth to aspire to. In other words, in liberal cosmopolitanism, people have different ends and you cannot possibly have a vision; it is just an end in itself: "The moment you establish liberal cosmopolitanism, your main challenge is to sustain the system. So, it resists any competitors."

Ethical cosmopolitanism is at the other end of the extreme. It is not interested in an end-free world, because it has a religious sense attached to it and religion is always interested in where you are going. And here is where the concept of authority comes in:

> Authority cannot be temporal, politically limited, subject to five year election cycles, etc. Because that serves no longer vision. It is simply vision-free and it drifts, whereas the whole point about an ethical cosmopolitanism is that it says yes it is good in itself but it takes us to a place that it also makes claims to humanism, individual harmony, spiritual transcendence, etc.[49]

Here is where it diverges from liberal cosmopolitanism and its thin description, because it simply deals with a constitution and does not require any underlying authority. And here there are differences in terms of its vision and its concepts of governance, accountability, and historical roots, none of which are interesting for a liberal cosmopolitan.

This theme is probably one of the most radical leaps connecting the AKDN, the Ismaili imamate and his authority to the idea of cosmopolitanism that he has in mind. But the question remains: Who is there to theorize this shift? I will address this under challenges and new pathways for the AKDN and the Ismaili imamate.

Toward a Humanistic Cosmopolitan Ethics: Ethics Prior to Religion?

The question of the relation between ethics and religion is an old one and its genealogy can be traced back to the early centuries of Islam with debates between the Muʿtazila and the Ashāʿira. Rationalist movements in Islam have had the tendency of arguing in favor of the priority of ethics—as an independent branch—over religion, which has been historically seen as the main reference point of ethics.[50] Ismailis, who have been historically the defendants of rationalism in the Muslim world, have contributions to this field (examples of it are found in Ṭūsī's *Akhlāq-i Nāṣirī*). In the modern period, the overall direction of the Ismaili imamate has been toward a rational and humanistic role of ethics, rather than an ethics which is exclusively dictated and defined by religion. In an interview with the Lebanese Broadcasting Corporation International, the Aga Khan says, "it is *not only on religious grounds* that I have to intervene, but *also on ethical grounds*" [emphasis mine].[51] The suggestion is more than clear: he views ethics not to be exclusively born out of religion. This point becomes clearer in another interview in 2008 where he says:

> It is necessary to develop the principle of *a cosmopolitan ethic, which is not an ethic oriented by faith, or for a society*. I speak of an ethic under which all people can live within a same society, and *not of a society that reflects the ethic of solely one faith*. I would call that ethic, quality of life. [Emphasis mine][52]

He finds cosmopolitan ethics interconnected with the quality of life, and, at the same time, he does not see it organically connected to

religion. In the same interview, he expresses doubts as about "ecumenical discourse," which clearly distinguished his position from certain movements in Muslim and Christian worlds:

> I have serious doubts about the ecumenical discourse, and about what it can reach, but I do not have any doubts about cosmopolitan ethics. I believe that people share the same basic worries, joys, and sadness. If we can reach a consensus in terms of cosmopolitan ethics, we will have attained something, which is very important.[53]

To the Aga Khan, belief in pluralism should not be confused with ecumenical discourses. His major concern is that interreligious dialogue might indeed lead to an exclusion of non-believers:

> Inter-religious dialogue, yes, but I would prefer that it be based upon a cosmopolitan ethic. *It would have to include non-believers.* Because I am talking about human society and I cannot judge an individual's belief at any given time, in his life or mine. [Emphasis mine][54]

This is a rare instance in which a religious leader is indeed recognizing the rights of non-believers in the context of a cosmopolitan ethics, which is deeply concerned about the quality of life of all people. Elsewhere, he expresses a similar concern:

> A possible common ground could be found if all the political forces accepted over-arching responsibility to nourish a cosmopolitan ethic among their peoples. This would be an ethic for all peoples, one that offers equitable and measurable opportunities for the improvement of their lives, measured in terms of their own criteria for quality living. Clearly, different peoples will have different visions about a desirable quality of life, in urban versus rural areas, for example.

He continues to speak of a "universal ethical system" connecting it with the agencies of the AKDN:

> But a commitment to *a universal ethical system* that welcomes and respects diversity will be of central importance. AKDN has sought to structure itself through its network of specialise agencies to optimise its contribution to civil society. These agencies are able to design various matrices for interventions, which can be adapted to as many situations as possible. [Emphasis mine][55]

Civil Society

Civil Society has been one of the other phrases that the Aga Khan has frequently and increasingly used. A part of this is clearly because his institutions form part of the Civil Society. His vision of Civil Society is closely interconnected with his perception of sustainable development—which is often coming up alongside the phrase "enabling environment"[56]—and as such a healthy and strong civil society is a key to the success of his work. It is not simply Civil Society being non-governmental organizations that interests him. This Civil Society has to be pluralist as well to accommodate the changes that can happen through his development work.

So, we see how interconnected these terms and themes are to his way of thinking. According to him, "the strengthening and enhancement of pluralist civil society, in all corners of the globe" will be "making a very significant contribution in an area which I believe will be critical to the development of humankind in the 21st century."[57]

His institutional activities have brought him face-to-face with predicaments of constraints of Civil Society. In a speech in Tashkent, Uzbekistan, he says,

> No country to my knowledge can achieve stable continuous growth if its civil society is constrained by inherent institutional instability. The need is universal. It exists in big countries and small countries, countries better endowed with natural resources, and those that have less, countries in the developing world, the developed world, and those in transition following the dissolution of the Soviet Union.[58]

As we can see from these words, the Aga Khan's concern for Civil Society is deeply rooted in his institutional work. It is here in the context of Civil Society that once again the ideas of pluralism and cosmopolitanism come back to us and the issue of ethics resurfaces once more. John Keane has highlighted this concern: "Empirical applications of the concept of global civil society—a concept whose emphasis upon pluralism sticks a pin in the bottom of cosmopolitan universalism—are virtually absent" (Keane, 2003: 125). And this is exactly why these debates recur in the words of the Aga Khan, as head of a development network who is also the Imam of a Shi'i Muslim Community.

So, to sum up what I have briefly touched upon so far, these terms, phrases, and the concepts that frequently appear in the words of the Aga Khan in his speeches create a matrix that runs through the work of the AKDN. If these were merely the concerns of the head of a development

organization, it would be probably an essential part of the work of a responsible leader who cares about the success of his work.

Another dimension, however, is added to this: his religious position is so deeply intertwined with his development work in the context of his interpretation of the role of the Imam. It is this interpretation that is the key to understanding how he thinks and how he acts. This interpretation is the hallmark of what I have called a transmutation or a shift. It is what clearly describes his bifocal leadership and an authority which is no longer bound by territorial nation-state constraints.

Democracy and Its Failures

For the past quarter of century, the Aga Khan has been touching on issues that have been of serious political importance. One of these issues has been democracy. His concern for the "failure of democracy" has not been simply a detached observation or critical remark. His positions often reflect themselves in the actual institutional work that he does. Like many other areas of his vision, some important areas of which are addressed in this chapter, issues relating to democracy are somehow embedded in the agencies that he has created. Details of these institutions appear in the next chapter, but as regards democracy itself, he made the following remarks in the Governor General's Conference in Gatineau in Canada in 2004:

> Much of the world's attention is periodically focussed on the phenomenon of so-called failed states. But of the global threats that face us today, apart from nuclear war or HIV/AIDS, the most preoccupying is not failed states. It is the failure of democracy. The global picture at the beginning of the twenty-first century is a story of failed democracies in the Muslim world, in Latin America, in Eastern Europe and in sub-Saharan Africa. A startling fact today is that nearly 40 per cent of UN member nations are failed democracies. The greatest risk to the West itself, and to its values, is therefore the accumulation of failed democracies, which, in turn, will cause deep undercurrents of stress, if not conflict, among societies.

After giving these figures, he draws attention to the idea that even democracy itself is not immune to failures and it can turn against itself:

> It is essential, in its own interest, that the West admit to itself that *democracy is as fragile as any other form of human governance.* It is essential that every nation and each society ask the following question: "If

democracy is failing, why is this the case?" They must make every effort to help correct the situation rather than referring dismissively to "failed states." To my knowledge, democracy can fail anywhere, at any time, in any society-as it has in several well-known and well-documented situations in Europe, as recently as the last fifty years. It is self-evident, in Europe and across the globe, that the existence of political parties and elections does not alone produce stable governments or competent leadership. [Emphasis mine][59]

These are not words of a politician or a political scientist; they are reflections of the leader of a Shi'i Muslim community who expresses genuine concern about the fate of a political system that "can work." He goes on to make his own suggestions as to what could help stabilize and strengthen democracy around the world:

Three concepts seem to me essential in creating, stabilizing and strengthening democracy around the world, including among the people of Africa and Asia with whom I have worked in the past. These concepts are meritocracy, pluralism and civil society. (Ibid.)

The three concepts that he introduces are the ones he had worked on and promoted for a very long time inside his own community among his followers and also in the institutions that he has built: (1) a healthy civil society: "It is an essential bulwark that provides citizens with multiple channels through which to exercise effectively both their rights and duties of citizenship"; (2) pluralism: "The rejection of pluralism is pervasive across the globe and plays a significant role in breeding destructive conflicts"; and (3) education:

A secure pluralistic society requires communities that are educated and confident both in the identity and depth of their own traditions and in those of their neighbours. Democracies must be educated if they are to express themselves competently, and their electorates are to reach informed opinions about the great issues at stake. Perhaps the greatest obstacle to pluralism and democracy, however, is the lacuna in the general education of the populations involved. (Ibid.)

In fact, it is not surprising at all that he finds his own institutions (the AKDN being the most visible of them) to be part of a vibrant civil society. I have earlier spoken about the place of pluralism for the Aga Khan. He has not only supported pluralism in word and in action, but he has also brought a much wider and more public embodiment to it by

establishing the GCP in Canada. The Centre can be seen as a physical expression of what the Aga Khan thinks. The architectural dimension of it is an unmistakable visible aspect of it, which fits within his vision of what a vibrant Muslim community can be.

In the way he addresses some of the most critical issues of our world, one can easily discern a certain set of vocabularies and a unique language rich with ideas, which shapes his thinking and the general direction of the institutions he has created. Let us have a look at the following paragraph from one of his speeches (in which he speaks about Canada):

> Whatever definition is used, a quality civil society is independent of government; it is pluralist, and it is led by merit-based, educated leadership. Not only does Canadian civil society eminently meet these three criteria, but I know of no country where civil society is more empathetic with the needs of civil society in the countries of Africa and Asia, countries in which I have been working for some forty-five years. I have therefore asked myself, not once but hundreds of times, if and how Canadian civil society can mobilize its resources more vigorously to help improve the quality of life of the peoples of Africa and Asia.
>
> Asked in these terms, the issue becomes that of sharing the many forms of human knowledge and experience that create and sustain a civil society of quality, rather than looking for a massive injection of monetary resources. There are, however, two obvious preconditions. First, that the governments and peoples of the developing world wish for, and welcome, the help being offered. This requires an enabling social, legal and fiscal environment. Second, that Canadian institutions and human resources must see real enrichment in life's purpose in their willingness to help.[60]

There is an obvious concern for a "quality civil society." We can see "pluralism" embedded in every facet of his thinking. He highlights the importance of "meritocracy." He speaks of "educated leaders," which reveals his preoccupation with the idea of good leadership and good governance. We also see the term "enabling environment," which he has used in his speeches for many years. These concepts are not accidentally present in his thinking.

They are ideas that have been carefully thought through and have been constantly polished and appraised by him. They have then found their expression in institutions with an ideal. Things do not remain simply on the level of just an ideal development network. Ideas are then placed in the context of a Muslim interpretation of faith. This sounds

like a very rare and strange Muslim leadership, but the fact is that one exists not only in terms of words but also in action and practice in agencies which have a history. He has put his words into action through institutional work.

We must note, however, that we only speak about how the AKDN functions. We must not confuse the views of the Aga Khan about democracy with how his Community institutions function. Even though there is a semi-democratic element in the appointments in community institutions—in that there is a limit on terms—it does not exactly fit a democratic model. There is no system of voting as such. The outgoing office bearers suggest names of the incoming ones to be chosen by the Imam (which I will come back to in chapter 4).

Counter-intuitive Political Statements or Re-politicizing the De-politicized?

The present Ismaili Imam, Aga Khan IV, is generally viewed as a shrewd leader who is very cautious about making political statements. Nonetheless, while remaining true to this policy, he has at times been vocal over certain critical issues. In a rather recent comment about the nuclear program of Iran, he is critical of the overall position of the West toward Iran to the extent that he calls it "technological colonization":

> Il me semble que, aujourd'hui, il y a une tendance à ériger en règle une «non-prolifération» qui concerne la totalité de la technologie nucléaire, à finalité civile comme militaire. En effet, les conditions posées à la vente du nucléaire civil ressemblent à une forme de colonisation par la technologie dans la mesure où les pays les plus avancés insistent pour conserver toutes les «clés». On est donc très loin d'une «démocratisation» de cette énergie! Peut-être suis-je naïf, mais je défends une autre approche, ce que j'appelle «prolifération positive». Je suis favorable à la diffusion de la technologie nucléaire civile. Naturellement, il faut mener à bien une réflexion pointue sur les conditions de cette «prolifération positive»: comment se mettre à l'abri des problèmes environnementaux? Comment éviter le détournement du nucléaire civil à des fins militaires? J'ai étudié l'histoire, comme vous le savez; eh bien, il n'y a jamais eu un progrès scientifique d'importance globale dont on ait pu stopper le développement. Cette prolifération positive que j'appelle de mes voeux repose sur un principe simple: oui à l'énergie, non aux armes.[61]

In the same interview, while on the subject of Iran, his comments about Ayatollah Khomeini (while being quite candid in his criticism

of the Shah) are rare, even though they do not necessarily signal any endorsement of the policies of Khomeini:

> La direction que prend l'Iran est un phénomène très préoccupant pour le monde entier, y compris pour les autres pays chiites. À mes yeux, la cause première de la révolution iranienne remonte à la gestion économique malheureuse du régime du Shah : je regrette de devoir dire que, de tous les chefs d'État que j'ai connus, il était probablement celui qui comprenait le moins bien les questions économiques—ou peut-être était-il profondément mal conseillé... Cette lacune a provoqué une multiplication de foyers d'opposition. Il a suffi que Khomeyni se présente pour que l'Histoire bascule. Moi qui suis chiite, lorsque j'ai écouté ses discours, je me suis dit que pas un chiite au monde ne resterait insensible à ses prêches![62]

It is, however, important to note that with regards the Rushdie affair, the Aga Khan is critical about the publication of the book and reactions to it at the same time. He believed that this book would offend any practicing Muslim, and its publication has been insensitive. He even mentions the blasphemy law in the UK in this regard:

> The law of blasphemy in England could have been looked at before the Rushdie book, and there may have been some way of dealing with the whole issue of what is blasphemy for any faith in the UK... That is a serious issue for them because the law of blasphemy applies only to the Church of England, not even to the Catholic Church. So they have a serious problem... But, of course, once you have a book like the Rushdie book, any debate on the issue becomes impossible.[63]

Yet, he believes that murder is a crime and the law of every land has to be respected. So, while he is critical of the whole incident, he does not go so far as to challenge the legal norms altogether, which is where his implicit criticism emerges in how the matter was dealt with. He is nonetheless, acutely conscious of the difference between his own position of authority and status as the "Imam" of a Shi'i community and a "jurist" whose position is lower than that of a Shi'i Imam.

In a different example, after George W. Bush made his notorious comment about North Korea, Iran, and Iraq, calling them the "axis of evil," the Ismaili Imam's response and reaction was blunt (interview dates January 30, 2002):

> I find it difficult to pass a moral judgement on all Iran or all Iraq. I will not do that. I have to tell you very frankly. I will not stigmatise a whole population as being evil. Whether they are Muslim, Christian, Jewish,

Hindu, I will not do it. It is, in my view, a very serious issue. I can't do that. If he wants to say that the people in government are responsible for things that he doesn't like, that's his prerogative. But don't stigmatise a whole country.[64]

Another instance of such counter-intuitive comments is providing a different angle for looking at Hamas and the conflict in the Middle East:

You have to work with whoever the population has elected as long as they are willing to respect what I call cosmopolitan ethics. Now, it's true that Hamas has a record of conflict . . . but it would not be the only time that movements that have such a record make it into parliament, and even end up in charge of government later on. Can I remind you of Jomo Kenyatta and his Mau Mau movement in Kenya, for example, or the ANC in South Africa? Take away the causes of extremism and extremists can come back to a more reasonable political agenda.[65]

The Aga Khan gives the context of democracy and the demand of the people to highlight the popularity of Hamas in the Palestinian regions despite the tense atmosphere of propaganda which depicts Hamas as a "terrorist" organization. He delicately avoids using such loaded terms as "terrorist" and simply describes them as having a "record of conflict." Then, Hamas is seen no different from other movements around the globe with a history of conflict—or violence—and at the same time he suggests his own way out of these deadlocks: taking away the causes of extremism. In other words, if roots of the conflict are not addressed, conflicts shall continue to remain there. It is also noteworthy that he does not fall into the trap reinforced by the mainstream media to label Hamas as "Islamist" as if "Islam" as a faith has been a motivation and source for conflict and violence, rather than political situations and agendas.

There are many more instances in which he expresses his opinions frankly and those opinions do not exactly fit with the numerous misperceptions about him; they are sometimes counterintuitive. He neither appears as a pro-Western Muslim leader who would submissively align himself with political powers, nor does he lean toward radical and aggressive positions. His political positions are well-balanced and in line with his style of leadership.

Positive Change and a Long-term Vision

One of the characteristics of the leadership of the Aga Khan has always been his patience and his long-term vision of what he does. He is

famously quoted to have said on a number of occasions that he does not believe in "instant coffee solutions." To him, development and change is a long-term endeavor. A part of this vision comes from the fact that the authority of the Ismaili Imam is not subject to periodic change. He does not have to worry about re-election. He has a lifetime ahead of him. However, this does not mean that a serious thinking process does not come into play.

In the interview I had with Tom Kessinger, I asked what makes the Aga Khan an effective leader, and his response touched upon this key characteristic of the Aga Khan:

> I think part of it is that he manages very effectively both through explicit guidance and commentary, but also the way that he conducts himself, to transcend many of the limiting considerations of other forms of leadership. I once said to him—and this is a development question and not a theological question—that you know I have been doing development almost as long as you have been the Imam and I have never met anybody who took the long-term view of the development process that you do. How do you account for your long-term vision? In response, he said two things: one is, "I have been engaged in development for almost 50 years and I have learned if real development can be accomplished, it has got to work over time. That positive change is not something that happens quickly. You could put something in place, but it has got to stay in place. Longevity to the change you achieve is one of the measures of the importance of the change.
>
> The second thing he said was "I have a life-time job. I don't have to run for office or satisfy external bodies. I don't have to respond to fads or artificial deadlines. I mean look at government policies, 24 months is forever. Foundations are supposed to take a long-term view. After five or six years they want to have a new plan or new strategy." This makes a difference, because he can afford, in terms of the basis of his authority, to stay with his ideas through ups and downs where the AKDN works. That's what I mean by "transcend." Those are real limits for even very powerful leaders, whether it is term limits or losing majorities or all the other things leaders have to contend. And of course, other religious leaders can have authority that lasts for a very extended periods of time, although most of them are limited by the structure of organized religion even in that sense, but political leaders, business leaders, and civil society leaders seldom can. This is what he has carved out and created. For example the respect with which he is held in the university world has got nothing to do with theology or being a religious leader. He is respected for what he has accomplished, and particularly what he has done in what are considered to be difficult circumstances. He is respected in the business world, sometimes with a certain amount of surprise, because he will take risks in countries

where most businessmen would avoid in the first instance and certainly not stay with after any adverse events... He will always look to the future. He will live through three, four, five years of bad performance, because he has made a commitment.

If we can sum up the areas that are captured so far, one can safely say that we are dealing with a visionary leader who is acutely aware of the issues of his time. He does not live in a dream world. His leadership style brings him in close contact with real issues, and the channels of gathering information are so diverse for him that a single source of information does not suffice for him to form a judgment. He has proved this through his deliberative form of leadership and the consultation process that he finds so crucial to his leadership. His language, as the language of a Muslim leader, has a signature of its own. Therefore, it would be no surprise to see his words being frequently quoted in the circles that have come to know him. I will end this chapter with a quotation from him, which has found its way on Wikiquote:

> You start with an idea, and then you let it grow. I think at the moment, there is a tendency to want to see political change occur in the developing world very rapidly, and I think this notion of consultation and democracy is all excellent, but I simply don't believe that Western forms of democracy are necessarily replicable throughout the developing world that I know, and indeed I would go so far as to say that, at the moment, one of our risks is to see democracies fail. [...] I think you have to be patient, careful, analytical, thoughtful, prudent, and build step-by-step. I don't think it can be done like mixing a glass of Nescafé.' (Interview with the Aga Khan, BBC World News America, November 13, 2007)[66]

CHAPTER 4

The AKDN: An Overview of the Ismaili Imamate's Institutional Endeavors

The role of institutions and institutional capacities has been of prime importance in the mind of the present Ismaili Imam. The seeds for this approach to institutions were planted by the previous Aga Khan who had already established a network of educational, health care, and financial institutions in the Ismaili community.

In order to understand how these institutions came into being and were transformed into the AKDN (or rather more widely as the Institutions of the Ismaili Imamat), one has to take one step back and see the context of the Ismaili community around the globe. Some of these points have already been discussed to some extent in earlier chapters in the context of more doctrinal issues. A little bit of history, here, helps clarify matters further.

The Ismaili community is a minority Shiʻi Muslim community scattered all around the world living in different countries in Asia, Europe, and America, with a greater proportion of its population residing in the developing countries. In a sense, one can say that the Ismaili community is something like a state without a land, with the great difference that in every territory where the Ismailis live, they are bound by their allegiance to their Imam to remain faithful and loyal to any government that undertakes their welfare. This implies political neutrality which works as a guarantee for the security and safety of this community in the face of political upheavals in any country.

Although this strategy has not always been a perfect solution to the issue of security for the Ismaili community (the counterexample being the mass expulsion of Ismailis along with other Asians from Idi Amin's

Uganda), it has at least been a basic point of departure for its safeguarding. It has been the advice of the present Imam to his followers that every Ismaili has two main commitments: one to his Imam, which is his/her oath of allegiance, and the other to the country, which provides for their safety and well-being.

The idea of Ismailis as "loyal citizens" of every country where they live is an important point for consideration given the nature of the activities of the Ismaili imamate institutions, which may sometimes be seen as a paradoxical commitment, particularly in light of the cosmopolitan nature of its work. However, this would only be paradoxical if we were to define the activities of the Ismaili imamate within a nation-state framework.

If the institutions of the Ismaili imamate were to be favorable to one nation-state as opposed to another and show any kind of discrimination as such, it would defeat the whole purpose of its being pluralistic and cosmopolitan. The Ismaili imamate, by the very fact of its current position, cannot give an ideological dimension to the loyalty of its followers toward the countries of which they are citizens. This loyalty is not an ideological loyalty which could lead to a confrontation between Ismailis of different nationalities.

Ismaili Diaspora and the Changed Concept of Nation

An important element for understanding the shift of authority in the leadership of the Ismaili community is its unique position in terms of demography and the pluralistic nature of the various groups around the globe that make up the global Ismaili community. This is indeed nothing new, it has existed in the past. However, with the establishment of nation-states, this position of the Ismaili community gains a different meaning and significance.

As mentioned earlier, following the guidance of the Ismaili Imam (the present Imam as well as the previous one), the Ismailis are bound by two major commitments: one is their spiritual allegiance (bay'a) to their Imam, as any Shia Ismaili Muslim would be by definition, and the other is their loyalty to the country, which provides security and welfare to them. Also, the Ismaili imamate has no political ambitions and as such the idea of an Ismaili "state" does not exist in the mindset of the Ismaili leadership.

While Ismailis come from different ethnic and geographical backgrounds, the concept of an Ismaili "nation" does not exist either. The absence of an Ismaili state and an Ismaili nation clearly puts the Ismaili

community in the position of existing across the frontiers and beyond the borders of nation-states. Some of the problems that might arise can be identified as originating in a possible conflict between the ideologies of certain states and the Ismaili doctrines. However, these conflicts would have to be resolved through the Ismaili Constitution and with discretion, without affecting the Ismaili identity.

The only publicly recorded instance, in the modern period, when an issue of Ismailis acquiring a land was ever raised—which could have some sort of a meaning of state—came up during the time of Aga Khan III. He writes in his memoirs:

> It had long been felt among the Ismaili community that it would be desirable to possess a national home—not a big, powerful State, but something on the lines of Tangier or the Vatican—a scrap of earth of their own which all Ismailis, all over the world, could call theirs in perpetuity, where they could practise all their customs, establish their own laws, and (on the material side) build up their own financial centre, with its own banks, investment trusts, insurance schemes, and welfare and provident arrangements. The idea of a territorial State made no particular appeal to me; but in view of the strength of Ismaili sentiment on the matter I made my approach to the Government of India. For reasons which I am sure were perfectly just and fair, the Government of India could not see their way to granting our request. The idea that they disapproved of me for having made it, or that I was hurt and disappointed by their refusal, is fantastic. (Aga Khan, 1954: 286)

And this is as far as it ever went. Later developments in the history of the Community all converged toward a non-state and transnational activity for the Community. As much as the idea of a territorial state may not have made any appeal to Aga Khan III, one can look at the current institutions of the Ismaili imamate and conclude that any attempt or desire to have a "scrap of earth" would be detrimental to the very way in which they function. Such an option seems to be completely unfathomable now, given the Ismaili imamate's developments.

The fact that Ismailis are scattered around the globe, while keeping a double loyalty to their Imam and their country of residence necessarily puts them in a position of a cosmopolitan community. Yet, Ismailis, wherever they are, are joined and united by their allegiance to their Imams. The Ismaili Constitution, as described in the earlier chapter, is in fact a "covenant" rather than a "contract," and it regulates the relationship between the Imam and members of his community (called *murīds*[1] in the Constitution).[2]

When we speak about the leadership of the Ismaili community, we are talking about a term that can be and is interchangeably used both for the Imam and the leaders appointed by him to run the affairs of the community. Although the leadership is not subject to elections or any sort of democratic apparatus, there is a rotation of power. Indeed, the leadership that is appointed by the Imam, regularly changes after three-year terms (with provisions of only a second term of appointment). Thus, although we do not see any structure of a nation-state, nor any democratic institution (as we would find in political entities), there is still some form of monitoring and an accountability process that is built into these institutions in terms of management and financial auditing.

Hierarchies of Power in Community Institutions

The Ismaili Community is hierarchical in nature and "power is vested in the formal leadership position, with the status of such a position reinforcing the power holder's opportunity to direct the community" (Walji, 1974: 86). Given the context in which the Ismaili Communities in East Africa developed—and the way the Constitution was introduced—as Walji notes, "those who attain high status have done so primarily by commanding administrative and economic power." And "since administrative power comes to those with economic power, status is ultimately associated with wealth" (Walji, 1974: 87–88). To this, Walji adds the role of kinship ties which "played an important part in raising men to leadership position" (Walji, 1974: 88).

This hierarchical structure makes the Community institutions difficult to be characterized as democratic. The only resemblance it has to a democratic institution is the limitation on terms in office. The situation today has changed, however, as compared with the case of the Community in East Africa (at the time when Walji wrote her thesis). There are more Ismaili Communities that have now emerged in the global settings of the Community, of non-Indian origins, like the Iranians, the Tajiks, the Syrians, and the Afghans which makes it difficult to implement this unspoken and unwritten rule of raising people of wealth to positions of leadership.

There are, however, newer measures that may secure a position of leadership in the Community, and these include education and managerial skills. The latter is still found among those members who have an entrepreneurial background, but the former is not limited to particular groups. These issues are, however, mostly applicable to Community institutions, and the rules governing AKDN institutions are different as

they have a global mandate and the character of NGOs. The hierarchies in the Community institutions and their mechanism do not, however, matter in the context of the decoupling of the Ismaili Community and the imamate from nation-states.

In terms of the Imam's leadership for the community, the first and foremost concern of the Ismaili imamate, as has often been explicitly stated in the words of the present and of past Ismaili Imams, has been the security and safety of the community. The idea of "loyal citizens" has been one strategy toward this end. There is another dimension to the security of the Community, which has some constitutional bearings and this has to do with dissent within the Community. Walji notes that

> the security of the community has been made more compelling than the right to dissent. These factors, along with the guidance of the Aga Khan and the Ismaili sense of religious community, have no doubt been major ones in holding together a community that continues its tradition, customs, and values at the same time that it leaves room for change in its constitutional provisions for maintaining social order. (Walji, 1974: 116)

The social, economic, and cultural issues of the Ismaili communities around the world are another matter that has been at the center of the concerns of contemporary Ismaili Imams (specifically Aga Khan III and the present Imam). As these areas of the life of the community have received a great deal of attention, one strategy to secure the continuation of the efforts of the Ismaili imamate to improve the living conditions of its *Jamā'at* around the world has been to provide services not only to the Ismaili community itself but also to the people among whom they live.

This approach has not only been seen for its own value, which is to avoid any undue tension or rivalry between the Ismailis and the people around them, but it has also an ethical expression and purpose of providing service to different communities around the globe.

In some instances the kind of services provided by the Ismaili imamate institutions and in particular the AKDN has gone beyond simply serving the Ismaili community to areas where there are no Ismaili constituencies. A very good example of one of such institution is the AKU, established in Pakistan, where the great majority of the beneficiaries are non-Ismailis.

With this brief reference, I think a most productive way of explaining the structure of the AKDN, given the central question of this thesis, would be to see how these institutions have been born out of the Imam's vision.

A New Perception of the Role of the Imam

As discussed in the earlier chapter, the Aga Khan finds the dichotomy between the world and the faith a false one. Therefore, getting involved in worldly matters (like building hotels and investment in tourism etc.) is by no means a deviation from his role as the Imam. Quite to the contrary, he finds it an integral part of his responsibility as the Imam and his mandate. Therefore, the institutions that he has created over the years are just a reflection of his vision for creating a balance between the faith and the world. Religion to him is not something private that should have no reflection in the public life of a Muslim, as opposed to a radical secularity that drives religion to a strictly private sphere. However, this public dimension of faith or the social responsibility of a Muslim as he has demonstrated through his institutional and development work is precisely the area where it makes it distinct from other forms of leadership in the Muslim world today.

I have described this perception of the imamate as "new," and I must explain why I have described it this way, because when you refer to the Aga Khan's vision, he does not find anything specifically new in it; to him, it is a continuation of the tradition of the Ismaili imamate, and this social responsibility has been a part and parcel of this tradition. It can be called "new" only in a context where we see tradition as dynamic; other forms of leadership in the Muslim world continuously refer to tradition, but the tradition they speak of is still an "old" tradition. The only element that gives a different perspective to this setting is the encounter of the Ismaili imamate with modernity that has left a lasting impression in the modernization of the Community.

The role that the Ismaili Imam has carved out for himself through institutional work and has earned over the years is a role that is distinctly different from the roles other leaders in the Muslim world identify themselves with.

Where the Ismaili Imam speaks about social responsibility and a serious commitment to the improvement of the quality of life of Muslims, which is a reflection of a sense of humiliation that echoes throughout the Muslim world, there are voices in the Muslim world who bring in a political dimension to this leadership, and it often fuels fundamentalist, aggressive, and radical reactions around the world to the "other."

Ethical Underpinnings of the AKDN

The following words by the Aga Khan describe the general framework of the AKDN:

The engagement of the Imamat in development is guided by the ethics of Islam which bridge faith and society, a premise on which I established the Aga Khan Development Network, known as the AKDN. Its cultural social and economic development agencies seek to improve opportunities and living conditions of the weakest in society, without regard to their origin, gender or faith.[3]

However, as far as it goes into the details of the work of the AKDN and the projects undertaken by it, there are always serious ethical considerations that run through the organization's work. These considerations have been formulated in a document that is known as the "AKDN Ethical Framework." This document is particularly important for understanding how the Ismaili imamate is articulating its vision in terms of Shi'i Muslim ideals. It also reflects the interpretation of the Imam on how a Muslim community should be in modern times. As such, we see also normative articulations of the work of the AKDN, which is critical in the consolidation of these institutions.

There are eight headings for this ethical framework:

- Ethic of Inclusiveness
- Ethic of Education and Research
- Ethic of Compassion and Sharing
- Ethic of Self-reliance
- Ethic of Respect for Life and Health Care
- Ethic of Sound Mind
- Ethic of Sustainable Environment
- Ethic of Governance

Each of the areas, which are covered in these headings, is traced back to traditional and historical values, with specific Ismaili interpretations of them, and they are explained either in the context of verses from the Qur'ān or the traditions of the Prophet or the Shi'i Imams.

Any project that is proposed at the AKDN institutions, or any institution that is created, eventually gets checked against these criteria. If any proposed project is not in line with these ethical considerations, it does not get approved. It is the practice of the Aga Khan to do this work within these principles. These principles are not exhaustive. There are clearly other ethical considerations that may be called Muslim ethical principles, but if we want to find something that is common to all the above headings, we can see that it contains some minimum ethical considerations to which the Ismaili Imam has given a specific name: "*cosmopolitan ethic*," which I discussed in chapter 3.

So what are these ethical principles? If we look at the AKDN, they are, in a sense, universal ethical principles which inspire and define the work of the AKDN. So, when projects are presented to the Aga Khan, they have to be argued on that basis:

> You would have to make a case to say that we think this programme should be supported because these ethical principles are being met and addressed by it. Or you have to counter-argue to say that we understand the risks of these things happening, for example dependency is created, but here is how we are going to underwrite that risk. Unless you can make that case, it will not be signed off (Interview with Shiraz Kabani[4]).[5]

Apart from these ethical considerations, there is of course a financial aspect to the decisions that are being made in these institutions. They would not invest in projects that are doomed to failure. Yet, there is an element of risk management and risk taking in the AKDN work that makes it distinct from other development agencies. As we proceed to describe the structure of the AKDN and what each agency is involved in, we can better see how these ethical principles are embedded in their mandates.

For this chapter, unlike the theoretical aspects of what we have been addressing so far and the more philosophical questions, there is a huge bulk of information available, in a transparent manner, on the AKDN agencies in the website of the AKDN. A helpful approach to describing the AKDN institutions would be to look at them based on areas of focus of these agencies.

If we look at the organizational chart of the AKDN below (see Figure 4.1), there are three major areas of focus in these institutions: economic development, social development, and culture. One immediate observation can be made by looking at these categories, and that has to do with "culture." There seems to be a conscious approach to this issue of culture to the effect that one cannot develop culture as such. It seems that the activities of the AKDN in the areas of culture do not include any form of "intervention" for change. Cultures are there and with the pluralistic understanding that is there, it does not make much sense to "develop" cultures. When asked about the role of culture in the AKDN, Farrokh Derakhshani, Director of the Aga Khan Award for Architecture (AKAA), responded:

> Social and economic development is not enough to ensure a holistic development and therefore the cultural branch of AKDN complements the

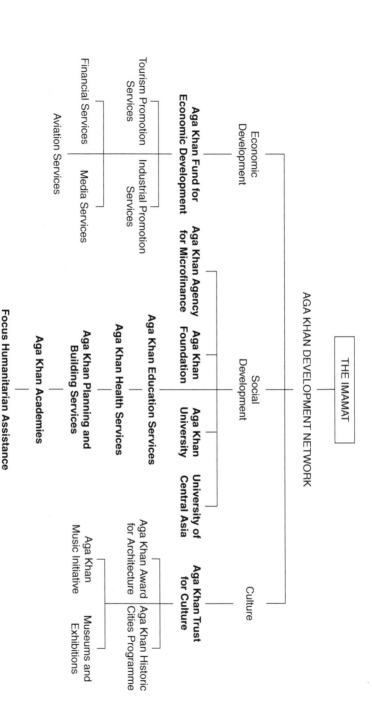

Figure 4.1 AKDN structure.

other two. The basis is how through culture you can help for a positive change in a society. One of the main aspects in a society is to understand its identity and how one can respond to the aspirations of the generations to come. You cannot have development without cultural issues. That's why, especially now, that the AKDN is becoming an interwoven network of institutions, we can see various programmes of the AKTC can be in the service of the other divisions. We can see it more and more how the institutions that existed before, now they have got to work together.[6]

So, there seems to be a clarity that culture is there as a platform for development. Hence, we see that the three major agencies in the AKDN for culture (The AKAA, the AKTC, the Aga Khan Historic Cities Program) take a very active role in development work.

The area of culture is one area that has found a very important place in the work of the imamate institutions during the time of the present Aga Khan. It is interesting to note that the institution that deals with culture is a "trust" and not a fund for development. The very use of the term "trust" suggest that culture is not dealt in the same manner as economics. The use of this term is deliberate. The earth and the physical environment has been given to man as a trust, and it is the duty of man to leave this place better than what it was given to him in the first place. This vision is also expressed in the words of the Aga Khan in regard to the AKTC's work.

In the other two areas (social development and economic developments), seeds of these institutions were there during the time of Aga Khan III and they have now developed into agencies, which are now part of the AKDN, with newer agencies later established.

If we have the above organizational chart as our guiding map to understanding the structure of this network, we can go further into the details of the agencies working under it. According to the AKDN website, the focus areas of the network are the following 12 areas: (1) Architecture; (2) Civil Society; (3) Culture, (4) Economic Development; (5) Education; (6) Health; (7) Historic Cities; (8) Humanitarian Assistance; (9) Microfinance; (10) Music; (11) Planning and Building; and (12) Rural Development.

It is not possible to go into details of each and every agency of the AKDN and their full history,[7] but we can pick a few of them and explore the way they function and how they are connected to other agencies in the AKDN. Going into the details of all of these institutions is beyond the scope of this research. I will only explore them so far as they help better understand the cornerstones of the AKDN, the vision of the Ismaili

imamate and the leadership of the Ismaili Imam. The areas I have selected below are mainly for the purpose of shedding light on the main question of this thesis. I begin our journey through the AKDN with the example of architecture which will also take us to other areas of the network and gives us a tour of the overall spirit of the AKDN.

Architecture

In chapter 3, I examined the vision of the Aga Khan and how he looks at architecture in his development work. The first agency with a focus on issues of architecture was the AKAA. The driving force behind this agency was the areas of concern that the Aga Khan had identified, (earlier mentioned) and it turned into an award for architecture, which was a tri-annual award to "set new standards of excellence in architecture, urban or regional design, conservation and landscape architecture." This award has now turned into the most prestigious award for architecture in the Muslim world, and according to the AKDN website,

> Prizes totalling up to US$ 500,000 are presented every three years to projects selected by an independent master jury. The award has completed ten cycles of activity since 1977, and documentation has been compiled on over 7,500 building projects located throughout the world. To date, 100 projects have received the award.[8]

One of the fascinating things about the AKAA is the trajectory of its development. This program in itself kick-started a number of other programs and initiatives that together have formed the Aga Khan Trust for Culture forming the "Culture" arm of the network.

Looking back to the history of the Awards, Farrokh Derakhshani says,

> The Award was somehow different to all other activities of the AK Foundation. It was not supposed to be philanthropic or educational. It was a new phenomenon. From its inception the Award was not just an award for architecture like the others which existed in the world those days. What was interesting was that it was a "search". And within this search, the whole idea is why we are giving the awards, is it to celebrate someone or to have an impact.[9]

This process of search that was further enhanced through the master juries and the steering committees of the awards brought in an

educational dimension to the awards which would later on have to be connected with other areas of the AKDN. This is one of the best examples in the work of these institutions that fully displays the "network" nature of these agencies.

Furthermore, Derakhshani continues to describe this process of "search" to show how new avenues were explored in the area of architecture with the awards:

> In 1980s nobody knew about what is happening architecturally in the Muslim world. And usually I repeat saying this that for an architect in India, it was very easy to know what is happening in London. For someone in Algeria, it was very easy to know what is happening in France, but an Algerian would never imagine what was happening in India or in Egypt or even in next door Morocco. So, this was a kind of making communication South-South as well, there was a real lack of information then[10].

This process of search and education led to the creation of a program called the Aga Khan Programme for Islamic Architecture at MIT. The question at the time was what to do with "Islamic architecture," and there was a need for education. There was also a series of publications, apart from the regular awards procedures, that was published in each cycle of the awards, and for a while a journal called *Mimar* was published, but was later stopped because there was no longer a need for it.

As the story of the awards continued, other matters emerged. Some of them were a response to a situation and some were contingent matters that happened and became part of the legacy of the awards. Derakhshani recounts the story as follows:

> His Highness, whenever he was going to the Award ceremonies and seminars, wanted to leave sometimes a gift, like in 1984 in Cairo, he decided to create a park as a gift. Later these became programs of their own, the Historic Cities Programme. The goal was that besides showing the good work of others through the Award programme we also do exemplary projects that others will see as a model. Intervening in the dilapidated historic cities and centers became a priority. HCP, the AKPIA programme, Mimar magazine all started as responses that the "search" identified through the Awards.[11]

If we follow the lines of the story, we can trace the development of an award for architecture into an array of agencies, which all together serve

the purpose of development but come together in a network of inter-connected institution working in synergy. Although the AKAA remains somewhat apart from the other agencies that are active in the AKTC, the other agencies are very much interconnected and working closely with one another.

One of the fascinating stories that describes the spirit and method of work in the AKDN is the Al-Azhar park project that was carried out by the AKTC. This is one of the best examples of the work of the AKDN in how one program leads to another and becomes a series of projects that may last for a couple of generations:

> First of all, the Azhar Park is very interesting, because the project has been growing on its own. A number of issues which you see now, today, in the Azhar Park were not initially a part of the program. So, it is a program which has evolved itself over time. It has taken a long time. So, the very first idea was to have a gift to the city of Cairo: a park. This was the first idea, in 1984, when His Highness was in Cairo for the Aga Khan Award for Architecture seminar, he used that occasion to initiate this program and expressed his wish that he would like to offer a park to the city of Cairo. Then, there was a process of how you do a park. What you do with it, in a historical area. And what has been very important is that it was supposed to be the state-of-the-art in landscape design, in design, etc. So, it was not just a simple design.[12]

As I explained earlier in the section on cosmopolitanism, the Al-Azhar Park is one of the areas that reflects the Ismaili Imam's vision about cosmopolitanism. Derakhshani explains the different elements that led to the creating of the park as follows:

> The Al-Azhar Park saw a lot of changes from its initial concept to the final project. A lot of time was spent on the design of the park and the elements which were going to be there. Many elements were added which were not known at the beginning. For example after initial excavations the Ayyubid wall was uncovered. It was not supposed to be there. So, it became an archaeological project. And by working in the park in that area, the idea came that there was a whole neighbourhood that had to benefit and what would be the relationship of this park with its neighbourhoods. We are not going to have something which is excluding the people who are the first users, at the same time it is a park for everyone. So, this pro-gram of Darb al-Ahmar started, which is the neighbourhood adjacent to the park, one of the oldest and poorest neighbourhoods in Cairo next to Khan al-Khalili.[13]

Here is where the element of culture, as part of a cosmopolitan approach, is infused into the AKTC work, enriching the project itself. Derakhshani explains how these elements were added to the park:

> So a series of projects were initiated in Darb al-Ahmar, both restoration of smaller buildings, such as mosques, and other dilapidated buildings bringing new functions to them. A number of streets and public spaces were also developed. This way the whole neighbourhood became better. You give added value to the neighbourhood. Secondly, there was a series of programs, training programs, because you had people who are working from the neighbourhood in doing the restoration work. There are schools and social programs. There is a very huge social program, which is associated with the Darb al-Ahmar project. And then, the AKDN's Microfinance programme came in to help implement these projects. So, it was a project that was not foreseen so multifaceted from the very beginning, but it became more and more complex as the needs were identified throughout the implementation and various potentials of the network were employed as necessary.[14]

The work on the Al-Azhar Park has not finished and newer elements are still being introduced into it:

> Now for example, we are adding a public parking to it which the area needs. So, it is a development program. When you look at it, a park, a simple park, became a development program and an economic program, because there are possibilities to add a hotels, museum etc., there as well. So, the whole thing is that it became an engine of enabling the whole area and the city of Cairo at large, economically and socially to develop. That's why it is a model. I must add that there here I can see the vision of His Highness to have a park and that he was ready to change the program when he sees that it was for the betterment of the people.[15]

This account is better reflected in the words of the Aga Khan himself:

> [W]e were creating not just a park . . . we were giving birth to a catalyst for social, economic and cultural renewal and improvement that would grow for many years to come. . . . [I]t would have far-reaching consequences for the urban fabric of one of the city's most historic, yet poorest neighbourhoods, touching some 200,000 individuals. . . . Al-Azhar Park has taught us important new lessons that will contribute to the international body of knowledge about preservation and development in world heritage cities, a substantial portion of them in the Muslim world. . . . A fundamental lesson . . . is that public-private partnerships can be effective mechanisms for

enhancing the value of underused, unappreciated or even unknown social, cultural and economic assets.[16]

The above description clearly describes how a learning process has taken place. The AKTC and the AKAA is important in the sense that it has opened new windows to the cosmopolitan nature and character of the AKDN, which in turn leads to further transformation as to how the leadership and the authority should adjust itself.

A related story which may describe the style of the Aga Khan's vision when it comes to building and architecture can be seen in the Ismaili Centers that are built around the world. At the moment, there are five Ismaili Centers in London, Burnaby, Lisbon, Dubai, and Dushanbe. These centers, as expected, are purpose-built with a rigorous architectural thinking behind them, are not just for the use of the members of the Ismaili community, but they are designed to become part of the fabric of the civil life of the area in which they are built. In his speech at the inauguration of the Ismaili Center in Dubai, the Aga Khan speaks of his vision for the Ismaili Centers and how they are seen in the context of the ethical principles that he has in mind:

> It would be appropriate to situate one of the functions of the Ismaili Centre in the tradition of Muslim piety. For many centuries, a prominent feature of the Muslim religious landscape has been the variety of spaces of gathering co-existing harmoniously with the *masjid*, which in itself has accommodated a range of diverse institutional spaces for educational, social and reflective purposes. Historically serving communities of different interpretations and spiritual affiliations, these spaces have retained their cultural nomenclatures and characteristics, from *ribat* and *zawiyya* to *khanaqa* and *jamatkhana*. The congregational space incorporated within the Ismaili Centre belongs to the historic category of jamatkhana, an institutional category that also serves a number of sister Sunni and Shia communities, in their respective contexts, in many parts of the world. Here, it will be space reserved for traditions and practices specific to the Shia Ismaili *tariqah* of Islam[17].

In this section, apart from describing the architectural trajectory of the Ismaili Centers, the Aga Khan is introducing a pluralistic dimension to spaces of worship, opening room for spaces other than the mosque in the context of Islamic rituals and practices. He continues to merge this with a secular aspect of the Ismaili Center:

> In the tradition of Muslim spaces of gathering, the Ismaili Centre will be a symbol of the confluence between the spiritual and the secular in Islam.

Architect El Dahan has drawn inspiration from the Fatimid mosques in Cairo. Like its functions, the Centre's architecture will reflect our perception of daily life whose rhythm weaves the body and the soul, man and nature into a seamless unity. Guided by the ethic of whatever we do, see and hear, and the quality of our social interactions, resonate on our faith and bear on our spiritual lives, the Centre will seek to create, Insh'allah, a sense of equilibrium, stability and tranquillity. This sense of balance and serenity will find its continuum in the wealth of colours and scents in the adjacent Islamic garden which the Aga Khan Trust for Culture will help to develop as a public park.[18]

The interesting thing is that the ethic that he speaks about, the architecture that he has passionately pursued all throughout his imamate and his leadership for his community is all physically and in practice demonstrated in these buildings. This practical and pragmatic aspect of his work is an element that has a strong resonance of what Taylor describes as a "social imaginary" (discussed earlier).

Other examples of where this interconnected agency collaboration of AKDN is physically and palpably seen around the world can be seen in the Serena Hotels. The Serena Hotels, which are now found in different parts of the world where the AKDN is active, are basically in the category of tourism and hospitality. Tourism Promotion Services is now under the Aga Khan Fund for Economic Development (AKFED) area of the AKDN forming the for-profit arm of the network. The Aga Khan's vision for these hotels puts their creation in the context that he intends. In 2006, on the occasion of the official opening ceremony of the Kampala Serena Hotel in Uganda, he said:

In all of these places, the Serena projects exemplify a larger strategy. In all of these places, our goal is not merely to build an attractive building or to fill its rooms with visitors, but also to make a strategic investment which many private investors might be reluctant to make, but which promises to produce a magnificent multiplier effect as its impact ripples through the local communities.

The multiplier effect is in part an economic one. It is measured in jobs—created in building, maintaining and operating the new facility. The impact is measured by the flow of visitors and their resources—and by the investments they are encouraged to make. It is measured by the returns it generates for local investors, as our projects achieve stability and their shares are placed on local stock exchanges. It is also measured in the motivating effect a successful new enterprise almost inevitably has on other local enterprises.

The Serena Hotels are part of the AKTC projects, but they are connected with the for-profit aspects of the AKDN; so it is both a cultural and an economic work and as finds itself in a network of interconnected agencies:

> But these ripple effects need not be limited to the economic sector. Their impact can also be a social and a cultural one, as this project works to re-enforce the values of hospitality and courtesy, of excellence and efficiency, of community and confidence, of self reliance and self improvement. We are proud that our projects exemplify the highest standards of corporate governance and human resource development. We also believe that, through the creative design of the hotel and through the activities it supports, this effort will help to nourish cultural pride, strengthen artistic expression, and renew traditional values.[19]

With the single example of the Kampala Serena Hotel, there are several things that could be said. The architectural aspect of the building is important, where there is collaboration with the AKTC. It is also part of the AKFED, with its financial benefits. The ethical principles that the Aga Khan has in mind are present in it ("this project works to re-enforce the values of hospitality and courtesy, of excellence and efficiency, of community and confidence, of self reliance and self improvement.") And interestingly Uganda is the very same country that expelled Ismailis in the 1970s: a country that was once a threat has now turned into an opportunity, and the Ismaili imamate has returned to it.

Education

The activities of the AKDN in the area of education fall under social development in the network. There is a history to this area. Aga Khan III, the previous Ismaili Imam, had built a large number of schools for the use of the Ismaili community. The idea behind them was clearly the promotion of education. It is important to understand the context in which Aga Khan III was pursuing his policies for educational development of his community. Speaking about the activities of Aga Khan III, Daftary writes:

> The Aga Khan had increasingly concerned himself with the affairs of the Muslim community of India, beyond the immediate interests of his own followers. As a result, he gained much popularity amongst the Indian Muslims and their spokesmen. He participated actively in the first All-India Muslim

Educational Conference, held at Bombay in 1903, and became the president of the second one, held at Delhi the following year...Aga Khan III campaigned most energetically for various educational projects, for Khojas and other Indian Muslims. He played a leading part in the elevation of the Muhammadan Anglo-Oriental College at Aligarh to university status, a measure that came about in 1912. (Daftary, 2007: 482)

So, we have a long history of the active engagement of the Ismaili imamate in the early twentieth century. The key and critical factor here is indeed the modernization aspect of the Aga Khan's work. The Aligarh University was not a traditional Muslim school or seminary, and indeed it faced stiff resistance when Sayyid Ahmad Khan was promoting the cause of Aligarh. The Aga Khan, who had had encounters with Europeans from an early age, was clearly in favor of these modern secular institutions of education and he followed it all throughout his life. His legacy continued to the time of his successor.

Here, it is perhaps timely to acknowledge the role of Aga Khan III in the issue of leadership/authority in the case of the Ismaili imamate and its institutions. To give a summary of Aga Khan III's role in what we see today as the institutions of the Ismaili imamate, we can have a quick look at Daftary's account of what he calls the "modernizing" efforts of Aga Khan III:

> During his long imamate, Aga Khan III devoted much of his time and financial resources to consolidating and organizing the Nizārī community, especially in South Asia and East Africa. He was particularly concerned with introducing socio-economic reforms that would transform his Shiʿi Muslim followers into a modern, self-sufficient community with high standards of education and welfare. The successful attainment of these objectives, however, required an appropriate administrative organization, over and beyond the existing traditional structure of the Nizārī community. Through such an organization the imam could implement his reform policies and modernize the Nizārī community without destroying its traditions and identity. The development of a new communal organization thus became one of Aga Khan III's major tasks.

Here, Daftary refers back to the legal cases of the Aga Khan, which as I have mentioned earlier has a modern element to it (with modern legal institutions at the center of it):

> The court decisions in Bombay had already laid the foundations in British India for the imam's institutional and administrative reforms. They had

delineated the Nizārī Khojas from those Khojas who preferred to be Sunnīs or Ithnā asharīs, while clarifying the status of the Aga Khan with respect to his followers and to all the communal property. At the same time, the deep devotion of the Nizārī Khojas to their imam permitted them to readily accept his reform policies.

Daftary then explains the grounds for the genesis of Ismaili constitutions:

> On the basis of such assets and the existing jamāʿat structure of the community, and enjoying the support of the British government of India, Aga Khan III developed an elaborate administrative system of councils for the Nizārīs of the Indian subcontinent and East Africa. The powers, functions and compositions of different categories of councils were in due course specified in written constitutions for the Nizārī Ismāʿīlīs of those regions, designated officially as the Shia Imami Ismailis. Similar constitutions were promulgated for the councils and jamāʿats of India and East Africa, and when India was partitioned in 1947 a separate but still similar constitution and council system was developed for Pakistan. The workings of the Ismāʿīlī administrative system of councils can perhaps be best shown in the case of the community in East Africa, where the Nizārī Khojas have been scattered through the independent states of Kenya, Uganda and Tanzania, formerly representing three colonial territories. (Daftary, 2007: 484)

I have already written about the constitutions and their background in the Ismaili community in my last chapter. The above paragraph from Daftary explains in very clear terms how crucial the role of Aga Khan III has been in laying the foundations for the existing institutions of the Ismaili imamate. Some of the key agencies of the AKDN are built upon the capacities that were created earlier by Aga Khan III and then developed during the imamate of the present Aga Khan.

If we go back to the case of education, we have the network of schools that were available from the time of Aga Khan III (known as Aga Khan Schools). These schools were created in almost all the places where the Ismailis lived. East Africa is probably one of the best places to see the development of this network of schools and a place where the genesis of the current form of the Ismaili imamate institutions began.

If we go back to the philosophy of the creation of these schools, we can look at other areas too. In the case of Iran, Aga Khan III had ordered his Ismaili followers to build schools using the imamate funds, which at the time were generally derived from the tithes paid to the Imam as part of the religious duty of Ismailis. At that time in Iran, the general religious community was hardly in favor of "modern" or "secular" schools

as they were understood at the time, and the very act of encouraging people to have an education different from the traditional education that mainly consisted of religious instruction, seemed like a revolutionary move. There is an Ismaili village in the north of Khurāsān in Iran, near Nīshabūr, called Dīzbād. This village was the first village in Iran to achieve a literacy rate of 100 percent in the entire country, thanks to the support and encouragement of the Aga Khan.[20]

With this brief background, one can easily identify a long-standing tradition in the area of education in the Ismaili community, which is now an inseparable part of the activities of the Ismaili imamate. A quick look at the various educational institutions, which now form an integral part of the AKDN, reveals that this is a crucial cornerstone for the development of the imamate institutions.

The oldest institution in the AKDN, which was the continuation of the work of Aga Khan III, is the Aga Khan Education Services (AKES). According to the latest figures at the time of writing this chapter, the AKES runs over three hundred educational institutions with a staff of over 4,800 and it has more than 61,000 students.

This agency with its current structure was created in 1986, but as earlier explained many of the infrastructures for it were already in place from the time of Aga Khan III.

There are other agencies in the educational sector of the AKDN namely the Aga Khan Foundation (est. 1967); the AKU (est. 1983); the University of Central Asia (UCA) (est. 2000); and Aga Khan Academies (est. 2000). Each of these institutions has several other structures or institutions under them. For example, the AKU, which was the first internationally chartered university in Pakistan, consists of a School of Nursing, Medical College, University Hospital, the Institute for Educational Development, Institute for the Study of Muslim Civilization (based in London), and an Examination Board.

Like many other agencies of the AKDN, each of these other institutions, which are born out of the AKU, has been a response to certain needs that have arisen due to the specific circumstances present. They have drawn on the support of other agencies of the AKDN too. The AKU is probably more independent of the Ismaili Community than other institutions. The description we read on the AKU website of the university is clear as to how it operates:

> Chartered in 1983 as a private international university, Aga Khan University (AKU is a self-governing institution currently operating in eight countries. The University is part of the Aga Khan Development

Network (AKDN), a group of private international development agencies working to *improve living conditions* and opportunities in the developing world through social, economic and cultural development. Like all Network institutions, the University is *non-denominational and admission to its academic programmes is based strictly on merit*. With 11 teaching sites spread over eight countries – Afghanistan, Kenya, Pakistan, Tanzania, Uganda, Syria, Egypt and the United Kingdom, AKU serves as an *agent of change*: developing skills and providing career advancement opportunities through programmes offered by its Medical College, School of Nursing, teaching hospitals, Institute for Educational Development and Institute for the Study of Muslim Civilisations. Future plans for AKU include an Institute of Human Development and a Faculty of Arts and Sciences with a curriculum based on a liberal arts model of undergraduate and post-graduate education. [Italics are mine.][21]

As we can see, the philosophy that runs through the AKU as an educational development organization contains the same tone dominant in the vision of the Aga Khan:

- It seeks to "improve living conditions."
- It is "non-denomination" and "merit-based," so there is no discrimination in it; it does not highlight the Ismaili leanings as a privilege.
- And it is "an agent of change."

To summarize these points, one can discern that some of the major qualities of this institution, as with other agencies of the AKDN, are based on a "developmental" outlook rather than being defined on sectarian grounds. The spirit of "pluralism" and "meritocracy" is part of its mandate. And it is an agent of change: it is not a political entity and yet its very nature is very much political. Its intervention for change is not driven by power or military force. It comes from a rich philosophical outlook which represents a profoundly different approach to the issues of the Muslim world.

The AKU is based in Pakistan but the AKDN's work overflows to other regions as well. If we look at other institutions within the AKDN, we can see how it responds to issues in every region through different institutional work. The UCA primarily serves the people of the mountainous regions in the countries of Central Asia. The Aga Khan Academies are more recent and they are in response to the issues of our times, at the heart of which is the issue of "leadership." The description of the Aga Khan Academies on the AKDN website, provides a very interesting

outlook on how important the development of "good leaders" is to the AKDN:

> The conviction that *home-grown intellectual leadership of exceptional cali-bre* is the best driver of society's future development led His Highness the Aga Khan to found an integrated network of residential schools in Africa, South and Central Asia, and the Middle East, known as the Aga Khan Academies. The Aga Khan Academies have a dual mission: *to offer exceptional girls and boys from all backgrounds*—irrespective of their families' ability to pay—an international standard of education from pre-primary to secondary levels with a *rigorous academic and leadership experience*; and to strengthen the profession of teaching by investing substantially in the professional development of teachers, locally and regionally. [Italics are mine.][22]

Like the AKU, we can again trace this thinking process and the framework of thinking prevalent in the vision of the Aga Khan in this new institution, which is scattered around the developing world.

In December 2003, in a speech at the Inauguration Ceremony of the Aga Khan Academy Kilindini (Mombasa, Kenya), the Aga Khan says:

> As the young men and women from this Aga Khan Academy, and over time from its sister schools, grow and assume leadership in their societies, it is my hope that it will be members of this new generation who, driven by their own wide knowledge and inspiration, will change their societies; that *they will gradually replace many of the external forces that appear, and sometimes seek, to control our destinies.* These young men and women, I am sure, will become *leaders in the governments and the institutions of civil society in their own countries, in international organizations* and in all those institutions, academic, economic and artistic that create positive change in our world. [Emphases are mine.][23]

As we can see here, the idea of "leadership" is quite prominent in the Aga Khan's vision, and he moves beyond just speaking about different forms of leadership, positively taking action in an institutional form to bring about this change in leadership.

As with most of the projects that the Aga Khan has been following throughout his imamate, he has had a long-term vision and the patience to see change; then, there would be no surprise at seeing an entirely new and different generation of leaders in 10 or 15 years' time. In the long term, the change that these educational institutions can bring to social and political settings can be potentially far-reaching.

This journey into the structure of the educational development side of the AKDN helps very much to put in the right context what the AKDN is doing around the world. There is a point that may also be repeated when we move to other areas of the AKDN, but it is important to include it here too.

If we look at the history of these institutions in education, it would perhaps not be easy to recognize the picture that we see today (for example, this concern for developing good leadership) in the terms that we speak about now. There is obviously a huge difference between what we saw in the Aga Khan Schools during the time of Aga Khan III and what we can see in the Aga Khan Academies. The early days of these institutions were merely laying foundations for what was to come in the future.

If we look at the case of Iran and the examples I gave above, it was, then, only a matter of "literacy." Now, these institutions go far beyond what is now clearly an achieved goal. The quality and degree of education has drastically changed over the twentieth century both inside the Ismaili community and globally. The questions have changed and other pressing matters are on the agenda. However, if these institutions had not been created in their early form during the time of Aga Khan III, it would probably be impossible for the Ismaili imamate today to pull off this huge and ambitious development enterprise as we see today.

Health

The Ismaili imamate's involvement in the area of health is almost like what we saw in the area of education. The seeds of the Aga Khan Hospitals were planted during the time of Aga Khan III and there were already some health care centers in place when the present Aga Khan assumed the imamate.

Like other agencies of the AKDN, as explained earlier, there is close collaboration between other agencies of the network and institutions in the area of health. If we look at the description appearing on the AKDN brochure (2007), we read:

> Building on the Ismaili Community's healthcare efforts during the first quarter of the twentieth century, AKHS has become one of the most comprehensive non-profit health-care systems in the developing world. It operates 168 health centres, dispensaries and other community outlets; 23 first-level referral facilities including diagnostic centres, rural medical and maternity care centres, as well as five general and four women's and

children's hospitals. It provides or supports primary healthcare services to populations totalling 1.7 million and handles approximately 1.8 million patient visits annually.

This vast network of institutions is not run on its own. The Aga Khan Health Services (AKHS) have a close collaboration with the AKU, which comes under the remit of educational development. As we saw earlier, the AKU has other institutions under it, apart from the university itself, whose mandates goes beyond just education. Hence, it can be easily understood from where the idea of a "network" is derived and how it works within the Ismaili imamate institutions. The institutions are not just isolated agencies doing their own work. It is true that there may be different degrees and levels of collaborations between different agencies, but the very concept of networking is crucial to the success of these institutions.

Economic Development

The activities of the Ismaili imamate in the area of economic development are very much under the umbrella of the AKFED. In the section on architecture earlier, I brought in the example of the Serena Hotels which are part of the tourism enterprises of the AKDN (under is Tourism Promotion Services) and are the for-profit sections of the network.

A useful description of the work of AKFED is found in the AKDN brochure. The AKFED is described as below:

> The only for-profit institution which is part of the Aga Khan Development Network, AKFED carries out AKDN's activities in economic development. Its network of companies and financial institutions are grouped by sector of activity under Industrial Promotion Services, Tourism Promotion Services, Financial Services, Aviation Services and Media Services. The Fund operates more than 90 separate project companies, employs over 30,000 people and has revenues of US $1.5 billion (p. 13).

AKFED is in a sense the driving engine for the work of the other agencies of the imamate institutions. On another note, I will give further details as to how the AKDN is operated internationally and how it works with other international partners to promote and pursue its work; but before going there let us consider the AKFED through the words of the Aga Khan himself:

> AKFED ... is neither a charitable foundation, nor a vehicle for the personal wealth of the Ismaili Imam of the time. It is a for-profit, international

development agency that, because of its *institutional background* and *social conscience*, invests in countries, sectors and projects, on criteria far different from those of a straightforward commercial investor. Investment decisions are based more on the *prospects for better lives for the constituencies of people* that will be impacted by the investments and their results *rather than on bottom line profitability...* The approach of the Imamat has always been to respond to the *development challenges* and *priorities of the countries in which it is engaged...* It has often meant taking *courageous but calculated steps to create opportunity in environments that are fragile and complex at the same time.* [Emphasis mine][24]

In the chapter 3, I quoted Tom Kessinger on how the Aga Khan's vision of managing risks and managing opportunities has been a driving force in the work of the AKDN when it comes to financial matters. If we look at the track record of the AKFED, we can see a very diligent financial manager who has a deep commitment to long-term change.

While he continues to manage the imamate's finances and the financial aspects of the success of the work, his own personal "adventure" (as Kessinger puts it) and his "ethical commitments" shape the fate of this part of the AKDN. If we rewind for a moment to one of the agencies, which is under the social development area of the AKDN, that is the Aga Khan Agency for Microfinance, we can see the same vision working through this institution:

Microcredit has helped millions of poor people in developing countries, but they remain at the mercy of a death or serious injury of a family member, the loss of a crop or livestock, or a natural disaster such as the recent tsunami. The assets of borrowers, accumulated through great effort over many years, can be destroyed overnight. Families are then forced to make the same difficult climb out of poverty a second or even third time. By creating a wider range of better targeted products such as micro-insurance, the poor will have the ability to protect their assets. Other products such as savings accounts, education and housing loans will help them improve their quality of life. The poor need access to just about every product and service that people and businesses need in the developed world. (Remarks at a Press Conference at the United Nations, February 22, 2005)[25]

If we take the above remarks in an isolated context and we are not aware of the huge network of the institutions that are run by him, we might just assume that this could have easily come from the mouth of someone at the World Bank. However, the important point is that there is an organic connection between these words and the vision which drives the rest of the network.

As regards the institutional impact of these agencies and their more philosophical implications, different agencies within the AKDN serve different roles and not all of them specifically serve to explain this transmutation in the authority of the Imam. On the case of Microfinance, Amy Sajoo notes that it is not comparable with the huge work of the AKTC and the AKAA, as setting up a microcredit organization "only requires someone with an economics degree"[26] and gives the example of Muhammad Yunus who has done a similar job in Bangladesh.

While we are still dealing with AFKED, it is perhaps timely to mention the Media Services of the AKDN. The Aga Khan established the Nation Media Group in the very early years of his imamate in 1960, and it has now turned into a huge network of media and press:

> The Group has six principal divisions. Nation Newspapers includes the daily and Sunday Nation and Taifa newspapers, the weekly Coast Express, and a regional weekly, The East African. The Nation Broadcasting Division operates Nation TV and Nation FM radio. The Group includes Monitor Publications Limited (Uganda), which publishes the daily and Sunday Monitor and operates Monitor FM radio. In Tanzania, Mwananchi Communications Limited publishes Mwananchi and has invested in Radio Uhuru. The Group encompasses Nation Marketing and Publishing Limited and the Nation Carriers Division. (AKDN Brochure, 16)[27]

There are several things to be said about this media group. First, that it is based in East Africa, where there was a strong institutional presence of the Ismaili community. The second is that this group emerged after the collapse of the colonial rule. The third is that media and the press are a focus of the Ismaili imamate's attention. The Aga Khan eloquently describes how his involvement with the media fits within his vision:

> My presence here today, in fact, grows directly out of my interest in the developing world and the forces that shape it, including the critical influence of the press.
>
> The intertwining of these two interests—the developing world and the newspaper world—began for me in Kenya nearly forty years ago, when the British government was moving away from its colonial role. It became clear to me that this weaning process, in the political realm, could never wholly succeed unless it was matched by a similar process in the realm of public education and journalism.
>
> At that time, East African journalism largely meant colonial journalism, and it was to help change that picture and with the encouragement of

young African pre-independence politicians that I entered the newspaper field.[28]

He goes further to touch upon "responsible journalism," "freedom of the press" raising a point about limits of freedom of speech, to which he had also reacted in the case of the Danish cartoons later:

> Freedom of the press does not mean the right of any journalist to write and to publish anything he or she wants to say. It is not acceptable for a reporter to cry "censorship" when an editor or a publisher questions his accuracy or his judgement. Nor is it acceptable for editors, managers and proprietors to slip their solemn responsibilities by invoking the same line of defence.
>
> They may sometimes say they don't want to "meddle" with the contents of their publications. This is a weak and dangerous excuse. And too often that comment really disguises an abdication of moral responsibility.
>
> This abdication is particularly troubling when it is used by proprietors or editors to mask their personal quest for financial gain or political influence, or to sustain divisive sectarian agendas. For in the final analysis, the press and those who manage it must also be held accountable to the collective judgements of the community.
>
> Responsible journalists and managers will not want to shield themselves from such judgements. To the contrary, they will eagerly seek them out. They will want to know what thoughtful readers are saying and how responsible advertisers are thinking. They will talk constantly with scholars and religious leaders, with artists and business leaders, with scientists and labour leaders, with educators and community leaders—and yes, with politicians and diplomats and governmental leaders as well. And through such continuing interaction they will develop and refine their sense of how the larger community can best be served.[29]

Here is another critical area of the work of the Ismaili imamate that comes under the umbrella of development but has serious political implications as well.

International Partnerships

The AKDN, as one of the most visible and successful development agencies in the world, is closely connected with other international and development institutions. Apart from the many institutions that collaborate with the Ismaili imamate, currently, the imamate has signed accords, protocols, treaties, agreements of cooperation, letters of intent,

and memoranda of understanding with more than 25 countries and international agencies. In Afghanistan, Cote d'Ivoire, Kenya, the Kyrgyz Republic, Mozambique, Portugal, Syria, Tajikistan, Tanzania and Uganda the Personal Representatives of the Ismaili imamate enjoy full diplomatic status and the AKDN Representatives enjoy status similar to that of a head of mission of an international organization.

The AKDN representatives have diplomatic status, while the Ismaili imamate is not heading a state, nor is it something like the Vatican. In this sense, it is one of the rare examples of diplomatic status for non-state actors.

A Delegation of Ismaili Imamat is established in Canada and (and one is to be established in Portugal). The Imam's vision, direction, and the ensuing imamate initiatives have been acknowledged and honored by governments as well as philanthropic and educational institutions.

These partnerships are also very important in understanding how the Aga Khan's leadership has transformed not only the Ismaili community, but also the leadership itself. The status of the Ismaili imamate's institution and its leadership is something that can hardly be compared with any other stage of the history of this community.

Religious Freedom and Political Agreements

The Ismaili imamate and the Portuguese Republic signed an agreement in May 2009, which is the first of its kind. Although the AKDN had signed different accords and agreements for its development work with various governments where the AKDN is active, this agreement with the government of Portugal is particularly significant because it moves beyond a simple agreement for development work.

This agreement grants some kind of protection for the Ismaili Community in Portugal which is rare in the examples we see in the European world. The Portuguese government has signed the contract within its Constitution and its Religious Freedom Act.

Given the sensitivities that we see in different countries toward Muslims and expressions of Muslim practices in various countries, from France to Switzerland and even Tajikistan now, the case of Portugal indeed seems a unique one. There is an expectation that such agreements may be signed with other governments too. Looking at the different articles of this agreement, we can see how different elements that form the Shi'i Ismaili Muslim identity of this Community as spelled out in the Ismaili Constitution is recognized in it.

Interestingly enough, this agreement does not talk about the AKDN, and its focus area is the religious dimension of the community and the authority of Aga Khan IV as the Imam of the Ismailis.

Scope and Impact

I have given figures of some of the agencies within the AKDN to give an idea of the scope of its work. The following details can also give us a picture of the impact of these institutions as they operate today:

- The AKDN has presence in 29 countries with annual not-for-profit expenditure of $320,000,000 and a staff of over 50,000.
- Aga Khan Foundation: Established in 16 countries; 2,800 staff; disbursed $128,500,000 in 2005.
- Aga Khan Foundation Scholarships: Awarded 845 scholarships to students from 30 countries, 151 PhD studies.
- Aga Khan Health Services: Over 200 hospitals, medical centers and clinics; over 9,000 staff; over 1,500,000 patients.
- AKES: Over 300 educational institutions; staff of over 4,800; over 61,000 students.
- AKFED: Over 90 project companies; over 30,000 staff across 16 countries; with revenues over $1,500,000,000.
- Aga Khan Agency for Microfinance: over $52,000,000 micro-loans; over 97,000 beneficiaries.
- AKU: Campuses in Pakistan, East Africa, and UK (School of Nursing; Faculty of Health Sciences, Institute for Educational Development, and Institute for the Study of Muslim Civilisations); over 4,000 alumni; over 4,500 faculty and staff.

Economy and the AKDN

One of the constraining factors in any corporate institution is the issue of funding. The Ismaili imamate has a number of sources of funding. One of these sources is the religious dues of believers, who have traditionally believed that they must pay a proportion of their income to their Imam, which is called *sahm-i imām* (the share of the Imam) or *māl-i wājibāt* (obligatory dues). This has been traditionally part of Shi'i doctrines and the following verse from the Qur'ān is often quoted in support of this tradition: "Take of their wealth a freewill offering, to purify them and to

cleanse them thereby, and pray for them; thy prayers are a comfort for them; God is All-hearing, All-knowing" (Qur'ān, 9:103).

This "freewill offering" has undergone changes in history and as part of the mandate of the imamate the offering has been spent, at the sole discretion of the Imam, in the service of the community. The most visible examples of where this offering has been spent can be seen in the institutions created by the Ismaili imamate.

While there are no precise figures as to how much money is offered and where exactly the money is spent, as it remains within the internal affairs of the community, one can discern a number of points that is worthy of attention in our case:

1) The Ismaili Imam has had his own personal business/wealth which comes from a family with ties to royal families. There have been marriages with royal families in the history of the Ismaili imamate in a number of cases. Some of them have occurred in medieval times when the family of the Imams was linked through marriage with the Safavid rulers of Iran. Again, during the Qājār period, the first Aga Khan married the daughter of Fatḥ ʿAlī Shah, the second Qājār monarch, who was the mother of Aga Khan II. Aga Khan II married Bībī Shams al-Mulūk, who was a Qājār princess and mother of Aga Khan III. These marriages have had their financial aspects as in any traditional society. Although there is little information available as to exact details of the wealth and estates of the family, there is definitely some wealth that comes from these sources and part of the business enterprises of the Ismaili Imams.[30] Here, of course, it is very difficult to distinguish exactly what is earned and spent where. The AKFED is the for-profit arm of the AKDN (discussed earlier) that supports the imamate institutions. There is not any clear information available as to where this distinction is made.

2) The offerings of the members of the community as part of a religious commitment in the context of their allegiance to the Imam have been and continue to be another source of funding. However, one of the elements increasingly highlighted, particularly during the imamate of Aga Khan IV, has been the voluntary nature of these offerings. There is no obligation for an Ismaili to pay these dues. There is no register as to who pays how much. Therefore, there is no mechanism according to which someone could judge whether an individual is a better Ismaili or not in terms of whether he makes any offerings or how much he pays.

3) Another source of funding comes from international agencies with which the AKDN is partner. The collaborations that have increased over the years in areas of the development projects of the imamate institutions have been a result of the quality of the work of these institutions and the number of various awards that they have won is evidence of how valued their work is.

4) There is one more source of funding that could be in a sense placed under point 2, but there are some differences in it that makes us treat it differently. There are various fundraising campaigns that occur in the community for different projects and initiatives that are undertaken by the imamate institutions whether they directly benefit the community or not. These offerings are collected just like any other fundraising campaign and take some sort of a civil action without any religious obligation. Although the ethical commitment still remains to be there and it is often contextualized within the Muslim ethical responsibility of engaging in the affairs of the world, they can still be seen as just any other fundraising that we see around us in the Western world.

As regards the sources of funding, there are several important points to be raised here. It is important to realize that the economic grounding of the Ismaili community has drastically changed over the past century. Although traditionally and in history, part of the Ismaili community has been engaged in businesses and had access to wealth, with the development and institutional efforts of the Ismaili imamate and the regular direction and guidance of the last two Aga Khans, overall the Ismaili community is now in a much better position than it was in the beginning of the twentieth century.

There are still a large number of Ismailis who live in the developing world and cannot be called rich at all, but concern for eradication of poverty has been and still is one of the foremost concerns of the Ismaili imamate.

One might safely say that the Ismaili imamate has reached a degree of economic independence such that it does not solely rely on members of the Ismaili community to manage its work. But the community is still present and it is still an integral part of the projects that are undertaken by the imamate. Therefore, it has been critical for the leaders of the community to gain the confidence and trust of the members so that when they need the support of the community and there is a fundraising project, they can reach the target they had set.

The Imam has been careful to advise the leaders of his community to gain the trust and confidence of the ordinary members of the community through transparent and good leadership. He has had a policy that the generosity of the community must not be abused. There have often been cases when during a fundraising, the target is reached and the Imam advises that it must be stopped and no further funds should be collected, as it would be an abuse of the generosity of the community. There have also been cases where certain targets for fundraisings have not been met, because the trust between the community and its leaders has been damaged (here we speak about the leaders at local levels and not the Imam himself).

Given the above account, we can see how good leadership is essential to maintaining the financial support for these institutions drawing on the support of the community. Here, the leader/led relationship is one of sponsorship and the sponsorship is maintained through building trust and confidence. The challenges are easy to see. Wherever there is a good quality of leadership, the support of the community can be found too. Poor quality of leadership results in less support from the community. Therefore, no appointed leader can claim that because they are appointed by the Imam they have the sole authority to do whatever they wish to do and can never be accountable for what they do.

There are also checks and balances both internally and externally to make sure everything is running smoothly. There are institutions inside the community, better known as *jamā'atī* institutions. The following chart (see Figure 4.2) gives an overview of the structure of these institutions.[31] As we can see in the following chart, there are national boards called the Grants and Review Boards that are in charge of financial and management auditing of the institutions working for the community. Mandates of each of these institutions are clearly defined in the Ismaili Constitution.

These checks and balances are not simply within the community and for the *jamā'atī* institutions. Other institutions of the Ismaili imamate, including the AKDN institutions, are also audited externally. A part of this is done by requirement of law in the countries where they are active and registered, as with any other institution. And they are also partly monitored by the Grants and Review coordinator at the Imam's secretariat in the Department of Jamati Institutions[32].

The AKDN is a development network and an NGO. The nature of the AKDN is, however, very much defined by the role and the authority of the Ismaili imamate. The way the AKDN functions and the visions that drive it are not simply of a transnational/NGO nature. The functions

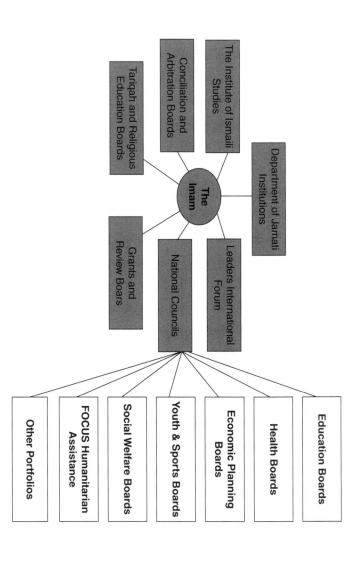

Figure 4.2 Jamāʿatī institutions and the imamate.

and the visions of the AKDN are defined by the vision of the Ismaili Imam as a person and as the holder of authority.

The imamate institutions, including the AKDN and the Community ones, are vehicles for the realization of the vision of the Imam. The Aga Khan created these institutions to ensure that his visions are implemented in a smooth, effective, and efficient manner. Therefore, the work of the AKDN cannot be seen in isolation of the role and authority of the Imam himself. There are some areas of the AKDN, like architecture, that are direct and immediate reflections of the Aga Khan as a person. There may be other areas of interest for the generations to come, but it is important to recognize that within the wider institutional context of the imamate and its institutions and the transformation of it in modern times, there are also elements that are peculiar to specific Imams.

Therefore, a simple categorization of the AKDN as an NGO would be an underestimation of its roles and failing to see the complexities involved. Susumu (2000) has addressed some part of this complexity putting the AKDN in the wider framework of Islamic revival movements, but it is important to note that the AKDN bears the signature of Aga Khan IV. It is his personal achievement in terms of a highly bureaucratic, efficient, and comprehensive institution reflecting the vision of the Ismaili imamate in the modern period.

Conclusion

We could still investigate other agencies of the AKDN and bring up details of other areas of the work of the Ismaili imamate to give us a yet more complete picture of the leadership style he has adopted. But the examples given above have made it apparent that if we follow the Aga Khan's vision through his institutional work, his ethical vision, and the work he has done in the past 50 years, built upon the leadership of his grandfather, we can see the picture with greater clarity.[33] What is highly palpable here is that we have a leadership of a minority Muslim religious community with a huge network of institutions functioning around the globe. It is like a state without any land. There is not one single nation where the Ismaili imamate is concentrated, nor has it adopted any nationalist ideology. It has distanced itself from radical aggressive political ideologies too. Although in some countries, like Canada or the UK, Ismailis are now in the higher echelons of political and financial administrations and part of the elite of these countries, the Ismaili imamate has maintained some form of political neutrality. The mixture of all these gives us a paradoxical image, which has no parallel elsewhere

in the world. There may be some development agencies that resemble the AKDN in some ways, but given the historical background of this community and the combination of different elements that shape the AKDN today, it is in a unique position to be a driving force of positive change in the developing world.

CHAPTER 5

Hybrid Leadership and the Case of the Ismaili Imamate

The Ismaili imamate and its institutions have come a very long way. If we look at the history of the genesis of the existing form of these institutions, the most visible form of which is now the AKDN, we can see how emerging issues of the Muslim world have been incorporated into the mandate and priorities of this development network. One of the qualities of these institutions is the way it keeps pace with the circumstances of the world. There is hardly any area of social and economic life that the AKDN does not make a contribution to.

If we look at how radical secularism looks at the role of religion in society, we can immediately feel the strong opposition that exists at the heart of secularization projects toward religion. The separation of church and state is fundamental to some projects of secularization. Even though the Muslim world did not follow a similar pattern and it did not develop its own political philosophy either (Abdel Razek, 2012: 46), there has been a constant debate about how the religion and state are related.

Given this picture of contrasting approaches to the role of religion in worldly affairs, and specifically in politics, we have the example of a kind of leadership whose base is religious authority, but employs quite successfully and extensively methods, ways, concepts, and terminologies that are generally considered "secular." As mentioned earlier, in chapter 3, this approach is not simply in using technologies of a Western, secular, and modern world in a passive way. It is engaging with the conceptual and philosophical matters that are part of it in a critical way rather than taking any passive or antagonistic position against them. In a sense, this engagement with the problem is one way of breaking this

secular/religious binary.[1] It seems like a subtle but carefully crafted critical approach in a world filled with misinformation about Muslims—and even greater misinformation about the Ismailis and the Ismaili imamate.

The Ismaili imamate, despite its glamorous success in its development endeavors and the work that continues, is still hardly mentioned in the mainstream media as an example of a Muslim institution which can argue to be a model for the life of Muslims in a multicultural world where the idea of borders and territorial nation-states are fading away in the midst of a globalized era. The calling cards are still in the hands of an extremist current that claims the destiny of the Muslim world. How can these conflicting images converge?

Leadership: New Pathways

In an assessment of the life of political leaders after they leave office, Keane notes that "the opening up of pathways that lead towards civil society serves as an important corrective to the undue dominance of state-centered definitions of leadership" (Keane, in Kane, Patapan, and 't Hart, 2009: 290). He justifies the involvement of former political officer bearers in politics in civil society leadership roles (which is effectively what the AKDN is doing with the exception that the Aga Khan has never been a "former political office bearer"), by highlighting some of the important merits of it.

These merits, according to him, include "challenging and pluralizing prevailing definitions of (good) leadership"; "stretching the boundaries and meaning of political representation," contributing to what he describes as "monitory" democracy in which the attention of the public is drawn to "the violation of public standards by governments, their policy failures or their general lack of political imagination" in handling "wicked" problems with no "readily agreed upon definitions let alone straightforward solutions"; and "helping both civil societies and governments to make sense of the growing complexity of democratic decision-making under conditions of dispersed power" (Keane, in Kane, Patapan, and 't Hart, 2009: 290–91).

There is a significant shift in the understanding of leadership today which stands in conflict with Weberian perspectives. As Keane notes:

Leadership no longer only means (as it meant ultimately in Max Weber's classic state-centred analysis) bossing and strength backed ultimately by

cunning and the fist and other means of state power—a Realpolitik under-standing of leadership that slides towards political authoritarianism (and until today has given the words *Führer* and *Führerschaft* a bad name in countries such as Germany) (Keane, in Kane, Patapan, and 't Hart, 2009: 292).

Leadership is further enhanced here with authority or, as Keane puts in different terms, "persuasive power":

Leadership instead comes to be understood as the capacity to mobilize "persuasive power" (as Archbishop Desmond Tutu likes to say). It is the ability to motivate citizens to do things for themselves, the learned capac-ity to win public respect by cultivating "narrative intelligence" (Denning 2007), an intelligence that includes (when leaders are at their best) a mix of formal qualities, such as level-headed focus; inner calm; courteousness; the refusal to be biddable; the ability to listen to others; poking fun at oneself; and a certain radiance of style (one of the confidants of Nelson Mandela explained to me his remarkable ability to create "many Nelson Mandelas around him"; the same thing is still commonly said of Jawarhalal Nehru). (Keane, in Kane, Patapan, and 't Hart, 2009: 292)

This quality of creating "many Nelson Mandelas" is also palpable in the leadership style of the Aga Khan, setting a benchmark for leader-ship in his own Community and the society at large. This ability is an element that comes with the transmutation that I have described. In a different tone, Keane describes it as "gestalt switching":

Such qualities also include the power to combine contradictory qualities (strength and vulnerability; singularity and typicality, etc.) simultane-ously, and apparently without effort, as if leadership is the embodiment of gestalt switching; and, above all, an awareness that leaders are always deeply dependent upon the people known as the led—that true leaders lead because they manage to get people to look up to them, rather than leading them by the nose. (Keane, in Kane, Patapan, and 't Hart, 2009: 292)

Much of the activities of the AKDN, in the projects that promote self-reliance and have an ethical underpinning to avoid making people dependent on leaders to manage their lives, suggest how the AKDN and the Ismaili imamate engenders this spirit among people. These qualities are neither articulated in Weberian terms nor were they on the horizon when Weber was developing his ideal types.

Hybrid Leadership

The jubilees, especially the Golden Jubilee, in commemoration of the Aga Khan's 50 years of imamate, sought to meet certain objectives, which included the consolidation of the institutions of the Ismaili imamate and ensuring that it was understood in modern terminology both by the Ismaili community and the wider public. A part of this understanding and consolidation had to do with raising awareness inside and outside the community of the role of the Imam. Where does this necessity come from?

The answer to the above question can be explained in terms of the question of this research. Traditionally, the Ismaili community has had a different understanding of the role of the Imam, and it is no wonder that even members of the community have not easily understood this shift. The emphasis that the Imam gave to education and health was such that sometimes there was a feeling that perhaps more attention should be paid to matters of faith. This is exactly where the shift is happening.

The emphasis on education and health, or, in other words, on the institutional development of the community and capacity building was seen by the Imam as part of his role and mandate. It was not seen as something distinct or separate from his religious role. This engagement with worldly matters was itself religious, from his perspective. Hence, we see that for the first time, the Ismaili Imam carves out a role and a function for himself that then appears to be different from his role as the Imam, when seen through the eyes of others.

Later developments, which are consolidated in the Ismaili Constitution, that is the "covenant" defining the relationship between the Ismailis and their Imam, were all in the spirit of establishing his interpretation of the faith of Islam which holds that the dichotomy between faith and world is a false one and has nothing to do with the faith of Islam. Therefore, his bifocal leadership is further developed in this way.

This has not been an easy undertaking. The supporting factor that has helped facilitate this shift has been the authority of the Ismaili Imam. Eventually, Ismailis are bound by their allegiance and submission to their Imam, and there has hardly been any subjective intervention by the members of the community to challenge the decisions of the Imam. No one disagreed with the Imam's policy of educational, health, and economic development. In fact, many members of the community now acknowledge how shrewd his decisions have been. Upheavals such as the one that happened in Uganda proved how farsighted his policies have been.

Here is where "hybrid leadership" plays a very crucial role. The authority of the Ismaili Imam was and still is a consolidated and established

authority. It is very unlikely that disagreements would break out in the decisions that he makes. He has tradition on his side and the full weight of the Ismaili history supporting him.

One of the Qur'ānic verses which are often quoted in Ismaili theological writings[2] to explain the functions of the imamate is verse 65 of Sura 4:

> But no, by thy Lord! They will not believe till they make thee the judge regarding the disagreement between them, then they shall find in themselves no impediment touching thy verdict, but shall surrender in full submission.[3]

To an Ismaili, this complete surrender is part and parcel of that faith. The only difference is that as time goes by and change occurs in the community, the level and degree of "surrender" changes too.

Again we come back to our question: how does the authority of the Imam change through time and how is it reinterpreted? Ismaili Imams have been facing different contingencies. Not all the Imams have been able to introduce all the changes they have wanted to.

One reason for different degrees of success in implementing the imamate probably goes back to the issue of longevity. Not all Imams have had a long life or indeed a long term of office. It is true that this position is for life, but there are few Ismaili Imams who have had long terms of office. And not all of them have been capable of consolidating their leadership as such.

If we take the example of al-Mustanṣir bi'llāh, the eighth Fatimid caliph, who had a long term of office as the Imam and Caliph, his reign coincided with great many problems. According to Daftary:

> The Fatimid state underwent a period of decline, accompanied by the breakdown of the civil administration, chaos in the army and the exhaustion of the public treasury ... In the meantime, Egypt was going through a serious economic crisis, marked by a shortage of food and even famine, which were caused by the low level of the Nile for seven consecutive years, from 457/1065 to 464/1072, as well as by the constant plundering and ravaging of the land by Turkish troops, all resulting in the total disruption of the country's agriculture. During these years, Egypt had become prey to the utmost misery. (Daftary, 2007: 193–94)

It was after the death of al-Mustanṣir that there was the split over the matter of succession. The simple point here is that although a long term in office helps in establishing and consolidating the agenda and vision

of an Imam, it is still not sufficient to guarantee a successful and strong leadership.

So, if we go back to our earlier question of what becomes of authority here and how would the shifts such as the one occurring in our time be completed successfully, my response would be that it is a combination of an established authority and good leadership. It is not merely the authority of the Ismaili Imam that guarantees the success of his work. It is not leadership alone. And that is why this hybrid element is important. There are many leaders who are good leaders but who are far less successful in their achievements. Here is where the dynamic link between authority and leadership can help explain the situation.

The Ismaili imamate has all the three Weberian elements of traditional, charismatic, and legal-bureaucratic authority on its side. The link with tradition is sufficiently explored in earlier chapters. The legal-bureaucratic authority is consolidated in the Constitutional framework of the Community. The proliferation of imamate institutions and the highly bureaucratic element of them further enhance this aspect.

The most outstanding and emerging feature of the leadership of the Aga Khan is the cosmopolitan dimension he has added to it through his institutional work. It has now gone beyond practice and it is increasingly approaching the realm of theory and articulation. As I discussed in the section on cosmopolitan ethic, this new approach is what bridges identity and citizenship through the work of the AKDN and the ethical principles it embodies. It is, moreover, in the context of NGOs and transnational organizations. All of these make this model of hybrid leadership distinct from all the existing Weberian types. The Weberian types were bound by territorial nation-states. There is no element of civil society in his articulations while civil society has now become a dominant theme of the AKDN work.

I have described this model of leadership as "hybrid" because it is a mixture of different elements; there are no pure types here. It is an offspring of various species of leadership, adjusted to the office of the Ismaili imamate in modern times.

Charismatic Leadership?

Following Max Weber's ideal types of leadership, we should now assess whether the Ismaili Imam's leadership is charismatic or not. Does the Ismaili Imam have charisma? Is his leadership a charismatic one? If so,

what has happened to his "charismatic leadership" with such a proliferation of institutions and agencies that are vehicles of the Ismaili imamate to do its work?

The answers to the above questions are quite simple, and unless one gets too confused with Weberian models, the entire leadership of the Ismaili imamate can be tested against the idea of charisma.

First, as to the question whether the Aga Khan has charisma, on a personal and spiritual level, the answer is positive. He definitely has charisma. This charisma can be seen in the eyes of his followers.[4] He has a very enchanting personality. His followers passionately love him, and he loves his followers too. This mutual relationship exists, and his charisma works in the area it ought to and can work. His charisma is also there for the wider public, and even though it may appear like the charisma of any celebrity, the public still detects an aura around the Aga Khan. So in this sense, his charisma is not different from what one can call "commercial charisma." But as far as his spiritual relationship with his followers is concerned, he definitely has charisma.

Is his leadership based on charisma? His leadership does not rest entirely and solely on charisma. In fact, charisma plays a minimal role in his leadership. It is true that his charisma helps, but there are few doors that charisma can open and it is definitely true for the Aga Khan too. In fact, where strong leadership works and yields results, there is little or no need at all to expend charisma.

Therefore, one thing can surely be said about his leadership style. It is definitely not charismatic leadership, although if we look at Weber's ideal types, he completely fits within Weber's categories. However, his leadership is not based on charismatic authority, even though one can call his community a charismatic community. There is a subtle difference between the Imam possessing charisma and the community being a charismatic community. The Community is charismatic only in the sense that it is conscious of its tradition of assigning this sacred role to the Imam and as such it is not easily distinguishable from a traditional community. Yet, the authority of the Ismaili Imam does not remain limited to his Community. He claims his authority in his institutions that are for the wider public. In those areas, he cannot claim his imamate the way he does it for his Community. So there is a shift here. The charismatic authority of the Aga Khan, if this is accurate enough, can only work within his own Community based on the Shiʻi Ismaili tradition. In the wider public, it rests entirely on a wider Muslim notion of leadership.

Will the community remain like this forever? If we read Weber's assessment of how charismatic authority leads to charismatic community, his line of argument is as follows:

> An organized group subject to charismatic authority will be called a charismatic community (*Gemeinde*). It is based on an emotional form of communal relationship (*Vergemeinschaftung*). The administrative staff of a charismatic leader does not consist of "officials"; least of all are its members technically trained. It is not chosen on the basis of social privilege nor from the point of view of domestic or personal dependency. It is rather chosen in terms of the charismatic qualities of its members. (Weber, 1978: 243)

This assessment clearly shows how the term "charismatic community" can only be applied to the Ismaili Community in a very limited sense. The emotional relationship is there, but the administrative staff is indeed officials with managerial skills, which has now become increasingly part of the institutions of the imamate. Moreover, even though rising to positions of leadership has undergone changes in the past 50 years, "social privilege" is still part of these mechanisms, as Walji had noted (1974). Charismatic qualities (let us call it loyalty to the Imam) definitely play a role, but bureaucratic, entrepreneurial, and managerial qualities have an important part in the structure of the institutions.

On charismatic authority, Weber says,

> The term "charisma" will be applied to a certain quality of an individual personality by virtue of which he is considered extraordinary and treated as endowed with supernatural, superhuman, or at least specifically exceptional powers or qualities. These are such as are not accessible to the ordinary person, but are regarded as of divine origin or as exemplary and on the basis of them the individual concerned is treated as a "leader." (Weber, 1978: 241)

This description prominently exists in the Ismaili doctrines and has been there for centuries. I have quoted a number of paragraphs from Ṭūsī earlier that resonate with the same idea. However, the authority of the Ismaili Imam is not an entirely charismatic authority, although he bears the same charisma that Weber speaks about.

This charisma has not influenced his leadership style in a manner that it would negatively impact his leadership such that it would lead to its routinization. It is indeed a fine example of the perpetuation of that

authority—as Dabashi puts it—without negatively impacting the leadership. This is one of those paradoxical cases where you would normally expect this kind of leadership to be charismatic; it is not.

Charismatic leadership would not sufficiently describe this kind of leadership. We need a better and more accurate term to describe it, which is not easy to find. I have earlier mentioned kaleidoscopic leadership and here I have highlighted the hybrid nature of it.

However, although the Aga Khan's leadership/authority is not a charismatic one, the charisma that is still there may be at risk. The question is whether it has diminished or not. This is a very difficult question to answer. One of the reasons for the difficulty of this question is that it has not been long since this level of institutional expansion happened and the Ismaili Imam himself has been so greatly visible and accessible. We have just seen in the examples above that the Weberian model has not worked here and cannot be used to explain what happens in the case of the Ismaili imamate and the AKDN. Can we argue that this charisma would become routinized and disappear?

Weber's opening paragraphs, when he talks about the routinization of charisma, has an alarming tone:

> In its pure form charismatic authority has a character specifically, foreign to everyday routine structures. The social relationships directly involved are strictly personal, based on the validity and practice of charismatic personal qualities. If this is not to remain a purely transitory phenomenon, but to take on the character of a permanent relationship, a "community" of disciples or followers or a party organization or any sort of political or hierocratic organization, it is necessary for the character of charismatic authority to become radically changed. Indeed, in its pure form charismatic authority may be said to exist only *in statu nascendi*. It cannot remain stable, but becomes either traditionalized or rationalized, or a combination of both (Weber, 1978: 246).

This description is at odds with the "everyday routine structures" of the Ismaili imamate's institutions. There is no interference of the Imam's charisma when he meets with different boards of his institutions, whose members are mixed and are not composed of only Muslims, let alone Ismailis. Weber continues:

> The following are the principal motives underlying this transformation: (a) The ideal and also the material interests of the followers in the continuation and the continual reactivation of the community, (b) the still stronger ideal and also stronger material interests of the members of the

administrative staff, the disciples, the party workers, or others in continuing their relationship. Not only this, but they have an interest in continuing it in such a way that both from an ideal and a material point of view, their own position is put on a stable everyday basis. This means, above all, making it possible to participate in normal family relationships or at least to enjoy a secure social position in place of the kind of discipleship which is cut off from ordinary worldly connections, notably in the family and in economic relationships.

These interests generally become conspicuously evident with the disappearance of the personal charismatic leader and with the problem of succession. The way in which this problem is met—if it is met at all and the charismatic community continues to exist or now begins to emerge—is of crucial importance for the character of the subsequent social relationships (Weber, 1978: 246, emphasis mine).

Some parts of what Weber tries to explain and formulate works in the case of the Ismaili imamate and the AKDN. We have the sublimation of the "personal imamate" to an "institutionalized imamate." The authority undergoes a shift, and the form of leadership greatly changes. However, charisma, and its role in leadership, becomes so greatly limited that one might as well ignore it in this case.

In response to a question about the relation between the charisma of the Imam and the community, Arkoun responded:

The charisma of the Imam himself is linked to the way the community is using or benefiting from this charisma. If the community is not at the level of that charisma, he can have all the charisma you wish, but he will not be able to move the community. You think charisma is going to do miracles all the time? Even the Qur'an didn't make any miracles.[5]

However, the existing structure of the AKDN and the role of the imamate itself still have their own challenges.

Visibility and Access

In the past 50 years something has happened, which is quite unprecedented in the history of the Ismaili imamate: the Ismaili Imam has never been as accessible and visible to his followers as now. Particularly, in the past decade when the AKDN has been far more active and fully engaged in its development work, the Aga Khan has been travelling extensively and he often meets his followers and goes among them. The frequency

of his contact with his followers has increased. In recent years, some members of the Ismaili community who had never seen an Ismaili Imam in their lifetime before have managed to see him a number of times in person. This immediate experience brings a different dimension to the psyche of his followers.

This visibility and close and direct access to him, although clearly not always and constantly possible as the nature of his work does not permit it (like any other senior manager anywhere), has not been limited to his followers alone. He has become even more visible in the media. The number of interviews with him has increased. His face is well known to the people who follow the news about him. Pictures of him are regularly posted on the AKDN website.

This may be something that is common to anybody else, be it a politician, a celebrity, a business manager, or a religious leader. The only big difference is that his position is something unique to his followers. Those who have seen him from outside can immediately sense that seeing this man breaks the stereotypes that one might have of a Muslim leader and specifically of a "Shi'i Imam." To his followers the Imam, who is always surrounded in an aura of mythical experience, is now physically present. Historically, this is the first time that this immediate access to him has been made possible. Thanks to technology and the shrinking of our world, this has become even simpler.

At the inauguration of his Golden Jubilee, the Ismaili community around the globe could watch the ceremony through a live webcast. In a sense, it resembles the way people would watch a head of state. The only difference in this case is that he is the Imam of a Muslim community with no land or nation, but his "virtual state" is out there. The institutions are so far reaching and all encompassing that it would not be difficult to conceive of this virtual state. When I say *virtual*, I only use it in terms of its being virtual as opposed to a territorial nation-state, otherwise everything else about the institution of the Ismaili imamate is very much *real*.

Now the question that arises here comes precisely out of this visibility and access. A religious figure who is not "absent" or not a "mythical" figure and is very much "human" and part of the breathing of life among human beings and his followers is a strange thing. It is strange because if we look at the Sunni world, the person in a position of authority in the manner that the Ismaili Imam is with his followers is akin to the Prophet, and no one else could be elevated to that position.

The Prophet of Islam is no longer physically present among Muslims. In the other larger branch of Shi'i Muslims, the Imam, who is also called "The Imam of the Time" is in concealment. He is believed to be alive and is expected to return at the end of the time and be the savior of mankind. Yet, at present, he is not accessible. He is not visible. He has no direct contact whatsoever with his followers. Yet, although the Ismaili Imam has never been in *ghayba* (absence or hiding) like the twelfth Imam of the Ithnā ʿasharīs, he had not been as accessible either.

As this veil of distance is lifted, partly because of the radically changed condition of mankind in modern times and the blessings of technology, the image of the Imam, which was very much mixed with enchantment, is becoming more human than ever. It is as if there is a flashback to the very early days of Islam when everyone could easily see the Prophet in the flesh.

In practice, this is what Ismailis have always been proud of. It is in their history, and their doctrinal books continuously raise the point that their Imam has always been there, even if they have not always been in direct contact with them. However, we have to ask the question whether this rapid demythologization of the Imam damages his charisma or his authority?

There is one area that cannot be easily judged or verified in this kind of research and that is the area of faith, simply because it is not testable using the methods of social sciences. Nonetheless, there is one way of giving at least a partial answer to this question. The Aga Khan has a secretariat where he works with different people, Ismaili and non-Ismaili. Those who are Ismailis have worked with him for a very long time and they regularly see him almost every day. This is a fact that was true even before the technological advancements of our time. Yet, among the people who work with him, there is no (or little) sign of any diminishing of authority or charisma. It is true that they may have become more comfortable with him, but access to him and his visibility does not seem to have affected this quality of his.

In terms of access, Arkoun finds this a strength in the Community, but he is skeptic whether the Community can fully benefit from it:

> What is interesting in the Ismaili community is that there is this reference to the Imam. This reference to the Imam doesn't exist anywhere else and the Imam has an open mind. He is not a tyrant ... So, with such a reference, if there is a community aware of its own responsibility, it has the privilege to refer to one person, not ten persons, like the states and many ministers and lobbies in the society operating.[6]

Arkoun finds the example of the Ismaili imamate "a very exceptional opportunity" for "intellectual reasons and for changing the Muslim mentality, because they are not harassed by totalitarian states. The Imam is not totalitarian," but as I quoted him before, he finds a discrepancy between the function and the language of the Imam and that of the members of the Community. The reason for this, according to Arkoun, is that the Ismailis are "involved in modernity" but they are "not yet initiated to what modernity is about":

> The Ismaili community is there, it exists. And the way it exists since the reactivation of the function of the Imam in 19th century is different because of the circumstances and the context in which Ismailis are involved today. They are involved in modernity but they are not yet initiated to what modernity is about, what modernity changes in the exercise of authority and in the exercise of politics.[7]

Sustainability of Hybrid Leadership

If we move past the "now," our questions would have to be directed toward the future. What is to become of this authority? Before we can answer this question, we must ask once again whether with all the developments that we have seen in the case of the Ismaili imamate, is it still appropriate to simply talk about authority as if it were something isolated. As I have shown earlier, this authority has undergone a shift. Therefore, "hybrid leadership" would be the best label, as I have explained, for capturing both aspects of the Ismaili imamate.

Then, our question would be this: how sustainable is this hybrid leadership? I will try to examine possible responses to this question as far as it is actually possible within our limits to provide an answer.

The model of hybrid leadership in the case of the Ismaili imamate today is a complex one. The many factors that contribute to the complexity of this model make it difficult, in one sense, but easier in another to assess the sustainability of this model of leadership. It is difficult because it does not resemble any existing model. There are always certain elements in this model that can never be replicated elsewhere. The very person of the Ismaili Imam as the forty-ninth hereditary Imam of Shīʿa Ismaili Muslims cannot be faked or coined anywhere else. History or tradition cannot be made up. This is a unique case in itself.

Whatever the reason that a certain authority asserts its legitimacy, the dynamic link between authority and leadership can be established

as long as the authority that is vested in a leader can be sustained by good leadership. In the case of the Ismaili imamate, we know that the authority of the Ismaili Imam is not derived from a democratic process. Different religious leaders from different traditions go through different processes of holding office, but none of them hold any form of public referendum to seek the consent of the people whom they are going to lead.

As regards the question of sustainability, one part of the issue is practical measures. In terms of practice, the AKDN has a brilliant track record of achievements and accomplishments. There is, however, another critical dimension that conditions the sustainability of this model and that is the theoretical aspect of it. As far as I have investigated, and this was also confirmed in the interview I had with Farhad Daftary,[8] there is no available theoretical discussion about how the AKDN functions. Traditional and classical scholarship is massive, but modern deliberations are very limited. Even the IIS does not yet seem to have the capacity to produce modern theoretical scholarship on these aspects.

This situation becomes even more sensitive, as almost the entire staff of the Imam consists of highly skilled managers and bureaucrats who have no sustained and rigorous religious, intellectual, or philosophical training. These qualifications are expected to be found in the IIS. But the discrepancy is still there. It seems that there is a real risk of the Weberian "iron cage" effect, and this is what Arkoun was also concerned about:

> He needs people to run and to transmit the language that he uses. But when it comes to the transmission of that authority, the people in charge of this use another language.[9]

Therefore, it seems that the entire responsibility of articulating these shifts often falls on the shoulders of the Imam himself, and the capacity to transmit the language he uses is weak in these institutions. This is one of the major challenges before this hybrid model of leadership.

The Leader and the Led

It is helpful to look at the issue of authority/leadership through the lens of the relationship between the leader and the led. If we take the case of state authority and the challenges faced by political leaders, we can see how the Ismaili Imam is looking at the issue:

Improved communication and education can be helpful, but we also must be realistic about public capabilities. I believe, for example, that publics are too often asked to vote on issues that bewilder them. In recent months, both in Africa and in Asia, new national constitutions have been left to the mercies of mass public referenda, posing complex, theoretical issues well beyond the ability of politicians to explain and publics to master. Nor is this matter unique to the developing world. We saw a similar pattern in 2005 when the French public rejected a new European constitutional treaty that was 474 pages long. Democracies need to distinguish responsibly between the prerogatives of the people and the obligations of their leaders. And leaders must meet their obligations. When democracies fail, it is usually because publics have grown impatient with ineffectual leaders and governments.[10]

The Aga Khan is highlighting the importance of education in cases where the public is indeed unaware of the complex theoretical issues. To him, there is a direct relationship between the prerogative of the people and their obligation to their leaders. Conversely, leaders have obligations too. It is also a matter of how responsible leaders are. In the words of the Aga Khan, one of the reasons for the failure of democracies is "ineffectual leaders and governments." Therefore, it is critical to add another quality for good leadership: being responsible and meeting one's obligations. The leaders who cannot deliver what they promise will eventually be labeled as "ineffectual" and "irresponsible."

On Weber's understanding of *Führer-Demokratie*, Turner says:

> The principal check on the stultifying consequences of bureaucracy is the charismatic figure of the demagogue, whose legitimacy is periodically ratified by a plebiscite. There is here further evidence of the continuity between Weber's sociological and political writings, since it was in *Economy and Society* that Weber discussed plebiscitary leadership as the "transformation of charisma in a democratic direction." The plebiscite is the "specified means of deriving the legitimacy of authority from the confidence of the ruled" (Weber 1978: 1, 267). As in the case of nationalist sources of state legitimacy, this "confidence" in the ability of the leader has highly irrational and unstable roots in the populace. Indeed, Weber claimed that it was wholly typical of *Führer-Demokratie* that political legitimacy should rest on "a highly emotional type of devotion." (Turner, 1993: 198)

When we speak of the "confidence" in the ability of the leader, it is either before a leader is appointed to the office or after it. Weber is

correct in saying that this confidence "has highly irrational and unstable roots in the populace," but this confidence can be put to test when a leader is in office. Even if the populace has irrationally trusted the leader, the leader can earn this confidence, and it all depends on how responsible and efficient he may be.

So far, there is nothing complicated in a leader earning the confidence of the led. It is a matter of how he does that and what methods he adopts to prove himself as someone who deserves this trust. However, when it comes to the case of the form of authority we see in the Ismaili imamate, complexities show themselves. The Imam has not earned his authority from the people, but his leadership might easily damage the trust of the led.

If the leaders keep jeopardizing this trust by mismanagement and irresponsible leadership, his authority may still be there and its source will still remain the same, but he can no longer gain the satisfaction of the people he leads as he might have done had he pursued a better form of leadership. And here is the point at which "hybrid leadership" can transform into "authoritarian leadership."

So, the equation is simple: even if the authority of the leader, as in this case, is not earned from the public and it remains solely at the discretion of the previous leader, in this case the Imam, he is still subject to an interaction with the led in such a way that his leadership produces satisfaction and confidence in him is maintained.[11] Although, theologically, the position and the authority of the Imam is assumed to be a God-given one, with the leader committing himself publicly to meeting objectives, he is already confining himself to a situation in which he is obliged to deliver what he promises.

The present Aga Khan has been one of the finest examples of maintaining this balance in the dynamic relationship between his authority and his leadership. In the very early days of his imamate, he made it clear in unequivocal terms that he wanted to dedicate his life to the improvement of the quality of life of his community. After 50 years, he has created a huge network of institutions and the quality of the life of his followers is incredibly different from what it was 50 years ago.

The Beginning or the End?

Thus far, we have a pretty clear grasp of what the institutions of the Ismaili imamate are about and how they function. The question is whether this system is sustainable. Are there any paradoxes? Are there inconsistencies? Is this sophisticated bureaucratization and institutional expansion

going to be a platform of longer durability, or would it crumble? Would there be any internal conflicts that might jeopardize the integrity of these institutions?

I have addressed some of these above but the answers to all of these questions are not simple. We cannot foresee the future. All we have at our disposal to assess them is what we see at the moment. From what we can see at the moment, these institutions have been functioning steadily for the past 50 years. There have been bumps on the road, but they have moved forward. Like any other institution, they inevitably face different kinds of challenges, which can become threats if they are not managed properly. The question of survival and sustainability is closely linked with how the Ismaili imamate deals with problems. The key is the resilience and fluidity of the Community and the approach of the imamate to these issues. This point is eloquently demonstrated in the words of Aga Khan III:

> Ismailism has survived because it has always been fluid. Rigidity is contrary to our whole way of life and outlook. There have really been no cut-and-dried rules, even the set of regulations known as the Holy Laws are directions as to method and procedure and not detailed orders about results to be obtained. (Aga Khan, 1954: 185)

One of the points that might form part of our answer to the above questions lies in the diversity of the Ismaili community. Before the collapse of the Soviet Union, the mainstream Ismaili Community, which contributed to the overall leadership of this Community, knew little or nothing about other communities with different backgrounds, languages, and traditions (even though the Imam himself was aware of these issues). After the fall of the Soviet Union and the removal of the Taliban regime, the Ismailis of Tajikistan and Afghanistan emerged into the global Ismaili community. The Tajiks, Afghans, and Iranians are a pool of people from different ethnic, linguistic, and historical background that are not as visible in the global leadership of the Ismaili community.

To this we can add the Syrian Ismaili community which comes from the Arabic tradition and language. One reason for this is clearly that they have had no contact with the mainstream community. Political situations and circumstances beyond their control have greatly hindered any attempt for integration hitherto.

As the world around these communities has opened, their contact with other Ismailis necessarily brought about some degrees of tensions.

As I mentioned earlier, one of the most prudent policies of the Ismaili Imam was to introduce the idea of pluralism reminding his followers of the diversity of their community and telling them that this pluralism is not a weakness but in fact a source of strength. I think the core of our question lies exactly here. What can be a source of weakness can be a source of strength and vice versa. There are many examples of what could have been something positive becoming its own antithesis. We have seen it in democracies and we have seen it in different forms of governments.

The question is how the Ismaili imamate responds to these challenges. One of the ways in which the issue has been dealt with has to do with the personal style of leadership of Aga Khan IV, which is special and unique to him. I have earlier spoken of his kaleidoscopic leadership style. We have spoken about his risk-taking nature and his courage in going to places others are not prepared to go. This is a personal characteristic. We do not know and it would be difficult to guess how the next Imam, whoever it may be, will respond to challenges.

The second way of dealing with these issues comes from an institutional culture. If the Ismaili imamate consolidates itself in such a way that through these institutions a generation of competent and good leaders and a cohort of highly qualified experts in theoretical and philosophical matters are nurtured and there is sufficient infrastructure to work on, a part of the problem is solved.

There are contingencies that are not predictable. Looking at the Ismaili history, we have at least two examples of a vast network of institutions that collapsed: one happened during the Fatimid times when the empire gradually declined, and the other one happened in Iran where the Alamūt state fell at the hand of the Mongols.

I think there have been lessons learned from the past and from the history of the Ismailis. The all-encompassing view of the Ismaili imamate on life has greatly helped it to see beyond parochial and short-term interests (this is quite clear from the leadership styles of Aga Khan III and Aga Khan IV). The political neutrality of the Ismailis around the world could also have been one means to safeguard this community and its institutions.

The synchronization of the AKDN institutions with their time is also a source of strength. If we bring together all the things that are keeping the integrity of these institutions, one easier way to answer the question would be to say that wherever these elements are missed or removed, there is a risk that these institutions could be endangered.

If we rule out unexpected and uncontrollable factors that can happen to any institution or leadership, the answer to the question whether this unprecedented development is the beginning of the end or the beginning of greater steps to be taken is that everything depends on good leadership and how this hybrid leadership functions in the flux of the events that surround it.

Conclusion

The transmutations which have occurred in the Ismaili imamate and the way it has led the Ismaili Community are mainly the result of two major factors. The first, which is of historical importance, is the migration of the Ismaili imamate from Persia to India, which led to the reactivation of the function of the Imam after a long period of absence from the social and political spheres following the fall of the Alamūt state. The migration of the Ismaili imamate to India opened many new doors for the imamate to start the engine of institutional development. A key factor in these developments was the socio-economic conditions of the Ismailis in the subcontinent and later in East Africa, which led to the introduction of legal-bureaucratic frameworks in the form of Ismaili Constitutions.

The second factor, which has a theoretical relevance, was the encounter of the Ismaili imamate with modernity and the modernization of the Community. Having access to greater financial resources in itself was not sufficient for this transmutation. The modernization of the Community touched areas of education, health, housing, and economic development. This arduous task was forcefully pursued by Aga Khan III who must be rightly credited for placing the Ismaili Community and the imamate on a platform that was never envisaged before.

The modernization of the Community brought with it some modern attitudes (which are best reflected in the legal framework of the Community), even though it retained its core traditional and spiritual values. The Ismaili Community, through the leadership of Ismaili Imams in the modern period, became gradually more secularized in a very subtle sense. This secularity was not of the kind of radical secularity that restricted any religious or spiritual engagement to the private sphere. Indeed, the Ismaili imamate treaded on a narrow path in a turbulent time to ensure that its religious background did not disappear in a sea of increasingly radical secular attitudes. This secularism, which also contained elements of modernity in it, was greatly reinforced by the highly

esoteric tradition that had remained in the Community's memory from earlier periods. The bifocal leadership of Aga Khan IV is the most important category when describing this particular "secularization," which is in effect creating and maintaining a balance between religion and the world. It also entailed a revival or reinvigoration of the role of intellect, at least in the language and practice of the Imam himself, when dealing with matters of faith. So there is also a stronger rational element now, as compared with the pre-modern era when Ismaili beliefs were shrouded in Sufi ideas, which was more than anything else a product of *taqiyya*.

In the time of the imamate of Aga Khan IV, these trends became more focused and found a more coherent and systematic expression. The situation had become more complex, and a number of key local and global events, such as the end of colonialism—in the midst of which the Ismaili Community had prospered and survived—and the end of the Cold War, were the backdrop of these developments. The Ismaili Community became more diverse in terms of its presence globally and its interconnectedness, with Ismailis from regions such as Iran, Afghanistan, and Tajikistan becoming more and more part of the global Ismaili Community.

A visible shift had started during the time of Aga Khan III when development had become the epitome of his imamate, particularly after his encounters with Europeans. It is during the imamate of Aga Khan III that the education of the Community on modern secular terms became central. It is also during his time that the emancipation of women becomes an integral part of his leadership. Conversely, dogmatic, narrow-minded, and thickly theological divisions began to fade away, even though demarcations on theological grounds continued to exist since the identity of the Ismaili Community had not yet fully formed and not been institutionalized yet. Nonetheless, during the imamate of Aga Khan III, we see much greater tolerance promoted among Ismailis toward those different from them, when compared with previous periods.

The imamate of Aga Khan IV is the time when institutionalization of the community and the imamate proceeds at a much faster pace. Moreover, development itself becomes much more significant to the extent that today the AKDN is an integral part of the public image of the Ismaili imamate, with which the Aga Khan identifies himself and his role as the Imam. Through these institutions, which reflect the vision of the Aga Khan, a new function and role was defined for the Imam. The wider label for this role is improving the quality of life for his Community and the people among whom they live, thus expanding the area of the Imam's responsibility. This is what I describe as bifocal leadership.

The introduction of these new functions, which are founded on his vision that there is no dichotomy between faith and the world (and between intellect and faith), brought new opportunities and new challenges with them. The vehicle for the implementation of the Imam's vision is his institutions within his Community and globally for humanity at large.

In this book, I have examined the historical background of the Community, its doctrines, and theological principles about the imamate, the Imam's authority, and his leadership. I used the Weberian ideal types to test them against models of traditional, legal-bureaucratic, and charismatic pure types of authority and leadership. This was done in the context of a predominantly Eurocentric scholarship about Muslim communities and the dynamics of their societies that had been very much under the influence of Orientalist approaches.

The critical study carried out in this research illustrates how Eurocentric scholarly work fails to recognize the complexities of Muslim communities and their encounters with modernity. In the case of the Ismaili imamate, I have demonstrated how tempting it is to assess these developments with a Weberian lens, as indeed there are many features in Weberian methodologies that can explain its developments and challenges.

Yet, Weberian ideal types have proved inadequate and inapplicable, despite their richness in other contexts, to describe the shift in the authority of the Ismaili imamate. This change in form and content of what the Ismaili imamate does through institutional work represented a shift also in leadership models. Weberian paradigms proved increasingly poor in describing these shifts, too. The Ismaili imamate today functions beyond divisions of nation-state and has in effect been decoupled from Weberian territorial divisions. Therefore, it further gives weight to the emergence of authority without territory. The authority of the Imam is no longer tied to or defined by territorial and nation-state divisions, nor is it influenced by nationalistic ideologies, which often beset Muslim populations around the globe today.

Some of the parameters that shed light on the inadequacy in Weberian ideal types are the increasingly global nature of the Ismaili imamate defying narrow local identities based on territorial nation-state divisions and its intense involvement in civil society as a form of NGO rooted in Muslim ethics, which also defines the role of the Ismaili Imam.

There are, however, important insights and lessons from Weberian approaches that can help identify the potential challenges before the institutions of the Ismaili imamate. With the modernization of the

Community, and the imamate, new strata of entrepreneurs and bureaucratic managers have become essential to the function of the imamate. In the process of shifting the stress from a thickly theologically defined identity for the Community to one driven by cultural and civilizational elements, a generation of entrepreneurs became an integral part of the functions of the imamate.

Even though there are institutions like the IIS and the AKU, which can help promote critical and theoretical debates about issues of concern for the imamate, the bureaucratization of the imamate itself poses a risk of the "iron cage" that Weber had warned about as a result of this modernization: "specialists without spirit, sensualists without heart; this nullity imagines that it has attained a level of civilization never before achieved" (Weber, 2001: 124).

There is a visible attempt on the side of the Ismaili imamate to bring more normative elements into the functions of the institutions. The most vivid example of it can be seen in what the Aga Khan has described as cosmopolitan ethic, which stands both as a rival to political secular cosmopolitanism and allows the AKDN to serve as a bridge for connecting identity with citizenship in a globalized world. These normative theoretical approaches are potentially rich and exciting with interesting prospects. They need, however, to be supported by strong, coherent, and methodological scholarly works that reflect a new metaphysics in light of modern developments of the Community and the imamate. What is now required is adapting the theology and the Imamology to this shift. This adaptation has happened at a minimal level and only tacitly in the Community. Understanding the imamate in new terms was one of the objectives for the Golden Jubilee of Aga Khan IV. This area seems to still need a lot of work in the future.

The imamate itself and its authority have been transcended into the "office of the imamate." Now, one can often find references made to the imamate or the office of the imamate rather than the Imam as a person. It is true that the personal qualities of the Imam have shaped these institutions, but this transcendence has actually been a consequence of institutionalization, which has worked as an enabling vehicle for the imamate to implement its visions.

With regard to the authority of the Imam in this transformed condition, institutions have strengthened this authority. The problem of succession has a solution to it, part of which is found in the traditional roots of the imamate and how a successor is appointed. The modern context of the imamate enables it to address these issues in a more competent manner. As we have seen in the case of Aga Khan III, the succession issue

was a smooth transition (noting how the Imam's will was recorded and read).

On the side of the Community, there is still great discrepancy between what the Imam says and does and what the Community understands. Being mindful of the privileged and special role and authority of the Imam, the kind of active and efficient exchange that can happen between members of the Community is hampered by institutions that have found an increasingly bureaucratic nature.

This is a point that Arkoun identified regarding the communication between the Imam and the Community:

> Authority is a free way of using language and a free way for the one who uses the language and for the receiver of the language. The receiver, when he listens to the one who is the voice of authority, should never feel constrained to accept or to obey what he is hearing from the voice of authority. The receiver is absolutely free in accepting it or not.[1]

This description is, of course, not static, and the image is constantly changing, even though the predominant institutional frameworks do not encourage this exchange. The moment this relation is translated into a requirement to obey blindly, authority turns into power. This is not how the imamate functions. This is a paradox and a challenge for the future to see how it is ensured that this free exchange can occur in a Community which has been so successfully transformed in the modern world.

The Ismailis do not have a territorial state, and it has been a privilege for them. The structure of the Ismaili imamate's institutions is such that it does not allow for falling short of cosmopolitan and transnational commitments. This decoupling of the imamate from nation-state has indeed enhanced the authority preventing it from being reduced to state-power politics.

I have proposed to minimally describe the leadership of the Aga Khan under the label "hybrid leadership" to overcome the limitations of Weberian approaches, and what we are encountering today is indeed "authority without territory." A critical and core element of this hybrid leadership is reflected in its ethical cosmopolitanism and pluralistic governance, which is so deeply engaged in civil society.

This book is the first comprehensive study of the modern institutions of the Ismaili imamate and its functions in the globalized and cosmopolitan world today. I have only highlighted the areas that need greater theoretical work in the future. I have addressed some of the

critical issues that play a role in opening new pathways. However, this kind of research is just the beginning of similar works to be done from different perspectives. This is a rich and promising area of research, which can be a source of great insight into questions about authority and leadership.

Notes

Introduction

1. The term *Imāmiyya* is common for both the Ismailis and the Ithnā ʿasharīs. Therefore, wherever I refer to the Imāmiyya and the historical context preceding the schism after Jaʿfar al-Ṣādiq, the term applies to both the Ismailis and the Ithnā ʿasharīs; it does not exclusively refer to the Ithnā ʿasharīs.

2. Muḥammad b. Ismāʿīl is also a figure of messianic importance for the early Ismailis as he is associated with the *qāʾim* and considered by early Ismailis to be the seventh *nāṭiq* (enunciator), based on the early doctrines of Ismailis about cyclical time.

3. The variation in the Imam's lists according to Ismailis and the Ithnā ʿasharīs comes from a doctrinal concept of imamate. For Ismailis, there are two types of Imams: the *mustaqarr* (consolidated or established) and the *mustawdaʿ* (given as a trust). The former are those Imams in whose bloodline the imamate shall continue, like Imam Ḥusayn b. ʿAlī; the latter are those Imams in whose descendants the imamate does not continue and the imamate is then transferred to the consolidated Imam, as in the case of Imam Ḥasan b. ʿAlī (see al-Shahrastānī, 2001: 226–37 and Badakhchani, 2005: 136–37).

4. In his edition of *Dīwān-i Qāʾimiyyāt*, Badakhchani gives his genealogy of Ḥasan II as being Ḥasan al-Qāhir b. Ḥusain al-Muntaṣir b. Ḥasan b. al-Muṣṭafā li-Dīn Allāh Nizār b. al-Mustanṣir bi'llāh (fn. 2, p. 32). In *Haft bāb*, Ḥasan-i Maḥmūd places Ḥasan II as the twenty-first Ismaili Imam (while in the official list, he is the twenty-third). In a later treatise named *Ḥaft bāb* by Abū Isḥāq-i Quhistānī, the official list is repeated, which explains the route from which the contemporary genealogy is adopted (p. 23, Persian text). In all likelihood, the three names which appear between Nizār and Ḥasan II might have been pseudonyms adopted by the descendants of Nizār.

5. For a detailed study of the post-Alamūt developments, see Virani (2007).

6. The terms *taqiyya* and *satr* are often interchangeably used by Ismailis in reference to (a) the concealment of the identity of the Imam, (b) concealment of the esoteric meanings of faith from the uninitiated, and (c) to make a distinction between the era of *sharīʿat* (which is the period of *satr*) and the era of *qiyāmat*

(which is the period of *kashf*). For an elaborate discussion on these usages in the overall Shi'i and specifically Ithnā 'asharī context (some of which is also shared by Ismailis), see Etan Kohlberg's "Taqiyya in Shī'ī Theology and Religion" (pp. 345–380) in Kippenberg and Stroumsa (1995) and Hermann Landolt's "Introduction" (pp. 1–2) in Ṭūsī (2005).

7. In his introduction to the edition of *Dīwān-i Qā'imiyyāt*, Shafī'ī Kadkanī notes that in order to refer to the mystical aspect of the Ismaili faith in earlier periods, one must look for a word different from "Sufism" or even "mysticism," and he suggests a closer term would be "Gnosticism" which bears both an allegorical and artistic encounter with religion and to some extent avoids the fatalism and antagonism with reason dominant in Sufism, see his "Introduction," in Badakhchani (2011).

8. M. Mu'izzī also briefly mentions the beginning of this affiliation during the Alamūt period in her MA thesis (1992: 373), but does not provide any detailed information.

9. For a detailed study of Aga Khan I's departure from Persia, see Daftary (2007), Algar (1969), and van Grondell (2009).

10. Arif Jamal's paper on the development of Ismaili law is a very important survey of the historical developments in Ismaili law and is particularly relevant for the institutional development of this community.

11. See Christian Jambet's elaboration on this term in his philosophical commentary to the *Paradise of Submission* in Badakhchani's edition and translation of this work attributed to Naṣīr al-Dīn al-Ṭūsī (Ṭūsī, 2005)

12. For an extensive narrative of the doctrine of *ta'līm*, look at Badakhchani's chapter titled "Shahrastānī's Account of Ḥasan-i Ṣabbāḥ's Doctrine of Ta'līm" (pp. 27–55) in Amir-Moezzi (2013).

13. The term leader in the contemporary Ismaili context is used in two ways. One is to refer to the single and unique leader, for which the most appropriate term in Shi'i Islam is the "Imam." The other is to refer to any of the individuals appointed by the Ismaili Imam to be members of his institutions and become office-bearers. These individuals are generally referred to as "leaders of the Jamā'at."

14. There is a dense passage in the *Paradise of Submission*, attributed to Ṭūsī, which fully captures this concept in the Ismaili doctrine: "The sacrosanct Divine Essence (*dhāt-i muqaddas*) has made the Imam—may salutations ensue upon the mention of him—the manifestation of the sublime Word (*maẓhar-i kalmia-yi a'lā*), the source of illumination (*manba'-i nūr*), the lamp of divine guidance (*mishkāt-i hidāyat*), the lantern of divine glory (*qandīl-i 'izzat-i ṣamadiyyat*), the scales of obedience and worship (*mīzān-i ṭā'at wa 'ibādat*), and the person who embodies this knowledge and love of Himself (*shakhṣ-i ma'rifat wa maḥabbat-i khud*)" (Ṭūsī, 2005: 120).

15. Weber explains these different types in *Economy and Society*: "It is primarily, though not exclusively, these extraordinary powers that have been designated by such special terms as 'mana,' 'orenda' and the Iranian 'maga' (the term from which our word 'magic' is derived). We shall henceforth employ the term 'charisma' for

such extraordinary powers...Where this appellation is fully merited, charisma is a gift that inheres in an object or person" (Weber, 1978: 400) and continues to explain how it is connected with leadership: "The term 'Charisma' will be applied to a certain quality of an individual personality by virtue of which he is considered extraordinary and treated as endowed with supernatural, superhuman, or at least specifically exceptional powers or qualities. There are such as are not accessible or the ordinary person, but are regarded as of divine origin or as exemplary, and on the basis of them the individual concerned is treated as a 'leader.'" (Weber, 1978: 241).

16. Even in the most recent work on authority, Furedi (2013), this Eurocentric tone is quite dominant and despite its fascinating narrative of authority, other civilizations are practically absent in his narrative.

17. Throughout this book, I have used the standard spelling of "imamate" instead of "Imamat." The latter is only used in cases that are either used institutionally or are direct quotations.

18. One can compare it, for instance, with the institution of *Marja'iyyat* in the clerical system of religious leaders in the Shi'i Iran.

19. Looking at the vision of Aga Khan III is beyond the scope of this book. A comprehensive collection of his speeches have been published by K. K. Aziz (1998), which covers a diverse range of issues and it can give a clear picture of his teachings.

1 Max Weber, Authority, and Leadership

1. Dabashi's hermeneutical approach is further explained in detail in his book on 'Ayn al-Qudāt Hamadānī (1999) and it continues in his other works as well. Dabashi's methodology (1999: 1–63) is particularly relevant in this research too.

2. A recent book by Liakat N. Takim, *The Heirs of the Prophet: Charisma and Religious Authority in Shī'īte Islam*, that deals with the issue of authority in Shi'i Islam is heavily relying on the Weberian tripartite typology of the modes of authority. However, apart from taking the Weberian typology for granted, his work, which bears the general title for Shi'i Islam, fails to consider the Shi'i Ismaili community and its long-standing institutions, which is not surprising at all: this institution does not sit well with Weberian typologies, and it proves to be a paradoxical and perplexing model when viewed from a Weberian angle.

3. In his PhD thesis, Bayhom-Daou gives further details of what the knowledge of the Imam includes and it is wider than simply knowledge of the Qur'ān, according to the Imāmiyya, and they encompass 'things such as knowledge of "the past and the future" or of "the secrets of heaven and earth" (Bayhom-Daou, 2001:189). He explains that they are thought to have originated among the *ghulāt*, but also refers to Amir-Moezzi who says these were characteristic of the early esoteric Shi'i teachings highlighting that there were no real doctrinal distinctions between the "moderates" and the *ghulāt*.

4. There is, of course, Joseph Schacht's article that talks about the Ismailis of East Africa: Schacht, Joseph (1965), "Notes on Islam in East Africa," *Studia Islamica*, no. 23, pp. 91–136.

5. This is an issue that Dabashi was acutely aware of while working with Weberian methodology to address the issue of charisma (1989: 36–53).

6. Turner notes that "Weber is best known for his study of Protestantism and the rise of European capitalism, which has been mistakenly treated as a study which claims that Calvinism caused capitalism" (Turner, 1998: 2) and in a note on this he believes that Tawney has presented narrow interpretations of Weber (1998: 185).

7. These are not direct quotations. I have paraphrased Taylor's points in his public lecture titled "Secularism and Multiculturalism" dated January 15, 2010 (London, University of Westminster).

8. Some of these elements are not unique to the Ismaili imamate. Others, however, such as the need for a present living Imam descended from the Prophet, seem unique compared with other Muslims.

9. There is a sentence attributed to Ḥasan II in his proclamation of the *qiyāmat* in which he says "*naḥnu al-ḥāḍirūn al-mawjūdūn*" that means "we are present and accessible people" (Quhistānī, 1959: 42). This is the very phrase that appears in the contemporary vocabulary of the Ismailis and even in the daily ritual prayers in reference to the Aga Khan (see Kassam in Curtis [2008: 358–67]). This continuity reflects the importance of the Alamūt period, theologically, even though it is not explicitly acknowledged.

10. I have explained above, while quoting Charles Taylor, why the application of the term "secular" to the Ismailis is just a clumsy generalization ignoring significant subtle differences.

11. According to Weber, a charismatic community is "an organised group subject to charismatic authority will be called a charismatic community (Gemeinde). It is based on an emotional form of communal relationship (Vergemeinschaftung)" (Weber, in Dabashi, 1989: 141).

12. A good example of it can be seen in the Alamūt period, when the sixth Lord of Alamūt, the third Ismaili Imam, Jalāl al-Dīn Ḥasan decided to conform to Sunnī Muslim patterns, and for this reason he was called "*naw musalmān*" (new Muslim). This period of conformity did not last long, and it was revoked at the time of his son. The effect of Ḥasan II's radical reforms have remained until our time in the Ismaili Community.

2 Imamate and the Question of Authority in the Muslim and Shiʿi Contexts

1. Some of the literature produced on the Ismailis in Western scholarship was very much under the influence of dominant perceptions about Muslims particularly during the Crusades. The best example of it can be seen in the myths about Ismailis of Alamūt, which brought the term "assassins" into Western literature (see Daftary, 1995).

2. See, for example, Ṣāliḥī Najafābādī (1971).

3. It is important to note that in Europe it took centuries until monarchy faced serious challenges with the execution of Louis XVI of France and Charles I of England; it is imperative here to see the parallels in European thought as to how concepts of leadership have developed in Europe and how monarchy has been understood

4. As I was finalizing the revisions of this work, I learned of the publication of an English translation of his work, by the Aga Khan University's Institute for the Study of Muslim Civilisations in 2012.

5. It is, however, important to take account of the political circumstances of his time. The Ottoman Empire was in crisis and ʿAbd al-Rāziq's writings were in resonance with the political realities of his own time.

6. For a more details study of this, see Amir Arjomand (1984: 89–100).

7. There are counter-narratives against the standard one that sometimes assumes that the entire Imāmī scholars lent their support to the Safavids. Notably, see Newman (1993) and Stewart (1996).

8. The transliterated terms in brackets are mine; they are not in the original version of the translated book.

9. I would have translated this as "divine inspiration" rather than support, but I have not modified Wickens' translation quoted here.

10. The original Persian word for this is *muḥaddithān*, but in his note on this term, Wickens (1964: 315) mentions it as *muḥdathān*, which may be wrong. The reference is to the use made by Muslims after the Greeks.

11. This term could also be translated as "the authority to amend the laws" with the "law" referring to the *sharīʿat*.

12. *The Nasirean Ethics*, translated by G. M. Wickens, p. 192.

13. In the chapter quoted above, we can, however, see very strong indications of the ideas of Aristotle in Ṭūsī's writings.

14. It is also important to note that there are certain differences in the English translation provided by Wickens both in terms of the equivalents used and it terms of the Farsi edition he had used for translation. Some of the sentences that are available in the above translation do not exist in the most recent edition of the Nasirean Ethics (*Akhlāq Nāṣirī*) edited by Mujtabā Mīnawī and ʿAlīriḍā Ḥaydarī. The reason for these variations is that after the fall of Alamūt at the hand of the Mongol hordes, Ṭūsī apparently relinquishes his Ismaili affiliations and in order to show that he is no longer related to the Ismailis, he gives a new edition of his book dropping certain explicitly Ismaili phrases, including the above.

15. In a critical remark on the way Muslim philosophers used the Greek corpus to define *The virtuous city*, according to Plato's and Aristotle's view, Arkoun believes that in spite of the fact that they "contributed to the enrichment of political thought, they did not initiate a cognitive shift from their Greek sources and higher authorities" (Arkoun, 2002: 205).

16. In his note to this section of his essay, Amir Arjomand adds: "The notion of authority—or more precisely *auctoritas* and its complement *potestas*—comes

from Roman law and has no equivalent in Arabic or Persian." He them approximates the meaning of it by the terms discussed in his chapter by the use of "some other terms such as *ḥukm* (command, verdict) and *siyāda* (authority, originally of the tribal chief)" (Amir Arjomand, 1988: 18).

17. See also: Mohammad Poor, Daryoush, "'Alī b. Abī Ṭālib" section on 'Alī and Walāya in Daftary and Madelung (2011); also, look at Dakake, Maria Massi (2007), *The Charismatic Community: Shi'ite Identity in Early Islam* (Albany: State University of New York Press).

18. It is interesting that when explaining this term, Amir Arjomand indicates that in the Qur'ān, the notion of authority refers, on the one hand, to *dīn* (religion) and, on the other hand, to *mulk* (temporal rule). He explains further that this *mulk*, according to the Qur'ān, belongs to God and thus "the invidious contrast between divine and human kingship in the Qur'ān could only delegitimize the latter. The term *mulk* was thus tainted and another Qur'ānic term, *sulṭān*, was employed to denote legitimate political authority" (Amir Arjomand, 1988, 1–2). In contrast to Amir Arjomand, al-Qāḍī al-Nu'mān's explanation of verse 4:54 of the Qur'ān in reference to those who have been given the *mulk* is again referring to imamate quoting Ja'far al-Ṣādiq (al-Nu'mān, 2002: 29).

19. There is also another problem with how *'aql* is translated and understood. It may mean "reason," "intellect," "intelligence," or even "science" or "discernment." Amir-Moezzi has written an extensive section on this putting it in the context of how this term has developed among the Imāmīs (Amir-Moezzi, 1994: 6–19).

20. For example, look at Macintyre's essays in *Ethics and Politics* (2006).

21. See, for example, the Aga Khan's lecture as part of the LaFontaine-Baldwin Lectures in Toronto in October 2010: AKDN website: http://www.akdn.org/Content/1018 (last accessed July 1, 2014).

22. See the website of the Institute of Ismaili Studies: http://iis.ac.uk/view_article.asp?ContentID=101444 (last accessed July 1, 2014).

23. As an example of applying reason to leadership, the Ismaili Imam asks his followers not to smoke. He has often told his followers that the reason I do not want you to smoke (or to drink alcohol) is that it is harmful to your health. He had once told his followers that if you do not believe me, look what is written on cigarette packs! He is very simply appealing to reason rather than telling them they should obey him because he is the Imam. Nor has he given any theological ruling or doctrinal justifications for it to discourage smoking. It is interesting to note that legal terms of the *fuqahā* such as *ḥalāl* and *ḥarām* in reference to what is allowed and what is forbidden in religion does not at all appear in the language of the Ismaili Imam, which is another sign of moving away from a theologically driven style of leadership.

24. The recent inauguration of the Delegation of the Ismaili imamate in Canada, in December 2008, is yet another symbolic expression of this transcendence.

25. See, for example, various chapters in Ṭūsī's *Rawḍa-yi Taslīm* (in Ṭūsī, 2005): chapters 22 and 24.

26. I will be explaining further how another epistemic shift had occurred in the Alamūt period in a later chapter when I speak about the messianic roots of the Ismaili doctrines, but it is perhaps important to indicate that a similar shift had once again occurred when the first Ismaili Imam of Alamūt declared the resurrection. So the very idea of this shift is not completely unprecedented. It is, however, the change in the ingredients and the substance of the new dominating themes of the Ismaili imamate that signals this change.

27. This idea of "distribution of power" is of course much more nuanced. It is not a state-like democratic institution, and the mechanisms in the Ismaili constitution for the distribution of power have some differences. I will note some of these in the section on the Ismaili Constitution.

28. Madelung explains the difference of approaches in the early years of the formation of the Caliphate: "It may be countered that the succession to Muḥammad cannot be compared to that of a ruler or king and that the classical Sunnite theory of the caliphate indeed sharply distinguishes between it and kingship, *mulk*, which it condemns in part for its principle of hereditary succession. But the classical theory is obviously posterior to the succession and its opposition to *mulk* and the principle of heredity presumably reflects in part its essential purpose of justifying the early historical caliphate" (1997: 5).

29. As a comparative study, it would be interesting to look at Asma Afsaruddin's *Excellence & Precedence: Medieval Islamic Discourse of Legitimate Leadership* (2002), which is a study of discourse of legitimate leadership, in a traditional setting, comparing Sunnī and Shiʿi Imāmī backgrounds drawing on the works of al-Jāḥiẓ and Ibn Ṭāwūs.

30. At the time of the Abbasid Caliph al-Qāhir, they gathered a group of scholars and theologians of different religious groups including some Shiʿi scholars to sign a declaration denying the blood relationship of the Fatimid Caliphs to ʿAlī and Fāṭima. Some of the Shiʿi scholars refused to sign this declaration, although some of them did.

31. Such categorizations first appear in Kirmānī's writings, although similar ideas are seen in the works of previous *dāʿī*s. However, the elaboration of these traits in Kirmānī's work is quite new. These treatises appear in the early stages of the consolidation of the Fatimid Empire in North Africa.

32. In a recent interview, Ismail Poonawala clearly says that infallibility is not an article of faith: "The infallibility of the Imam is a concept, it is only a theoretical adjunct, and it grew out of the circumstances and needs of the times. You have to analyse those circumstances. Infallibility is not an article of faith." See: http://dawoodi-bohras.com/news/1683/107/Bohra-scholar-who-speaks-truth-to-power/d,pdb_detail_article_comment/ (last accessed March 22, 2014).

33. Here, the translator has used "logical necessity" but the original text only speaks about "necessity" and there is no reference to its being "logical." The passage above seems to be direct quotations from an Ismaili Imam of the Alamūt period, possibly *Ḥasan ʿAlā dhirihi'l salām*.

34. These are, however, metaphysical statements and irrefutable in nature; there is no way of critically testing these statements with human reason.

35. See my earlier footnote in the Introduction regarding genealogy and the number of the Imams.

36. Both these frameworks existed among Muslims from early times. Philosophers used Greek thought to define the virtuous city according to Aristotelian and Platonic views (which I will mention later when quoting from Ṭūsī), while theologians and jurists drew on the definitions and concepts provided by the traditions and the Qurʾān.

37. AKDN Webstie: http://www.akdn.org/about_akdn.asp (last accessed July 1, 2014).

38. Peter Mandaville's article challenges the "widely held assumption that transnational Islam is not conducive to discourses of political civility, pluralism, and democracy" (in Hefner, 2005: 302).

39. On the role of the ʿulamā and the constructions of authority, see Zaman (2002); also see Zaman, "Pluralism, Democracy and the ʿUlama" (in Hefner, 2005: 60–86).

40. In Turkey, the Gülen movement promotes moderate Islam and as such it is radically different from militant networks. Even though it is a successful and progressive model, there are still visible differences between the language of Gülen and the Aga Khan (regardless of the difference of the position and authority of the Aga Khan as a Shiʿi Imam); while Gülen would write a book on essentials of the Islamic faith, we have never seen such kind of a book or treatise produced by the Aga Khan with similar content or language. For a detailed sociological study of the Gülen movement, see Edbaugh (2010).

41. AKDN Website: http://www.akdn.org/Content/924 (last accessed May 29, 2011).

3   The Aga Khan: A Visionary Leader

1. This is a fairly new approach. We do not have any precedent of an Imam *explaining* to his followers *why* he has made a certain choice. This change, mutation, or shift seems to have been triggered during the life of Aga Khan III in conceptualizations and articulations as we see it expressed in the will.

2. At the time of the death of the Aga Khan III on July 11, 1957, his family members were in Geneva. Otto Giesen, a solicitor with the firm of Slaughter and May, brought the Will of the Aga Khan III to Geneva from Lloyds Bank, London, and read it at Barkat Villa before the Imam's family.

3. All the quotations from the Aga Khan in this book are from his speeches which are either published or publicly available on the Internet. There are *farmāns* by the Aga Khan, which are specifically addressed to the Community, but I could not get permission for reproducing those. However, apart from the general religious recommendations, the themes are practically the same as those of the speeches with the difference that they are more sophisticated in terms

of language in public speeches. Apart from the AKDN website, a fairly comprehensive collection of the speeches of the Aga Khan can be found in the Nanowisdom website: http://www.nanowisdoms.org/nwblog/.

4. The Avestan term saoshyant ("future benefactor"; MPers...sōshans) designates the savior of the world, who will arrive at a future time to redeem humankind. The concept of the future savior is one of the fundamental notions of Zoroastrianism, together with that of dualism; it appears as early as in the Gāthas. Zarathushtra (Zoroaster), as prophet of the religion, is himself a Saoshyant, one who performs his works for the Frashōkereti, the end of the present state of the world, when existence will be "rehabilitated" and "made splendid" (Gnoli, 2005: 260).

5. For example, see Ansari, Hassan (2011), "Abū al-Khaṭṭāb" *Encyclopaedia Islamica.* Editors-in-Chief: Wilferd Madelung and Farhad Daftary (Leiden: Brill).

6. Compare this idea with the assessment of a similar idea in the Ithnā ʿasharī faith by Modarresi Tabatabaee.

7. Throughout this book, wherever we talk about the Ismaili Imams and their sequence, the Shiʿi Imami Ismaili Muslims mean the followers of Aga Khan IV, unless otherwise expressed.

8. See: "al-Mahdī." *Encyclopaedia of Islam, Second Edition*, eds. P. Bearman, Th. Bianquis, C. E. Bosworth, E. van Donzel, W. P. Heinrichs. Brill Online, 2014. Reference. Institute Of Ismaili Studies Ltd. July 1, 2014 http://brillonline.nl/entries/encyclopaedia-of-islam-2/al-mahdi-COM_0618; first appeared online: 2012; first Print Edition: isbn: 9789004161214, 1960–2007.

9. The emphasis is mine; the italics on terms are Daftary's.

10. The case of ʿAyn al-Quaḍāt Hamadānī is particularly relevant because of his affiliations with Ismailis. I have made some references to these instances earlier. See also, Hermann Landolt's article on this topic in Alí-de-Unzaga (2011:369–386).

11. It is interesting to note that in that particular episode of the Ismaili history, the politics of communication and dialogue with the rest of the Muslim communities around them had failed in the midst of all hostilities and the increased persecution of Ismailis. The Ismaili state, then, was for sure an isolated island in a sea of hostilities.

12. During his time, it has recently been discovered that reading the essential treatise of ʿAlā Dhikrihi'l Salām called "*Fuṣūl-i muqaddas*" (The sacred chapters) had been banned as one can infer from the subtle reference in *Rawḍa-yi taslīm* to "an epoch of concealment (*satr*) and prudence (*taqiyya*)" (Ṭūsī, 2005: 118).

13. Here he compares the Aga Khan with Gaddafy, which is a matter of poor taste, and there is hardly a proper context in which the two could be compared.

14. For a detailed account of the conflict, see Algar (1969).

15. It is important to note that in these court cases, the Aga Khan was the defendant. It was the other side who had taken the dispute to the court and eventually lost the case.

16. See also the speech of the Aga Khan's lawyer, Edward Howard (1866), at the High Court.
17. The quotations are from Daftary; the sentences in italics are my emphasis.
18. For a detailed study of the gender policies of Aga Khan III and Aga Khan IV, see Zayn R. Kassam "The Gender Policies of Aga Khan III and Aga Khan IV," in Daftary, 2011. Also, see Keshavjee (2004).
19. It is important to note that sometimes throughout this book, the terms "leadership" and "community" may be used interchangeably because apart from a historical correlation between the "*Jamāʿat*" and the "*Imam*" (see Ṭūsī), particularly in modern times, this distinction seems to be blurred at some points.
20. It is important to note the theological and philosophical problem of attributing the same quality to God and to human beings in a similar way. Early Ismaili philosophers such as Abū Yaʿqūb al-Sijistānī had tried to deal with this problem by making a distinction between them.
21. See http://iis.ac.uk/view_article.asp?ContentID=101094 (last accessed March 24, 2014).
22. At a speech for the Opening of Alltex EPZ Limited (Athi River, Kenya, December 19, 2003) Last accessed on the AKDN website on October 30, 2011: http://www.akdn.org/Content/596.
23. Interview with Mohammed Arkoun, April 29, 2008.
24. Ibid.
25. Ibid.
26. Aga Khan IV (1985), *Silver Jubilee Speeches*.
27. The myths surrounding his grandfather's jubilees, weighing him with gold, diamond, and platinum, did create its own negative impact at the time, but what we see today in the institutions of the Ismaili Community is closely connected with the financial engine that started running as a result of these jubilees that were a public and voluntary expression of gratitude by the Ismaili Community for their Imam.
28. Remarks Made by His Highness the Aga Khan Upon Receiving the Carnegie Medal for Philanthropy (Edinburgh, Scotland, October 4, 2005), last accessed on the AKDN website on October 30, 2011: http://www.akdn.org/Content/117.
29. See also: Karim H. Karim (in Cherry, 2014: 155).
30. Address by His Highness the Aga Khan to the Tutzing Evangelical Academy upon receiving the "Tolerance" award (Tutzing, Germany, May 20, 2006), last accessed on the AKDN website on October 30, 2011: http://www.akdn.org/speeches_detail.asp?id=605.
31. Aga Khan I was the son-in-law of Fatḥ ʿAlī Shah, and Aga Khan II was also married to a Qājār princess, who was the mother of Aga Khan III.
32. Speech at the University of Virginia in 1984.
33. Interview in London on July 18, 2008.
34. Interview with Tom Kessinger in London on July 18, 2008.
35. Taken from the Persian word *Khʷāja* meaning lord and master (see Hirji, in Daftary, 2011: 130).

36. Last accessed on the AKDN website on October 30, 2011: http://www.akdn.org/Content/373.

37. From the mission statement of the Global Centre for Pluralism: http://www.pluralism.ca/the-centre/mission.html last accessed on September 29, 2012.

38. Remarks by His Highness the Aga Khan at Evora University Symposium: "Cosmopolitan Society, Human Safety and Rights in Plural and Peaceful Societies" (Evora, Portugal, February 12, 2006); last accessed on the AKDN website on October 30, 2011: http://www.akdn.org/Content/228.

39. Last accessed on the IIS website on October 30, 2011: http://www.iis.ac.uk/view_article.asp?ContentID=109417.

40. Lecture by His Highness the Aga Khan: The LaFontaine-Baldwin Lecture (Toronto, Canada, October 15, 2010); last accessed on the AKDN website on October 30, 2011: http://www.akdn.org/Content/1018.

41. We can see a very clear Socratic tone in this statement, which comes very close to how critical rationalists view knowledge.

42. AKDN website: http://www.akdn.org/Content/483 (last accessed on October 30, 2011).

43. Speech by His Highness the Aga Khan at the Nobel Institute on Democratic Development, Pluralism and Civil Society (Oslo, Norway, April 7, 2005); last accessed on the AKDN website on October 30, 2011: http://www.akdn.org/Content/599.

44. For example, see Farshid Moussavi, "Cosmopolitanism and Architecture," in *Intervention Architecture: Building for Change*, pp. 166–67.

45. Amyn Sajoo is a scholar-in-residence in Simon Fraser University. He has been working with the IIS in various capacities and as visiting research fellow.

46. Interview with Amyn Sajoo, May 21, 2008.

47. Ibid.

48. Ibid.

49. Ibid.

50. For a thorough and detailed analysis of these, see Fanāʾī (2005). Fanāʾī's work, which is only in Persian, is one of the rare works of scholarly quality written investigating the relation between religious ethics and secular ethics.

51. The Nanowisdom website: http://www.nanowisdoms.org/nwblog/6073/ (last accessed March 25, 2014).

52. Nanowisdom website: http://www.nanowisdoms.org/nwblog/8861/ (last accessed 25th March 2014).

53. Ibid.

54. Ibid.

55. The Nanowisdom website, "A Life in the Service of Development," published in *Politique Internationale,* Winter 2011/2012 (Paris, France): http://www.nanowisdoms.org/nwblog/10062/ (last accessed March 25, 2014).

56. His remarks at the Prince Claus Fund's Conference on Culture and Development (Amsterdam, The Netherlands, September 7, 2002) is quite interesting here: "Phrases like, 'civil society,' 'poverty alleviation,' and 'sustainable development'

are familiar to many of you, as is 'enabling environment' for which I must carry responsibility, since it was the Enabling Environment Conference in Nairobi sponsored by the Aga Khan Development Network, the World Bank and others which brought that phrase into common use."

57. Keynote Speech by His Highness the Aga Khan Concluding the Prince Claus Fund's Conference on Culture and Development (Amsterdam, The Netherlands, September 7, 2002); last accessed on the AKDN website on October 30, 2011: http://www.akdn.org/Content/354.

58. Speech by His Highness the Aga Khan at the Annual Meeting of The European Bank for Reconstruction and Development (Tashkent, Uzbekistan, May 5, 2003); last accessed on the AKDN website on October 30, 2011: http://www.akdn.org/speeches_detail.asp?id=591.

59. Last accessed on the AKDN website on October 30, 2011: http://www.akdn.org/Content/238.

60. Address by His Highness the Aga Khan at the Convocation of the University of Toronto's Ontario Institute for Studies in Education (Toronto, Canada); last accessed on the AKDN website on October 30, 2011: http://www.akdn.org/Content/598.

61. Interview with *Politique Internationale* (March 2010): http://www.politiqueinternationale.com/revue/article.php?id_revue=127&id=909&content=synopsis (last accessed March 27, 2014). The English translation of the quote: "It seems to me that rules of non-proliferation are now applied to all nuclear technology for both civilian and military purposes. In fact, the conditions for the sale of civilian nuclear energy is like some kind of technological colonisation, insofar that the most advanced nations make a point of holding on to all the 'keys.' From this point of view, we are a long way from the democratisation of nuclear energy. Maybe I'm naive but I advocate another approach, which I call 'positive proliferation.' I am in favour of the widespread distribution of civilian nuclear power. Of course, careful thought must be given to the conditions under which positive proliferation would operate. How to avoid environmental problems? How to prevent the misappropriation of civilian nuclear power for military purposes? As you know, I have studied history and it has never been possible to halt any globally significant scientific advance. The positive proliferation that I would dearly love to see happen is based on a simple principle: yes to energy, no to arms" (from http://www.nanowisdoms.org/nwblog/9473/ last accessed March 17, 2014).

62. Ibid. The English translation: "The direction in which Iran is moving is very worrying for the whole world, including other Shia nations. In my view, the chief cause of the revolution in Iran originated in the regrettable mismanagement of the economy under the Shah's regime. I regret to say that, of all the heads of state I have known, he was probably the one with the worst understanding of economic issues—or he was poorly advised. This ineptitude led to growing numbers of pockets of resistance. Khomeini only had to arrive on the scene for the course of history to change radically. I am a Shia and when I heard

his speeches I thought that no Shia on earth could remain unmoved by his preachings" (from http://www.nanowisdoms.org/nwblog/9473/ (last accessed March 17, 2014).

63. See http://www.nanowisdoms.org/nwblog/4527/ (last accessed March 27, 2014).

64. See http://www.nanowisdoms.org/nwblog/6120/ (last accessed March 27, 2014).

65. Interview with Spiegel Online, October 12, 2006 (http://www.nanowisdoms .org/nwblog/7900/; last accessed July 18, 2014).

66. http://en.wikiquote.org/wiki/Aga_Khan_IV (last accessed May 14, 2010).

4 The AKDN: An Overview of the Ismaili Imamate's Institutional Endeavors

1. The very use of terms such as *murīd* reflects how remnants of the earlier interactions of the Ismailis with Sufis are now preserved in their literature.

2. This distinction was made by a senior administrator at His Highness the Aga Khan's secretariat at Aiglemont in an interview in London on September 18, 2008.

3. Address at the Annual Conference of German Ambassadors, Berlin, September 6, 2004; last accessed on the AKDN website on October 30, 2011: http://www. akdn.org/Content/583.

4. Shiraz Kabani was the former Head of Finance and Operations at the IIS and he is currently Head of the Department of Community Relations at the IIS. He has a long history of service in the Ismaili institutions.

5. In London on January 18, 2010

6. Interview in London on September 25, 2008

7. A full and detailed account of all these are available in Malise Ruthven's article in *A Modern History of the Ismailis* (Daftary, 2011); see earlier chapters and the bibliography.

8. AKDN website, last accessed on October 30, 2011: http://www.akdn.org/ Content/937Aga-Khan-Award-for-Architecture-Announces-Master-Jury-for-2010.

9. Interview with Farrokh Derakhshani, September 25, 2008.

10. Ibid.

11. All quotations are from my interview with Derakhshani on September 25, 2008.

12. Ibid.

13. Ibid.

14. Ibid.

15. Derakhshani interview, September 25, 2008.

16. Speech by His Highness the Aga Khan at the Inauguration of Al-Azhar Park (Cairo, Egypt, March 25, 2005), last accessed on the AKDN website on October 30, 2011: http://www.akdn.org/Content/187.

17. Speech by His Highness the Aga Khan at the Foundation Laying Ceremony of the Ismaili Centre (Dubai, United Arab Emirates, December 13, 2003), last accessed on the AKDN website on October 30, 2011: http://www.akdn.org/Content/594/Foundation-Laying-Ceremony-of-the-Ismaili-Centre-Dubai.
18. Ibid.
19. Remarks by His Highness the Aga Khan at the Official Opening of the Kampala Serena Hotel (Kampala, Uganda, November 10, 2006), last accessed on the AKDN website on October 30, 2011: http://www.akdn.org/Content/586/Official-Opening-of-the-Kampala-Serena-Hotel.
20. For some of the references and detailed examination of the case of Iran, see Rezaee (2008).
21. Last accessed on the AKU website on a version before the upgrade on October 30, 2011 at: http://202.3.130.27/ismc/ismc-aku.shtml.
22. Last accessed on the AKDN website on October 30, 2011: http://www.akdn.org/academies.
23. AKDN website: http://www.akdn.org/speech/595/Inauguration-Ceremony-of-the-Aga-Khan-Academy-Kilindini-Mombasa (last accessed June 15, 2010).
24. At a speech in the Opening of Alltex EPZ Limited (Athi River, Kenya, December 19, 2003). Last accessed on the AKDN website on October 30, 2011: http://www.akdn.org/Content/596.
25. AKDN website, last accessed on October 30, 2011: http://www.akdn.org/Content/684.
26. Interview with Amy Sajoo, May 21, 2008.
27. AKDN website, last accessed on October 30, 2011: http://www.akdn.org/publications/2007_akdn.pdf.
28. Speech by His Highness the Aga Khan at the Commonwealth Press Union Conference in Cape Town, South Africa, October 17, 1996. Last accessed on the AKDN website on October 30, 2011: http://www.akdn.org/Content/979.
29. Speech by His Highness the Aga Khan at the Commonwealth Press Union Conference in Cape Town, South Africa, October 17, 1996. Last accessed on the AKDN website on October 30, 2011: http://www.akdn.org/Content/979.
30. Frischauer has given a list of the different financial assets and industries of the Aga Khan family in his book and has conspicuously titled it *The Aga Khan Empire* (1970: 275–76). He has put them under seven different categories, some of which are now part of the AKDN, and it includes the imamate's private enterprises such as studs and stables and the Sardinia resort.
31. These institutions did not exist in the current institutional form at the time when Walji was doing her PhD work, and such details as this are not reflected in her work.
32. See also: Karim H. Karim (in Cherry, 2014).
33. In order to get a full understanding of what the Aga Khan thinks, it is probably essential to look at all his speeches very carefully. The instances that I have quoted or explained so far have been for the purpose of capturing the most important elements in his words that signal this shift or transmutation in the

nature of his authority. It can certainly be done by highlighting other areas to prepare a more comprehensive draft of his thoughts.

5 Hybrid Leadership and the Case of the Ismaili Imamate

1. For a lengthy discussion of this secular/religious binary, see Dabashi (2013: 19–41).
2. See for example Ṭūsī (1998: 47).
3. Arberry's translation: website of http://tanzil.net/ (last accessed July 2, 2014).
4. In my interviews with various administrators and senior figures in the Community, almost all of them have confirmed that this sense of "charisma" does exist as the Aga Khan's followers literally "eat from the palm of his hand". This is, of course, not in contrast with the existence of "dissent" within the community, although this dissent, at an intellectual level, does not take any radical or disruptive form.
5. Interview with Mohammed Arkoun, April 29, 2008.
6. Ibid.
7. Ibid.
8. Interview conducted on May 12, 2009.
9. Interview with Mohammed Arkoun, April 29, 2008.
10. Address by His Highness the Aga Khan to the School of International and Public Affairs, Columbia University (New York, May 15, 2006); last accessed on the IIS website on October 30, 2011: http://www.iis.ac.uk/view_article. asp?ContentID=109422.
11. This has not always been a constant. Back in the early episodes of the Shi'i—and Ismaili imamate—during the time of Imam Ja'far al-Ṣādiq, there were some of his followers who were growing impatient with his conservative political stances that avoided confrontation with the Abbasid establishment. These issues could also lead to dissatisfactions among the community.

Conclusion

1. Interview with Mohammed Arkoun, April 29, 2008.

Bibliography

Primary Sources

Aga Khan, Prince Karim (1985), *Silver Jubilee Speeches* (London: Islamic Publications Ltd.).

—— (2008), *Where Hope Takes Root* (Vancouver: Douglas & McIntyre).

Aga Khan, Sir Sultan Muhammad Shah (1918), *India in Transition: A Study in Political Evolution* (London: Phillip Lee Warner).

—— (1954), *The Memoirs* (London: Cassel and Company Ltd.).

Aga Khan Award for Architecture (2007), *Intervention Architecture: Building for Change* (London, I.B. Tauris & Co Ltd.).

Algar, Hamid (1969), "The Revolt of Āghā Khān Maḥallātī and the Transference of the Ismāʿīlī Imamate to India", *Studia Islamica*, no. 29, pp. 55–81.

Alí-de-Unzaga, Omar (2011), *Fortresses of the Intellect: Ismaili and other Islamic Studies in Honour of Farhad Daftary* (London: I.B. Tauris).

Al-Husayni, Shihāb al-Dīn Shāh (1947), *Risāla dar ḥaqīqat-i Dīn*, ed. Ivanow, W. (Mumbai: Thacker & Co. Ltd).

—— (1963), *Khiṭābāt-i ʿālīya*, ed. Ujāqī, Hūshang (Tehran: Tehran University Press).

Aubin, Jean and Lombard, Denys (1999), ed., *Asian Merchants and Businessmen in the Indian Ocean and the China Sea* (New Delhi: Oxford University Press).

Aziz, K. K. (1998), *Aga Khan III: Selected Speeches and Writings of Sir Sultan Muhammad Shah* (London: Kegan Paul International).

Badakhchani, S. Jalal (2011), *Dīwān-i Qāʾimiyyāt* (Tehran: Miras-e Maktoob).

Bocock, Robert J. (1971), "The Ismailis in Tanzania: A Weberian Analysis," *The British Journal of Sociology*, vol. 22, no. 4 (Dec. 1971), pp. 365–80.

Clarke, Peter B. (1976), "The Ismailis: A Study of Community", *The British Journal of Sociology*, vol. 27, no. 4 (Dec. 1976), pp. 484–94.

—— (1998), *New Trends and Developments in the World of Islam* (London: Luzac Oreintal).

Corbin, Henry (1962), *History of Islamic Philosophy* (London and New York: Kegan Paul International in association with Islamic Publications for The Institute of Ismaili Studies).

Cotran, Eugene (2000–2001), *Yearbook of Islamic and Middle Eastern Law*, Vol. 7 (The Hague/London/New York: Kluwer Law International).

Curtis, Edward E., ed. (2008), *The Columbia Sourcebook of Muslims in the United States* (New York: Columbia University Press).

Daftary, Farhad (2007), *The Ismāʿīlīs: Their History and Doctrines,* 2nd edn. (Cambridge: Cambridge University Press).

—— (2011), *A Modern History of the Ismailis: Continuity and Change in a Muslim Community* (London: I.B. Tauris in association with the Institute of Ismaili Studies).

—— (1995), *The Assassin Legends: Myths of the Ismaʿilis* (London: IB Tauris).

Daftary, Farhad and Madelung, Wilferd (2011), *Encyclopaedia Islamica*, Vol. 3 (Leiden and Boston: Brill).

Frischauer, Willi (1970), *The Aga Khans* (London: The Bodley Head Ltd).

Gellner, Ernst (1981), *Muslim Society* (Cambridge: Cambridge University Press).

Green, Nile (2011), *Bombay Islam: The Religious Economy of the West Indian Ocean, 1840–1915* (Cambridge: Cambridge University Press).

Gupte, Pranay (1999), "Venture Capitalist to the Third World," in *Forbes Magazine*, dated May 31, 1999.

Hamdani, Abbas (1999), "Brethren of Purity, a Secret Society for the Establishment of the Fatimid Caliphate," in M. Barrucant, ed., *L'Égypte Fatimide: Son art et son histoire* (Paris: Presses de l'Université de Paris-Sorbonne).

Hodgson, Marshall G. (1955), *The Order of the Assassins: The Struggle of the Early Nizārī Ismāʿīlīs against the Islamic World* (Chicago: University of Chicago Press).

Howard, E. I. (1866), *The Shia School of Islam and Its Branches, Especially That of the Imamee-Ismailies,* a speech delivered in the Bombay High Court (Mumbai: Oriental Press).

Interview with Dr. Amyn Sajoo, London, May 21, 2008.

Interview with Mr. Farrokh Derakhshani, September 25, 2008.

Interview with Professor Mohammed Arkoun, London, April 29, 2008.

Interview with Mr. Shiraz Kabani, London, January 18, 2010.

Interview with Mr. Tom Kessinger, London, July 18, 2008.

Ivanow, Wladimir (1938), "A Forgotten Branch of the Ismailis," *Journal of the Royal Asiatic Society* (New Series), 70, pp. 57–79.

Jodidio, Phillip (2007), *Under the Eaves of Architecture: The Aga Khan: Builder and Patron* (Munich, Berlin, London, New York: Prestel).

Kaiser, Paul (1996), *Culture, Transnationalism and Civil Society: Aga Khan Social Service Initiatives in Tanzania* (Connecticut: Praeger Publishers).

Kassam, Tazim R. (2003), "The Aga Khan Development Network: An Ethic of Sustainable Development and Social Conscience," in Foltz, Richard C. et al., ed., *Islam and Ecology: A Bestowed Trust* (Cambridge, MA: Harvard University Press).

Keshavjee, Rashida (2004), *The Redefined Role of the Ismaili Muslim Women through Higher Education and the Professions* (PhD thesis, University of Toronto).

Kippenberg, H. G. and Stroumsa, G. G. (1995), *Secrecy and Concealment: Studies in the History of Mediterranean and Near Eastern Religions* (Leiden, New York Köln: Brill).

Al-Kirmānī, Ḥamīḍ al-Dīn (1953), *Rāḥat al-ʿaql*, ed., Muḥammad Kāmil Ḥusayn and Muḥammad Muṣṭafā Ḥilmī (Leiden: Brill)

—— (2007), *Master of the Age: An Islamic Treatise on the Necessity of the Imamate*, English translation and edition of *al-Maṣābīḥ fī ithbāt al-imāma* by Walker, Paul (London: I.B. Tauris and Institute of Ismaili Studies).

Muʿizzī, Maryam (1992), *Ismāʿīliyān-i Iran: az suqūṭ-i Alamūt tā imrūz bā takya bar dawrān-i muʿāṣir* (PhD thesis, Ferdwosy University of Mashhad).

Nanji, Azim (1974), "Modernization and Change in the Nizari Ismaili Community in East Africa: A Perspective," *Journal of Religion in Africa*, vol. 6, fasc. 2, pp. 123–39.

Nasr, Seyyed Hossein, ed., (1977), *Ismāʿīlī Contributions to Islamic Culture* (Tehran: Imperial Iranian Academy of Philosophy).

Al-Nuʿmān, al-Qāḍī (2002), *The Pillars of Islam*: Volume I, *Acts of Devotion and Religious Observances*, tr. Asaf A. A. Fyzee, revised and annotated by Ismaili K. Poonawala (New Delhi: Oxford University Press).

Purohit, Teena (2012), *The Aga Khan Case: Religion and Identity in Colonial India* (Cambridge, London: Harvard University Press).

Quhistānī, Abū Isḥāq, *Haft bāb-i Abū Isḥāq* (1959), ed. and English trans. by Wladimir Ivanow (Mumbai, Ismaili Society).

Rezaee, Maryam (2008), *Women and Higher Education: An Analysis of the Relationship between Higher Education and Women's Empowerment with Special Reference to the Ismaili Women of the Two Major Cities of Tehran and Mashhad in Iran* (PhD thesis, The University of York).

Schacht, Joseph (1965), "Notes on Islam in East Africa," *Studia Islamica*, no. 23, pp. 91–136.

Al-Shahrastānī, Muḥammad b. ʿAbd al-Karīm (2001), ed. Fāʿūr, ʿAlī Ḥasan and Mahnā, Amīr ʿĀlī, *al-Milal wa al-niḥal*, vol. I (Beirut: Dār al-Maʿrifa).

Steinberg, Jonah (2011), *Ismaʿili Modern: Globalization and Identity in a Muslim Community* (Chapel Hill: The University of North Carolina Press).

Susumu, Nejima (2000), "The Ismaili Imam and NGOs: A Case Study of Islamic Civil Society," *Bulletin of Asia-Pacific Studies*, no. X, pp. 149–63.

The Constitution of the Shia Imami Ismaili Muslims (Lisbon, 1998).

Ṭūsī, Naṣīr al-Dīn, (1977), *Akhlāq-i Nāṣirī*, ed. Mujtabā Mīnuwī and ʿAlīriḍa Ḥaydarī (Tehran: Khāʷrazmī).

—— (1964), *The Nasirean Ethics*, tr. G. M. Wickens (London: George Allen & Unwin).

—— (1998), *Contemplation and Action: The Spiritual Biography of a Muslim Scholar*, ed. and trans. Badakhchani, J. (London: I.B. Tauris and Institute of Ismaili Studies).

—— (2005) *Paradise of Submission: A Medieval Treatise on Ismaili Thought*, ed. and trans. Badakhchani, J. (London: I.B. Tauris and Institute of Ismaili Studies).

Van Grondelle, Marc (2009), *The Ismailis in the Colonial Era* (London: C. Hurst).

Virani, Shafique (2007), *The Ismailis in the Middle Ages: A History of Survival, a Search for Salvation* (Oxford: Oxford University Press).

Walji, Shirin Remtulla (1974), *A History of the Ismaili Community in Tanzania* (PhD thesis, University of Wisconsin, Madison).

Walker, Paul (1993), "The Ismaili Daʿwa in the Reign of the Fatimid Caliph Al-Ḥākim," *Journal of the American Research Center in Egypt*, vol. 30, pp. 161–82.

Website of the Aga Khan Development Network, www.akdn.org

Website of the Institute of Ismaili Studies, www.iis.ac.uk

Website of the Ismaili.Net: www.ismaili.net

Website of The Nanowisdoms of Imamat Speeches, Interviews and Writings, http://www.nanowisdoms.org/nwblog/

Website www.tanzil.net (Qurʾān and its translations)

Secondary Sources

ʿAbd al-Rāziq, ʿAlī (2000), *al-Islām wa uṣūl al-ḥukm*, ed. Muḥammad ʿImāra (Amman: Dār al-Fāris).

Abdel Razek, Ali (2012), *Islam and the Foundations of Political Power*, tr. Maryam Loutfi, ed. Abdou Filaly-Ansary (Edinburgh: Edinburgh University Press in association with The Aga Khan University).

Afsaruddin, Asma (2002), *Excellence and Precedence: Medieval Islamic Discourse on Legitimate Leadership* (Leiden: Brill).

Amir Arjomand, Said (1998), *Authority and Political Culture in Shiʿism* (New York: State University of New York).

—— (1984), *The Shadow of God and the hidden Imam* (Chicago: The University of Chicago Press).

Amir-Moezzi, Mohammad Ali (1994), *The Divine Guide in Early Shiʿism: The Sources of Esotericism in Islam*, tr. David Streight (Albany: State University of New York Press)

—— (2013), *Islam: Identité et Altérité: Hommage à Guy Monnot, O.P.* (Turnhout: Brepols).

Ansari, Hassan (2011), "Abu al-Khaṭṭab", *Encyclopaedia Islamica*. Editors-in-Chief: Wilferd Madelung and Farhad Daftary (Leiden: Brill).

Arendt, Hannah (1961), *Between Past and Future: Six Exercises in Political Thought* (New York: The Viking Press)

Arkoun, Mohammed (2002), *The Unthought in Contemporary Islamic Thought* (London: Saqi Books).

—— (2006), *Islam: To Reform or to Subvert?* (London: Saqi Books).

Atamaj, Dwi S., Martin, Richard C. and Woodward, Mark R. (1997), *Defenders of Reason in Islam: Muʿtazilism from Medieval School to Modern Symbol* (Oxford: One World Publications).

Bayhom-Daou, Tamima (2001), "The Imam's Knowledge and the Quran according to al-Faḍl b. Shādhān al-Nisābūrī (d. 260 AH/874 AD)," in *Bulletin of the School of Oriental and African Studies*, vol. 64, no. 2, pp. 188–207.

Bayat, Asef (2007), *Making Islam Democratic* (Stanford, CA: Stanford University Press).

Beck, Ulrich (2006), *The Cosmopolitan Vision*, tr. Cronin, Ciaran (Cambridge: Polity Press, reprint).

Cherry, Stephen M. (2014), *Global Religious Movements Across Borders: Sacred Service* (Farnham, Surrey: Ashgate Publishing Limited).

Curtis, Michael (2009), *Orientalism and Islam: European Thinkers on Oriental Despotism in the Middle East and India* (Cambridge: Cambridge University Press).

Dabashi, Hamid (1989), *Authority in Islam: From the Rise of Muhammad to the Establishment of the Ummayads* (New Jersey: Transaction Publishers).

—— (2013), *Being a Muslim in the World* (New York: Palgrave Macmillan)

—— (2008), *Islamic Liberation Theology: Resisting the Empire* (New York: Routledge).

—— (1999), *Truth and Narrative: The Untimely Thoughts of ʿAyn al-Quḍāt al-Hamadānī* (Richmond, Surrey: Curzon Press).

Dakake, Maria Massi (2007), *The Charismatic Community: Shiʿite Identity in Early Islam* (Albany: State University of New York Press).

Edbaugh, Helen Rose (2010), *The Gülen Movement: A Sociological Analysis of a Civic Movement Rooted in Moderate Islam* (Heidelberg, London, New York: Springer).

Eickelman, Dale F. and Piscatori, James (1996), *Muslim Politics* (Princeton: Princeton University Press).

Eisenstadt, Shmuel N., Hoexter, Miriam, and Letzion, Nehemia (2002), *The Public Sphere in Muslim Societies* (Albany: State University of New York Press).

Fanāʾī, Abulqāsim (1384 Sh./2005), *Dīn dar tarāzū-yi akhlāq* (Tehran: Muʾassisa-yi Farhangi-yi Ṣirāṭ).

Friedrich, Carl J. (1972), *Tradition and Authority* (London: The Pall Mall Press).

Furedi, Frank (2013), *Authority: A Sociological History* (Cambridge: Cambridge University Press).

Gadamer, Hans Georg (2004), *Truth and Method* (London: Continuum).

Global Center for Pluralism (GCP) (2012), *Defining Pluralism*, Pluralism papers No. 1 (http://www.pluralism.ca/resources/pluralism-papers.html).

Gnoli, Gherardo (2005), "Saoshyant", *Encylopedia of Religion*, ed. Lindsey Jones, 2nd edn. (Detroit: Macmillan Reference).

Haley, Peter (1980), "Rudolph Sohm on Charisma," *The Journal of Religion*, vol. 60, no. 2 (April 1980), pp. 185–97.

Hamadānī, ʿAyn al-Quḍāt (1983), *Nāmah-ha*, Vols 1 and 2, ed. Munzawī, ʿAlīnaqī and ʿUsayrān, ʿAfīf (Tehran: Manūchihrī).

—— (1998), *Nāmah-ha*, Vol. 3, ed. Munzawī, ʿAlīnaqī (Tehran: Asāṭīr).

Al-Hamidi, Jabir Habib Jabir (1991), *Modern Islamic Theories of the State with Special Reference to Rashid Ridha and ʿAli ʿAbdul-Raziq* (PhD thesis, University of Dundee).

Hanks, Patrick and Pearsall, Judy, (2001), ed., *The New Oxford Dictionary of English* (New York: Oxford University Press).

Hefner, Robert W., ed., (2005), *Remaking Muslim Politics: Pluralism, Contestation, Democratization* (Princeton and Oxford: Princeton University Press).

Huff, Toby E. and Schluchter, Wolfgang, ed., (1999), *Max Weber & Islam* (New Brunswick and London: Transaction Publishers).

Iqbal, Mohammad (1934), *The Reconstruction of Religious Thought in Islam* (London: Oxford University Press).

Kahlberg, Stephen, ed., (2005), *Max Weber: Readings and Commentary on Modernity* (Oxford: Blackwell).

Kane, John, Patapan, Haig, and 't Hart, Paul (2009), *Dispersed Democratic Leadership: Origins, Dynamics and Implications* (Oxford: Oxford University Press).

Karim, Karim H. (2000), *Islamic Peril: Media and Global Violence* (Montreal: Black Rose Books).

Keane, John (2003), *Global Civil Society* (Cambridge: Cambridge University Press).

—— (1984), *Public Life and Late Capitalism: Towards a Socialist Theory of Democracy* (Cambridge: Cambridge University Press).

Kuhn, Thomas (1966), *The Structure of Scientific Revolutions*, 3rd edition (Chicago: The University of Chicago Press).

Macintyre, Alasdair (2006), *Ethics and Politics* (Cambridge: Cambridge University Press).

Madelung, Wilferd (1997), *The Succession to Muhammad: A Study of the Early Caliphate* (Cambridge: Cambridge University Press).

—— (2012), "al-Mahdī", *Encyclopaedia of Islam, Second Edition* (Brill Online).

Marsh, David and Stoker, G. (2002), *Theory and Methods in Political Sciences*, 2nd edn. (New York: Palgrave Macmillan).

Modarresi, Hossein (1993), *Crisis and Consolidation in the Formative Period of Shi'ite Islam* (New Jersey: Darwin Press).

Newman, Andrew J. (1993), "The Myth of the Clerical Migration to Safawid Iran: Arab Shiite Opposition to 'Alī al-Karakī and Safawid Shiism," *Die Welt des Islams* (New Series), vol. 33, issue 1, pp. 66–112.

Rūmī, Jalāl al-Dīn Muḥammad (1935), *Mathnawī ma'nawī*, ed. Nicholson, R. A. (Leiden: Brill).

Said, Edward (2003), *Orientalism* (London: Penguin).

Sajoo, Amyn B., ed., (2008), *Muslim Modernities: Expressions of the Civil Imagination* (London: I.B. Tauris).

Ṣāliḥī Najafābādī, Ni'mat Allāh (1971), *Shahīd-i jāwīd* (Qumm: n.p).

Soroush, Abdolkarim (2001), "Mahdawiyyat wa iḥyā-yi dīn," *Aftāb Magazine*, vol. 12, pp. 60–63.

Spencer, Martin E. (1970), "Weber on Legitimate Norms and Authority," *The British Journal of Sociology*, vol. 21, no. 2 (Jun. 1970), pp. 123–34.

—— (1973), "What is Charisma," *The British Journal of Sociology*, vol. 24, no. 3 (Sep. 1973), pp. 341–54.

Stewart, Devin J. (1996), "Notes on the Migration of 'Āmilī Scholars to Safavid Iran," *Journal of Near Eastern Studies*, vol. 55, no. 2, pp. 81–103.

Takim, Liyakat N. (2006), *The Heirs of the Prophet: Charisma and Religious Authority in Shī'ite Islam* (Albany: State University of New York Press).

Taylor, Charles (2004), *Modern Social Imaginaries* (Durham and London: Duke University Press).

—— (2007), *A Secular Age* (Cambridge and London: The Belknap Press of Harvard University Press).

Turner, Bryan S. (1993), *Max Weber: From History to Modernity* (New York: Routledge).

—— (1998), *Max Weber Classic Monographs vol. VII: Weber and Islam* (New York: Routledge).

Weber, Max (1978), *Economy and Society: An Outline of Interpretative Sociology*, eds. Guenther Roth and Claus Wittich, 2 vols (Berkeley: University of California Press).

—— (2001) *The Protestant Ethic and the Spirit of Capitalism*, tr. Talcott Parsons (London and New York: Routledge).

—— (2008) *Max Weber's Complete Writings on Academic and Political Vocations*, ed. and intro. Dreijmanis, John, trans. Wells, Gordon, C. (New York: Algora Publishing).

—— (1949), *The Methodology of Social Sciences*, ed. and trans. Finch, Henry, A., Shils, Edward, A. (Illinois, Glencoe: The Free Press).

—— (1961) *General Economic History*, trans. Frank H. Knight (New York: Collier Books).

Zaman, Muhammad Qasim (2002), *The Ulama in Contemporary Islam: Custodians of Change* (Princeton and Oxford: Oxford University Press).

Index

LaVergne, TN USA
07 April 2010
178491LV00001B/19/P